This edition written and researched by

Paula Hardy, Duncan Garwood & Robert Landon

## SYMBOLS IN THIS BOOK

Top Tips | History & Culture | Essential Photo
Link Your Trips | Family | Walking Tour
Tips from Locals | Food & Drink | Eating
Trip Detour | Outdoors | Sleeping

Telephone Number
Opening Hours
Parking
Nonsmoking
Air-Conditioning
Internet Access
Wi-Fi Access
Vegetarian Selection
Swimming Pool
English-Language Menu
Family-Friendly
Pet-Friendly

## MAP LEGEND

**Routes**
Trip Route
Trip Detour
Linked Trip
Walk Route
Tollway
Freeway
Primary
Secondary
Tertiary
Lane
Unsealed Road
Plaza/Mall
Steps
Tunnel
Pedestrian Overpass
Walk Track/Path

**Boundaries**
International
State/Province
Cliff
Wall

**Population**
Capital (National)
Capital (State/Province)
City/Large Town
Town/Village

**Transport**
Airport
Cable Car/ Funicular
Parking
Train/Railway
Tram
Underground Train Station

**Trips**
1 Trip Numbers
9 Trip Stop
Walking Tour
Trip Detour

**Route Markers**
E44 E-Road Network
M100 National Network

**Hydrography**
River/Creek
Intermittent River
Swamp/Mangrove
Canal
Water
Dry/Salt/ Intermittent Lake
Glacier

**Areas**
Beach
Cemetery (Christian)
Cemetery (Other)
Park
Forest
Urban Area
Sportsground

# PLAN YOUR TRIP



# ON THE ROAD

# CONTENTS

# Contents cont.



## ROAD TRIP ESSENTIALS

# Classic Trips

**Look out for the Classic Trips stamp on our favourite routes in this book.**

**Tuscany** Landscapes of rolling hills, golden fields and snaking lines of cypress trees

# WELCOME TO ITALY

**Italy, the *bel paese* (beautiful country), is one of Europe's great seducers.** Blessed with an unparalleled cultural heritage, food that's imitated the world over and a landscape that combines Alpine peaks, stunning coastlines and remote wildernesses, it's been beguiling travellers for centuries. And still today it casts a powerful spell.

Many travellers restrict themselves to the country's star cities, but with a car you'll discover there's more to Italy than Michelangelo masterpieces and Roman ruins. The 38 trips in this book run the length of the country, from the northern Alps to southern Sicily, and cover a wide range of experiences.

So whether you want to tour gourmet towns and historic vineyards, picture-perfect coastlines or pristine national parks, we have a route for you. And if you've only got time for one trip, make it one of our nine Classic Trips, which take you to the very best of Italy. Turn the page for more.

# ITALY

# Classic Trips

STEPHEN STAKS/GETTY IMAGES ©

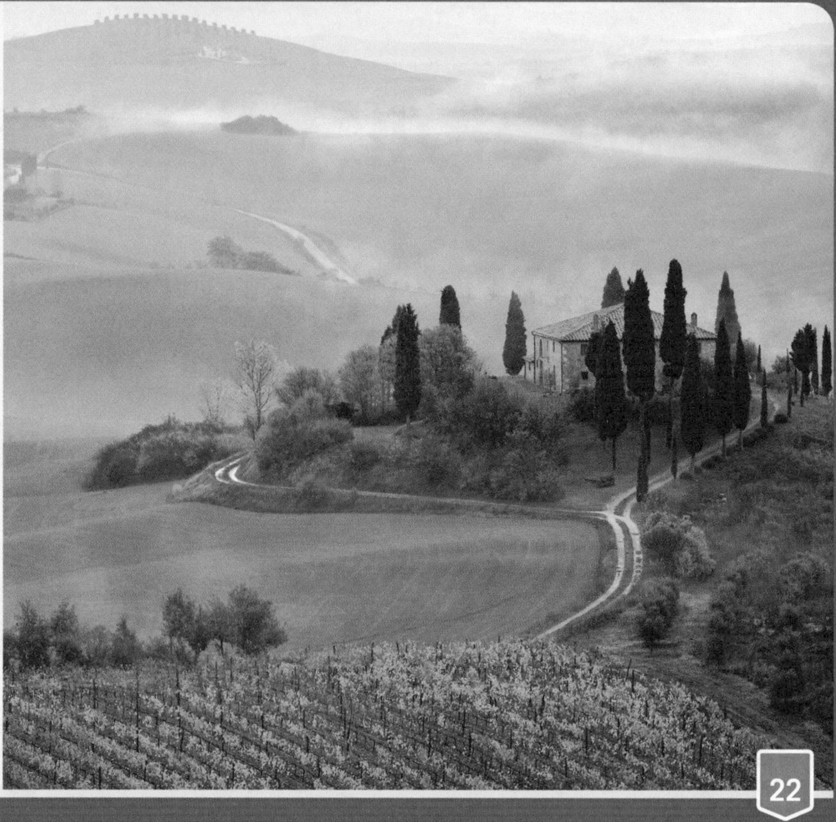


MAXIM BOLOTNIKOV/GETTY IMAGES ©

## What is a Classic Trip?

All the trips in this book show you the best of Italy, but we've chosen nine as our all-time favourites. These are our Classic Trips – the ones that lead you to the best of the iconic sights, the top activities and the unique Italian experiences. Turn the page to see the map, and look out for the Classic Trip stamp throughout the book.

27 **Amalfi Coast** Italy's most dazzling seafront stretch is made for road trips.

22 **Tuscan Wine Tour** An intoxicating blend of scenery, acclaimed restaurants and top-notch wine.

12 **Grande Strada delle Dolomiti** The pink-hued Dolomites form a picture-perfect backdrop.

GLENN VAN DER KNIJFF/GETTY IMAGES ©

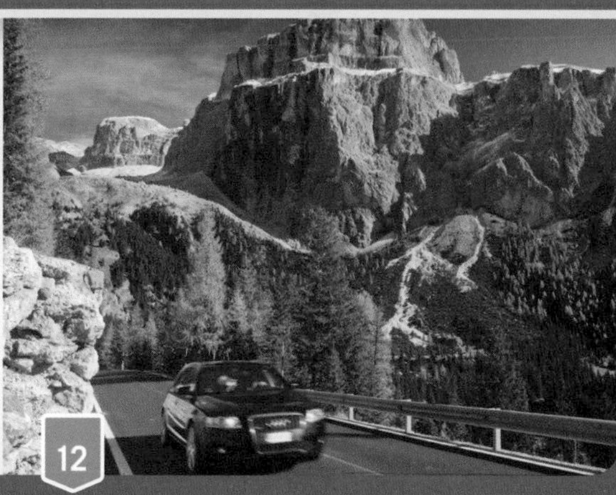

# ITALY Classic Trips

**8 The Graceful Italian Lakes** Destination of choice for Goethe, Hemingway and George Clooney. **5–7 DAYS**

**12 Grande Strada delle Dolomiti** Tour the rock amphitheatre of the Dolomites. **7–10 DAYS**

**13 A Venetian Sojourn** Glide along the Brenta Canal to splendid frescoed villas. **4–5 DAYS**

**1 Grand Tour** The classic cultural tour – part pilgrimage, part rite of passage. **12–14 DAYS**

**15 World Heritage Wonders** Discover the Unesco-listed treasures of Italy's art cities. **14 DAYS**

**22 Tuscan Wine Tour** Red wine fuels this jaunt around historic Chianti vineyards and Tuscan cellars. **4 DAYS**

MOLISE
Nazionale del Gargano
Monte Cavo (949m)
Isernia
Campobasso
PUGLIA
Golfo di Manfredonia
Bari
Capo Circeo
CAMPANIA
Golfo di Gaeta
Mt Vesuvius (1281m)
Olbia
Sassari
Naples
Salerno
Potenza
Matera
Brindisi
Taranto
Ischia
Golfo di Napoli
Capri
Golfo di Salerno
Lecce
Nuoro
BASILICATA
Parco Nazionale del Cilento e Vallo di Diano
Sapri
Parco Nazionale del Pollino
Golfo di Taranto
Gallipoli
Parco Nazionale del Golfo di Orosei e del Gennargentu
Monte Pollino (2248m)
Oristano
Punta La Marmora (1834m)
Tyrrhenian Sea
Golfo di Policastro
Capo Santa Maria di Leuca
SARDINIA
CALABRIA
Cosenza
San Pietro
Cagliari
Crotone
Sant'Antioco
Catanzaro
Capo Malfatano
Golfo di Sant'Eufemia
Golfo di Squillace
Capo Rizzuto
Aeolian Islands
Capo Vaticano
Messina
Reggio Calabria
Trapani
Palermo
Tyrrhenian Coast
Parco Naturale dell'Etna
Ionian Coast
Ionian Sea
Pizzo Carbonara (1979m)
Mt Etna (3340m)
SICILY
Enna
Catania
Agrigento
Syracuse
Gela
Ragusa
MEDITERRANEAN SEA
25
Shadow of Vesuvius
Head from Naples' tumult to Pompeii's long-buried mysteries.
2–3 DAYS
33
Wonders of Ancient Sicily
Palermo's Arab roots to Taormina's Greek splendours.
12–14 DAYS
27
Amalfi Coast
A stunning coastline of vertical landscapes and chic resort towns.
7 DAYS
0 200 km
0 100 miles

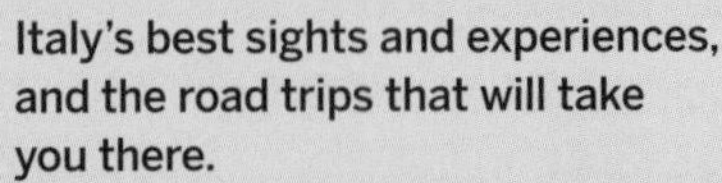

Italy's best sights and experiences, and the road trips that will take you there.

# ITALY HIGHLIGHTS

## Rome

All roads lead to Rome (Roma) and **Trip 1: Grand Tour** is one such, stopping off at the Eternal City en route from Turin (Torino) to Naples (Napoli). The one-time *caput mundi* (capital of the world) is a mesmerising city, home to celebrated icons – the Colosseum, Pantheon, Trevi Fountain, Michelangelo's Sistine Chapel – and spectacular works of art. Even strolling its romantic lanes and operatic piazzas is a thrill to remember.

**TRIPS**  1 15

**Rome** The city's iconic Trevi Fountain

HIGHLIGHTS ★

**Venice** Gondola on the Grand Canal

## Venice

Drive **Trip 15: World Heritage Wonders** and the road runs out in Venice (Venezia), where highways give way to waterways. Venice is absolutely unique and it's a soul-lifting experience to explore its backstreets and piazzas, revelling in East-meets-West architecture. Art treasures abound, but for sheer 'wow' factor little can compare with the Basilica di San Marco and its 24-carat-gold mosaics.

**TRIPS** 1 7 13 15    

## Pompeii

A once-thriving Roman port frozen in its 2000-year-old death throes, Pompeii is an electrifying spectacle. Head down on **Trip 25: Shadow of Vesuvius** and wander its fantastically preserved streets, exploring the forum, the city brothel, the 5000-seat theatre and the frescoed Villa dei Misteri. Body casts of victims add a sense of menace as Vesuvius looms darkly on the horizon.

**TRIPS** 1 25 

## The Dolomites

One of the great soul-stirring sights of northern Italy, the Dolomites are the stars of **Trip 12: Grande Strada delle Dolomiti**. Their pink-hued granite summits form the majestic backdrop for this epic drive along Italy's most famous mountain road between Bolzano and Cortina d'Ampezzo. Stop off en route to admire sweeping panoramas and explore the Alpine villages of the Alta Badia and Alpe di Siusi.

**TRIP** 12

**Cinque Terre** The village of Vernazza

## BEST ROADS FOR DRIVING

**Grande Strada delle Dolomiti** Epic road through exhilarating Alpine scenery. **Trip** 12

**SS17bis** Traverses Abruzzo's awe-inspiring Campo Imperatore plateau in the shadow of the Gran Sasso. **Trip** 18

**SP146** A panoramic drive through classic landscapes in Tuscany's Unesco-listed Val d'Orcia. **Trips** 22 23

**SS163** Also known as the Nastro Azzurro, this road weaves along the precipitous Amalfi Coast. **Trip** 27

## Cinque Terre

Tackle the Unesco-listed Cinque Terre on **Trip 6: Cinematic Cinque Terre**. An idyllic stretch of coastline named after five villages – Riomaggiore, Manarola, Corniglia, Vernazza and Monterosso al Mare – the Cinque Terre offers superb walking. A coastal path snakes along cliffs and hills, while up above, trails traverse shrub-covered mountains as they lead to ancient sanctuaries and heavenly views.

**TRIP** 

**Florence** Views across the city and Arno river from Piazzale Michelangelo

RICHARD I'ANSON/GETTY IMAGES ©

## Florence

From Brunelleschi's red-domed Duomo to Michelangelo's *David* and Botticelli's *The Birth of Venus*, Florence (Firenze) boasts priceless masterpieces and a historic centre that looks much as it did in 1550, with stone towers and cypress-lined gardens. Art aside, the city's captivating centre sets the perfect scene for alfresco dining and relaxed wine drinking. Lap it all up on **Trip 15: World Heritage Wonders** and **Trip 21: Piero della Francesca Trail**.

**TRIPS** 1 15 21 22

## BEST MUSEUMS & GALLERIES

**Vatican Museums** Michelangelo's Sistine Chapel, Raphael frescoes and much, much more. **Trip** 1

**Galleria degli Uffizi** Florence gallery housing Italy's finest collection of Renaissance art. **Trips** 1 15 21

**Peggy Guggenheim Collection** Striking modern art in a classic Venetian setting. **Trip** 13

**Museo Archeologico Nazionale** Naples' premier museum with breathtaking classical sculpture and mosaics from Pompeii. **Trips** 1 25

RICHARD I'ANSON/GETTY IMAGES ©

**Amalfi Coast** Views of Positano

RICHARD I'ANSON/GETTY IMAGES ©

**Lake Como** Waterside Villa Melzi D'Eril

## Amalfi Coast

The quintessential Mediterranean coastline, the Amalfi Coast is Italy's most dazzling seafront stretch. Its single road – detailed in **Trip 27: Amalfi Coast** – curves sinuously along the coast, linking the area's steeply stacked towns and rocky inlets. All around, cliffs sheer down into sparkling blue waters, lemons grow on hillside terraces, and towering *fichi d'India* (prickly pears) guard silent mountain paths.

**TRIP** 27

## Lake Como

The most picturesque and least visited of Italy's main northern lakes, Lake Como (Lago di Como) is a highlight of **Trip 8: The Graceful Italian Lakes**, a scenic jaunt around Lakes Maggiore, Orta and Como. Set in the shadow of the Rhaetian Alps, Lake Como's banks are speckled with Liberty-style villas and fabulous landscaped gardens that burst into blushing colour in April and May.

**TRIP** 8

## Valle d'Aosta

Italy's smallest and least populous region is also one of its most spectacular. Follow **Trip 11: Valle d'Aosta** as it inches up a narrow mountain valley ringed by the icy peaks of Europe's highest mountains, including Monte Bianco (Mont Blanc), Monte Cervino (the Matterhorn), Monte Rosa and Gran Paradiso. Leave your car and take to the slopes for exhilarating hiking and hair-raising skiing.

**TRIP** 11

## Mt Etna

Europe's largest volcano, Etna is a foreboding presence just outside the Sicilian city of Catania. Eruptions are regular, and while many barely register, some light up the sky with dramatic pyrotechnic displays and towering showers of lava. To set your heart racing, take **Trip 35: Sicilian Island Hop**, climb to the craters at the black, barren summit and survey the vast views that unfurl beneath you.

**TRIP** 35

## Tuscan Landscapes

Picture in your mind's eye the ideal Italian landscape – golden fields, haughty cypress trees, and hills capped by medieval towns. You're imagining Tuscany, whose fabled panoramas have inspired everybody from Renaissance artists to overwrought poets and modern motorists. Drive **Trip 23: Tuscan Landscapes** or **Trip 22: Tuscan Wine Tour** and give yourself up to its soothing beauty and delicious vino.

**TRIPS**  

MARK BOLTON/GETTY IMAGES ©

(left) **Tuscan Landscapes** The golden fields of the Val d'Orcia

(below) **Milan** The city's cathedral

MARK HORN/GETTY IMAGES ©

## Milan

With its designer boutiques, cool aperitif bars and chic restaurants, Italy's fashion and financial capital is a city for urbanites with a sense of style. Milan (Milano) is also a cultural heavyweight, home to Europe's most famous opera house, a gloriously fairy-tale Gothic cathedral and da Vinci's celebrated mural *The Last Supper*. Discover all this on **Trip 1: Grand Tour** or **Trip 7: Northern Cities**.

**TRIPS** 

## BEST HILLTOP TOWNS

**Matera** Basilicata town famous for its primitive *sassi* (cave houses). **Trip** 31

**Urbino** A Renaissance gem in off-the-radar Le Marche. **Trip** 21

**Orvieto** Proud clifftop home of a stunning Gothic cathedral. **Trip** 23

**Montalcino** Tuscan producer of Brunello di Montalcino, one of Italy's top red wines. **Trip** 22

Delectable pasta dishes await

## Food & Wine

With its superb produce, culinary traditions and world-beating wine, Italy is a food-lover's dream destination. Whether it's eating wood-fired pizza at a Neapolitan pizzeria, dining alfresco on a medieval piazza, or tasting Chianti at a Tuscan vineyard, great foodie experiences await at every turn.

3 **Gourmet Piedmont** Feast on chocolate, cheese and wine in Italy's Slow Food heartland.

22 **Tuscan Wine Tour** Mull over Tuscany's great reds in Chianti vineyards.

24 **Foodie Emilia-Romagna** Discover the towns that put the Parma into ham and the Bolognese into spag bol.

33 **Wonders of Ancient Sicily** Forget baroque basilicas and gorge on devilish Sicilian *dolci* (sweets).

## Art & Architecture

Boasting an unparalleled artistic and architectural legacy, Italy is home to some of the Western world's most celebrated masterpieces. Works by Renaissance heroes and baroque maestros grace the country's churches, museums and galleries, many of which are works of art in their own right.

1 **Grand Tour** Take in the Scrovegni Chapel, *The Last Supper*, the Galleria dell'Accademia et al.

7 **Northern Cities** Admire Giotto frescoes and medieval cityscapes.

21 **Piero della Francesca Trail** From Urbino to Florence, follow the trail of frescoes left by the Renaissance master.

36 **Sicilian Baroque** Swoon over extravagant baroque architecture in southeastern Sicily.

## Ancient Relics

Everywhere you go in Italy you're reminded of the country's long and tumultuous past. Etruscan tombs and Greek temples stand testament to pre-Roman civilisations, while amphitheatres, aqueducts, even whole towns, testify to the ambition of ancient Rome's rulers and the genius of its architects.

15 **World Heritage Wonders** Rome's Colosseum and Verona's Arena headline on this classic cross-country drive.

19 **Etruscan Tuscany & Lazio** Duck into underground tombs decorated with ancient frescoes.

25 **Shadow of Vesuvius** Wander around Pompeii and Herculaneum, the most celebrated victims of Vesuvius' volcanic fury.

33 **Wonders of Ancient Sicily** Sicily's ancient Greek temples are the best you'll see outside Greece.

**Selinunte** Explore ancient Greek ruins (Trip 33)

# Islands & Beaches

From the cliffs of the Amalfi Coast to the villages of the Cinque Terre, and from Sicily's volcanic seascapes to Sardinia's dreamy beaches, Italy's 7600km-long coastline is as varied as it is enticing. Add crystal-clear waters in a thousand shades of blue and you've got the perfect summer recipe.

6 **Cinematic Cinque Terre** Cruise one of Italy's most picture-perfect coastal stretches.

27 **Amalfi Coast** Italy's most celebrated coastline is a classic Mediterranean pin-up.

35 **Sicilian Island Hop** Revel in the volcanic beauty of the Unesco-listed Aeolian Islands.

37 **Emerald Coast** Sardinia's northern coast boasts dazzling beaches and heavenly waters.

# Outdoor Activities

With its pristine seas, Alpine peaks, hills, lakes and rivers, Italy offers great year-round sport. Mountain resorts in the Alps and Apennines offer the full gamut of winter sports as well as superb hiking, climbing and cycling. Offshore, there's fabulous diving and full-on windsurfing.

10 **Roof of Italy** Hike the 100 glaciers of the Stelvio and hit the spa amid mountain peaks in Merano.

11 **Valle d'Aosta** A spectacular Alpine region and stunning outdoor playground.

18 **Abruzzo's Wild Landscapes** Trek amid wolves and bears in Abruzzo's national parks.

37 **Emerald Coast** Superb diving and windsurfing await in Sardinia's glorious seas.

# Villas & Palaces

Ever since the days of the Roman Empire, Italy's ruling dynasties have employed the top artists and architects of their day to design their homes. The results are imperial palaces and royal residences, Renaissance mansions and aristocratic villas.

2 **Savoy Palace Circuit** Tour the Savoy family's royal palaces in Turin and the Piedmont countryside.

8 **The Graceful Italian Lakes** For grace, style and floral exuberance, head to the villas and gardens of Italy's northern lakes.

13 **A Venetian Sojourn** Stop at Unesco-protected Palladian villas as you drive Veneto's wine country.

15 **World Heritage Wonders** Explore imperial palaces and art-filled *palazzi* (mansions) in Rome, Siena, Florence and Venice.

# NEED TO KNOW

## CURRENCY
Euros (€)

## LANGUAGE
Italian

## VISAS
Generally not required for stays of up to 90 days (or at all for EU nationals); some nationalities need a Schengen visa (p411).

## FUEL
You'll find filling stations on autostradas and all major roads. Reckon on €1.93 for unleaded petrol and €1.81 for diesel, per litre.

## RENTAL CARS
**Avis** (www.avis.com)

**Europcar** (www.europcar.com)

**Hertz** (www.hertz.com)

**Maggiore** (www.maggiore.it)

## IMPORTANT NUMBERS
**Ambulance** (☎118)

**Emergency** (☎112)

**Police** (☎113)

**Roadside Assistance** (☎803 116; ☎800 116800 from a foreign mobile phone)

## Climate

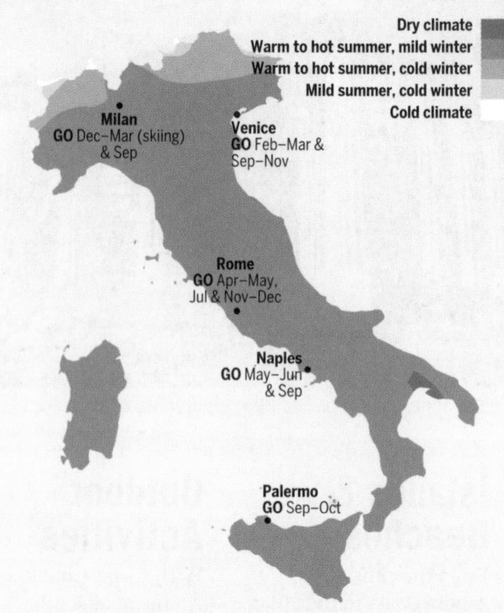


## When to Go

### High Season (Jul–Aug)
» Prices high on the coast; accommodation discounts available in some cities in August.

» Prices rocket for Christmas, New Year and Easter.

» Late December to March is high season in the Alps and Dolomites.

### Shoulder Season (Apr–Jun & Sep–Oct)
» Good deals on accommodation, especially in the south.

» Spring is best for festivals, flowers and local produce.

» Autumn provides warm weather and the grape harvest.

### Low Season (Nov–Mar)
» Prices at their lowest – up to 30% less than in high season.

» Many sights and hotels closed in coastal and mountainous areas.

» A good period for cultural events in large cities.

## Daily Costs

### Budget: Less than €100

» Double room in a budget hotel: €50–€100

» Pizza or pasta: €6–€12

» Excellent markets and delis for self-catering

### Midrange: €100–€200

» Double room in a midrange hotel: €80–€180

» Lunch and dinner in local restaurants: €25–€45

» Museum admission: €5–€15

### Top End: More than €200

» Double room in a four- or five-star hotel: €200–€450

» Top-restaurant dinner: €50–€150

» Opera tickets: €15–€150

## Eating

**Restaurants (Ristoranti)** Formal service and refined dishes, with prices to match.

**Trattorias** Family-run places with informal service and classic regional cooking.

**Vegetarians** Most places offer good vegetable starters and side dishes.

Price indicators for a meal with *primo* (first course), *secondo* (second course), *dolce* (dessert) and a glass of house wine:

| | |
|---|---|
| **€** | less than €25 |
| **€€** | €25–€45 |
| **€€€** | more than €45 |

## Sleeping

**Hotels** From luxury boutique palaces to modest family-run *pensioni* (small hotels).

**B&Bs** Rooms in restored farmhouses, city *palazzi* (mansions) or seaside bungalows.

**Agriturismi** Farmstays range from working farms to luxury rural retreats.

Price indicators for a double room with bathroom:

| | |
|---|---|
| **€** | less than €100 |
| **€€** | €100–€200 |
| **€€€** | more than €200 |

## Arriving in Italy

### Leonardo da Vinci (Fiumicino) Airport (Rome)

**Rental cars** Agencies are near the multilevel car park. Look for signs in the Arrivals area.

**Trains & buses** Run every 30 minutes from 6.30am to 11.40pm.

**Night buses** Hourly departures from 12.30am to 5am.

**Taxis** Set fare €48; 45 minutes.

### Malpensa Airport (Milan)

**Rental cars** In Terminal 1 agencies are on the 1st floor; in Terminal 2 in the Arrivals hall.

**Malpensa Express & Shuttle** Runs every 30 minutes from 5am to 11pm.

**Night buses** Limited services from 12.15am to 5am.

**Taxis** Set fare €90; 50 minutes.

### Capodichino Airport (Naples)

**Rental cars** Agencies are located in the main Arrivals hall.

**Airport shuttles** Run every 20 minutes from 6.30am to 11.40pm.

**Taxis** Set fare €19 to €23; 30 minutes.

## Mobile Phones (Cell Phones)

Local SIM cards can be used in European, Australian and unlocked, multiband US phones. Other phones must be set to roaming.

## Internet Access

Wi-fi is available in many lodgings and city bars, often free. Internet cafes are thin on the ground and typically charge €2 to €6 per hour.

## Money

ATMs at airports, most train stations and in towns and cities. Credit cards accepted in most hotels and restaurants. Keep cash for immediate expenses.

## Tipping

Not obligatory but round up the bill in pizzerias and trattorias; 10% is normal in upmarket restaurants.

## Useful Websites

**Italia** (www.italia.it) Official tourism site.

**Michelin** (www.viamichelin.it) A useful route planner.

**Agriturismi** (www.agriturismi.it) Guide to farmstays.

**Lonely Planet** (www.lonelyplanet.com/italy) Destination lowdown.

**For more, see Road Trip Essentials (p396).**

## ROME

Even in a country of exquisite cities, Rome (Roma) is special. Pulsating, seductive and utterly disarming, it's a mesmerising mix of artistic masterpieces and iconic monuments, theatrical piazzas and haunting ruins. If your road leads to Rome, give yourself a couple of days to explore its headline sights.

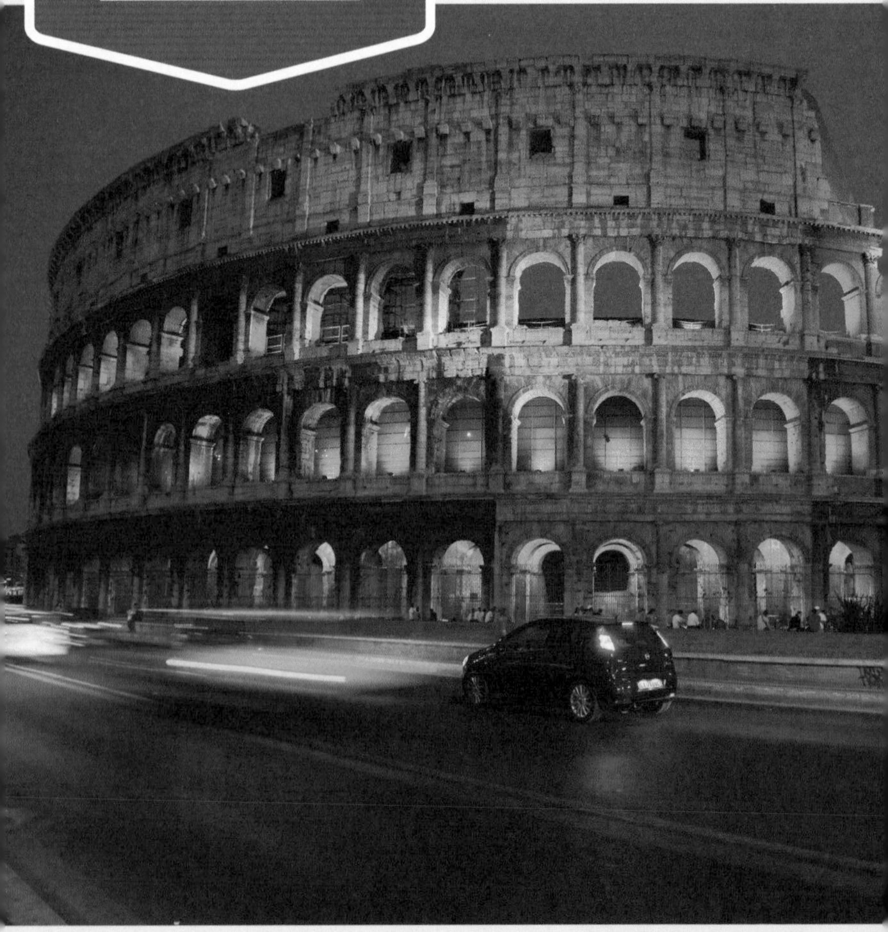

**Rome** The Colosseum at night

## Getting Around

Driving is not the best way to get around Rome. Traffic can be chaotic and much of the *centro storico* (historic centre) is closed to non-authorised traffic on weekdays and weekend evenings. You're better off using public transport; a day pass is €6.

## Parking

On-street parking, which is expensive and scarce, is denoted by blue lines. There are a few car parks in the centre, which charge about €15 to €20 per day. Some top-end hotels offer parking, usually at extra charge.

JUAN SILVA/GETTY IMAGES ©

## Discover the Taste of Rome

For authentic nose-to-tail Roman cooking check out the trattorias in Testaccio, and for traditional Roman-Jewish cuisine head to the atmospheric Jewish Ghetto.

## Live Like a Local

The most atmospheric, and expensive, place to stay is the *centro storico*, where you'll have everything on your doorstep. Night owls will enjoy Trastevere, while Tridente offers refined accommodation and designer shopping. The Vatican is also popular.

## Useful Websites

**060608** (www.060608.it) Official tourist website.

**Pierreci** (www.pierreci.it) Information and ticket booking for Rome's monuments.

**Lonely Planet** (www.lonelyplanet.com/rome) Destination lowdown, hotels and traveller forum.

## Trips Through Rome: 

# TOP EXPERIENCES

### ➡ Get to the Heart of the Ancient City

Thrill to the sight of the Colosseum, Roman Forum and Palatino, where Romulus and Remus supposedly founded the city in 753 BC.

### ➡ Gaze Heavenwards in the Sistine Chapel

File past kilometres of priceless art at the Vatican Museums to arrive at the Sistine Chapel and Michelangelo's fabled frescoes. (www.vatican.va)

### ➡ Villa Borghese's Baroque Treasures

Head to the Museo e Galleria Borghese to marvel at a series of exhilarating sculptures by baroque maestro Gian Lorenzo Bernini. (www.galleriaborghese.it)

### ➡ Admire the Pantheon's Dome

The Pantheon is the best preserved of Rome's ancient monuments, but it's only when you get inside that you get the full measure of the place as its dome soars above you.

### ➡ Pay Homage at St Peter's Basilica

Capped by Michelangelo's landmark dome, the Vatican's showpiece church is a masterpiece of Renaissance architecture and baroque decor.

### ➡ Live the Trastevere Dolce Vita

Join the evening crowds in Trastevere to eat earthy Roman food, drink in the many bars and pubs, and parade up and down the streets.

### ➡ Hang Out on the Piazzas

Hanging out on Rome's piazzas is part and parcel of Roman life – having an ice cream on Piazza Navona, people-watching on Piazza del Popolo and posing on Piazza di Spagna.

**Florence** City views from Piazzale Michelangelo

# FLORENCE

**An essential stop on every Italian itinerary, Florence (Firenze) is one of the world's great art cities, boasting Renaissance icons and a wonderfully intact *centro storico*. Beyond the Michelangelo masterpieces and Medici *palazzi* (mansions), there's a buzzing bar scene and great shopping in artisan workshops and designer boutiques.**

## Getting Around

Non-resident traffic is banned from the centre of Florence for most of the week, and if you enter the Limited Traffic Zone (ZTL) you risk a €150 fine. Rather than drive, walk or use the city buses; tickets cost €1.20 or €2 on board.

## Parking

There is free street parking around Piazzale Michelangelo (park within the blue lines). Pricey (around €20 per day) underground parking can be found around Fortezza da Basso and in the Oltrarno beneath Piazzale di Porta Romana. Otherwise, ask if your hotel can arrange parking.

## Discover the Taste of Florence

Florence teems with restaurants, trattorias, *osterie* (casual taverns) and wine bars catering to all budgets. Top neighbourhoods include Santa Croce, home to some of the city's best restaurants, and over-the-river Oltrarno.

## Live Like a Local

To be right in the heart of it, go for the Duomo and Piazza della Signoria areas, which have some excellent budget options. Near the train station, Santa Maria Novella has some good midrange boutique/design hotels.

## Useful Websites

**Firenze Turismo** (www.firenzeturismo.it) Official tourist office site; comprehensive and up to date.

**The Florentine** (www.theflorentine.com) For accommodation, sights information and practical advice.

**Firenze Musei** (www.firenzemusei.it) Book tickets for the Uffizi and Accademia.

## Trips Through Florence: 1 15 21 22

**Naples** Church on a city piazza

# NAPLES

**Naples (Napoli) is an exhilarating sprawl of bombastic baroque churches, Dickensian alleyways and electrifying street life. Its in-your-face vitality can be overwhelming, but once you've found your feet you'll discover a city of regal palaces, world-renowned museums, superb pizzerias and sweeping seascapes.**

## Getting Around

Neapolitan traffic is so anarchic that even Italians balk at the idea of driving here. Much of the city centre is closed to non-resident traffic, so try to leave your car as soon as you can and use public transport (bus, metro and funicular).

## Parking

Street parking is not a good idea – car theft is a problem – and few hotels offer it. There's a 24-hour car park east of the city centre at Via Brin, otherwise ask your hotel for advice.

## Discover the Taste of Naples

To taste authentic Neapolitan pizza, head to the *centro storico* where you'll find a number of hard-core pizzerias serving the genuine article. For a more refined meal, make for seafront Santa Lucia and the cobbled lanes of Chiaia.

## Live Like a Local

For maximum atmosphere, consider the *centro storico*. Seaside Santa Lucia is home to some of the city's most prestigious hotels, and Chiaia is cool and chic. For lofty views and a chilled-out vibe, hit Vomero.

## Useful Websites

**I Naples** (www.inaples.it) The city's official tourist-board site.

**Napoli Unplugged** (www.napoliunplugged.com) Attractions, up-to-date listings, articles and blog entries.

**Turismo Regione Campania** (www.turismoregionecampania.it) Events listings, as well as audio clips and itineraries.

## Trips Through Naples:

# VENICE

**A magnificent, unforgettable spectacle, Venice (Venezia) is a hauntingly beautiful city. For 1000 years it was one of Europe's great sea powers and its unique cityscape reflects this, with golden Byzantine domes and great Gothic churches, noble *palazzi* and busy waterways.**

## Getting Around

Venice is off-limits to cars, leaving you to walk or take a boat. You'll inevitably get lost at some point but directions to Piazza San Marco, the Rialto and Accademia are posted on yellow signs. *Vaporetti* (small ferries) ply the city's waterways; a one-way ticket costs €7.

## Parking

Once you've crossed the Ponte della Libertà bridge from Mestre, you'll have to park at Piazzale Roma or Tronchetto car parks; bank on up to €26 for 24 hours.

BUENA VISTA IMAGES/GETTY IMAGES ©

**Venice** Grand Canal

## TOP EXPERIENCES

### ➡ Cruise the Grand Canal

Whet your sightseeing appetite by taking a *vaporetto* (small ferry) along the Grand Canal.

### ➡ Basilica di San Marco Mosaics

Step inside Venice's signature basilica, an architectural hybrid of Byzantine domes, Gothic windows and Egyptian walls, to gape at golden dome mosaics. (www.basilicasanmarco.it)

### ➡ Compare Titian & Tintoretto

Soaring I Frari is home to Titian's masterpiece, *Assumption*. Nearby, the Scuola Grande di San Rocco boasts stunning frescoes by Tintoretto. (www.scuolagrandesanrocco.it)

### ➡ Modern Art at the Guggenheim

Step inside the palatial home of Peggy Guggenheim to peruse canvases by Jackson Pollock and the giants of modern art. (www.guggenheim-venice.it)

## Discover the Taste of Venice

Venice's version of tapas, bar snacks called *cicheti* are served in *osterie* across town at lunch and between 6pm and 8pm.

## Live Like a Local

Many Venetians open their historical homes as B&Bs – check the Turismo Venezia website for lists. Dorsoduro and San Polo are charming areas to stay in, near major museums and with plenty of bar action. Cannaregio is another good option, relatively untouristy and in parts very picturesque.

## Useful Websites

**Turismo Venezia** (www.turismovenezia.it) The city's official tourism site.

**A Guest in Venice** (www.unospitedivenezia.it) Hotelier association that provides information on upcoming exhibits, events and lectures.

**Veneto Inside** (www.venetoinside.com) Book entry to the Basilica di San Marco, guided visits and water taxis.

## Trips Through Venice: 

# ITALY BY REGION

Driving in Italy is a thrilling way to experience the country in all its varied beauty. To help you on your way, we've divided the country into three areas and outlined what each has to offer.

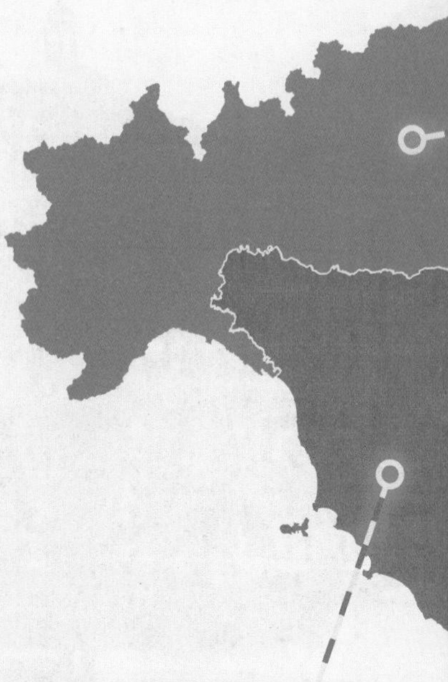

## Central Italy (p177)

In central Italy the road leads to heavyweight destinations such as Rome, Florence and Assisi, as well as frescoed Etruscan tombs, remote Tuscan monasteries and national parks in Abruzzo. Foodies can indulge their passions in the gourmet towns of Emilia-Romagna and Tuscany's historic vineyards.

**Discover Etruscan treasures on Trip** 19

**Taste wine on Trip** 

## Northern Italy (p35)

Revel in spectacular scenery as you drive epic Alpine roads, stunning coastlines and gorgeous lakesides. Our northern Italian trips take in everything from the wine-rich hills of Piedmont to exotic lakeside gardens, the pink-hued Dolomites and Venetian villas, as well as great cities such as Genoa, Turin and Milan.

**Tour art-rich cities on Trip 7**

**Motor through the Dolomites on Trip 12**

## Southern Italy (p269)

Get off the beaten track in the rugged wilds of Calabria and Basilicata and enjoy coastal thrills on Sardinia and the Amalfi Coast. In Sicily you can feast on exuberant art, decadent food and smoking volcanoes, while near Naples, Mt Vesuvius broods menacingly over ruined Pompeii.

**Enjoy the Amalfi Coast on Trip 27**

**Explore Greek ruins on Trip** 

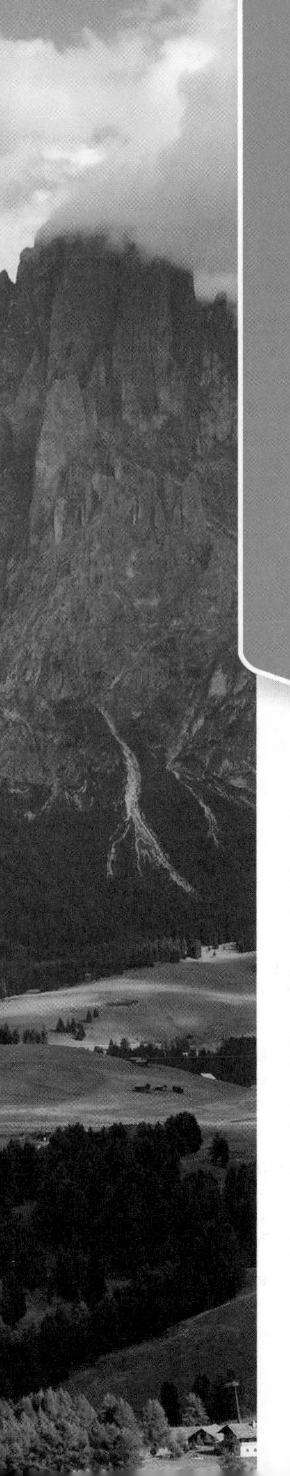

# Northern Italy

**FROM THE SNOWY SLOPES OF THE MILKY WAY TO VILLAS FRAMED BY GAZEBOS** and mould-breaking art and architecture, northern Italy is as action packed as it is artful. Its mountains, lakes and coastal villages have been luring artists, celebrities and moneyed Mitteleuropeans since the days of the Grand Tour, and it's easy to see what drew them here: world-class art, an embarrassment of culinary riches, cult wines and a slew of sophisticated cities.

While Venice's city of palaces dazzles and Milan's Golden Quad rapidly helps to relieve you of your hard-earned cash, you're never far from a rural hinterland that still moves with the rhythm of the seasons and that seems largely untouched by modern tourism.

**Alpe di Siusi** Europe's highest alpine pastures, framed by the magnificent Dolomites (Trip 12)
DENNIS K JOHNSON/GETTY IMAGES ©

*Classic Trip*

**1 Grand Tour 12–14 Days**
The classic cultural tour – part pilgrimage, part rite of passage. (p39)

**2 Savoy Palace Circuit 3–4 Days**
The impressive property portfolio of the frivolous Dukes of Savoy. (p55)

**3 Gourmet Piedmont 6 Days**
Bold Barolos, white truffles and Asti spumante put fizz in this food tour. (p63)

**4 Meandering the Maritime Alps 7 Days**
Ski the Milky Way and hike old salt routes in the Gran Paradiso park. (p71)

**5 Italian Riviera 4 Days**
Seaside bastions, palm-fringed promenades, Belle Époque villas. (p79)

**6 Cinematic Cinque Terre 5–7 Days**
Tour maritime vineyards and secret coves to the Gulf of Poets. (p87)

**7 Northern Cities 7–10 Days**
Visit grand-slam cultural sites amid the rice paddies of the Po valley. (p97)

*Classic Trip*

**8 The Graceful Italian Lakes 5–7 Days**
The destination of choice for Goethe, Hemingway and George Clooney. (p109)

**9 A Weekend at Lake Garda 4 Days**
The ultimate lakeside tour through vineyards, orchards and olive groves. (p121)

**10** **Roof of Italy 6 Days**
Dare to drive Europe's highest Alpine pass for the spa on the other side. (p129)

**11** **Valle d'Aosta 5 Days**
Hike the Gran Paradiso and ascend Monte Bianco, Europe's highest peak. (p137)

*Classic Trip*
**12** **Grande Strada delle Dolomiti 7–10 Days**
Admire the rocky amphitheatre of the rose-coloured Dolomites. (p145)

*Classic Trip*
**13** **A Venetian Sojourn 4–5 Days**
Glide along the Brenta Canal to splendid frescoed villas. (p157)

**14** **Trieste to Tarvisio 7 Days**
From Italo-Austrian Trieste zigzag through vineyards to Alpine Tarvisio. (p169)

### Scrovegni Chapel
See the Renaissance blossoming through the tears in Giotto's moving frescoes for the Scrovegni Chapel on Trips 1 7 13

### Portofino Peninsula
Steel a march on Cinque Terre hikers and walk the quiet pathways on the Portofino peninsula, ending with a Spritz at Caffè Excelsior on Trip 6

### Truffles
Strike gastronomic gold in Alba, and dine on prized white truffles on Trip 3

### Terme Merano
Dip in and out of hot and cold pools amid stunning mountain scenery, just as Austrian royals, and Kafka, have done before you on Trip 10

### Walking the Alta Vie
Walk on the roof of the Dolomites through Alpine meadows strewn with wildflowers on Trip 12

***Florence*** *Step back into the 15th century in this Renaissance wonderland*

Classic Trip

# Grand Tour

1

*The gap-year journey of its day, the Grand Tour is a search for art and enlightenment, adventure and debauchery.*

## TRIP HIGHLIGHTS

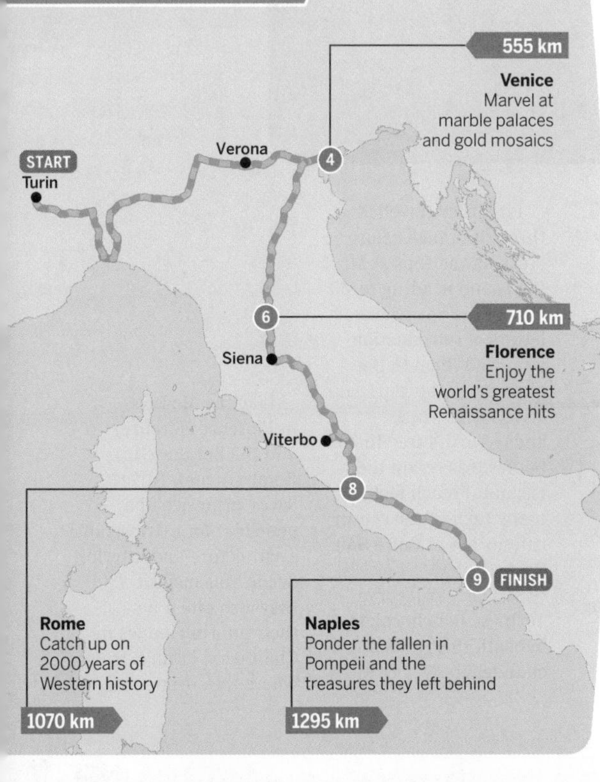

**12–14 DAYS**
**1295KM / 804 MILES**

**GREAT FOR...**

**BEST TIME TO GO**

Spring (March–May) is perfect for urban sightseeing.

**ESSENTIAL PHOTO**

Florence's multicoloured, marble *duomo* (cathedral).

Rome, the repository of over 2500 years of European history.

Classic Trip

# 1 Grand Tour

From the Savoy palaces of Turin and Leonardo's *Last Supper* to the dubious drinking dens of Genoa and the pleasure palaces of Rome, the Grand Tour is part scholar's pilgrimage and part rite of passage. Offering a chance to view some of the world's greatest masterpieces and hear Vivaldi played on 18th-century cellos, it is a rollicking trip filled with the sights, sounds and tastes that have shaped European society for centuries.

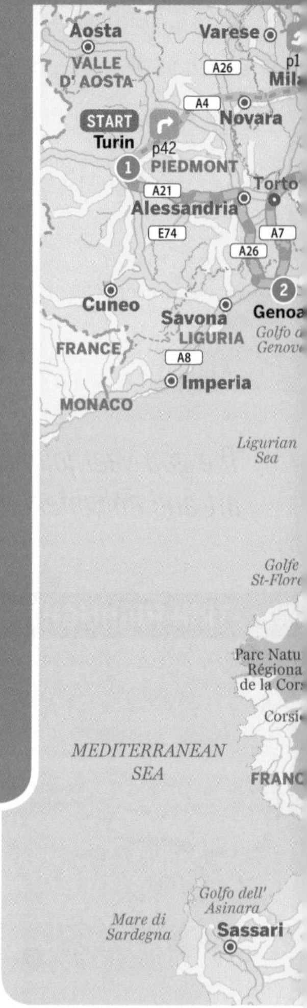

## 1 Turin

In his travel guide, *Voyage through Italy* (1670), travel writer and tutor Richard Lassels advocated a grand cultural tour of Europe, and in particular Italy, for young English aristocrats, during which the study of classical antiquity and the High Renaissance would ready them for future influential roles shaping the political, economic and social realities of the day.

First they travelled through France before crossing the Alps at Mt Cenis and heading to Turin (Torino), where letters of introduction admitted them to the city's agreeable Parisian-style social whirl. Today Turin's tree-lined boulevards retain their elegant, French feel and many turn-of-the century cafes, such as **Caffè San Carlo** (Piazza San Carlo 156; ⌚8am-1am), still serve Torinese hot chocolate beneath their gilded chandeliers.

Like the Medicis in Florence (Firenze) and the Borghese in Rome (Roma), Turin's Savoy princes had a penchant for extravagant architecture and interior decor. You suspect they also pined for their hunting lodges in Chambéry, France, from where they originated, as they invited André le Nôtre, Versailles landscaper, to design the gardens of **Palazzo Reale's** (Piazza Castello; adult/reduced €6.50/3.25; ⌚8.30am-7.30pm Tue-Sun) in 1697.

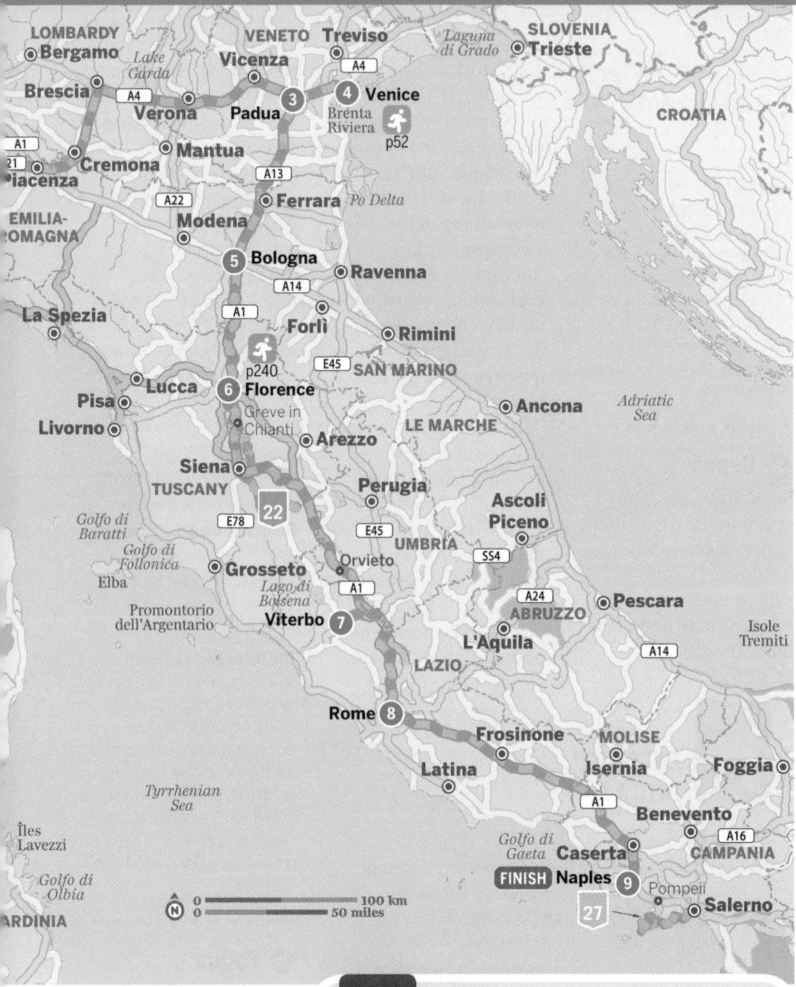

p50

**The Drive »** The two-hour (170km) drive to Genoa is all

**LINK YOUR TRIP**

**22 Tuscan Wine Tour**
Linger in the bucolic hills around Florence and enjoy fine gourmet dining and world-renowned wine-tasting (p243).

**27 Amalfi Coast**
Play truant from high-minded museums and head south from Naples for the Blue Ribbon drive on the Amalfi Coast (p291).

on autostrada, the final stretch twisting through the mountains. Leave Turin following signs for the A55 (towards Alessandria), which quickly merges with the A21 passing through the pretty Piedmontese countryside. Just before Alessandria turn south onto the A26 for Genoa/ Livorno.

## 2 Genoa

Some travellers, shy of crossing the Alps, might arrive by boat in Genoa (Genova). Despite its superb location, mild microclimate and lush flora, the city had a dubious reputation. Its historic centre was a warren of dark, insalubrious *caruggi* (alleys), stalked by prostitutes and beggars, while the excessive shrewdness of the Genovese banking families earned them a reputation, according to author Thomas Nugent, as 'a treacherous and over-reaching set of people'.

And yet with tourists and businessmen arriving from around the world, Genoa was, and still is, a cosmopolitan place. The Rolli Palaces, a collection of grand mansions originally meant to host visiting popes, dignitaries and royalty, made Via Balbi and Strada Nuova (now Via Giuseppe Garibaldi) two of the most famous streets in Europe. Visit the finest of them, the **Palazzo Spinola** (Galleria Nazionale; www.palazzospinola.it; Piazza Superiore di Pellicceria 1; adult/reduced €5/3; ⏲9am-8pm Tue-Sat, 2-8pm Sun) and the **Palazzo Reale** (www.palazzorealegenova.it; Via Balbi 10; adult/child €4/2; ⏲9am-7pm Thu-Sun, to 1.30pm Tue & Wed). Afterwards stop for sweets at **Pietro Romanengo fu Stefano** (www.romanengo.com; Via Soziglia 74r); see p44.

p50

**The Drive »** This 365km drive takes most of the day, so stop for lunch in Cremona (p50). Although the drive is on autostrada, endless fields of corn line the route. Take the A7 north out of Genoa and at Tortona exit onto the A21 around industrial Piacenza to Brescia. At Brescia, change again onto the A4 direct to Padua.

## 3 Padua

Bound for Venice (Venezia), Grand Tourists could hardly avoid visiting Padua (Padova), although by the 18th century international students no longer flocked to **Palazzo del Bò** (☎049 827 30 47; Via VIII Febbraio; adult/reduced €5/3.50; ⏲tours 9.15am, 10.15am & 11.15pm Tue, Thu & Sat, 3.15pm, 4.15pm & 5.15pm Mon, Wed & Fri),

### DETOUR: MILAN

**Start: 1 Turin**

No Grand Tour would be complete without a detour up the A4 to Milan (Milano) to eyeball Leonardo da Vinci's iconic **Il Cenacolo** (The Last Supper; www.cenacolovinciano.net; Piazza Santa Maria delle Grazie 2; adult/reduced €6.50/3.25; ⏲8.15am-7pm Mon-Sat). Advance booking is essential (booking fee €1.50).

From his *Portrait of a Young Man* (c 1486), to portraits of Duke Ludovico Sforza's beautiful mistresses, *The Lady with the Ermine* (c 1489) and *La Belle Ferronière* (c 1490), Leonardo transformed the rigid conventions of portraiture to depict highly individual images imbued with naturalism. Then he evolved concepts of idealised proportions and the depiction of internal emotional states through physical dynamism *(St Jerome)*, all of which cohere in the masterly *Il Cenacolo*.

While you're here, step out on our Milan walking tour (p106).

the Venetian Republic's radical university where Copernicus and Galileo taught class.

You can visit the university's claustrophobic, wooden anatomy theatre (the first in the world), although it's no longer *de rigueur* to witness dissections on the average tourist itinerary. Afterwards don't forget to pay your respects to the skulls of noble professors who donated themselves for dissection because of the difficulty involved in acquiring fresh corpses. Their skulls are lined up in the graduation hall.

Beyond the university the melancholy air of the city did little to detain foreign visitors. Even Giotto's spectacular frescoes in the **Scrovegni Chapel** (www.cappelladegliscrovegni.it; Giardini dell'Arena; adult/reduced €13/8; ⏲9am-7pm), where advance reservations are essential, were of limited interest given medieval art was out of fashion, and only devout Catholics ventured to revere the strange relics of Saint Anthony in the **Basilica di Sant'Antonio** (www.basilicadelsanto.org; Piazza del Santo; ⏲6.30am-7.45pm, to 6.45pm Nov-Mar).

**The Drive »** Barely 50km from Venice, the drive from Padua is through featureless areas of light industry along the A4 and then the A57.

TRIP HIGHLIGHT

## 4 Venice

Top of the itinerary, Venice at last! Then, as now, *La Serenissima's* watery landscape captured the imagination of travellers. At **Carnivale** (www.carnivale.venezia.it) in February numbers swelled to 30,000; now they number in the hundreds of thousands. You cannot take your car onto the lagoon islands so leave it in a secure garage in Mestre, such as **Garage Europa** (www.garageeuropametre.com; per day €14), and hop on the train to Venice Santa Lucia where water taxis connect to all the islands.

Aside from the mind-improving art in the **Galleria dell'Accademia** (www.gallerieaccademia.org; Campo della Carità 1050; adult/reduced €6.50/3.25; ⏲8.15am-2pm Mon, to 7.15pm Tue-Sun), extraordinary architectural follies such as the **Palazzo Ducale**, the **Campanile** and Longhena's **Chiesa di Santa Maria della Salute**, as well as the glittering Eastern domes of **Basilica di San Marco** (www.basilicasanmarco.it; Piazza San Marco; basilica entry free; ⏲9.45am-5pm Mon-Sat, 2-4pm Sun), Venice was considered, according to author Bruce Redford, the 'locus of decadent Italianate allure'. Venetian wives were notorious for keeping handsome escorts *(cicisbeo)*, courtesans held powerful positions at court and much time was devoted to frequenting casinos and coffeehouses. **Caffè Florian** (www.caffeflorian.com; Piazza San Marco 56/59; drinks €8-12; ⏲10am-midnight Thu-Tue) still adheres to rules established in the 1700s.

So do as the Venetians would do, glide down the **Grand Canal** on the **No 1 vaporetto** (small passenger ferry; ticket €6.50) for an architectural tour of 50 *palazzi* (mansions), gossip in the balconies of the **Teatro La Fenice** (☎reservations 041 24 24; www.teatrolafenice.it; Campo San Fantin 1965; audiotours adult/reduced €7/5), or listen for summer thunderstorms in Vivaldi's *Four Seasons*, played by **Interpreti Veneziani** (www.interpretiveneziani.com; Chiesa San Vidal, San Marco 2862; adult/reduced €25/20; ⏲8.30pm).

For more earthly pleasures take a tour of Venice's centuries-old markets with our gourmet food walk (p52).

✕ 🛏 p50

**The Drive »** Retrace your steps to Padua on the A57 and A4 and navigate around the ring road in the direction of Bologna to pick up the A13 southwest for this short 1½-hour drive. After Padua the dual carriageway dashes through wide-open farmland and crosses the Po river that forms the southern border of the Veneto.

Classic Trip

BRUNO MORANDI/GETTY IMAGES ©

CHARLES BOWMAN/GETTY IMAGES ©

## LOCAL KNOWLEDGE
MARIO PIETRACCETTA, HOTELIER, VILLA ROSMARINO

In Genoa you must get a box of *canditi* (candied fruit) from Pietro Romanengo fu Stefano (p42). The idea of sugared goods came to Genoa from the Middle East. They were originally created so sailors could take some fruit to sea, but Stefano Romanengo turned them into an art form in the 18th century with his Parisian-style marron glacé. The shop on Via Soziglia hasn't changed since 1814 and the candies still come in the original blue-paper packaging.

Top: Piazza Maggiore, Bologna
Left: Basilica di Sant'Antonio, Padua
Right: Diners in Rome

GARY YEOWELL/GETTY IMAGES ©

### 5 Bologna

Home to Europe's oldest university (established in 1088) and once the stomping ground of Dante, Boccaccio and Petrarch, Bologna had an enviable reputation for courtesy and culture. Its historic centre, complete with 20 soaring towers, is one of the best-preserved and largest medieval cities in the world. In its **Basilica di San Petronio** (Piazza Maggiore; admission free; ⌚7.45am-12.30pm & 3.30-6pm), originally intended to dwarf St Peter's in Rome, Giovanni Cassini's sundial (1655) proved the problems with the Julian calendar giving us the leap year, while Bolognesi students advanced human knowledge in obstetrics, natural science, zoology and anthropology. You can peer at their strange model waxworks and studiously labelled collections in the **Palazzo Poggi** (www.museopalazzopoggi.unibo.it; Via Zamboni 33; ⌚10am-1pm & 2-4pm Tue-Fri, 10.30am-1.30pm & 2.30-5.30pm Sat & Sun).

In art as in science, the School of Bologna gave birth to the Carracci cousins Ludovico, Agostino and Annibale, who were among the founding fathers of Italian baroque and were deeply influenced by the Counter-Reformation.

See their emotionally charged blockbusters in the **Pinacoteca Nazionale** (Via delle Belle Arti 56; admission €4; 9am-7pm Tue-Sun).

p50

**The Drive »** Bologna sits at the intersection of the A1, A13 and A14. From the centre navigate west out of the city, across the river Reno, onto the A1. From here it's a straight shot into Florence for 110km, leaving the Po plains behind you and entering the low hills of Emilia-Romagna and the forested valleys of Tuscany.

TRIP HIGHLIGHT

## 6 Florence

From Filippo Brunelleschi's red-tiled dome atop Florence's **Duomo** (www.duomofirenze.it; Piazza del Duomo; admission €8; 10am-5pm Mon-Wed & Fri, to 4.30pm Thu, to 4.45pm Sat, 1.30-4.45pm Sun) to Michelangelo's and Botticelli's greatest hits, *David* and *The Birth of Venus*, in the **Galleria dell'Accademia** (055 294 883; Via Ricasoli 60; adult/reduced €6.50/3.25; 8.15am-6.50pm Tue-Sun) and the **Galleria degli Uffizi** (www.uffizi.firenze.it; Piazza degli Uffizi 6; adult/reduced €6.50/3.25, with temporary exhibition €11/5.50; 8.15am-6.50pm Tue-Sun), Florence, according to Unesco, contains 'the greatest concentration of universally renowned works of art in the world'.

Whereas Rome and Milan have torn themselves down and been rebuilt many times, incorporating a multitude of architectural whims, central Florence looks much as it did in 1550, with stone towers and cypress-lined gardens. Enjoy the best of it with our leg stretcher on p240.

p51

**The Drive »** The next 210km, continuing south along the A1, travels through some of Italy's most lovely scenery. Just southwest of Florence the vineyards of Greve in Chianti harbour some great farmstays (p51), while Arezzo is to the east. At Orvieto exit onto the SS71 and skirt Lago di Bolsena for the final 50km into Viterbo.

## 7 Viterbo

From Florence the road to Rome crossed the dreaded and pestilential campagna (countryside), a swampy, mosquito-infested low-lying area. Unlike now, inns en route were uncomfortable and hazardous, so travellers hurried through Siena stocking up on wine for the rough road ahead. They also stopped briefly in medieval Viterbo for a quick douse in the thermal springs at the **Terme dei Papi** (07 61 35 01; www.termedeipapi.it; Strada Bagni 12; pool €12, Sun €25; 9am-7pm Wed-Mon, plus 9.30pm-1am Sat), and a tour of the High Renaissance spectacle that is the **Villa Lante** (07 612 88 008; admission €2; 8.30am-1hr before sunset Tue-Sun).

**The Drive »** Rejoin the A1 after a 28km drive along the rural SS675. For the next 40km the A1 descends slowly into Lazio, criss-crossing the river Tevere and keeping the ridge of the Apennines to the left as it darts through tunnels. At Fiano Romano exit for Roma Nord

### TOP TIP: JUMP THE QUEUE IN FLORENCE

In July, August and other busy periods such as Easter, long queues are a fact of life at Florence's key museums. For a fee of €4 each, tickets to the Uffizi and Galleria dell'Accademia (where *David* lives) can be booked in advance. To organise your ticket, go to www.firenzemusei.it or call **Firenze Musei** (Florence Museums; 055 29 48 83; booking line 8.30am-6.30pm Mon-Fri, 8.30am-12.30pm Sat), which also has **ticketing desks** (8.30am-7pm Tue-Sun) at the Uffizi and Palazzo Pitti.

onto the A1dir for the final 20km descent into the capital.

TRIP HIGHLIGHT

##  Rome

In the 18th century Rome, even in ruins, was still thought of as the august capital of the world. Here more than anywhere the Grand Tourist was awakened to an interest in art and architecture, although the **Colosseum** (Piazza del Colosseo; adult/reduced incl Roman Forum & Palatino €12/7.50; 8.30am-1hr before sunset) was still filled with debris and the Palatine Hill was covered in gardens, its excavated treasures slowly accumulating in the world's oldest national museum, the **Musei Capitolini** (www.museicapitolini.org; Piazza del Campidoglio 1; adult/reduced €12/10; 9am-8pm Tue-Sun).

Arriving through the Porta del Popolo, visitors first espied the dome of **St Peter's** (Piazza San Pietro; audioguides €5; 7am-6pm) before clattering along the *corso* to the customs house. Once done, they headed to **Piazza di Spagna**, the city's principal meeting place where Keats penned his love poems and died of consumption.

Although the **Pantheon** (Piazza della Rotonda; admission free; 8.30am-7.30pm Mon-Sat, 9am-6pm Sun) and **Vatican Museums** (www.vatican.va; Viale Vaticano; adult/reduced €14/8; 9am-6pm Mon-Sat) were a must, most travellers preferred to socialise in the grounds of the **Borghese Palace** (www.galleriaborghese.it; Piazzale del Museo Borghese 5; adult/reduced €8.50/5.25; 9am-7pm Tue-Sun, prebooking necessary).

Follow their example and mix the choicest sights with more venal pleasures such as fine dining at **Open Colonna** (06 478 22 641; Via Milano 9a; meals €20-80; noon-midnight Tue-Sat, lunch Sun) and souvenir shopping at antique perfumery **Officina Profumo Farmaceutica di Santa Maria Novella** (Corso Rinascimento 47).

p51

**The Drive »** Past Rome the landscape is hotter and drier, trees give way to Mediterranean shrubbery and the grass starts to yellow. Beyond the vineyards of Frascati, just 20km south of Rome, the A1 heads straight to Naples (Napoli) for 225km, a two-hour drive that often takes much longer due to heavy traffic.

### TOP TIP: ROME INFORMATION LINE

The Comune di Roma (city council) runs a free multilingual **information line** (06 06 08; www.060608.it; 9am-9pm), providing information on culture, shows, hotels, transport etc. You can also book theatre, concert, exhibition and museum tickets on this number. The call centre, open 24 hours, has staff who speak English, French, Arabic, German, Spanish, Italian and Chinese available from 4pm to 7pm.

TRIP HIGHLIGHT

##  Naples

Only the more adventurous Grand Tourists continued south to the salacious southern city of Naples. At the time **Vesuvius** (www.parconazionaledelvesuvio.it; crater tours €8; 9am-6pm Jul & Aug, to 5pm Apr-Jun & Sep, to 4pm Mar & Oct, to 3pm Nov-Feb) glowed menacingly on the bay, erupting no less than six times during the 18th century and eight times in the 19th century. But Naples was the home of opera and *commedia dell'arte* (improvised comedic drama satirising stock social stereotypes), and singing lessons and seats at **Teatro San Carlo** (box office 081 797 23 31, guided tours 081 553 45 65; www.teatrosancarlo.it; Via San Carlo 98; tours €5; 10am-5.30pm Mon-Sat, prebooking necessary) were obligatory.

Then there were the myths of Virgil and Dante to explore at Lago d'Averno and **Campi Flegrei** (the Phlegrean Fields). And, after the discovery of **Pompeii** (☎081 861 90 03; entrances at Porta Marina & Piazza Anfiteatro; adult/reduced €11/5.50; ⏰8.30am-7.30pm Apr-Oct, 8.30am-5pm Nov-Mar) in 1748, the unfolding drama of a Roman town in its death throes drew throngs of mawkish voyeurs. Then, as now, it was the most popular tourist sight in Italy and its priceless mosaics, pornographic frescoes and colossal sculptures filled the **Museo Archeologico Nazionale** (☎081 44 01 66; Piazza Museo Nazionale 19; admission €6.50; ⏰9am-7.30pm Wed-Mon).

p51

BOCCALUPO PHOTOGRAPHY/GETTY IMAGES ©

**Turin** View over the rooftops

# Eating & Sleeping

## Turin 1

**Fiorio** Cafe €

(Via Po 8; 8.30am-1am Tue-Sun) Garner literary inspiration in Mark Twain's old window seat as you contemplate the gilded interior of a cafe where 19th-century students once plotted revolutions and the Count of Cavour deftly played whist.

## Genoa 2

**Trattoria della Raibetta** Trattoria, Genovese €€

(www.trattoriadellaraibetta.it; Vico Caprettari 10-12; meals €20-30; lunch & dinner Tue-Sun) The stone columns in Raibetta's dining room date back a century, and for nearly 300 years food has been served at its tables. Now art-loving Carlo and Chiara Buzzo plate up Ligurian staples such as stewed baby octopus and fish *alla ligure* (with pine nuts and olives).

## Cremona

**La Sosta** Cremonese €€

(0372 45 66 56; Via Vescovo Sicardo 9; meals €30-35; Tue-Sat, lunch Sun Sep-Jun) Surrounded by violin-makers' workshops, this is a good place to feast on regional delicacies, such as *cotechino* (boiled pork sausage) with polenta and Cremona's sweet mustard.

## Venice 4

**Dalla Marisa** Venetian €€

(041 720 211; Fondamenta San Giobbe 652b; set menu €30-35; 11am-3pm & 7-11pm Tue & Thu-Sat) Like a friend, you'll be seated where there's room and get no menu, but you will be informed that the menu is meat- or fish-based when you book, and house wine is included in the price. Venetian regulars confess Marisa's *fegato alla veneziana* (Venetian calf's liver) is better than their grandmothers'.

**Ristorante Oniga** Venetian €€

(041 522 44 10; www.oniga.it; Campo San Barnaba 2852; meals €18-30; noon-3pm & 7-10pm Wed-Mon) Purists come to Ristorante Oniga for chef Annika's Venetian seafood platter with exemplary *sarde in saor* (sardines in tangy onion marinade), vegetarians are spoiled for choice with seasonal pastas (try broccoli rabe, pecorino and breadcrumbs), and everyone appreciates the selection of 150 wines.

**Ca' Angeli** B&B €€

(041 523 24 80; www.caangeli.it; Calle del Traghetto de la Madonnetta, San Polo 1434; d €80-250; ) Brothers Giorgio and Matteo inherited this Grand Canal mansion and converted it into an antique showplace, with original Murano glass chandeliers, namesake angels from the 16th century and a restored Louis XIV sofa in the canalside reading room.

## Bologna 5

**Marco Fadiga Bistrot** Seafood €€

(051 22 01 18; www.marcofadigabistrot.com; Via Rialto 23; meals €35-40; dinner Tue-Sat) With its Parisian air and elegant *fin de siecle* decor, and a menu specialising in seafood, Marco Fadiga is a Grand Tourist's dream. Impress other diners and order the Grand Plateau Royal, an extravagant seafood platter.

**Il Convento dei Fiori di Seta** Boutique Hotel €€€

(051 27 20 39; www.silkflowersnunnery.com; Via Orfeo 34; r €130-270, ste €280-440; ) Finding reliable accommodation en route to Rome was always fraught with danger

and disappointment so lodgings in religious establishments were highly sought. Luckily these days convents, such as the 14th-century Fiori di Seta, come with plush beds, sleek linens and modern art.

## Florence 6

### I Due Fratellini — Panetteria €

(www.iduefratellini.com; Via dei Cimatori 38r; 9am-8pm Mon-Sat) This hole in the wall has been in business since 1875. Wash *panini* (sandwiches) down with a beaker of wine and leave the empty on the wooden shelf outside.

### Il Santo Bevitore — Contemporary Tuscan €€

(055 211264; www.ilsantobevitore.com; Via di Santo Spirito 64-66r; meals €35; lunch & dinner Sep-Jul) Dress for dinner at stylish Santo Bevitore, where you'll dine by candlelight on classics such as hand-chopped beef tartare, chestnut *millefeuille*, and lentils and acacia honey *bavarese*.

### Palazzo Guadagni — Palazzo, B&B €€

(055 265 83 76; www.palazzoguadagni.com; Piazza Santo Spirito 9; d €100-150, f per person €35; ) You may no longer be able to pick up a room on Piazza Santo Spirito for 150 *scudi* a year, but you can make yourself at home on the romantic loggia of the 16th-century Palazzo Guadagni, where Zefferelli shot scenes for *Tea with Mussolini*.

## Greve in Chianti

### Fattoria di Rignana — Agriturismo €€

(www.rignana.it; Val di Rignana 15, Rignana; s/d in fattoria €100/110, in villa €120/140; P @ ) Thankfully things have moved on since the 18th century and the countryside south of Florence is no longer full of shabby inns and thieving beggars, but instead has stylish *agriturismi* (farmstays) like Rignana. Here you can lodge in a historic setting and enjoy glorious views over the Chianti countryside.

## Rome 8

### Ar Galletto — Roman, Osteria €€

(06 686 17 14; www.ristoranteargallettoroma.com; Piazza Farnese 102; meals €35-40; Mon-Sat) Located on Piazza Farnese, one of Rome's loveliest squares, this long-running *osteria* (casual tavern) is the real thing, with good, honest Roman food, a warm atmosphere and dazzlingly set exterior tables. Roast chicken, as the name suggests, is the house speciality.

### Salotto Locarno — Hotel Bar €€

(www.hotellocarno.com; Via della Penna 22; noon-3am) Part of the art deco Hotel Locarno, Salotto has an Agatha Christie–era feel, and a vine-shaded outdoor terrace in summer. It attracts fashionistas and stylish Romans for chichi cocktails and *aperitivo* (aperitifs) at sundown.

### Hotel Scalinata di Spagna — Hotel €€

(06 699 40896; www.hotelscalinata.com; Piazza della Trinità dei Monti 17; d €150-190; ) Right next to the Spanish Steps, with a very friendly price tag, the Scalinata might be a warren but it has a great roof terrace and old-fashioned, romantic rooms with gilt-edged mirrors and plush furnishings. Book early for a room with a balcony.

## Naples 9

### Pizzeria Gino Sorbillo — Pizzeria €

(Via dei Tribunali 32; pizzas from €2.30; Mon-Sat) The clamouring crowds say it all: Gino Sorbillo is king of the pizza pack. Head in for gigantic, wood-fired perfection, best followed by a velvety *semifreddo* (semi-frozen dessert).

### Grand Hotel Vesuvio — Luxury Hotel €€€

(081 764 00 44; www.vesuvio.it; Via Partenope 45; s €230-370, d €290-450; @ ) End the tour in style at the Vesuvio. Known for bedding legends such as Rita Hayworth and Humphrey Bogart, this five-star heavyweight is a wonderland of dripping chandeliers, period antiques and opulent rooms.

# STRETCH YOUR LEGS VENICE

**Start/Finish** Rialto Market

**Distance** 3.5km

**Duration** Three hours

Venice's cosmopolitan outlook has kept the city ahead of the locavore curve and makes local cuisine anything but predictable. Take this tour of the city's famous markets and backstreet *bacarie* (bars) to sample the unique fusion of flavours in Venice (Venezia).

**Take this walk on Trips**

## Rialto Market & Pescaria

Any tour through Venice's gourmet history starts where great Venetian meals have begun for centuries: the 600-year-old **Rialto Market** (⌚7am-2pm Tue-Sun). Hear the chant of grocers singing the praises of island-grown produce. Nearby fishmongers call out the day's catch at the **Pescaria** (fish market). You cannot take your car onto the lagoon islands so leave it in a secure garage in Mestre, such as **Garage Europa** (www.garageeuropametre.com; per day €14) and hop on the train to Venice Santa Lucia where you can pick up a *vaporetto* (water taxi) to Rialto-Mercato.

**The Walk »** Around the corner from the Pescaria, on Ruga degli Spezieri, glimpse the treasures that made Venice's fortune: trade-route spices, in mounds in the windows of Drogheria Mascari (No 381). Down the road, duck into Calle dell'Arco.

## All'Arco

At **All'Arco** (☎041 520 56 66; Calle dell'Arco, San Polo 436; cicheti €1.50-4; ⌚noon-8.30pm Mon-Sat Apr-Jun & Sep, to 3.30pm Oct-Mar) father and son chefs Francesco and Matteo invent Venice's best *cicheti*, the dainty bar snacks that are Venice's version of tapas. If you wait patiently, they'll invent a seasonal speciality for you.

**The Walk »** Pick up Calle Raspi and weave your way northwest over the Rio di San Cassiano, past Veneziastampa, on Campo Santa Maria Mater Domini, and on to Palazzo Mocenigo.

## Palazzo Mocenigo

Costume dramas unfold in the **Palazzo Mocenigo** (www.museicivicivenezіana.it; Salizada di San Stae 1992; adult/reduced €5/3.30; ⌚10am-5pm), once the Mocenigo's swanky pad and now a showcase for the fashions of Venice's elite. Necklines plunge in the Red Living Room, lethal corsets come undone in the Contessa's bedroom and men's paisley knee-breeches show some leg in the dining room.

**The Walk »** Continue up Calle del Tintor and across the Ponte del Megio. Right after you cross the bridge turn left and then first right into the Campo San Giacomo dell'Orio.

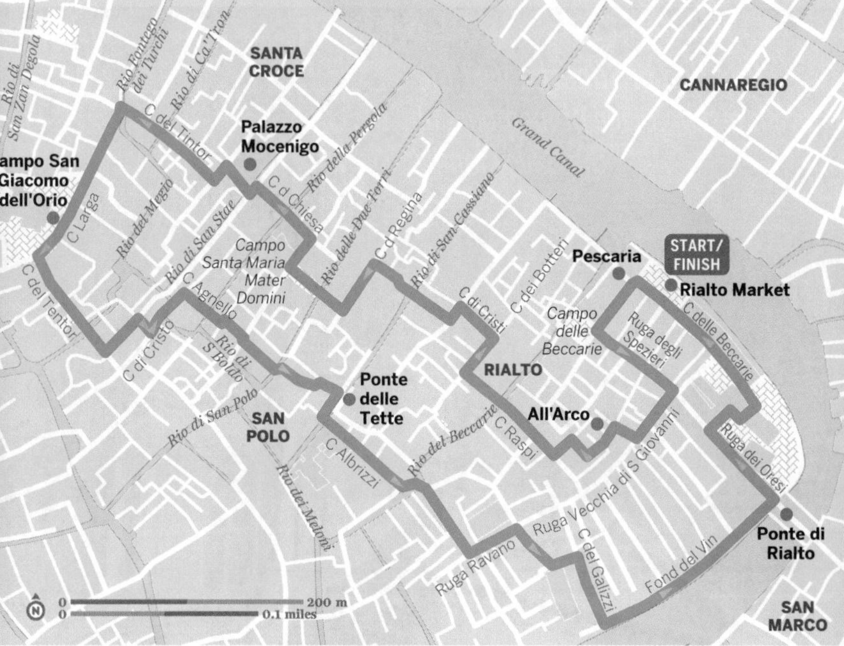


## Campo San Giacomo dell'Orio

You can pop your head into the church, but the real attraction of this *campo* is **Al Prosecco** (www.alprosecco.com; Campo San Giacomo dell'Orio, Santa Croce 1503; ⌚9am-9pm Mon-Sat), where from 9am they're popping corks and raising glasses of *vini naturi* (natural process wines) and *ombre* (wine by the glass).

**The Walk »** Head south of Campo San Giacomo, quickly crossing a small canal and turn left on Calle di Cristo and then right down Calle Agnello, which will bring to you to the high-arched Ponte delle Tette.

## Ponte delle Tette

No one remembers the original name of the Ponte delle Tette, known since the 15th century as 'Tits Bridge'. Back in those days, the shadowy porticos flanking this bridge were a designated red-light zone where prostitutes displayed their wares. For educated conversation, *cortigione* (courtesans) might charge 60 times the basic rates of the average prostitutes. Fees were set by the state and posted in Rialto brothels, and the height of platform shoes was limited to a staggering 30cm.

**The Walk »** Continue down Calle Albrizzi across the Rio de Beccarie at Ponte Storte and dog-leg down Ruga Ravano and Calle del Galizzi towards the waterfront; then turn left along the Fond del Vin. In front of you, you'll be greeted by the splendid sight of the Ponte di Rialto.

## Ponte di Rialto

An amazing feat of engineering in its day (1592), Antonio da Ponte's marble Ponte di Rialto was for centuries the only land link across the Grand Canal. The construction cost 250,000 gold ducats, a staggering sum that puts cost overruns for the new Calatrava bridge into perspective. The southern side faces San Marco, and when shutterbugs clear out around sunset it offers a romantic long view of gondolas pulling up to Grand Canal *palazzi* (mansions).

**The Walk »** To return to the Rialto market head north up Ruga dei Oresi, past the Hotel San Salvadore and right down Sestiere San Polo.

***Basilica di Superga*** *Visit the lavish resting place of members of the Savoy family*

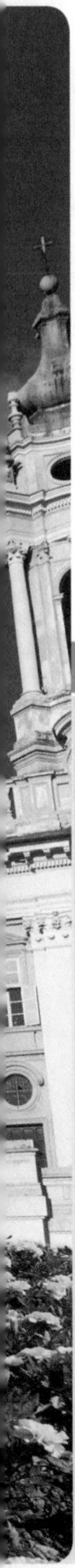

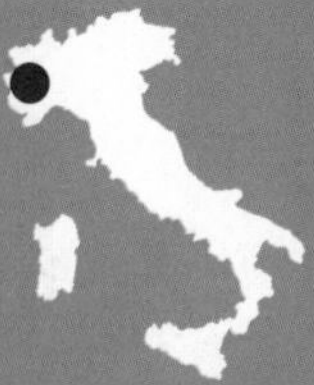

# Savoy Palace Circuit

2

*Bisected by the Po and overshadowed by the Alps, Turin has an air of importance, adorned as it is with sumptuous Savoy palaces, grand hunting lodges and Napoleonic boulevards.*

## TRIP HIGHLIGHTS

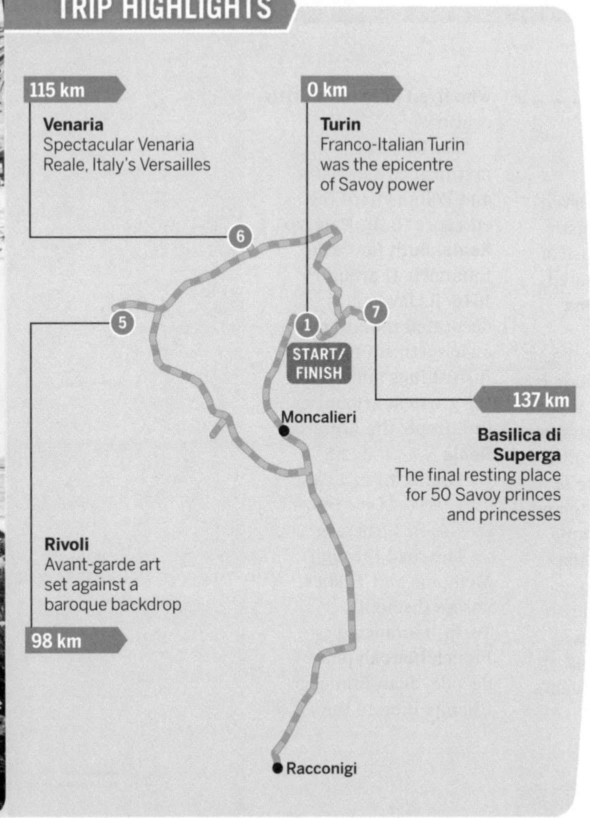

115 km
**Venaria**
Spectacular Venaria Reale, Italy's Versailles

0 km
**Turin**
Franco-Italian Turin was the epicentre of Savoy power

START/FINISH

Moncalieri

137 km
**Basilica di Superga**
The final resting place for 50 Savoy princes and princesses

**Rivoli**
Avant-garde art set against a baroque backdrop
98 km

Racconigi

**3–4 DAYS**
**148KM / 92 MILES**

**GREAT FOR...**

**BEST TIME TO GO**

April to October, when the castles are open for viewing.

**ESSENTIAL PHOTO**

The classical facade of the Basilica di Superga.

Palazzo Carignano, where key events leading to Italian unification took place.

# 2 Savoy Palace Circuit

The Savoys abandoned their old capital of Chambéry in France in 1563 and set up home in Turin (Torino). To make themselves comfortable they spent the next 300 years building an array of princely palaces (many of them designed by Sicilian architect and stage-set designer Filippo Juvarra), country retreats and a grand mausoleum. They encircle Turin like an extravagant baroque garland and make for fascinating day trips or an easy long-weekend tour.

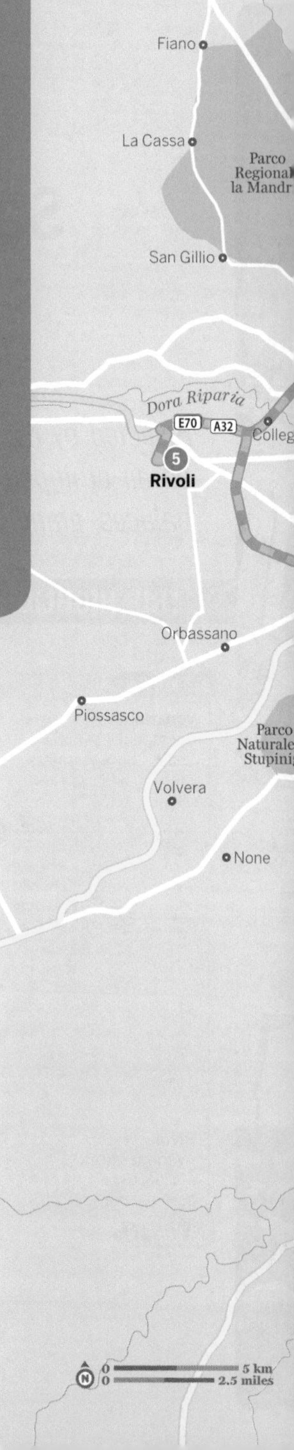

## 1 Turin

**Piazza Castello** served as the seat of dynastic power for the House of Savoy. It is dominated by **Palazzo Madama** (Piazza Castello; www.palazzomadamatorino.it; adult/reduced €7.50/6; ⏲10am-6pm Tue-Sat, to 8pm Sun), a part-medieval, part-baroque castle built in the 13th century on the site of the old Roman gate and named after Madama Reale Maria Cristina (widow of Vittorio Amedeo I, also known as the Lion of Susa and nominally King of Cyprus and Jerusalem), who lived here in the 17th century.

Nearby statues of mythical twins Castor and Pollux guard the entrance to the **Palazzo Reale**. Built for Carlo Emanuele II around 1646, its lavishly decorated rooms house an assortment of gilded furnishings and one of the greatest armouries in Europe, the **Armeria Reale** (www.artito.arti.beniculturali.it; Piazza Castello; adult/reduced €4/2; ⏲9am-2pm Tue-Fri, 1-7pm Sat & Sun).

'The road through Memphis and Thebes passes through Turin,' trumpeted French hieroglyphic decoder Jean-François Champollion in the

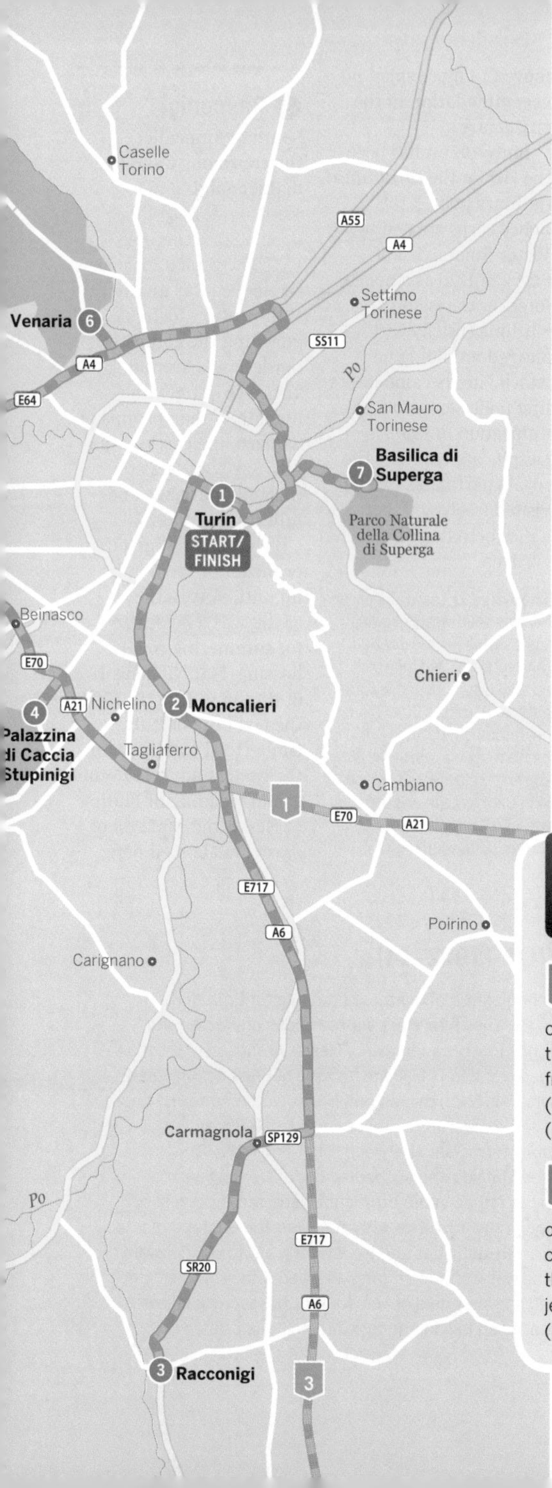

19th century, and he wasn't far wrong. The **Palazzo dell'Accademia delle Scienze** houses the most important collection of Egyptian treasure outside Cairo in the **Museo Egizio** (Via Accademia delle Scienze 6; www.museoegizio.org; adult/reduced €7.50/3.50; ⌚8.30am-7.30pm Tue-Sun). Also in the *palazzo* (mansion) is the **Galleria Sabauda** (adult/reduced €4/2; ⌚8.30am-2pm Tue, Fri, Sat & Sun, 2-7.30pm Wed & Thu), which contains the Savoy art collection.

Opposite, **Palazzo Carignano** is where Carlo Alberto (1798–1849) and the first King of Italy, Vittorio Emanuele II (1820–78), were born, and it provided the seat for Italy's first parliament. Now it houses the unmissable

## LINK YOUR TRIP

### 1 Grand Tour

From Italy's first capital to a Grand Tour of the peninsula, continue from Turin to Genoa (Genova) on the A21 and A7 (p39).

### 3 Gourmet Piedmont

Head south of Turin on the A6 to tour the rich culinary hinterland of the Langhe, Piedmont's jealously guarded larder (p63).

**Museo Nazionale del Risorgimento Italiano** (www.museorisorgimentotorino.it; Via Accademia delle Scienze 5; adult/reduced €7/5; ⌚9am-7pm Tue-Sun), which charts the course of the modern nation state.

 p61

**The Drive »** Drive south along Corso Unitá d'Italia. This busy dual carriageway turns into Corso Trieste and then Via Custoza. Take a right for Moncalieri, beneath the A6 and across the river Po on Via Martiri della Libertá. Turn right on Via Arduino and you'll arrive at the castle after about 9km.

## 2 Moncalieri

The 12th-century **Castello di Moncalieri** (Via del Castello 2) was the first fortress built by Thomas I of Savoy just south of the centre of Turin, commanding the southern access to the city. The family then upped sticks and moved to more splendid accommodation in the city centre.

Since 1921 it has been the HQ for the *carabinieri* (military police), the police corps created by Victor Emanuele I of Savoy in 1726 as a police force for the island of Sardinia (briefly within Savoy dominion) and which later became Italy's first police force following unification in 1861. Despite appearances the royal apartments can be visited freely and there's a nice belvedere over the gardens.

**The Drive »** Leave Moncalieri heading southwest, following signs saying *tutte le direzioni* (all directions) and then pick up the A6 southbound towards Savona/Piacenza. Drive 15km on the autostrada, then exit for Carmagnola, which will put you first on the SP129 (as you skirt Carmagnola) and then on the SR20 towards Racconigi, a further 12km southwest.

## 3 Racconigi

South of Moncalieri, the enormous **Castello di Racconigi** (www.ilcastellodiracconigi.it; Via Morosini 3; adult/reduced €5/2.50; ⌚9am-6.30pm Tue-Sun Apr-Oct) was another 12th-century fortress, guarding the contested borderlands around Turin. Originally the domain of the Marquis of Saluzzo, the castle came into Savoy possession through marriage and inheritance.

Inhabited by various branches of the family up until WWII, the castle was a favourite for summering royals, hosting Tsar Nicholas II of Russia in 1918. In 1904 the last king of Italy, Umberto II, was born in the castle and in 1925 the grand wedding of Philip of Hesse and Mafalda of Savoy was hosted here.

### MAFALDA OF SAVOY (1902–44)

Mafalda of Savoy was the second of four daughters of King Victor Emmanuel III of Italy and Elena of Montenegro. Known for her cultured, pious character, she made a grand marriage to Prince Philip, Landgrave of Hesse, grandson of German Emperor Frederick III and great-grandson of Queen Victoria of England. Affiliated with the German National Socialist (Nazi) movement, Philip, with his international connections, rose rapidly in the Nazi hierarchy, becoming a trusted member of the Reichstag and acting as an intermediary between Hitler and Mussolini. But Hitler distrusted the outspoken Mafalda and suspected her of working against the German war effort. When her father, Victor Emmanuel, ordered the arrest of Mussolini in July 1943 and signed the armistice with the Allies, the Gestapo reacted by arresting Mafalda for subversive activities and transferring her to Buchenwald concentration camp. There she was wounded during an Allied attack on the camp's munitions factory in 1944, and she later died of her wounds, beseeching fellow prisoners to remember her not as an Italian princess, but an Italian sister.

Palazzina di Caccia Stupinigi

Tragically, Mafalda later died in the death camp of Buchenwald. Now you can wander the strangely intimate apartments of kings and queens – full of elegant furnishings, family photos and personal objects – and enjoy the grand portrait gallery with its 1875 dynastic portraits. You can even take a carriage ride through the gardens.

✕ p61

**The Drive »** The 38km drive north to Palazzina di Caccia Stupinigi retraces much of the previous journey, first on the SR20 and then the A6. However, after 14km on the autostrada, before you reach Moncalieri, take the exit for the E70 (Tangenziale) towards Aosta. Now heading northwest, drive a further 8.5km and then take the exit for Stupinigi. The Viale Torino runs right up to the *palazzina* (hunting lodge).

## 4 Palazzina di Caccia Stupinigi

The Savoy's finest hunting park, the **Palazzina di Caccia Stupinigi** (☎011 358 12 20; Piazza Principe Amedeo 7; adult/reduced €12/8; ⏰10am-6.30pm Wed-Mon Jul-Dec) was cleverly acquired by the almost landless Emanuele Filiberto, Duke of Savoy from 1553 to 1580. Known as *Testa di Ferro* ('Ironhead') due to his military prowess, Emmanuele was the only child of Charles III, Duke of Savoy, and Beatrice of Portugal, who left him little more than his title when they died. However, through diligent service in the armies of the Austro-Hungarian empire he slowly and surely reclaimed Savoyard lands, including the Stupinigi park and Turin, where he moved the family seat in 1563.

The fabulous *palazzina* came later, thanks to Vittorio Amadeo II, who set Filippo Juvarra to work in 1729. He enlisted decorators from Venice to attend to the interiors covering the 137 rooms and 17 galleries in trompe l'oeil hunting scenes such as the *Triumph of Diana* in the main salon. Now the rooms accommodate the **Museo di Arte e Ammobiliamento**, a fabulous museum of arts and furnishings, many of them original to the lodge.

**The Drive »** Continue on the Turin periphery (E70) heading further northwest towards Fréjus for the 21km drive to Rivoli. You'll be on the E70 for 11km before exiting at Rosta/Avigliana. From here it's a short 4km drive before exiting on the SS25 towards Rivoli. Brown signs direct you to the castle.

TRIP HIGHLIGHT

## 5 Rivoli

Works by Franz Ackermann, Gilbert and George, and Frank Gehry would have been beyond the wildest imagination of the Savoy family, who used the 17th-century **Castello di Rivoli** as one of their country retreats.

Since 1984, the cutting edge of Turin's contemporary art scene has been housed here in the **Museo d'Arte Contemporanea** (www.castellodirivoli.org; Piazza Mafalda di Savoia, Rivoli; adult/reduced €6.50/4.50; ⏲10am-5pm Tue-Fri, to 7pm Sat & Sun), creating shocking juxtapositions between the classical architecture and the art: witness Maurizio Cattelan's taxidermy horse suspended from the rococo ceiling.

As well as its permanent collection, the castle also hosts bold temporary exhibits such as Thomas Shütte's *Frauen* in 2012.

✕ p61

**The Drive »** Return to the Tangenziale via the SS25 and A32 and continue northeast in the direction of Aosta/Monte Bianco/Milano. This puts you on the E64 for 9km. Then take the exit for Venaria and at the traffic lights turn left onto Corso Giuseppe Garibaldi, from where you'll see the palace signposted.

TRIP HIGHLIGHT

## 6 Venaria

The **Reggia de Venaria Reale** (Piazza della Repubblica; www.lavenariareale.it; adult/reduced €15/6, gardens €5/3; ⏲9am-5pm Tue-Fri, to 8pm Sat & Sun) is a Unesco-listed palace complex built by Amadeo di Castellamonte for Carlo Emanuele II between 1667 and 1690. It's one of the biggest royal residences in the world and lengthy restoration works were concluded in late 2010. The full trajectory of the buildings stretches 2km. Highlights include the Galleria Grande, the Cappella di Sant'Uberto and the Juvarra stables.

Outside, there's more: 17th-century grottoes, the Fontana del Cervo (stag fountain), the Rose Garden and the 17th-century Potager Garden, all of which took eight years to restore and required the replanting of 50,000 plants. It's all set against the 3000-hectare La Mandria park.

✕ p61

**The Drive »** First return to the E64 and continue northeast for 6km, then take the Falchera exit for Torino Nord. Follow the signs for Torino Centro and merge southwards onto the A4 for 2.5km. Before you hit the river Po, turn left onto Lungostura Lazio, which skirts the river before crossing over it. The next 5km are through a natural park until you reach the suburb of Sassi where you turn left onto the Strada Comunale Superga.

TRIP HIGHLIGHT

## 7 Basilica di Superga

In 1706 Vittorio Amedeo II promised to build a basilica to honour the Virgin Mary if Turin was saved from besieging French and Spanish armies. Like a religious epiphany, the city was saved, so Duke Amadeo once again commissioned Juvarra to build the **Basilica di Superga** (www.basilicadisuperga.com; Strada della Basilica di Superga 73) on a hill across the Po river in 1717.

Magnificently sited as it is, with a crowning dome 65m high, it is visible for miles around and in due course it became the final resting place for 50 members of the Savoy family. Their lavish tombs make for interesting viewing. In their company, at the rear of the church, lies a tomb commemorating the Gran Torino football team, all of whom died in 1949 when their plane crashed into the basilica in thick fog.

**The Drive »** To return to the city centre, descend down Strada Comunale Superga and take a left along Corso Casale for 4km. Cross the river right over the Ponte Vittorio Emanuele I onto Via Po, which brings you once again to Piazza Castello.

# Eating & Sleeping

## Turin 1

### Porta di Savona — Trattoria, Piedmontese €€

(Piazza Vittoria Veneto 2; meals €25; lunch & dinner Wed-Sun, dinner Tue) An unpretentious trattoria with a deserved reputation for superb *agnolotti al sugo arrosto* (Piedmontese ravioli in a meat gravy), and *gnocchi di patate al gorgonzola* (potato gnocchi with gorgonzola).

### Ristorante del Cambio — Gastronomic €€€

(011 54 66 90; Piazza Carignano 2; set menu from €60; Mon-Sat) Crimson velvet, glittering chandeliers and a timeless air greet you at this grande dame of the Turin dining scene, regularly patronised by Count Cavour in his day. It first opened its doors in 1757, and classic Piedmont cuisine still dominates the menu.

### Ai Savoia — B&B €€

(339 1257711; www.aisavoia.it; Via del Cazmine 1b; r €95-125; P) Occupying an 18th-century townhouse, this modest boutique hotel has grand pretensions. Rooms, named after members of the Savoy dynasty, are decorated in Napoleonic style: chandeliers, swagged curtains and self-important portraits.

### Grand Hotel Sitea — Hotel €€€

(011 517 01 71; www.sitea.thi.it; Via Carlo Alberto 35; d €220-350; P) The Grand Hotel sits in a neoclassical *palazzo* proudly boasting gilded Empire-style decor, large French windows and a wood-panelled American bar. Service is old-style, too: charming and unobtrusive.

## Racconigi 3

### La Caffetteria dei Cavallini — Cafe €

(0172 82 08 80; Castello di Racconigi, Via Morosini 3; 10am-6pm Tue-Sun Apr-Oct) Located in the centre of the Racconigi park, between Swan Lake and the Russian dacha, is the Scuderia where the ponies of the Savoy princes were stabled. Now it houses a cafe, which serves a selection of Piedmontese goodies from the Terre di Savoia.

## Rivoli 5

### Combal.Zero — Gastronomic, Contemporary €€€

(011 956 52 25; www.combal.org; Piazza Mafalda di Savoia; meals €80-140; Tue-Sat) In the glass-fronted restaurant overlooking the courtyard of Castello di Rivoli, creative genius Davide Scabin has been upsetting traditionalists for years with his unorthodox, conceptual gastronomy. Humorous takes on the classics include Empire State peppers in six solutions and sunny-side-up San Remo prawns.

## Venaria 6

### Caffè degli Argenti — Cafe €

(10am-4.30pm Tue-Fri, to 7.15pm Sat & Sun) Tucked behind the Grand Gallery you'll find a cafe in the glorious, gold-on-black lacquer Sala Cinese. Indulge in an *aperitivo* (aperitif) or order a salty *bresaola panini* (cured-beef sandwich) and wander out to the terrace, which overlooks the Grand Parterre garden.

### Chiosco delle Rose — Ice Cream €

(Piazza della Repubblica; noon-4.30pm Sat, to 6.30pm Sun Apr-Oct) The Venaria's ice-cream parlour is located in the Rose Garden in the 19th-century summerhouse. Choose from artisanal flavours and enjoy a picnic beneath the pergolas.

***Alba*** *Sample the town's famous truffles*

CHRISTOPHER PILLITZ/GETTY IMAGES ©

# Gourmet Piedmont

*Immersed in tradition as old as the towns that fostered it, Piedmont's cuisine is the toast of Italy. It is also home to the Slow Food movement, Alba truffles and big-hitting Barolo wines.*

## TRIP HIGHLIGHTS

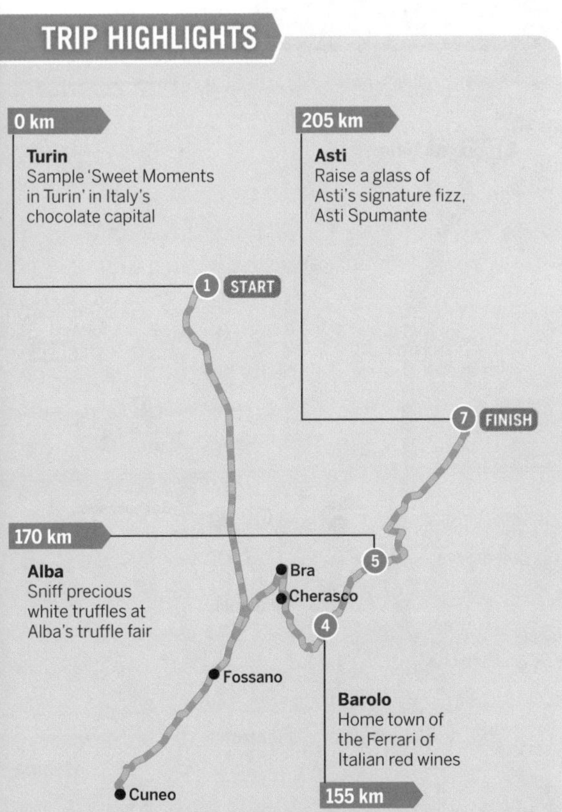


**6 DAYS**
**205KM / 127 MILES**

**GREAT FOR...**

**BEST TIME TO GO**

September to November for autumn food festivals.

**ESSENTIAL PHOTO**

Endless vistas of vines in Barolo or Barbaresco.

**BEST FOR OENOPHILES**

Sampling glasses of Barolo for only €5 at Castello Falletti.

# 3 Gourmet Piedmont

The rolling hills, valleys and towns of Piedmont are northern Italy's specialist pantry, weighed down with sweet hazelnuts, rare white truffles, Arborio rice and Nebbiolo grapes that metamorphose into Barolo and Barbaresco wines. Out here in the damp Po river basin they give out Michelin stars like overzealous schoolteachers give out house points, and with good reason. Trace a gourmet route, and counter the calorific overload with rural walks and bike rides.

TRIP HIGHLIGHT

## 1 Turin

The innovative Torinese gave the world its first saleable hard chocolate, perpetuated one of its greatest mysteries (the Holy Shroud) and played a key role in the creation of the Italian state. You can follow the epic story in the **Museo Nazionale del Risorgimento Italiano** (www.museorisorgimentotorino.it; Via Accademia delle Scienze 5; adult/reduced €7/5; ⏲9am-7pm Tue-Sun). Aside from

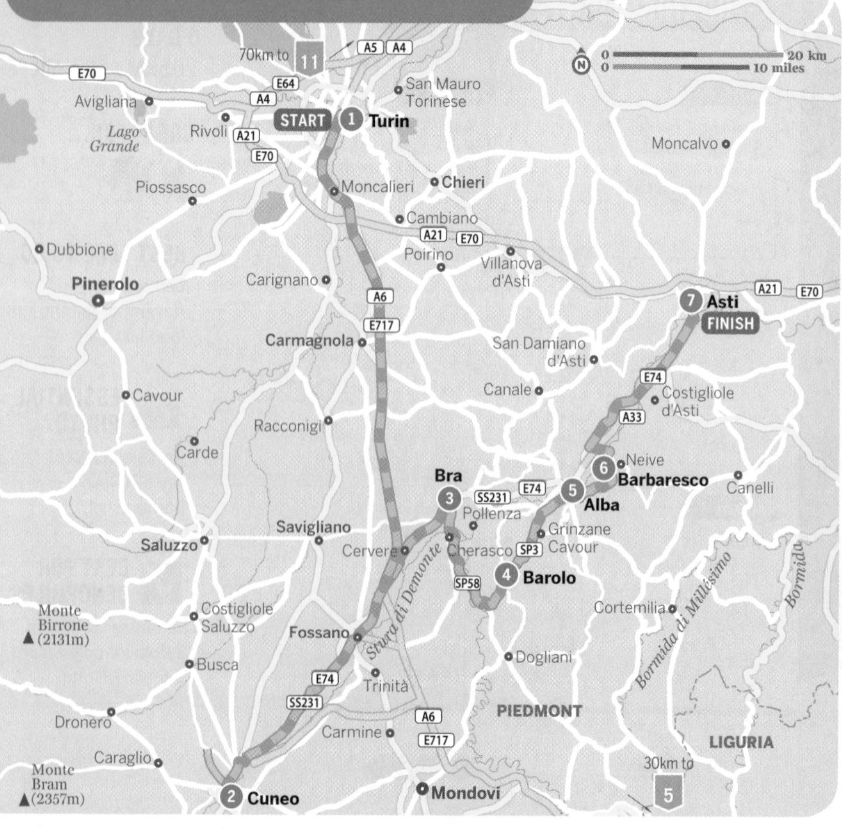

the national narrative and the intriguing Shroud of Turin, on display in the **Duomo** (Piazza San Giovanni), you've come to Turin for chocolate.

Planning your trip in March when the **CioccolaTÒ** (www.cioccola-to.it) festival is in full swing is a good start. Otherwise visit **Al Bicerin** (Piazza della Consolata 5; ⌚8.30am-7.30pm Mon, Tue, Thu & Fri, 8.30am-1pm & 3.30-7.30pm Sat & Sun), named from *bicerin*, a caffeine-charged hot drink of chocolate, coffee and cream. Then there's **Peyrano** (www.peyrano.com; Corso Vittorio Emanuele II 76), specialist chocolatiers since 1912 and creators of *Dolci Momenti a Torino* (Sweet Moments in Turin).

**LINK YOUR TRIP**

**5 Italian Riviera**

From Bra continue south along the A6 to enjoy a tour of the olive groves and gardens along the Italian Riviera (p79).

**11 Valle d'Aosta**

Cheese-lovers beware: the A5 from Turin takes you into the heart of the Valle d'Aosta, where days of hiking end with *fontina* fondues (p137).

Beyond the chocolate, Turin is home to Slow Food's groundbreaking 'supermarket', **Eataly** (www.eatalytorino.it; Via Nizza 230; ⌚10am-8pm Tue-Sun). Housed in a converted factory, it showcases a staggering array of sustainable food and beverages and hosts regular tastings and cookery workshops.

✕ p69

**The Drive »** Cuneo lies 90km south of Turin, virtually a straight shot down the A6 autostrada. Head out of Turin on Corso Unitá d'Italia and across the river Po. Then join the autostrada for 55km. Exit at Fossano and join the SS231/E74 for the final 20km.

## 2 Cuneo

A condensed version of Turin, Cuneo is a genteel town with an impressive Renaissance square, the grand arcaded **Piazza Galimberti**, where market stalls set up every Tuesday. It's a good place for festivals, too, such as the **music festival** in June, the **Tour de France** in July, the **Chestnut Fair** in autumn and the regional **Cheese Fair** in early November. The city's signature rum-filled chocolates though, can be sampled year-round.

Cuneo also has some wonderfully dark and zealous churches. The oldest is the deconsecrated San Francisco convent and church which today houses the **Museo Civico di Cuneo** (Via Santa María 10; admission €2.60; ⌚9am-1pm & 3-5.30pm Tue-Thu, to 7pm Fri & Sat), tracking the history of the town and province.

✕ 🛏 p69

**The Drive »** The 44km journey to Bra retraces much of the previous drive along the SS231/E74. Head back to Fossano, but instead of reconnecting with the A6, take the periphery north and continue northeast through Cervere and Bergoglio, where the countryside opens out into green fields.

## 3 Bra

Up on the 1st floor of a recessed courtyard, the little **Osteria del Boccondivino** (☎0172 42 56 74; www.boccondivinoslow.it; Via Mendicità Istruita 14; set menu €26-28; ⌚Tue-Sat), lined with wine bottles, was the first restaurant to be opened by Slow Food in the 1980s (see p68). The food is predictably excellent, and the local Langhe menu changes daily. In the same courtyard you'll find the **Slow Food headquarters** (www.slowfood.it), which includes a small bookshop selling guides to all of Italy's Slow Food–accredited restaurants and heritage producers.

Just outside Bra, in the village of Pollenza, 4km southeast, is the Slow Food **Università di Scienze Gastronomiche**

ROSTISLAV GLINKSY/ALAMY ©

(University of Gastronomic Sciences; www.unisg.it; Piazza Vittorio Emanuele 9). It offers three-year courses in gastronomy and food management. Also here is the acclaimed **Guido Ristorante** (☎0172 45 84 22; www.guidoristorante.it; set menu €75; ⏰Tue-Sat, closed Jan & Aug) that people have been known to cross borders to visit, especially for the veal. Next door is the **Banca del Vino** (www.bancadelvino.it; Piazza Vittorio Emanuele II 13), and a wine-cellar 'library' of Italian wines. Reserve for free guided tastings.

**The Drive »** From Bra to Barolo is a lovely 20km drive through the gentle Langhe hills. Head east along the SS231 for 3km before turning southeast onto the SP7, then the SP58. The latter passes through orchards and vineyards and offers up photogenic views of old stone farmhouses.

## SNAILS, GLORIOUS SNAILS

Set within the Langhe's lush wine country, Cherasco, just south of Bra, is best known for *lumache* (snails). Snails in this neck of the woods are dished up *nudo* (shell-free). They can be pan-fried, roasted, dressed in an artichoke sauce or minced inside ravioli. Piedmontese specialities include *lumache al barbera* (snails simmered in Barbera wine and ground nuts) and *lumache alla Piemontese* (snails stewed with onions, nuts, anchovies and parsley in a tomato sauce).

Traditional trattorias serving such dishes include **Osteria della Rosa Rossa** (☎0172 48 81 33; Via San Pietro 31; meals €30-35; ⏰12.30-2pm & 8-9pm Fri-Tue).

Piedmontese vineyards

TRIP HIGHLIGHT

## 4 Barolo

Wine-lovers rejoice! This tiny 1800-hectare parcel of undulating land immediately southwest of Alba knocks out the Ferrari of Italian reds, Barolo. Many argue it is Italy's finest wine.

The eponymous village is dominated by the **Castello Falletti** (www.baroloworld.it; Piazza Falletti), once owned by the powerful Falletti banking family. Today it houses the **Museo del Vino** (www.wimubarolo.it; adult/reduced €7/5; ⌚10.30am-7pm Fri-Wed Mar-Dec) where multimedia displays tell the story of wine through history, art, music, films and literature.

Also, in the cellars, the **Enoteca Regionale del Barolo** (⌚10am-12.30pm & 3-6.30pm Fri-Wed) is run by the region's 11 wine-growing communities. It offers three Barolo wines for tasting each day, costing €2 each or all three for €5.

🛏 p69

**The Drive »** The short 16km hop from Barolo to Alba is another stunning drive through Barolo's vineyards as you head northeast along the SP3. Then join the A33 for just 2.5km and exit into Alba.

TRIP HIGHLIGHT

## 5 Alba

Alba's fertile hinterland, the vine-striped Langhe Hills, radiates out from the town, an undulating vegetable garden replete with grapes, hazelnut groves and vineyards. Exploring them on foot or with two wheels is a rare pleasure. Alba's **tourist office** (www.langheroero.it; Piazza Risorgimento 2; ⌚9am-6.30pm Mon-Fri, 10am-6.30pm Sat & Sun) can organise an astounding number of Langhe/Roero valley excursions. Highlights include a 10km **walk** (2½ hours, €15) through the chestnut groves, **winery tours** (€80 to €100) and **truffle-hunting excursions** (price depends on group).

In October and November the town hosts its renowned **truffle fair** (every weekend), and the equally ecstatic *vendemia* (grape harvest).

 p69

**The Drive »** Barbaresco sits in the hills just 10km northeast of Alba. Exit Alba along Viale Cherasca and then pick up the narrow, winding SP3 as it loops through the pretty residential suburb of Altavilla and out into the countryside.

## 6 Barbaresco

Only a few kilometres separate Barolo from Barbaresco, but a rainier microclimate and fewer ageing requirements have made the latter into a softer, more delicate red.

Sample it at the atmospheric **Enoteca Regionale del Barbaresco** (Piazza del Municipio 7; per tasting €1.50; ⌚9.30am-6pm Thu-Tue), housed inside a deconsecrated church. The *enoteca* (wine bar) also has information on walking trails in the vicinity.

If you haven't had your fill of wine yet, head a further 4km east to the pin-drop-quiet village of Neive, where you'll find the **Bottega dei Quattro Vini** (☎0173 67 70 14; Piazza Italia 2). This two-room shop was set up by the local community to showcase the four 'DOC' wines (Dolcetto d'Alba, Barbaresco, Moscato and Barbera d'Alba) produced on Neive's hills.

 p69

**The Drive »** The final 30km stretch to Asti leaves Barbaresco's vineyards behind on the SP3 and rejoins the A33 for an uninterrupted drive to Asti. Although it's a two-lane highway, it slices through more unspoilt farmland.

TRIP HIGHLIGHT

## 7 Asti

Asti and Alba were fierce medieval rivals ruled over by feuding royal families, who built Asti's legendary 150 towers. Of these only 12 remain, and only the **Torre Troyana o dell'Orologio** (Piazza Medici; admission free; ⌚10am-1pm & 4-7pm Apr-Sep, 10am-1pm & 3-6pm Sat & Sun Oct) can be climbed. Asti's rivalry with Alba is still recalled in the annual **Palio d'Asti**, a bareback horserace on the third Sunday of September that commemorates a victorious battle.

The 10-day **Douja d'Or** (a *douja* being a terracotta wine jug unique to Asti), in the first or second week in September, is complemented by the **Delle Sagre** food festival on the second Sunday of September. Otherwise you can sample the city's eponymous wine, Asti Spumante, at the **Enoteca Boero di Boero Mario** (Piazza Astesano 17; ⌚9am-noon & 3-8pm Tue-Sun, 9am-noon Mon).

Like Alba, the countryside around Asti contains precious black and white truffles. Asti's **truffle fair** is in November.

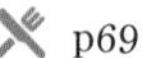 p69

### SLOW FOOD

**Slow Food** (www.slowfood.it) was the 1980s brainchild of a group of disenchanted Italian journalists from the Piedmontese town of Bra who, united by their taste buds, successfully ignited a global crusade against the fast-food juggernaut whose tentacles were threatening to engulf Italy's gastronomic heritage. Their mantra was pleasure over speed and taste over convenience in a manifesto that promoted sustainability, local production and the protection of longstanding epicurean traditions. Today, Slow Food has 100,000 members in 153 countries.

# Eating & Sleeping

## Turin 1

### Andrea Perino — Bakery €

(Via Cavour 10; snacks from €4) Cult Slow Food–baker Andrea Perino knocks out generous portions of freshly baked focaccia and tasty snacks at this bakery-cum-cafe situated near Piazza San Carlo.

## Cuneo 2

### Osteria della Chiocciola — Piedmontese €€

(0171 6 62 77; Via Fossano 1; meals €28-33; Mon-Sat) Lack of outside signage testifies to an inner confidence at Chiocciola's, where seasoned cooks perform small miracles. The restaurant is Slow Food–affiliated, and offers a wine bar and light menu of platters on the ground floor and in an upstairs dining room.

### Hotel Royal Superga — Hotel €

(0171 69 32 23; www.hotelroyalsuperga.com; Via Pascal 3; s €59-89, d €79-109; P) This old-fashioned hotel mixes some regal touches with a raft of complimentary items. Bank on free wi-fi, free DVDs to watch in your room, free *aperitivo* (aperitifs), and free city bikes for guests.

## Barolo 4

### Villa Carita B&B — B&B €€

(0173 50 96 33; www.villacarita.it; Via Roma 105, La Morra; s/d €90/120; P) This B&B not only has vineyard views from every room (and its panoramic terrace), but romantic nighttime views of La Morra's lights. Tucked below the main building, one suite is hidden in the hillside with its own private terrace.

## Alba 5

### Piazza Duomo-La Piola — Gastronomic €€€

(0173 44 28 00; www.piazzaduomoalba.it; Piazza Risorgimento 4; meals €20-30, set menu €60-80; lunch Tue-Sun) A two-in-one culinary extravaganza in Alba's main square. Downstairs, La Piola sports local specials, such as *vitello tonnato* (chilled, sliced veal in a tuna-flavoured cream sauce). Upstairs, the theme is international in chef Enrico Crippa's Michelin-starred restaurant decorated with frescoes by artist Francesco Clemente.

### Hotel San Lorenzo — Boutique Hotel €€

(0173 36 24 06; www.albergo-sanlorenzo.it; Piazza Rossetti 6; s/d €85/100; P) Take 11 rooms in a refurbished 18th-century house, stick it footsteps from the cathedral, call it a boutique hotel and add a unique downstairs pastry shop, Golosi, selling butter-/egg-/dairy-free confectionery. The result: one of those only-in-Alba moments.

## Barbaresco 6

### Ristorante Rabayà — Piedmontese €€

(0173 63 52 23; Via Rabayà 9, Barbaresco; set menu €30-45; Fri-Wed, closed mid-Feb–early Mar) Rabayà has the ambience of dining at a private home. Its antique-furnished dining room has a roaring fire, but when the sun's shining, there's no better spot than its terrace set high above the vineyards. Try the signature rabbit.

## Asti 7

### Pompa Magna — Piedmontese €€

(www.pompamagna.it; Via Aliberti 65; set menu €20-30; Tue-Sun) This split-level brasserie is a great spot for a bruschetta and glass of very good wine (they also own an *enoteca* at Corso Alfieri 332; closed Mondays). But the chef-prepared menus and *bônnet* (an elaborate chocolate pudding) are also worthwhile.

**Sestriere** *One of Europe's most glamorous ski resorts*

# Meandering the Maritime Alps

*In the Susa Valley and Maritime Alps you'll encounter a rich diversity of marmots, ibex and grouse. That's when you're not skiing the Milky Way or hiking old salt routes.*

## TRIP HIGHLIGHTS

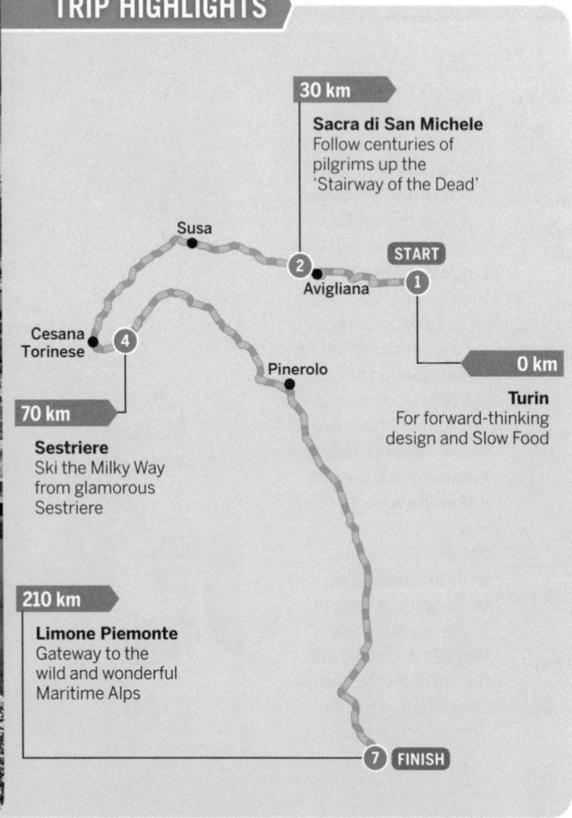

**7 DAYS**
**210KM / 130 MILES**

**GREAT FOR...**

**BEST TIME TO GO**

October to January for food fairs, hiking and skiing.

**ESSENTIAL PHOTO**

The red-tiled rooftops of Saluzzo from the Torre Civica.

**BEST FOR SKIING**

The 400 spotless kilometres of the Milky Way.

# 4 Meandering the Maritime Alps

Shoehorned between the rice-growing plains of Piedmont and the sparkling coastline of Liguria lie the brooding Maritime Alps – a unique pocket of dramatically sculpted mountains that rise like a stony-faced border guard along the frontier of Italy and France. Traverse their valleys and peaks to gaze in mirror-like lakes, ski the spotless Milky Way and hike amid forests rich with chestnuts.

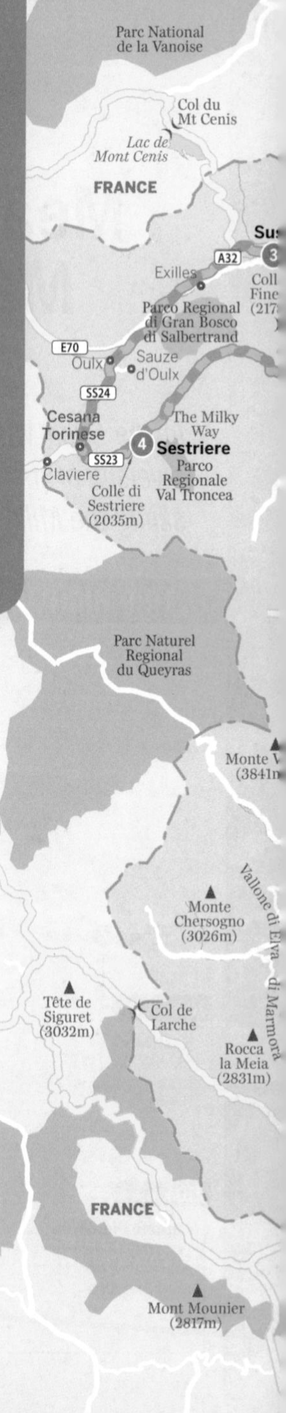

TRIP HIGHLIGHT

## 1 Turin

In 2008 Turin (Torino) held the title of European Capital of Design, and no wonder; the city's architecture mirrors its trajectory from the baroque elegance of the **Palazzo Reale** (Piazza Castello; adult/reduced €6.50/3.25; ⏰8.30am-7.30pm Tue-Sun), seat of the monarchic House of Savoy, to the futuristic steel-and-glass **Mole Antonelliana**, symbol of the city's industrial rebirth and now the repository for the **Museo del Cinema** (www.museonazionaledelcinema.org; Via Montebello 20; adult/reduced €7/5; ⏰9am-8pm Tue-Fri & Sun, to 11pm Sat). Take the panoramic lift (€9) to the roof terrace for 360-degree views.

From the Mole you may just be able to spy **Lingotto Fiera** (www.lingottofiere.it; Via Nizza 294), Turin's former Fiat factory, redesigned by Renzo Piano into an exhibition centre. It also houses the 'treasure chest' rooftop gallery **Pinacoteca Giovanni e Marella Agnelli** (Via Nizza 230; admission €4; ⏰10am-7pm Tue-Sun), with masterpieces by Canaletto, Manet, Matisse and Picasso. Equally dazzling are the stalls in the famous Slow Food supermarket,

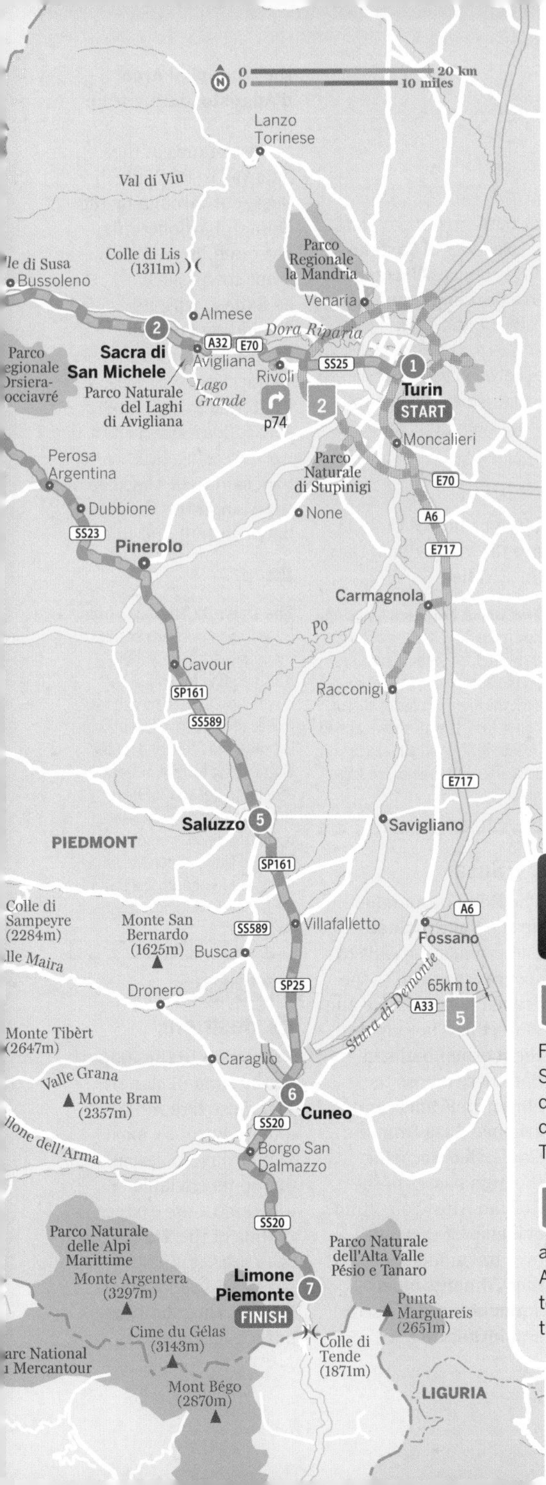

**Eataly** (www.eatalytorino.it; ⏲10am-8pm Tue-Sun) next door.

✂🛏 p77

**The Drive »** Leave Turin westwards along Corso Vittorio Emanuele II following signs for the A32/E70 to Bardonecchia/Fréjus. Join the autostrada for 11km and then take exit 2, Avigliana Est. From here pick up the SS25 for 4km, following signs towards San Michele, which you can see on a peak to your left.

---

TRIP HIGHLIGHT

## 2 Sacra di San Michele

Brooding above the A32, once a key stretch of the Via Francigena pilgrim path from Canterbury through Rome to Monte Sant'Angelo in Puglia, is the **Sacra di San Michele** (www.sacradisanmichele.com; admission/reduced €5/4;

### 2 Savoy Palace Circuit

For more bombastic Savoy palaces and castles continue from Rivoli on a circuit around Turin on the Tangenziale (p55).

### 5 Italian Riviera

From Cuneo cut across eastwards along the A33 and then down the A6 to Savona for a cruise along the Italian Riviera (p79).

## DETOUR: RIVOLI

**Start: 1 Turin**

Works by Franz Ackermann, Gilbert and George, and Frank Gehry now sit amid the splendour of **Castello di Rivoli**, once the home of Savoy princes and now the venue for the **Museo d'Arte Contemporanea** (www.castellodirivoli.org; Piazza Mafalda di Savoia, Rivoli; adult/reduced €6.50/4.50; 10am-5pm Tue-Fri, 10am-7pm Sat & Sun). The startling contrasts between the historic house and the avant-garde art are worth the trip. You can mix contemporary art with contemporary food at Combal.Zero (p77).

9.30am-12.30pm & 2.30-6pm Tue-Fri, 9.30am-noon & 2.40-6pm Sat & Sun, to 5pm Oct-Mar). This Gothic-Romanesque abbey has kept sentry atop Monte Pirchiriano (962m) since the 10th century and exerted enormous power over abbeys throughout Italy, France and Spain, including Mont'Sant Michel in France. It looks familiar, because Umberto Eco used it as the basis for the abbey in *The Name of the Rose.*

Approach as pilgrims would up the **Scalone dei Morti** (Stairway of the Dead), flanked by arches that would once have held the skeletons of dead monks. At the top enter through the whimsical, 12th-century Zodiac Door. Within the walls, the complex houses a frescoed church and the remnants of the monastery, crowned by the **Torre della Bell'Alda** (Tower of Beautiful Alda). More beautiful though are the views down the Susa Valley.

**The Drive »** Return to the A32 down the SS25 for the 35km drive to Susa. Although you're on the autostrada the entire way, the journey passes through dense forests with snow-capped peaks slowly rising ahead of you. Just after Bussoleno, exit for Susa Est.

---

### 3 Susa

The Romans marched up the **Valle di Susa** and crossed the Alps to secure a passage to the French ports of Nice and Marseille. They enjoyed the thermal baths in Belvédère across the border in France, and grabbed Susa from the Gauls, thus securing the high passes of the Cottian Alps. You'll find evidence of them all over town, including the remnants of an **aqueduct**, a still-used **amphitheatre** and the triumphal **Arco d'Augusto**, dating from 9 BC.

Susa stands at the gateway to the Valle di Susa, cut through by the Dora di Bardonecchia river and littered with stone towns such as Exilles, with its forbidding **Forte di Exilles** (www.fortediexilles.it; Via degli Alpini; adult/reduced €10/8; 10am-7pm Tue-Sun Apr-Sep, 10am-2pm Tue & Fri, 2-6pm Wed, Thu, Sat & Sun Oct-Mar), said to be the keep of the Man in the Iron Mask between 1681 and 1687.

p77

**The Drive »** The 44km from Susa to Sestriere is a scenic mountain drive. Rejoin the A32, heading for Fréjus, for 20km (you'll pass the exit for Exilles after 12km). Exit at Oulx Est onto the SS24 and follow the gushing torrent of Dora-Riparia to Cesana Torinese (alternatively you can head uphill and base yourself in Sauze d'Oulx). When the road forks, veer left onto the SS23 for the final winding ascent to Sestriere.

---

TRIP HIGHLIGHT

### 4 Sestriere

Developed in the 1930s by the Agnelli clan of Fiat, Sestriere ranks among Europe's most glamorous ski resorts due to its enviable location in the eastern realms of the **Via Lattea** (www.vialattea.it; daily ski pass €34) ski area. Neither chocolate bar nor a galaxy of stars,

ROSTISLAV GLINSKY/ALAMY ©

Limone Piemonte

the Via Lattea, or Milky Way, incorporates some 400km of piste and five interlinked ski resorts: Sestriere (2035m), Sauze d'Oulx (1509m), Sansicario (1700m), Cesana Torinese (1350m) and Claviere (1760m) in Italy; and Montgenèvre (1850m) in neighbouring France.

Outside of ski season the **tourist office** (www.sestriere.it; Via Louset; ⌚9am-12.30pm & 2.30-7pm) has information on every conceivable summer activity, including golfing on Europe's highest golf course, walking, free climbing and mountain biking.

**The Drive »** The longest journey on this tour is the 86km out of the mountains to Saluzzo. Continue on the winding SS23 through mountain towns for 33km and descend southeast to Pinerolo. Then take the ramp to the SS589 (towards Cuneo), which brings you to Saluzzo after 29km.

## 5 Saluzzo

Situated at the foot of Monte Viso, Saluzzo was once a powerful marquisate that lasted four centuries until the Savoys won it in a 1601 treaty with France. Its historic significance – although diminished – has left a stirring legacy in its old centre.

The imposing castle, known locally as **La Castiglia** (Piazza Castello; adult/reduced €5/3; 3-7pm Sun Mar-Oct), overlooks the cobbled alleys and Gothic and Renaissance mansions of the old town, which cluster around the **Salita al Castello**, literally 'the ascent to the castle'. Nearby are the Town Hall and the **Torre Civica** (Via San Giovanni; admission €2, incl Museo Civico di Casa Cavassa €6; 10.30am-12.30pm & 2.30-6.30pm Fri-Sun), which you can climb for views over the burnt red-tiled rooftops.

p77

**The Drive »** It's a short 27km drive from Saluzzo to Cuneo, first on the SP161 and then on the SP25 after Villafalleto. Dropping into low-lying plains, the road passes through vineyards and orchards and across mountain torrents.

## 6 Cuneo

Sitting on a promontory between the Gesso and Stura di Demonte rivers, Cuneo enjoys excellent Alpine views framed by the high pyramid-shaped peak of Monte Viso (3841m). To the southwest lie the Maritime Alps, a rugged outdoor-adventure playground. After a hard day out hiking, you'll be thankful for the heart-warming buzz of a *cuneesi al rhum* – a large, rum-laced praline, which you can lay your hands on at 1920s-vintage chocolatier **Arione** (www.arione-cuneo.com; Piazza Galimberti 14; 8am-8pm Tue-Sat, 8am-1pm & 3.30-8pm Sun), located in magnificent **Piazza Galimberti**.

Cuneo also has some wonderfully dark and zealous churches. The oldest is the deconsecrated San Francisco convent and church which today houses the **Museo Civico di Cuneo** (Via Santa María 10; admission €2.60; 9am-1pm & 3-5.30pm Tue-Thu, to 7pm Fri & Sat), tracking the history of the town and province.

p77

**The Drive »** The final 34km to Limone Piemonte provide another picturesque mountain road. Leave Cuneo heading southwest on the SS20 to Borgo San Dalmazzo, where you veer left (keeping on the SS20) across the Torrente Gesso and up into the mountains.

TRIP HIGHLIGHT

## 7 Limone Piemonte

To the southwest of Cuneo lies the **Parco Naturale delle Alpi Marittime** (www.parcoalpimarittime.it). Despite their diminutive size, there's a palpable wilderness feel to be found among these Maritime peaks. The park is a walker's paradise, stocked with ibex, chamois and whistling marmots, which scurry around rocky crags covered in mist above a well-marked network of mountain trails, some of them old salt routes, others supply lines left over from two world wars.

The best-equipped town for access to the park is picturesque **Limone Piemonte** (www.limonepiemonte.it). One of the oldest Alpine ski stations, Limone has been in operation since 1907 and maintains 15 lifts and 80km of runs.

p77

### MARGUAREIS CIRCUIT

The Marguareis Circuit is a 35km, two-day hike that starts in Limone Piemonte and tracks up across the mountain passes and ridges to the **Rifugio Garelli** (0171 73 80 78; dm €36; Jun-Sep). The peaks of the Argentera and Cime du Gélas massifs are clearly visible from the summit of Punta Marguareis (2651m), the highest point in the park. On Day 2, 4km of the trek passes through a mountainous nodule of France before swinging back round into Italy.

# Eating & Sleeping

## Turin 1

**Gofri Piemontèisa** Snacks €

(www.gofriemiassepiemontesi.it; Via San Tommaso 4a; 11.30am-7.30pm) *Gofri* are thin waffles made from flour, water and yeast and placed in hot irons. They originate in the Piedmontese mountains and make for a delicious fast food. Try the house *gofre* with ham, soft cheese and rocket.

**Le Meridien Lingotto** Luxury Hotel €€€

(011 664 20 00; www.lemeridienlingotto.it; Via Nizza 262; d €270-300; P) This industrial-luxe hotel is situated within the Fiat car factory, which was built in the 1920s and renovated by Renzo Piano in the 1980s. Guests can jog around the former car-testing circuit on the roof, which was featured in the 1969 film *The Italian Job.*

## Rivoli

**Combal.Zero** Gastronomic, Contemporary €€€

(011 956 52 25; www.combal.org; Piazza Mafalda di Savoia; meals €80-140; Tue-Sat) Davide Scabin has been tossing out food conventions for years with his conceptual gastronomy. Humorous takes on the classics include 'Zuppizza', a liquid pizza reconstructed from the bottom up featuring a mozzarella soup topped with tomato and miniature basil leaves.

## Susa 3

**Hotel Susa & Stazione** Hotel €

(0122 62 22 26; www.hotelsusa.it; Corso Stati Uniti 4/6; s/d €62/85; P) The lemon-yellow Hotel Susa sits opposite the station and has been welcoming Alpine-bound travellers and Tour de France cyclists for years. Rooms, recently renovated, are neat and modern, and staff are happy to prepare packed lunches for hikers and cyclists.

## Sauze d'Oulz

**Chalet Chez Nous** Chalet, B&B €€

(0122 85 97 82; www.chaletcheznous.it; Frazione Jouvenceaux 41; s €60-80, d €90-120; Dec-Jul; P) Located in Jouvenceaux, the old part of Sauze, barely five minutes from the chair lift, Chalet Chez Nous is not only superbly located but warm and friendly. Rooms feature exposed oak beams and traditional furnishings, and hosts Andrea, Roberto and Laura are on hand to help with shuttles and ski hire.

## Saluzzo 5

**Terra Gemella** Piedmontese €€

(347 642 72 61; Via Seminario 28; meals €20-35; Wed-Sun, dinner only Tue) Terra Gemella is a wonderful '50s throwback, with pistachio-green walls, chandeliers and traditional tiled floors. Owners Omar and Romina take care of everything personally, and the small menu, featuring classics like gnocchi with gorgonzola, changes frequently.

## Cuneo 6

**Delle Antiche Contrade** Gastronomic €€€

(0171 48 04 88; www.antichecontrade.it; Via Savigliano 11; meals €60; lunch & dinner Tue-Sat, lunch Sun) This former 17th-century postal station is the culinary workshop of Ligurian chef Luigi Taglienti, who melds the fish of his home region with the meat and pasta of the mountains. The result: a Michelin star.

## Limone Piemonte 7

**Hotel Marguareis** Hotel €

(0171 92 75 67; Via Genova 30; s/d €48/96) A small, family-run hotel in the centre of Limone, well located for an early-morning start on the Marguareis Circuit. Rooms are small, neat and retro-Alpine in style.

**Alassio** *Enjoy the town's colonial character and pastel-hued villas*

# Italian Riviera

5

*Curving west in a broad arc, backed by the Maritime Alps, the Italian Riviera sweeps down from Genoa through ancient hamlets and terraced olive groves to the French border at Ventimiglia.*

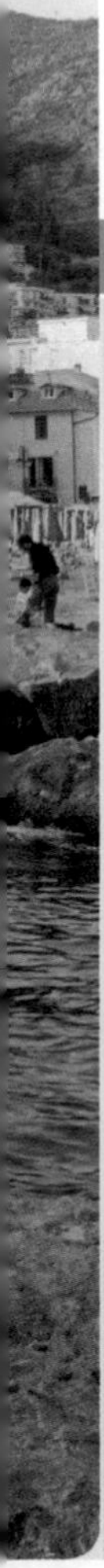

## TRIP HIGHLIGHTS

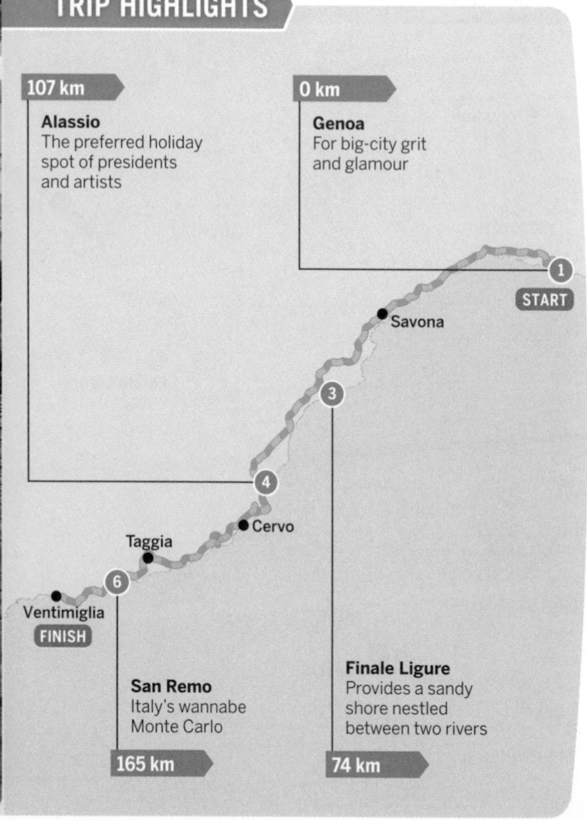

107 km
**Alassio**
The preferred holiday spot of presidents and artists

0 km
**Genoa**
For big-city grit and glamour

74 km
**Finale Ligure**
Provides a sandy shore nestled between two rivers

165 km
**San Remo**
Italy's wannabe Monte Carlo

Savona, Cervo, Taggia, Ventimiglia — START, FINISH

**4 DAYS**
**188KM / 117 MILES**

**GREAT FOR...**

**BEST TIME TO GO**

April, May and June for flowers and hiking; October for harvest.

**ESSENTIAL PHOTO**

Cascading terraces of exotic flowers at Villa Hanbury.

**BEST FINE DINING**

Purple San Remo prawns on the terrace of San Giorgio.

# 5 Italian Riviera

The contrast between sun-washed, sophisticated coastal towns and a deeply rural, mountainous hinterland, full of heritage farms, olive oil producers and wineries, gave rise to the Riviera's 19th-century fame, when European expatriates outnumbered locals. They amused themselves in lavish botanical gardens, gambled in the casino of San Remo and dined in style in fine art-nouveau villas, much as you will on this tour.

TRIP HIGHLIGHT

## ❶ Genoa

Like Dr Jekyll and Mr Hyde, Genoa (Genova) is a city with a split personality. At its centre, medieval *caruggi* (alleyways) untangle outwards to the **Porto Antico** and teem with hawkers, merchants and office workers. Along Via Garibaldi and Via XXV Aprile is another Genoa, one of Unesco-sponsored palaces, smart shops and grand architectural gestures like **Piazza**

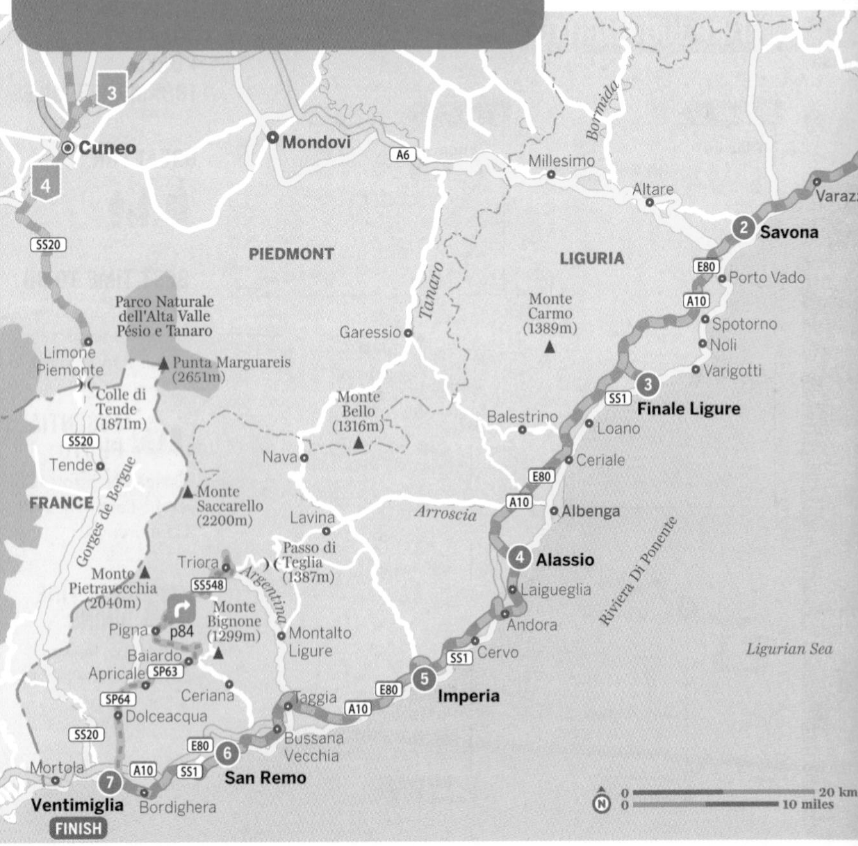

**de Ferrari** with its monumental fountain, art nouveau **Palazzo Borsa** (once the city's stock exchange) and the neoclassical **Teatro San Carlo** (www.carlofelice.it; Passo Eugenio Montale 4).

Join the well-dressed *haute bourgeoisie* enjoying high-profile art exhibits in the grand Mannerist halls of the **Palazzo Ducale** (www.palazzoducale.genova.it; Piazza Giacomo Matteotti 9; admission €5-10; ⏲exhibitions 9am-9pm Tue-Sun), then retire to sip Spritz amid Bernardino Strozzi's 17th-century frescos at **Cambi Café** (www.cambicafe.com; Vico Falamonica 1r; ⏲8am-11pm).

 p85

**The Drive »** Exit Genoa westward, through a tangle of flyovers and tunnels to access the A10 for the first 48km drive to Savona. Once out of the suburbs the forested slopes of the Maritime Alps rise to your right and sea views peep out at you as you duck through tunnels.

## 2 Savona

Don't be put off by Savona's horrifying industrial sprawl; the Savonesi were a powerful maritime people and the town centre is unexpectedly graceful. Standing near the port are three of the many medieval towers that once studded the cityscape. Genoa's greatest rival, the town was savagely sacked in 1528, the castle dismantled and most of the population slaughtered, but somehow the **Fortezza del Priamàr** (Piazza Priamar) and the **Cattedrale di Nostra Signora Assunta** (Piazza Cattedrale) survived.

But you're not here for the architecture – you're here for the food. The covered **market** (Via Pietro Giuria; ⏲7am-1.30pm Mon-Sat) is crammed with fruit-and-veg stalls and fish stands stacked with salt cod. **Grigiomar** (Via P Giuria 5-2; ⏲Tue-Sun) salts its own local anchovies. Then there are the local *amaretti* biscuits, made with bitter and sweet almonds, available at **Pasticceria Besio** (www.amarettibesio.com; Via Sormano 16r; ⏲Tue-Sat), and the *farinata di grano* (wheat-flour pancakes) at **Vino e Farinata** (Via Pia 15; ⏲Tue-Sat).

**The Drive »** Rejoin the A10 and leave the industrial chimneys of Savona behind you. For the first 13km the A10 continues with views of the sea, then at Spotorno it ducks inland for the final 15km to the Finale Ligure exit. Descend steeply for 3km to the Finale hamlets on the coast.

### LINK YOUR TRIP

**3 Gourmet Piedmont**

Up the A6 from food-town Savona is Slow Food HQ Bra and the start of a gourmet tour of the Langhe (p63).

**4 Meandering the Maritime Alps**

From Ventimiglia slice through France on the SS20 to Limone Piemonte to start an adventure in the Maritime Alps (p71).

TRIP HIGHLIGHT

## 3 Finale Ligure

Finale Ligure comprises several seaside districts. The marina is narrow and charming, spreading along the sandy shore between two small rivers, the Porra and the Sciusa. East of the Sciusa is Finale Ligure Pia, where you'll find **Alimentari Magnone** (Via Moletti 17), which stocks excellent extra virgin olive oils from local growers. Nearby the Benedictine abbey houses the **Azienda Agricola Apiario Benedettino** (Via al Santuario 59; ⌚Mon-Sat), where you can buy honey, grappa and organic beauty products.

At the other end of town, **Finalborgo** is the old medieval centre. Each year in March, Finalborgo's cloisters are home to the **Salone dell'Agroalimentare Ligure**, where local farmers hawk seasonal delicacies and vintages.

On Thursday it's worth driving 9km up the coast to picturesque **Noli** for the weekly outdoor market on Corso d'Italia.

✕ 🛏 p85

**The Drive »** Once again take the high road away from the coast and follow the A10 for a further 35km to Alassio. At Albenga you'll cross the river Centa and the broad valley where dozens of hothouses dot the landscape.

TRIP HIGHLIGHT

## 4 Alassio

Less than 100km from the French border, Alassio's popularity among the 18th- and 19th-century jet set has left it with an elegant colonial character. Its pastel-hued villas range around a broad, sandy beach, which stretches all the way to **Laigueglia** (4km to the west). American president Thomas Jefferson holidayed here in 1787 and Edward Elgar composed *In the South* inspired by his stay in 1904. **Il Muretto**, a ceramic-covered wall, records the names of 550 celebrities who've passed through.

Follow the local lead and promenade along Via XX Settembre or the unspoilt waterfront. Take coffee at **Antico Caffè Pasticceria Balzola** (www.balzola.net; Piazza Matteotti 26; ⌚Tue-Sun Dec-Oct) and enjoy gelato on the beach beneath a stripy umbrella.

✕ 🛏 p85

**The Drive »** If you have time take the scenic coast road, SS1 (Via Roma), from Alassio through Laigueglia, to Andora, before rejoining the autostrada. It adds about 5km to the journey but is a scenic jaunt when traffic is light. From Andora it's a further 16km on the A10 to Imperia.

## 5 Imperia

Imperia consists of two small seaside towns, Oneglia and Porto Maurizio, on either side of the Impero river.

Oneglia, birthplace of Admiral Doria, the Genoese Republic's greatest naval hero, is the less attractive of the two, although **Piazza Dante**, with its arcaded walkways, is a great place for artisanal coffee at **Caffè Piccardo** (Piazza Dante 1; ⌚6.30am-8.30pm). This is also where the great olive-oil dynasties made their name. Visit the **Museo dell'Olio**

**Coastal road** Views across the Ligurian sea

(www.oliocarli.it; admission free; ⏰9am-12.30pm & 3-6.30pm Mon-Sat) in the landscaped grounds of the Fratelli Carli factory, where a pair of 1000-year-old olive trees guard the entrance to 18 spot-lit caverns detailing the history of the Ligurian industry. You can buy oil here or at award-winning **Ranise** (www.ranise.it; Via Nazionale 30, Oneglia).

West of Oneglia is pirate haven **Porto Maurizio**, perched on a rocky spur that overlooks a yacht-filled harbour.

**The Drive »** Rejoining the A10 at Imperia, the landscape begins to change. The olive terraces are dense, spear-like cypresses and umbrella pines shade the hillsides, and the fragrant *maquis* (Mediterranean scrub) is prolific. Loop inland around Taggia and then descend slowly into San Remo.

TRIP HIGHLIGHT

## 6 San Remo

San Remo, Italy's wannabe Monte Carlo,

### SAN GIORGIO

Cult restaurant **San Giorgio** (☎0183 40 01 75; www.ristorantesangiorgio.com; Via A Volta 19, Cervo; ⏰lunch & dinner Wed-Mon Feb-Dec) has been quietly wowing gourmets with its authentic Ligurian cooking since the 1950s when mother-and-son team Caterina and Alessandro opened the doors of their home in the *borgo* (medieval town) of **Cervo Alta**. Dine out on the bougainvillea-draped terrace in summer, or in intimate dining rooms cluttered with family silverware and antiques in winter. Below the restaurant, in an old oil mill, is the less formal wine bar and deli **San Giorgino**.

is a sun-dappled Mediterranean resort with a grand Belle Époque **casino** (www.casinosanremo.it; Corso degli Inglesi; 10am-late) and lashings of Riviera-style grandeur.

During the mid-19th century the city became a magnet for European exiles such as Czar Nicolas of Russia, who favoured the town's balmy winters. They built an onion-domed **Russian Orthodox church** (Via Nuvoloni 2; admission €1; 9.30am-noon & 3-6pm) reminiscent of Moscow's St Basil's Cathedral, which still turns heads down by the seafront. Swedish inventor Alfred Nobel also maintained a villa here, the **Villa Nobel** (Corso Felice Cavallotti 112; 11am-12.30pm Tue-Fri), which now houses a museum dedicated to him.

Beyond the waterfront, San Remo hides a little-visited old town, a labyrinth of twisting lanes that cascade down the Ligurian hillside. Curling around the base is the **Italian Cycling Riviera**, a path that tracks the coast as far as Imperia. For bike hire, enquire at the **tourist office** (www.rivieradeifiori.org; Largo Nuvoloni 1; 8am-7pm Mon-Sat, 9am-1pm Sun).

p85

**The Drive »** For the final 17km stretch to Ventimiglia take the SS1 coastal road, which hugs the base of the mountains and offers uninterrupted sea views. In summer and Easter, however, when traffic is heavy, your best bet is the A10.

## DETOUR: L'ENTROTERRA

**Start: 7 Ventimiglia**

The designation 'Riviera' omits the pleated, mountainous interior – *l'entroterra* – that makes up nine-tenths of Liguria. Harried by invasions, coast-dwellers took to these vertical landscapes over a thousand years ago, hewing their perched villages from the rock face of the Maritime Alps. You'll want to set aside two extra days to drive the coiling roads that rise up from Ventimiglia to **Dolceacqua**, **Apricale** and **Pigna**. If you make it all the way to **Triora**, book into the **Colomba d'Oro** (0184 9 40 51; www.colombadoro.it; d €70-110; P). It's worth it for the breakfast and the see-forever panoramas.

## 7 Ventimiglia

Despite its enviable position between the glitter of San Remo and the Côte d'Azur, Ventimiglia is a soulful but disorderly border town, its Roman past still evident in its bridges, amphitheatre and ruined baths. Now it's the huge **Friday market** (Piazza della Libertà; 9am-sunset) that draws the crowds.

If you can't find a souvenir here then consider one of the prized artisanal honeys produced by **Marco Ballestra** (www.mielepolline.it; Via Girolamo Rossi 5; Tue-Sat), which has hives in the hills above the Valle Roya. There are over a dozen different types.

To end the tour head over to the pretty western suburb of Ponte San Ludovico to the **Giardini Botanici Hanbury** (www.giardinihanbury.com; Corso Montecarlo 43, La Mortola; adult/reduced €9/7.50; 9.30am-6pm), the 18-hectare estate of English businessman Sir Thomas Hanbury; he planted it with an extravagant 5800 botanical species from five continents.

p85

# Eating & Sleeping

## Genoa 1

**Antica Trattoria Sà Pesta** Trattoria, Genovese **€**

(010 246 8336; Via Giustiniani 16r; meals €10-15; lunch Mon-Sat) A landmark trattoria serving classic Genovese *farinata* in seasoned antique pans, alongside traditional pasta dishes such as *pansòti* filled with wild greens.

## Finale Ligure 3

**Chiesa** Deli, Trattoria **€**

(019 69 25 16; Via Pertica 15; daily May-Oct, Mon-Sat Nov-Apr) Presided over by Laura Chiesa, this delicatessen offers a huge array of seafood salads, salamis, cheeses and gnocchi with pesto, of course. Order what you like in the shop and eat it at the *tavola calda* ('warm table', a casual eatery) round the corner on Vico Gandolino.

**Paradiso di Manù** Diffusion Hotel **€€**

(019 749 0110; www.paradisodimanu.it; Via Chiariventi 35, Noli; d €120-160; P @ ) Overlooking the Gulf of Spotorno, this 'diffusion' hotel is a revitalised hamlet with six elegant Provençal-style rooms located in a variety of stone buildings overlooking florid terraces, one with a large, inviting pool.

**Hotel Florenz** Hotel **€**

(019 69 56 67; www.hotelflorenz.it; Via Celesia 1; s €52-75, d €74-120; closed Nov & Feb; P @ ) Just 800m from the sea, this 18th-century former convent just outside Finalborgo's village walls provides atmospheric accommodation and offers a host of thoughtful family-friendly facilities (cots, a parents' kitchen and secure children's garden).

## Alassio 4

**Osteria dei Matetti** Osteria **€€**

(0182 64 66 80; Via Daniele Hanbury 132; Tue-Sun Sep-Jun, dinner daily Jul-Aug) A friendly *osteria* (casual tavern), serving *farinata* in winter and minestrone with homemade pesto in summer. Fish depends on the catch, but could include stuffed and baked anchovies, stewed octopus with tomatoes, and squid filled with pine nuts and herbs.

**Villa della Pergola** Boutique Hotel **€€€**

(0182 64 61 30; www.villadellapergola.com; Via Privata Montagu 9/1; d €240-310; P ) Sitting in a tropical garden that rivals the famous Villa Hanbury, Villa della Pergola was the home of eminent Victorian, General McMurdo. He bought the plot in 1875 and designed the villa in Anglo-Indian style with large airy rooms, broad verandas and cascading terraces with peerless sea views.

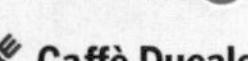

## San Remo 6

**Caffè Ducale** Cafe **€**

(Via Matteotti 145; lunch menu €18-22; 7.30am-midnight) Italian panache with a dash of San Remo swankiness makes this cafe-*enoteca-salon de thé* one of the most refined joints east of the Côte d'Azur. Enjoy a few *aperitivi* (aperitifs) under the weighty chandeliers before heading off to the casino.

## Ventimiglia 7

**Hotel Seagull** Hotel **€**

(0184 35 17 26; www.seagullhotel.it; Passeggiata Marconi 24; s/d from €55/75; P ) A 10-minute stroll along the seafront from Ventimiglia's town centre, this family-run hotel has simple but appealing sky-blue-and-white rooms, a fragrant garden and a breezy terrace.

***Monterosso al Mare*** *Bask on a postcard-perfect beach*

JOSEPH SPANTI

# Cinematic Cinque Terre

*From the Portofino peninsula, via the Cinque Terre's cliff-side villages to Portovenere, this trip exudes Riviera glamour. But amid billionaire motor yachts you'll find a hard-working community.*

## TRIP HIGHLIGHTS

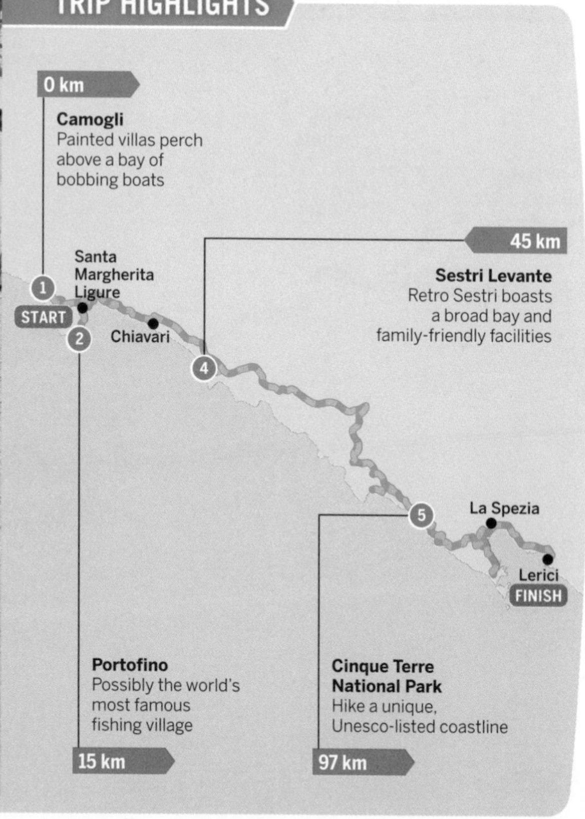

0 km
**Camogli**
Painted villas perch above a bay of bobbing boats

Santa Margherita Ligure

START

Chiavari

45 km
**Sestri Levante**
Retro Sestri boasts a broad bay and family-friendly facilities

La Spezia

Lerici

FINISH

**Portofino**
Possibly the world's most famous fishing village
15 km

**Cinque Terre National Park**
Hike a unique, Unesco-listed coastline
97 km

### 5–7 DAYS
### 165KM / 102 MILES

### GREAT FOR...

### BEST TIME TO GO

Balmy days in April and October are perfect for hiking and swimming.

### ESSENTIAL PHOTO

Views over pastel-coloured Camogli from San Rocco.

### BEST FOR HIKING

Any one of the Cinque Terre's sanctuary walks.

# 6 Cinematic Cinque Terre

Challenged by a landscape of soaring mountains, Ligurian farmers have been reclaiming the Levante's wild slopes with neatly banded stone terraces for over 2000 years. The work that went into them took centuries and is comparable, it is said, to the building of the Great Wall of China. Planted with olives, grapes, basil and garlic, they snake from sea level to crest gravity-defying precipices and are now protected as a Unesco World Heritage Site.

TRIP HIGHLIGHT

## 1 Camogli

Still an authentic fishing village with tall, trompe-l'oeil painted villas and a broad curving beach, Camogli's name is said to derive from *case delle mogli* (the wives' houses) for the women left behind by their fisherfolk husbands. In the 19th century it had the largest merchant fleet in the Mediterranean, but now it's a charming holiday spot for weekending Milanese who shop

for supplies in the Wednesday **market** (Via 20 Settembre; ⌚8am-1pm).

Fishing traditions also continue here, such as the *tonnara di Punta Chiappa*, a large, complex fishing net between Camogli and San Fruttuoso, which is used for the trapping of tuna between April and September. It's been here since the 1600s and during the season it's pulled up by hand once or twice a day. Boats leave from Via Garibaldi to the **Punta Chiappa** where you can swim and sunbathe in summer. In May the village celebrates the **Sagra del Pesce** (Fish Festival) with a huge fry-up – hundreds of fish are cooked in 3m-wide pans along the busy waterfront.

For the best views in town, take a short drive up to **San Rocco di Camogli**, a small hamlet wrapped in olive groves with panoramic views. Trailheads crossing **Monte di Portofino** start here.

p94

**The Drive »** Climb out of Camogli and pick up the SS1 in the direction of Santa Margherita Ligure. The cypress-lined road sweeps around the headland past gloriously grand villas. Just past San Lorenzo della Costa, exit right and descend steeply into Santa Margherita. When you hit the waterfront turn right on Corso Marconi (SP227), past Villa Durazzo, and follow the waterfront 5km to Portofino.

TRIP HIGHLIGHT

## 2 Portofino

With its striking setting and pastel-hued villas framed by the dense pine-covered slopes of the peninsula, Portofino ranks among the world's most famous fishing villages. A favourite destination of billionaires and celebrities, it has long been exclusive and expensive. In the late 16th century, aristocratic traveller Giambattista Confalonieri complained, 'You were charged not only for the room, but for the very air you breathed'.

Surprisingly, though, the best experience in Portofino is free: a hike along one of the 60km of trails that crisscross the natural **park** (www.parks.it/parco.portofino). Enquire at the tourist office for maps. You can walk the full 18km from Portofino to Camogli, via San Fruttuoso. Otherwise take the Salita

### LINK YOUR TRIP

**7 Northern Cities**
Swap the coastal scenery for the cultural cities of the Po plain by driving north to Milan (Milano) on the A7 (p97).

**24 Foodie Emilia-Romagna**
From Lerici, head up the A15 to Parma to sample the gourmet hams, cheese and pasta of Emilia-Romagna (p261).

San Giorgio stairs from the harbour, past the **Chiesa di San Giorgio**, to Portofino's unusual **Castello Brown** (www.portofinoevents.com; Via alla Penisola 13a; admission €3.50). In 1867 it became the private home of British diplomat Montague Yeats Brown, who no doubt derived endless pleasure from the spectacular views from its garden.

p94

**The Drive »** This short 9km seafront drive is fantastically scenic. Taking the only road out of town (SP227) follow its path back to Santa Margherita, where you can take a quick stroll in the gorgeous gardens of Villa Durazzo. The rest of the journey wends it way through Santa Margherita, which merges almost seamlessly with Rapallo.

JOSEPH SPANTI

## 3 Rapallo

WB Yeats, Max Beerbohm and Ezra Pound all garnered inspiration in Rapallo and it's not difficult to see why. Set on a curving bay lined with striped umbrellas and palm trees, and backed by the 1900m Montallegro, Rapallo is the picture of Riviera living.

On Thursday the historic centre comes alive when weekly market stalls fill **Piazza Cile**. Otherwise stroll the gorgeous **Lungomare Vittorio Veneto**, explore temporary exhibitions in the castle and take the 1934-vintage **cable car** (Piazzale Solari 2; one way/return €5.50/8; 9am-12.30pm & 2-6pm) up to the **Santuario Basilico di Montallegro** (612m), built on the spot where the Virgin Mary was reportedly sighted in 1557. Given the heavenly view, it's hardly surprising.

p94

**The Drive »** You can do the 25km drive from Rapallo to Sestri Levante all along the autostrada if you're pressed for time. Otherwise, it's worth taking the more scenic route out of Rapallo along the coast road (SS1) through Zoagli and rejoining the autostrada just before Chiavari (famous for its *farinata* flat bread; see p94). From here it's a further 13km to Sestri Levante.

**Cinque Terre National Park** The village of Vernazza

TRIP HIGHLIGHT

## 4 Sestri Levante

Set in a broad flat valley with a long sandy beach and two sheltered bays, Sestri, as the locals call it, has something of a 1950s feel. This might have something to do with the striped umbrellas that dot the beach, the old-style refreshment kiosks, play areas and amusements along the waterfront and the meandering cycle paths where well-dressed ladies pedal with brightly coloured towels in their baskets. Many of the beachfront apartments are owned by Milanese and Genovese families, so you can be sure of a high standard of restaurants, cafes and ice-cream shops in the densely packed historic centre, which sits squeezed between the **Baia del Silenzio** (Bay of Silence) and the **Baia della Favola** (Bay of Fairytales), the latter named after fairytale author Hans Christian Andersen, who lived in Sestri in the early 19th century.

Aside from the fabulous beachfront,

Sestri is surrounded by olive trees, and family-owned **Frantoio Bo** (www.frantoio-bo.it; Via della Chiusa 70; ⏲Mon-Sat) makes some of the finest oil on the Riviera. The top of the line is called Le Due Baie (The Two Bays) and is composed of handpicked Lavagnina, Razzola and Pignola olives.

 p95

**The Drive »** From Sestri head southeast onto the A12 autostrada for the 42km drive to the Monterosso al Mare. The first 23km are uneventful, but once you exit onto the SP566dir to Monterosso you descend steeply through the forested mountains along an improbable mountain road. The views, across deep valleys to the sea, are superb. Park in the guarded parking lot off Via Fegina (€12).

TRIP HIGHLIGHT

## 5 Cinque Terre National Park

Five dramatically perched seaside villages – **Monterosso al Mare**, **Vernazza**, **Corniglia**, **Manarola** and **Riomaggiore** – make up the five communities of the Unesco-protected **Parco Nazionale delle Cinque Terre** (parconazionale5terre.it). A site of genuine and marvellous beauty, it may not be the undiscovered Eden it was 100 years ago, but frankly – who cares? Sinuous paths traverse seemingly impregnable cliffs, while a 19th-century railway line cuts through coastal tunnels linking village to village. Cars are banned, so park in Monterosso or Riomaggiore, and take to the hills on foot or skirt the spectacular cliffs by boat.

Rooted in antiquity, the Cinque Terre's five towns date from the early medieval period, and include several castles and a quintet of illustrious parish churches. Buildings aside, the Cinque Terre's most unique feature is the steeply terraced cliffs banded by a complicated system of fields and gardens that have been chiselled, shaped and layered over the course of two millennia. The 12km **Sentiero Azzurro** (Blue Path; No 2 on maps) links all five villages by foot. To walk it you must first purchase a Cinque Terre card (see p92). If you don't fancy walking the full length then aim for quiet Corniglia, the only one of the five with no direct access to the sea, and return by train, snapping the perfect picture from the rocky promontory **Punta Buonfiglio** before you go.

From late March to October, the **Consorzio Marittimo Turistico Cinque Terre Golfo dei Poeti** (www.navigazionegolfodeipoeti.it; daily ticket adult/reduced €25/15) runs daily shuttle boats between the villages.

 p95

**The Drive »** If the roads are busy take the longer, 67km autostrada route via the A12 and A15. However, if you have more time you can take the more scenic, but winding SP51 and SP370 through the mountains of the Cinque Terre National Park until you hit the coast just south of La Spezia. From here turn southwards on the SS530 for the final 12km coastal drive into Portovenere.

### TOP TIP: CINQUE TERRE CARD

The best way to get around the Cinque Terre is with the Cinque Terre card, which gives you unlimited use of walking paths and electric village buses, as well as the elevator in Riomaggiore and cultural exhibitions (one/two days €5/9, four-person family card €15). With the addition of train travel, a one-/two-day card is €10/19, while a four-person family card costs €26.

Cards are sold at all Cinque Terre park **information offices** (www.parconazionale5terre.it; ⏲7am-8pm), located in the village train stations.

## ❻ Portovenere

If the Cinque Terre had to pick an honorary sixth member, Portovenere would surely be it. Perched on the western promontory of the Gulf of Poets (Shelley and Byron were regulars here), the village's century-old house towers form a citadel around **Castello Doria** (admission €2.20; ⏲10.30am-1.30pm & 2.30-6pm). No one knows the origins of the castle, although Portus Veneris was a Roman base en route from Gaul to Spain, but the current structure dates from the 16th century and offers wonderful views from its terraced gardens. Just off the promontory you'll spy the tiny islands of Palmaria, Tino and Tinetto.

The wave-lashed **Chiesa di San Pietro** sits atop a Roman temple dedicated to the goddess Venus (born from the foam of the sea) from whom Portovenere takes its name. At the end of the quay a Cinque Terre panorama unfolds from the **Grotta Arpaia**, a former haunt of Lord Byron, who once swam across the gulf to Lerici to visit his fellow romantic, Shelley.

**The Drive »** Return to La Spezia via the SS530 and cross through town to exit eastwards on the SP331. Driving along waterfront boulevards lined with umbrella pines you'll pass La Spezia's marina, then go through suburbs such as San Terenzo, until at Pugliola you turn right onto the SP28 and climb up the villa-lined road into Lerici.

### SANCTUARY WALKS

Each of Cinque Terre's villages is associated with a sanctuary perched high on the cliff sides. Reaching these religious retreats used to be an act of penance, but these days the walks are for pure pleasure.

» **Monterosso to Santuario della Madonna di Soviore** Follow trail No 9 up through forest to Liguria's oldest sanctuary.

» **Vernazza to Santuario della Madonna di Reggio** Follow trail No 8 past 14 sculpted Stations of the Cross to this 11th-century chapel with a Romanesque facade.

» **Corniglia to Santuario della Madonna delle Grazie** Ascend the spectacular Salla di Comeneco on trail No 7 to this church with its adored image of the Madonna and Child.

» **Manarola to Santuario della Madonna delle Salute** The pick of all the sanctuary walks is this breathtaking traverse (trail No 6) through Cinque Terre's finest vineyards.

» **Riomaggiore to Santuario della Madonna di Montenero** Trail No 3 ascends to this frescoed 18th-century chapel that sits atop an astounding viewpoint.

## ❼ Lerici

Magnolia, yew and cedar trees grow in the 1930s public gardens at Lerici, an exclusive retreat of handsome villas that cling to the cliffs along its beach. In another age Byron and Shelley sought inspiration here and gave the Gulf of Poets its name. The Shelleys stayed at the waterfront Villa Magni (closed to visitors) in the early 1820s but sadly Percy drowned here when his boat sank off the coast in 1822.

From Lerici a scenic 4km stroll takes you south past the magnificent bay of Fiascherino to **Tellaro**, a fishing hamlet with pink-and-orange houses cluttered about narrow lanes and tiny squares. Sit on the rocks at the **Chiesa San Giorgio** and imagine an octopus ringing the church bells – which, according to legend, it did to warn the villagers of a Saracen attack.

✕ 🛏 p95

# Eating & Sleeping



## Camogli 1

### La Bossa di Mario — Wine Bar €€

(0185 77 25 05; www.labossa.it; Via della Repubblica 124; meals €25-35; Thu-Tue) La Bossa takes Goethe's quote 'Life is too short to drink mediocre wine' seriously, and you'll drink your fill of over 130 fine local and Italian wines in this elegant bar. To accompany it, choose something off the seasonal menu, such as Camogli tuna on a bed of the sweetest vine tomatoes, or the raw fish of the day with a squeeze of citrus and fragrant coriander.

### La Cucina di Nonna Nina — Trattoria, Ligurian €€

(0185 77 38 55; Viale Franco Molfino 126, San Rocco di Camogli; meals €35-50; Thu-Tue) In the leafy heights of San Rocco di Camogli you'll find the only Slow Food–recommended restaurant along the coast. It's named for grandmother Nina, whose heirloom recipes have been adapted with love by Paolo Delphin, and your culinary odyssey will include fabulous traditional dishes such as air-dried cod stewed with pine nuts, potatoes and local Taggiasca olives, and *rossetti* (minnow) and artichoke soup.

### Villa Rosmarino — Villa, B&B €€€

(0185 77 15 80; www.villarosmarino.com; Via Figari 38; d €140-240; Dec-Oct; P) A self-styled *maison de charme* (boutique hotel), this elegant 1907 pink villa with its swirling terrazzo floors and gorgeous garden was a passion project for Milanese duo Mario and Fluvio, and it shows. Their modernist taste and the sleek 21st-century fittings and finish make this the most stylish B&B on the coast.

### La Rosa Bianco — B&B €€

(0185 77 66 66; www.larosabiancodiportofino.com; Via Mortola 37; d €120; P @) Gorgeously sited on the slopes of San Rocco di Camogli, inside the Portofino park amid olive and lemon trees, La Rosa Bianco is a genuine B&B in the home of Marco and Laura. Rooms are furnished in a friendly, family style with plenty of personal touches, while breakfast is served in the old mill room with its enormous grinding stone.

## Portofino 2

### Caffè Excelsior — Cafe €€

(Piazza Martiri dell'Olivetta 54) Standard €1.30 cappuccinos are a pipe dream here, but what you're paying for isn't the coffee, but the exclusive perch with alfresco booths where Greta Garbo used to hide behind dark glasses.

### Eden — Hotel €€€

(0185 26 90 91; www.hoteledenportofino.com; Vico Dritto 18; d €140-280; P) You've arrived in heaven so you might as well stay there. Eden is an apt word on the quiet cobbled side streets a stone's throw from Portofino's idyllic harbour front, where this home-style hotel does a good job at looking posh without being too pretentious.

## Rapallo 3

### uGiancu — Osteria, Ligurian €€

(0185 260 505; www.ugiancu.it; Via San Massimo 78; meals €30-45; dinner Thu-Tue Dec-Oct) About 5km inland in the hamlet of San Massimo di Rapallo, this cult restaurant is run by comic-book collector Fausto Oneto, and half of his collection decorates the walls. Away from the coast, the cooking focuses on meat and vegetables, including an incredibly succulent herb-battered suckling lamb with field greens from the kitchen gardens.

## Chiavari

### Luchin — Osteria €

(0185 30 10 63; www.luchin.it; Via Bighetti 53; meals €10-25; Mon-Sat Dec–mid-Oct) It really is worth stopping in to centuries-old Luchin to sample its peerless *farinata*, baked over olive wood in copper pans. Modestly they'll say they don't serve anything 'unique', just authentic Genovese dishes. But see for yourself when you slurp the savoury minestrone (simmered for three hours) or bite into the raisin-sweet chestnut-flour tart with fennel seeds. Then pack your bags with as many goodies as you can from the deli counter.

## Sestri Levante ❹

**Trattoria della Mandrella** Trattoria, Ligurian €€

(0185 4 27 16; Via Dante 37; meals €25-40; 7.30am-midnight) Mandrella's rough, working-class atmosphere belies the seriously good food served in hearty portions. Fresh pasta and daily fish dishes are chalked on the board, and include a pitch-perfect linguine with clams, stewed cuttlefish and the house special, a fragrant basil gnocchi with grand, pink shrimps and butterfly clams.

**Hotel Helvetia** Hotel €€€

(0185 41 1 75; www.hotelhelvetia.it; Via Cappuccini 43; d €170-250; P @) Leaning over the invisible edge of the swimming pool and gazing down on the Baia del Silenzio and the broad curve of the beach you have to agree, few hotels can rival the views of the Helvetia. Then there's the private beach, the terrace restaurant and cool white rooms with balconies or garden views.

## Cinque Terre National Park ❺

**Gianni Franzi** Seafood €€

(0187 82 10 03; www.giannifranzi.it; Piazza Matteotti 5, Vernazza; meals €22-30; s/d €70/100; mid-Mar–early Jan) Traditional Cinque Terre seafood (mussels, seafood, ravioli, lemon anchovies) has been served up in this harbourside trattoria since the 1960s. More recently they've been renting rooms with views, all of which share a communal terrace. Cheaper single rooms with a shared bath go for €45.

**Colle del Telegrafo** Restaurant, Ligurian €€

(0187 76 05 61; Località Colle del Telegrafo; meals €35-45; lunch & dinner) Perched on a ridge where the old telegraph line used to be strung, the views from the Colle del Telegrafo are spectacular. But they don't overshadow the carefully prepared dishes of pasta with Cinque Terre cooperative pesto, white bean soup and super-fresh whitebait.

**La Poesia** B&B €€

(0187 81 72 83; www.lapoesia-cinqueterre.com; Via Genova 4, Monterosso; d €90-180) Shoehorned up a backstreet in the older part of town, La Poesia's three rooms (named Clizia, Annetta and Aspasia after the women Nobel Prize–winning poet Eugenio Montale dedicated his poems to) occupy an early-17th-century house. Breakfast is served on a terrace surrounded by lemon trees and the house has a regal quality missing elsewhere in Cinque Terre.

## Lerici ❼

**I Pescatori** Trattoria, Seafood €€

(0187 96 55 34; Via Andrea Doria 6; meals €35; Tue-Sun) Located in an alley that leads on to the hiking trail to Montemarcello, I Pescatori is devoted to fresh seafood, hence the lack of a menu as you simply get what's fresh that day. Pace yourself though for the multicourse onslaught, which features a wonderful selection of clams and shrimp with gnocchi, grilled fillet of fish and fried fish platters.

**Locanda Miranda** Inn, Gastronomic €€€

(0187 96 40 12; www.miranda1959.com; Via Fiascherina 92; d €120, d with half-board €180, set menu €40-60; P) Tellaro is home to this gourmands' hideaway, an exquisite seven-room inn with art- and antique-decorated rooms, and a Michelin-starred restaurant specialising exclusively in seafood.

**Bergamo**
*Wander the enchanting alleys of the old town*

# Northern Cities

*The Po valley, with its waving fields of corn and rice paddies, hosts some of Italy's most handsome and prosperous towns, from Milan and Bergamo in the west to Verona and Venice in the east.*

## TRIP HIGHLIGHTS

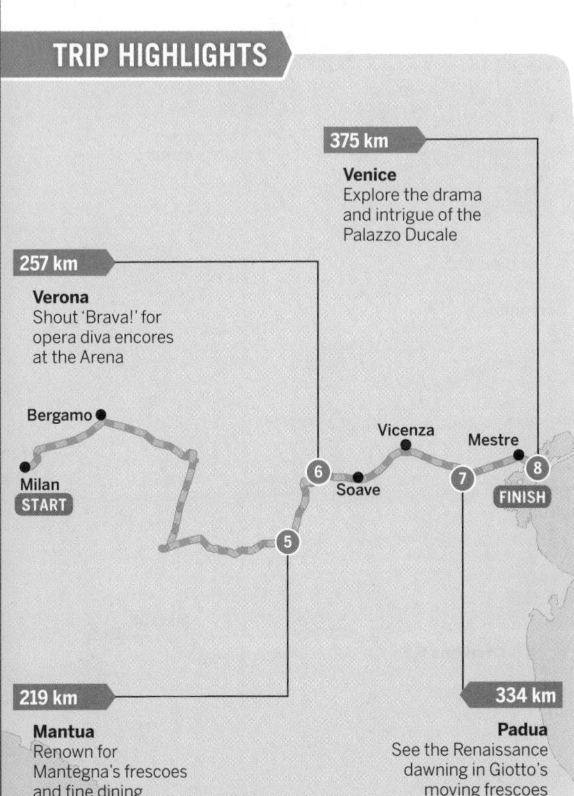


**7–10 DAYS**
**375KM / 233 MILES**

**GREAT FOR...**

**BEST TIME TO GO**

September to May to avoid the crowds.

**ESSENTIAL PHOTO**

The golden domes and precious mosaics of San Marco in Venice.

**BEST FOR SURPRISES**

The little-known treasures in Bergamo's Accademia Carrara.

# 7 Northern Cities

Ever since Julius Caesar granted Roman citizenship to the people of the plains, the Po valley has prospered. Wend your way through the cornfields from the Lombard powerhouse of Milan to Roman Brixia (Brescia), the Gonzaga stronghold of Mantua and the serene Republic of Venice. This is a land of legends spun by Virgil, Dante and Shakespeare, where grand dynasties fought for power and patronised some of the finest works of art in the world.

## 1 Milan

From Charlemagne to Napoleon, and even Silvio Berlusconi, mercantile Milan (Milano) has always attracted the moneyed and the Machiavellian. Follow the city's changing fortunes through the frescoed halls of the **Castello Sforzesco** (www.milanocastello.it; Piazza Castello; adult/reduced €7/3.50; ⌚9am-5.30pm Tue-Sun), some of them decorated by Leonardo da Vinci, where exquisite sculptures, paintings

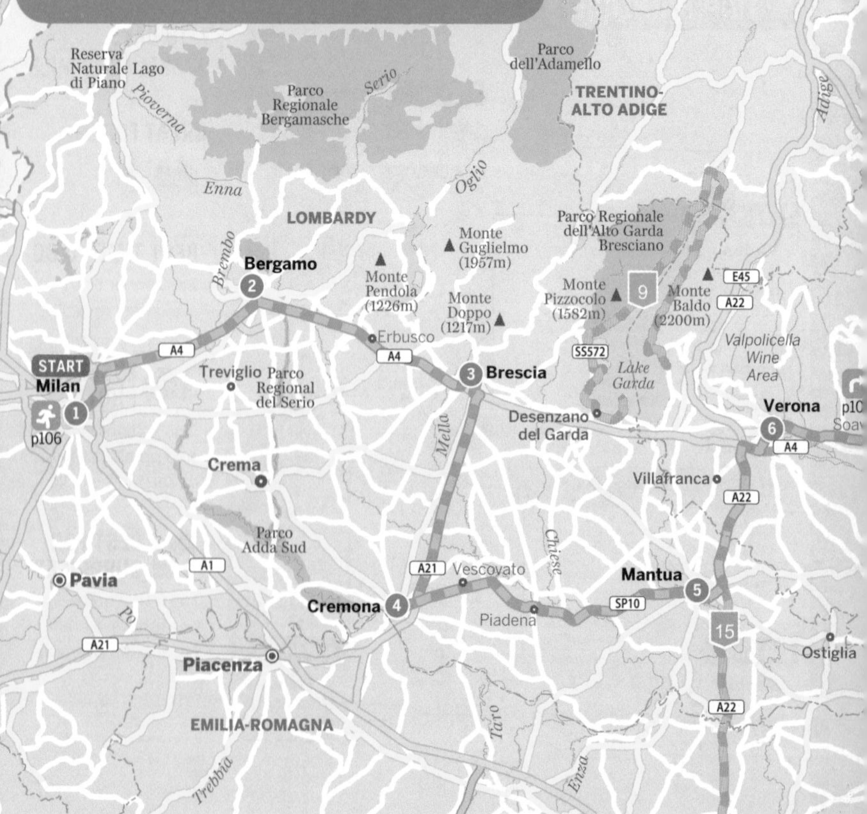

and weapons tell the turbulent tale of the city. From its ramparts, look out over the **Parco Sempione** and spy the pearly pinnacles of the **Duomo** (www.duomomilano.it; Piazza del Duomo; roof stairs/lift €7/12; ⌚9am-5.30pm). Begun in 1387 it took six centuries to build, rushed to completion in the 19th century so that Napoleon could crown himself King of Italy in its cavernous interior.

True to Milan's spirit of free enterprise, one of the city's finest art collections is the private collection of **Museo Poldi-Pezzoli** (www.museopoldipezzoli.it; Via Alessandro Manzoni 12; adult/reduced €9/6; ⌚10am-6pm Wed-Mon), where priceless Bellinis and Botticellis hang in Pezzoli's 19th-century *palazzo* (mansion). From here it's a few steps to the city's 'Golden Quadrangle' of designer shops, which you can explore on our walk (p106).

✕ p104

**The Drive »** Make your way northeast out of town along Corso Venezia, or via the A52 ring road, depending on where you're staying in town. Merge with the A4 Milan–Brescia autostrada for an uneventful 56km drive to Bergamo.

## 2 Bergamo

Beautiful Bergamo, its domes and towers piled on a promontory at the foot of the Alps, is one of the most arresting urban views in Italy. Le Corbusier found its **Piazza Vecchia** 'the most beautiful square in Europe', the magnificent ensemble of medieval and Renaissance buildings much influenced by Venetian fashions, with the lion of St Mark's emblazoned on the **Palazzo della Ragione**. The latter currently hosts works from the **Accademia Carrara** (www.accademiacarrara.bergamo.it;

### LINK YOUR TRIP

#### 9 A Weekend at Lake Garda

Got an urge for the outdoors? Jump off the A4 before Verona to Desenzano del Garda and mess around Lake Garda for a weekend.

#### 15 World Heritage Wonders

Further the tour of artistic and architectural blockbusters by continuing on the A22 from Mantua to Modena.

Piazza Carrara 82a; adult/reduced €5/3; ⏲10am-9pm Tue-Sun Jun-Sep, 9.30am-5.30pm Mon-Fri, 10am-6pm Sat & Sun Oct-Apr), one of Italy's great art repositories, currently closed for restoration until 2013.

Through the arches of the Palazzo della Ragione you'll glimpse a second square, the **Piazza Duomo**, fronted by the extraordinary polychromatic marble facade of the **Cappella Colleoni** (⏲9am-12.30pm & 2-4.30pm Tue-Sun Nov-Feb, 9am-12.30pm & 2-6.30pm Mar-Oct), the mausoleum-cum-chapel of Venice's most famous mercenary commander, Bartolomeo Colleoni (1696–1770).

p104

**The Drive »** Leave Bergamo via the *citta bassa* (lower town) southwards and rejoin the A4 in the direction of Brescia. Surprisingly this 55km stretch is relatively scenic, especially as you drive through the wine region of Franciacorta. Consider stopping in Erbusco for a Michelin-starred meal (see p104).

## 3 Brescia

Despite its seedy urban periphery, Brescia's old town contains some of the most important Roman ruins in Lombardy and an extraordinary, circular Roman church, the **Duomo Vecchio** (Piazza Paolo VI; ⏲9am-noon & 3-7pm Tue-Sun), built over the ancient Roman baths.

From here the Via dei Musei, the ancient *decumanus maximus* (east–west main street), leads to the heart of Roman Brixia, **Piazza del Foro**, which sits beneath the columns of the **Tempio Capitolino**, erected by Vespasian in AD 73 and preserved for posterity by a medieval mudslide. Next to the ruined temple is the unexcavated *cavea* (semicircular, tiered auditorium) of the **Teatro Romano**, and beside that the **Monastero di Santa Giulia** (www.bresciamusei.com; Via dei Musei 81b; adult/reduced €8/6; ⏲10am-6pm Tue-Sun May-Sep, to 5.30pm Oct-Apr), a vast monastery complex and museum that charts the layers of Brescian history. Best of all are the two Roman houses, which were absorbed wholesale into the monastery. Their mosaic floors and frescoes are real highlights.

p104

**The Drive »** Wend your way southwards out of Brescia's complicated suburbs following signs for the A21. Smaller and less heavily trafficked than the A4, the 53km drive to Cremona takes you through some unspoilt farmland dotted with the occasional farmhouse.

## 4 Cremona

Famous for violins, nougat and the tallest bell tower in Italy (111m), Cremona is a charming stopover. The stout-hearted can climb the 487 steps to the top of the *campanile* for scenic views. The **cathedral** (www.cattedraledicremona.it; Piazza del Comune; bell tower adult/reduced €5/4; ⏲10am-12.30pm & 2.30-5.30pm) next door is one of the most exuberant expressions of Lombard Romanesque architecture.

Aside from the views, Cremona made a name for itself as the violin capital of Europe, after Andrea Amati discovered in 1566 that with a bit of adjustment his old medieval fiddle could be made to sing the sweetest tunes. By the 18th century Andrea's son, Nicolò Amati, his pupil Antonio Stradivarius and Giuseppe Guarneri were crafting the best violins ever. See the originals in climate-controlled cases in the **Collezione Gli Archi di Palazzo Comunale** (http://musei.comune.cremona.it; Piazza del Comune 8; adult/reduced €6/4; ⏲9am-6pm Tue-Sat, 10am-6pm Sun). Afterwards visit the **Museo Civico** (Via Ugolani Dati 4; adult/reduced €7/5; ⏲9am-6pm Tue-Sat, 10am-6pm Sun) to see how they are crafted.

**The Drive »** You're off the main roads between Cremona and Mantua. Take Via Mantova east out of town and join the SP10. The tree-lined single

MATTEO COLOMBO/GETTY IMAGES ©

**Verona** The banks of the Adige river

carriageway passes through cornfields and the small towns of Vescovato and Piadena before reaching the watery outskirts of Mantua.

TRIP HIGHLIGHT

## 5 Mantua

The Latin poet Virgil was born just outside Mantua (Mantova) in 70 BC, and the modern town preserves its antique timeline in its art and architecture. Ruled by the Gonzaga dynasty for three centuries, the court attracted artists of the highest calibre, including Pisanello, Rubens and, more famously, Andrea Mantegna, who was court painter from 1460 until his death in 1506. It's their dazzling frescoes that decorate the **Palazzo Ducale** (www.mantovaducale.beniculturali.it; Piazza Sordello 40; adult/reduced €6.50/3.25; ⏲8.15am-7.15pm Tue-Sun). During busy periods you may have to book to see the biggest draw – Mantegna's 15th-century frescoes in the **Camera degli Sposi** (Bridal Chamber).

Hardly more modest in scale is the Gonzaga's suburban villa, the **Palazzo Te** (www.palazzote.it; Viale Te; adult/reduced €8/5; ⏲1-6pm Mon, 9am-6pm Tue-Sun). Mainly used by Duke Federico II as a place of rendezvous with his mistress, Isabella Boschetti, it is decorated in playboy style with playful motifs and encoded love symbols.

✕ 🛏 p104

**The Drive »** From Mantua head almost directly north for Verona. Leave town on Via Legnago, crossing the causeway that separates Lago di Mezzo from Lago Inferiore, then pick up the A22 autostrada for an easy 30km drive to Verona.

TRIP HIGHLIGHT

## 6 Verona

Shakespeare placed star-crossed Romeo Montague and Juliet Capulet in Verona for good reason: romance, drama and fatal family feuds have been the city's hallmark for centuries.

From the 3rd century BC, Verona was a Roman trade centre, with ancient gates, a forum (now Piazza delle Erbe) and a grand **Roman Arena** (www.arena.it; Piazza Brà; free with Verona Card, adult/reduced €6/4.50; ⏲1.30-7.30pm Mon, 8.30am-7.30pm Tue-Sun), which still hosts live summer opera performances. But Shakespearean tragedy came with the territory.

After Mastino della Scala (aka Scaligeri) lost re-election to Verona's commune in 1262, he claimed absolute control, until murdered by his rivals. On the north side of **Piazza dei Signori** stands the early-Renaissance **Loggia del Consiglio**, the 15th-century city council. Through the archway you'll find the **Arche Scaligere** – elaborate Gothic tombs of the Scaligeri family, where murderers are interred next to the relatives they killed.

Paranoid for good reason, the fratricidal Cangrande II (1351–59) built the **Castelvecchio** (☎045 806 26 11; Corso Castelvecchio 2; free with Verona Card, adult/reduced €6/4.50; ⏰1.30-7.30pm Mon, 8.30am-7.30pm Tue-Sun) to guard the river Adige, which snakes through town. Now it houses Verona's main museum with works by Tiepolo, Carpaccio and Veronese.

For discounted entry to all of Verona's major monuments, museums and churches, plus unlimited travel on city buses, consider purchasing a Verona Card (two/five days €15/20), on sale at most major tourist sights as well as tobacconists.

✕ 🛏 p105

**The Drive »** The 90km drive from Verona to Padua is once again along the A4. This stretch of road is heavily trafficked by heavy-goods vehicles. The only rewards are glimpses of Soave's crenulated castle to your left and the tall church spire of Monteforte d'Alpone. You could extend your trip with a stop to take in the World Heritage architecture of Vicenza – see it on our walking tour (p166).

## DETOUR: SOAVE

**Start: 6 Verona**

East of Verona, Soave serves its namesake DOC white wine in a storybook setting. Built by Verona's fratricidal Scaligeri family, the **Castello di Soave** encompasses an early Renaissance villa, grassy courtyards and the **Mastio** – a defensive tower apparently used as a dungeon. More inviting is the **Azienda Agricola Coffele** (☎045 768 00 07; www.coffele.it; Via Roma 5; ⏰9am-12.30pm & 2-7pm Mon-Sat), a family-run winery across from the church in the old town, where you can taste the lemon-zesty DOC Soave Classico and the bubbly DOCG Recioto di Soave, both bearing the regional quality-control standard of the Denominazione di Origine Controllata (DOC). Or try Locanda Lo Scudo (p105).

TRIP HIGHLIGHT

### 7 Padua

Dante, da Vinci, Boccaccio and Vasari all honour Giotto as the artist who officially ended the Dark Ages. Giotto's startlingly humanist approach not only changed how people saw the heavenly company, it changed how they saw themselves; not as lowly vassals but as vessels for the divine, however flawed. This humanising approach was especially well suited to the **Scrovegni Chapel** (☎049 201 00 20; www.cappelladegliscrovegni.it; Giardini dell'Arena; adult/reduced €13/8; ⏰9am-7pm by reservation only, call centre 9am-7pm Mon-Fri & 9am-6pm Sat), the chapel in Padua (Padova) that Enrico Scrovegni commissioned in memory of his father, who as a moneylender was denied a Christian burial. Think how radical the scenes must have been for medieval churchgoers witnessing familiar situations such as exhausted new dad Joseph asleep in the manger or onlookers gossiping as middle-aged Anne tenderly kisses Joachim.

Afterwards, tour the **Musei Civici agli Eremitani** (☎049 820 45 51; Piazza Eremitani 8; adult/reduced/child under 6 €10/8/free; ⏰ 9am-7pm Tue-Sun) for pre-Roman

Padua downstairs and a pantheon of Veneto artists upstairs.

 p105

**The Drive »** The 40km drive from Padua to Venice is through a tangle of suburban neighbourhoods and featureless areas of light industry along the A4 and then the A57.

---

TRIP HIGHLIGHT

### 8 Venice

Like its signature landmark, the **Basilica di San Marco** (www.basilicasanmarco.it; Piazza San Marco; basilica entry free; 9.45am-5pm Mon-Sat, 2-4pm Sun), the Venetian empire was dazzlingly cosmopolitan. Armenians, Turks, Greeks and Germans were neighbours along the **Grand Canal**, and Jewish communities persecuted elsewhere in Europe founded publishing houses and banks. By the mid-15th century, Venice (Venezia) was swathed in golden mosaics, imported silks and clouds of incense.

Don't be fooled though by the Gothic elegance: underneath the lacy pink cladding the **Palazzo Ducale** (Doges' Palace; www.museicivicivenezianі.it; Piazzetta San Marco 52; adult/reduced incl Museo Correr €14/8; 8.30am-7pm Apr-Oct, to 5.30pm Nov-Mar) ran an uncompromising dictatorship. Discover state secrets on the **Itinerari Segreti** (041 4273 0892; adult/reduced €18/12; tours in English 9.55am, 10.45am & 11.35am), which takes you to the sinister Trial Chamber and Interrogation Room.

Centuries later, Napoleon took some of Venice's finest heirlooms to France. But the biggest treasure in the **Museo Correr** (www.museicivicivenezianі.it; Piazza San Marco 52; 10am-7pm Apr-Oct, to 5pm Nov-Mar) couldn't be lifted: Jacopo Sansovino's **Libreria Nazionale Marciana**, covered with larger-than-life philosophers by Veronese, Titian and Tintoretto.

For more visual commentary on Venetian high life, head for the **Gallerie dell'Accademia** (www.gallerieaccademia.org; Campo della Carità 1050; adult/reduced €6.50/3.25; 8.15am-2pm Mon, to 7.15pm Tue-Sun), whose hallowed halls contain more murderous intrigue and forbidden romance than most Venetian parties. Alternatively, immerse yourself in the lagoon larder with our leg stretcher (p52).

You cannot take your car onto the lagoon islands so leave it in a secure garage in Mestre, such as **Garage Europa** (www.garageeuropamestre.com; per day €14), and hop on the train to Venice Santa Lucia, where water taxis connect to all the islands.

p105

## THE ORIGINAL GHETTO

In medieval times, the Cannaregio outpost in Venice housed a *getto* (foundry) – but as the designated Jewish quarter from the 16th to 18th centuries, this area gave the word a whole new meaning. In accordance with the Venetian Republic's 1516 decree, Jewish lenders, doctors and clothing merchants were allowed to attend to Venice's commercial interests by day, while at night and on Christian holidays, most were restricted to the gated island of **Ghetto Nuovo**.

When Jewish merchants fled the Spanish Inquisition for Venice in 1541, there was no place to go in the Ghetto but up: around **Campo del Ghetto Nuovo**, upper storeys housed new arrivals. Despite a 10-year censorship order issued by the church in Rome in 1553, Jewish Venetian publishers contributed hundreds of titles popularising new Renaissance ideas on religion, humanist philosophy and medicine.

# Eating & Sleeping

## Milan 1

### Giacomo Arengario — Bistrot €€

(☎02 7209 3814; Via Guglielmo Marconi 1; meals €25-35; ⏲lunch & dinner) Located on the 3rd floor of Mussolini's Arengario (now the Museo del Novecento), Giacomo's art-deco dining room has front-row views of the Duomo's spires and an elegant bistro menu featuring grand fish platters.

### Trattoria da Pino — Trattoria, Milanese €

(☎02 7600 0532; Via Cerva 14; meals €20-25; ⏲lunch Mon-Sat) Pino's is a working man's trattoria. Join diners at cafeteria-style tables shouting orders off the hand-printed menu. Cooking is *cucina casalinga* (home cooking), and includes staples such as *bollito misto* (mixed boiled meats).

## Bergamo 2

### Enoteca Zanini — Wine Bar €€

(☎035 22 50 49; www.enotecazanini.com; Via Santa Caterina 90a, Città Bassa; meals €30-35; ⏲lunch & dinner Tue-Sat, lunch Sun) Run by two accredited sommeliers, this is a great place to sample regional wine by the glass. The red-brick interior makes for a cosy atmosphere and the menu features dishes such as ravioli stuffed with Taleggio and creamed rucola with toasted pine nuts.

### Hotel Piazza Vecchia — Hotel €€

(☎035 428 42 11; www.hotelpiazzavecchia.it; Via Colleoni 3; s €140-180, d €160-200; ❄@) Carved out of a 13th-century building a few steps off Piazza Vecchia, the 13 rooms here are hung with the owner's paintings, amusing takes on the works of great artists. Some also have exposed beams while others have balconies.

## Erbusco

### Ristorante Gualtiero Marchesi — Contemporary Gourmet €€€

(☎030 776 05 62; www.marchesi.it; Via Vittorio Emanuele 23; meals €150-200; ⏲lunch & dinner Tue-Sat, lunch Sun) Housed in the ivy-clad Relais & Chateaux L'Albereta Hotel is Gualtiero Marchesi's temple of gastronomy. Sit in the gold-on-beige dining room gazing out of floor-to-ceiling windows onto a sea of greenery and sample some of Italy's finest contemporary cooking.

## Brescia 3

### Osteria al Bianchi — Osteria €

(☎030 29 23 28; www.osteriaalbianchi.it; Via Gasparo da Salò 32; meals €20; ⏲Thu-Mon) Crowd inside this old bar – in business since 1880 – and try for a seat at one of a handful of marble tables. Or head out back for a plate of *pestöm* (minced pork served with polenta).

## Mantua 5

### Il Cigno — Mantuan €€€

(☎0376 32 71 01; Piazza d'Arco 1; meals €55-65; ⏲Wed-Sun) The building is as beautiful as the food is elegant: a lemon-yellow facade with shutters and dining rooms adorned with antiques and Venetian glassware. Order the delicately steamed risotto with spring greens or poached cod with polenta.

### C'A Delle Erbe — B&B €€

(☎0376 22 61 61; www.cadelleerbe.it; Via Broletto 24; r €60-180; ❄📶) This 16th-century town house sits on Piazza delle Erbe. The sensitive conversion teams ancient, exposed-brick walls and beams with modern art and bathrooms fitted with huge rain showers.

## Verona 6

### Osteria del Bugiardo — Osteria €

(045 59 18 69; Corso Portoni Borsari 17a; 11am-11pm, to midnight Fri & Sat) On busy Corso Portoni Borsari, traffic converges at Bugiardo for glasses of upstanding Valpolicella bottled specifically for the *osteria* (casual tavern). Polenta and *sopressa* (aged salami) make worthy bar snacks for the powerhouse Amarone.

### Hotel Gabbia d'Oro — Hotel €€€

(045 59 02 93; www.hotelgabbiadoro.it; Corso Porta Borsari 4a; d from €220; P) One of the city's top addresses and one of its most romantic, the Gabbia d'Oro features luxe rooms inside an 18th-century *palazzo* that manages to be both elegant and cosy.

## Soave

### Locanda Lo Scudo — Modern Italian €€

(045 768 07 66; www.loscudo.vr.it; Via Covergnino 9; meals €35-45; lunch & dinner Tue-Sat) Arrive early and order fast – or miss out on daily fish specials or risotto made with Verona's zesty Monte Veronese cheese. Half country inn and half high-powered gastronomy, the owners rent out four bright, lovely rooms (singles/doubles €75/110).

## Padua 7

### Caffè Pedrocchi — Cafe €

(049 878 12 31; www.caffepedrocchi.it, in Italian; Via VIII Febbraio 15; 9am-10pm Sun-Wed, to 1am Thu-Sat) Since 1831 this neoclassical landmark has been a favourite of Stendhal and other pillars of cafe society for heart-poundingly powerful coffee and elaborate *caffè correto* (coffee 'corrected' with a shot of grappa).

### Osteria Dal Capo — Osteria €€

(049 66 31 05; Via degli Obizzi 2; meals €25-35; lunch & dinner Tue-Sat) Rub elbows with locals at tiny tables piled with traditional Venetian seafood and a few inspired novelties, such as *caviale di melanzane con bufala* (eggplant caviar with buffalo mozzarella atop crispy wafer bread). Reservations and a sociable nature advised.

## Venice 8

### I Figli delle Stelle — Modern Italian €€

(041 523 00 04; www.ifiglidellestelle.it; Zitelle 70; meals €25-40; 12.30-2.30pm & 7-10pm Tue-Sun mid-Mar–mid-Nov) A creamy fava-bean soup with chicory and fresh tomatoes coats the tongue in a naughty way, and the mixed grill for two with langoustine, sole and fresh sardines is a commitment – though given the cuisine and waterfront views of San Marco, this is a surprisingly cheap date.

### Osteria L'Orto dei Mori — Modern Italian €€

(041 524 36 77; Campo dei Mori 3386; meals €20-40; 12.30-3.30pm & 7.30pm-midnight Wed-Mon) Not since Tintoretto lived next door has this sleepy neighbourhood stayed up so late, thanks to this smart new *osteria*. Sicilian chef Lorenzo makes fresh pasta daily, including squid atop spinach tagliolini.

### Domus Orsoni — B&B €€

(041 275 95 38; www.domusorsoni.it; Corte Vedei 1045; s incl breakfast €80-150, d €100-250; @) Surprise: along a tranquil back lane near the Ghetto are five of Venice's most stylish guest rooms. In summer, breakfast is served in the garden near the Orsoni mosaic works, located here since 1885.

# STRETCH YOUR LEGS MILAN

**Start/Finish** Caffè Cova

**Distance** 2.5km

**Duration** Two hours

For anyone interested in the fall of a frock or the cut of a jacket, a stroll around the Quadrilatero d'Oro, the world's most famous shopping district, is a must. Even if you don't have the slightest urge to sling a swag of glossy carrier bags over your arm, the people-watching is priceless.

**Take this walk on Trips**

## Caffè Cova

Coffee and pastries at **Caffè Cova** (www.pasticceriacova.com; Via Montenapoleone 8; ⌚8.30am-8pm Mon-Sat) provides a glimpse into the world of the Quad: aggressively accessorised matrons crowd the neoclassical bar, barking pastry orders at the aproned staff. This is the oldest cafe in Milan (Milano), opened in 1817 by Antonio Cova, a soldier of Napoleon.

**The Walk »** Cova sits on the corner of Via Montenapoleone and Via Sant'Andrea, on the other side of which you'll spy G. Lorenzi. Walk north up Monte Nap past lavish window displays in old aristocratic mansions, such as the Palazzo Melzi di Cusano at number 18.

## Via Montenapoleone

Via Montenapoleone has always been synonymous with elegance and money – it was where Napoleon's government managed loans – and now it is the most important street of the Quad, lined with global marques such as Etro, Armani and Prada. Among the giants, remnants of the area's discreet past persist, such as men's grooming temple **G. Lorenzi** (www.lorenzi.it; Via Montenapoleone 9; ⌚Tue-Sat).

**The Walk »** Halfway up Via Montenapoleone, beside the glowing windows of Acqua di Parma, you'll see the narrow opening of Via Gesù. Head down there, past the hallowed doors of the Brioni atelier and in front of the Four Seasons you'll find the entrance to the Bagatti Valsecchi mansion.

## Il Salumaio di Montenapoleone

When **Il Salumaio** (www.ilsalumaiodimontenapoleone.it; Via Gesù 5; ⌚noon-11pm Mon-Sat) first opened on Via Montenapoleone in 1957 there was an outcry from aristocratic locals who thought a delicatessen would lower the tone of the neighbourhood. No matter, the deli opened and won them over with mouth-watering displays and exclusive products. Now housed in the same mansion as the **Museo Bagatti Valsecchi** (www.museobagattivalsecchi.org; Via Gesù 5; adult/reduced €8/4; ⌚1-5.45pm Tue-Sun), you can dine in the Renaissance courtyard.

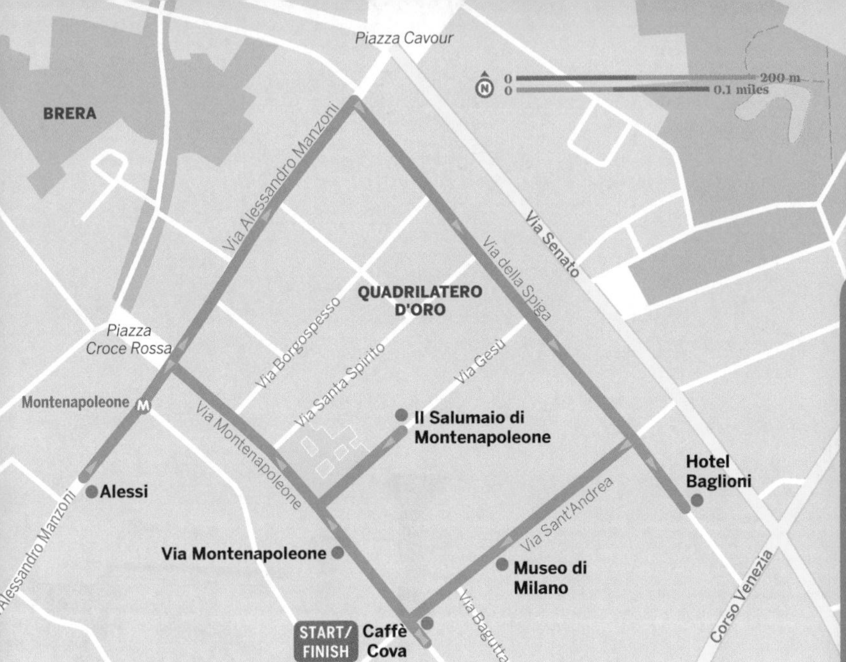


**The Walk »** Retrace your steps and head north to the top of Via Montenapoleone to the intersection with bigger, busier Via Alessandro Manzoni. Turn left here and after a few metres you'll find Alessi on your left.

## Alessi

Established on the shores of Lago d'Orta in Omegna in 1921, **Alessi** (www.alessi.com; Via Manzoni 14-16; ⌚Tue-Sun) has gone on to transform modern homes with over 22,000 crafted utensils. Some of the best examples now reside in the V&A in London and New York's MoMA, but you can just pop into the flagship store refitted by Martí Guixé.

**The Walk »** Exit Alessi and turn right, retracing your footsteps. Continue past Via Montenapoleone, past the Teatro Manzoni and take the next right down Via della Spiga. Walk almost the whole length of it, past Sermoneta and Tiffany, to reach the back door of the Baglioni.

## Hotel Baglioni

Who wouldn't love shopping on pedestrianised Via della Spiga, once the domain of bakeries. But if the cobbles are making those killer heels pinch, take the back door into **Hotel Baglioni** (www.baglionihotels.com; Via della Spiga 8) for a Campari and soda in its cafe. Decked out like a 19th-century drawing room, it's a favourite haunt with ladies who lunch.

**The Walk »** Exit the Baglioni back onto Via della Spiga, turn right and walk to Via Sant'Andrea and take a left. Walk a few metres down Via Sant'Andrea and you'll see the board for the Museo di Milano.

## Museo di Milano

For a glimpse of the Quad as it was during its 18th-century heyday, wander around the Palazzo Morando Attenolo Bolognini. Housing the collections of Contessa Bolognini, the apartments are also hung with the **Museo di Milano** (Via Sant'Andrea 6; ⌚2-5.30pm Tue-Sun) art collection, which provides a picture of the city as it was during Napoleonic times.

**The Walk »** It's a short walk back to Cova from the Museo di Milano. Turn left down Via Sant'Andrea and you'll find it just past Via Bagutta on your left.

**Varenna** Stroll Villa Monastero's extravagant, exotic gardens

Classic Trip

# The Graceful Italian Lakes

8

*Writers from Goethe to Hemingway have lavished praise on the Italian lakes, dramatically ringed by snow-powdered mountains and garlanded by grand villas and exotic, tropical flora.*

## TRIP HIGHLIGHTS

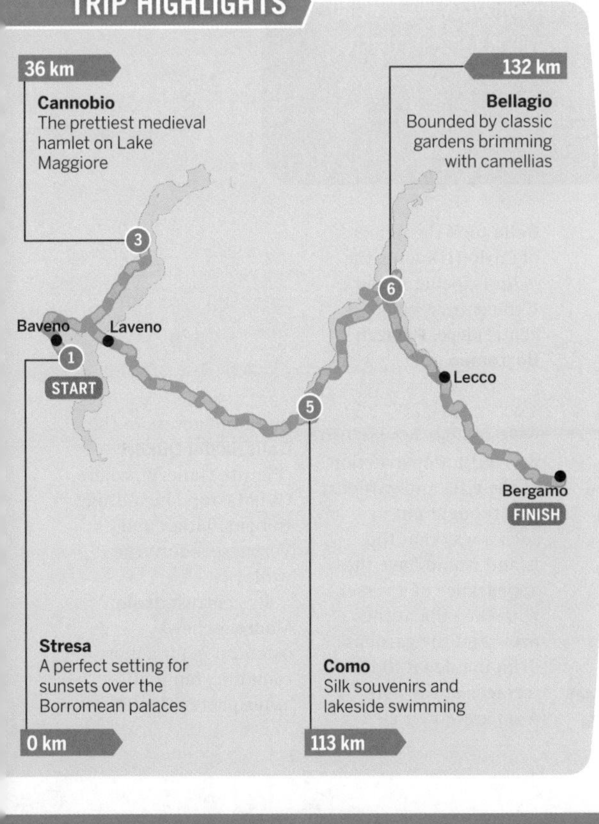

36 km
**Cannobio**
The prettiest medieval hamlet on Lake Maggiore

132 km
**Bellagio**
Bounded by classic gardens brimming with camellias

Baveno
Laveno
START
Lecco
Bergamo
FINISH

**Stresa**
A perfect setting for sunsets over the Borromean palaces
0 km

**Como**
Silk souvenirs and lakeside swimming
113 km

**5–7 DAYS**
**206KM / 128 MILES**

**GREAT FOR...**

**BEST TIME TO GO**

April to June, when the camellias are in full bloom.

**ESSENTIAL PHOTO**

The cascading gardens of Palazzo Borromeo.

**BEST FOR GLAMOUR**

Touring Bellagio's headland in a mahogany cigarette boat.

Classic Trip

# 8 The Graceful Italian Lakes

Formed at the end of the last ice age, and a popular holiday spot since Roman times, the Italian lakes have an enduring natural beauty. At Lake Maggiore (Lago di Maggiore) the palaces of the Borromean Islands lie like a fleet of fine vessels in the gulf, their grand ballrooms and shell-encrusted grottoes once host to Napoleon and Princess Diana, while the siren call of Lake Como (Lago di Como) draws Arabian sheikhs and Hollywood movie stars to its discreet forested slopes.

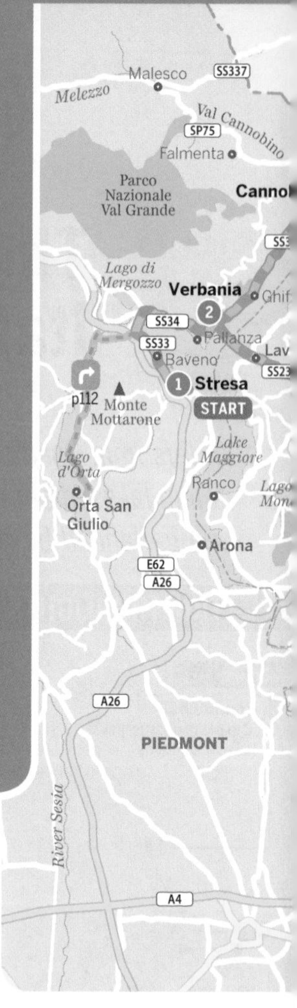

TRIP HIGHLIGHT

## 1 Stresa

More than Como and Garda, Lake Maggiore has retained the Belle Époque air of its early tourist heyday. Attracted by the mild climate and the easy access the new 1855 railway provided, the European *haute bourgeoisie* flocked to buy and build grand lakeside villas.

The star attractions are the Borromean Islands (Isole Borromee) and their palaces. **Isola Bella** took the name of Carlo III's wife, the *bella* Isabella, in the 17th century, when its centrepiece, **Palazzo Borromeo** (☎0323 3 05 56; www.borromeoturismo.it; adult/child €12.50/5.50; ⏲9am-5.30pm Apr–mid-Oct), was built. Construction of the villa and gardens was thought out in such a way that the island would have the appearance of a vessel, with the villa at the prow and the gardens dripping down 10 tiered terraces at the rear. A separate €4 ticket gives you access to the **Galleria dei Quadri** (Picture Gallery), where Old Masters, including Rubens, Titian and Veronese, adorn the walls.

By contrast, **Isola Madre** eschews ostentation for a more romantic, familial atmosphere. The 16th- to

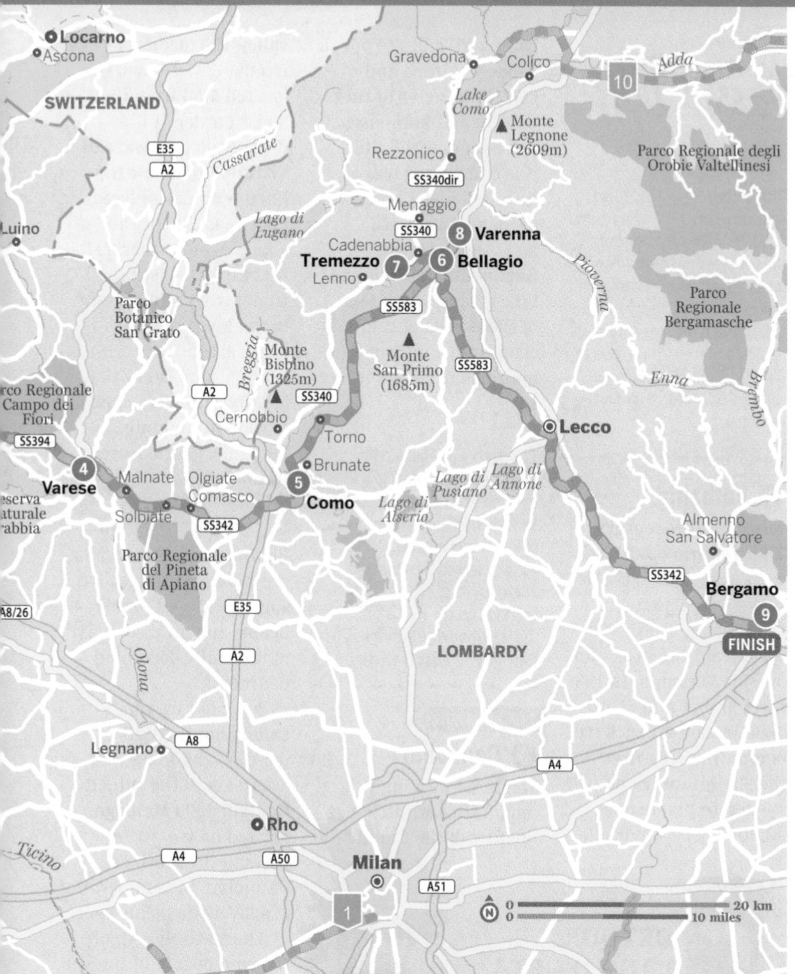


18th-century **Palazzo Madre** (☎0323 3 05 56; adult/child €10.50/5.50; ⏲9am-5.30pm Mar-Oct) includes a 'horror' theatre with a cast of devilish marionettes, while Chinese pheasants stalk the English gardens.

✕ p119

## LINK YOUR TRIP

### 1 Grand Tour

From Stresa take the A8 to Milan (Milano) from where you can commence your own Grand Tour of Italy (p39).

### 10 Roof of Italy

From Como take the SS340 to Gravedona from where you plunge eastwards into the Valtellina vineyards and over the Alps to Merano (p129).

Classic Trip



**The Drive »** Leave Stresa eastwards on the Via Sempione (SS33) skirting the edge of the lake for this short, 14km drive. Pass through Baveno and round the eastern edge of the gulf through the greenery of the Fondo Toce natural reserve. When you reach the junction with the SS34, turn right for Verbania.

## 2 Verbania

The late-19th-century **Villa Taranto** (☎0323 40 45 55; www.villataranto.it; Via Vittorio Veneto; adult/child €9.50/5.50; ⌚8.30am-6pm Mar-Sep, to 5pm Oct) sits just outside Verbania. In 1931, royal archer and Scottish captain Neil McEacharn bought the villa from the Savoy family and started to plant some 20,000 species. With its rolling hillsides of purple rhododendrons and camellias, acres of tulip flowers and hothouses full of equatorial lilies it is considered one of Europe's finest botanical gardens. During the last week in April, **Settimana del Tulipano** takes place, when tens of thousands of tulips erupt in magnificent multicoloured bloom.

✕ p119

**The Drive »** Pick up the SS34 again, continuing in a northeasterly direction out of Verbania, through the suburbs of Intra and Pallanza. Once you've cleared the town the 20km to Cannobio are the prettiest on the tour, shadowing the lakeshore the entire way with views across the water.

TRIP HIGHLIGHT

## 3 Cannobio

Sheltered by a high mountain and sitting at the foot of the Cannobino valley, the medieval hamlet of Cannobio is located 5km from the Swiss border. It is a dreamy place. **Piazza di Vittorio Emanuele III**, lined with pastel-hued houses, is the location of a huge Sunday market that attracts visitors from Switzerland. Right in the heart of the historic centre, in a 15th-century monastery that later became the home of the Pironi family, is the atmospheric **Hotel Pironi** (☎0323 7 06 24; www.pironihotel.it; Via Marconi 35; s €100-120, d €130-180; P). Behind its thickset walls are rooms with frescoed vaults, exposed timber beams and an assortment of tastefully decorated bedrooms.

You can hire small **sailing boats** (€120 per day) and make an excursion to the ruined **Castelli della Malpaga**, located on two rocky islets to the south of Cannobio. In summer it is a favourite picnic spot.

Alternatively, explore the wild beauty of the Val Cannobino up the SP75, following the surging Torrente Cannobino stream into the heavily wooded hillsides to Malesco. Just 2.5km along the valley, in Sant'Anna, the torrent forces its way powerfully through a narrow gorge known as the **Orrido di Sant'Anna**, crossed at its narrowest part by a Romanesque bridge.

### DETOUR: LAGO D'ORTA

**Start: 1 Stresa**

Separated from Lake Maggiore by Monte Mottarone (1492m) and enveloped by thick, dark-green woodlands, Lago d'Orta would make a perfect elopers' getaway. At 13.4km long by 2.5km wide you can drive around the lake in a day. The focal point is the captivating medieval village of **Orta San Giulio**, which sits across from Isola San Giulio where you'll spy the frescoed, 12th-century **Basilica di San Giulio** (⌚2-5pm Mon, 9.30am-6.45pm Tue-Sun Apr-Sep, to 5pm Oct-Mar). Come during the week and you'll have the place largely to yourself.

**The Drive »** The next part of the journey involves retracing the previous 22km drive to Verbania-Intra to board the cross-lake ferry to Laveno. Ferries run every 20 minutes (one-way tickets cost €7 to €11.60 for car and driver). Once in Laveno pick up the SS233 and then the SS394 for the 23km drive to Varese.

## LAGO MAGGIORE EXPRESS

The **Lago Maggiore Express** (www.lagomaggiore express.com; adult/child €32/16) is a picturesque day trip you can do without the car. It includes train travel from Arona or Stresa to Domodossola, from where you get the charming *Centovalli* train, crossing 100 valleys, to Locarno in Switzerland and a ferry back to Stresa. The two-day version is perhaps better value if you have the time, costing €40/20 per adult/child.

## 4 Varese

Spread out to the south of the Campo dei Fiori hills, Varese is a prosperous provincial capital. From the 17th century onwards, Milanese nobles began to build second residences here, the most sumptuous being the **Palazzo Estense**, completed in 1771 for Francesco III d'Este, the governor of the Duchy of Milan. Although you cannot visit the palace you are free to wander the vast Italianate **gardens** (8am-dusk).

To the north of the city sits another great villa, **Villa Panza** (0332 28 39 60; Piazza Litta 1; adult/reduced €8/3; 10am-6pm Tue-Sun), donated to the state in 1996. Part of the donation were 150 contemporary canvases collected by Giuseppe Panza di Biumo, mostly by post-WWII American artists. One of the finest rooms is the 1830 **Salone Impero** (Empire Hall), with heavy chandeliers and four canvases by David Simpson (born in 1928).

**The Drive »** The 28km drive from Varese to Como isn't terribly scenic, passing through a string of small towns and suburbs nestled in the wooded hills. The single-lane SS342 passes through Malnate, Solbiate and Olgiate Comasco before reaching Como.

TRIP HIGHLIGHT

## 5 Como

Built on the wealth of its silk industry, Como is an elegant town and remains Europe's most important producer of silk products. The **Museo della Seta** (www.museosetacomo.com; Via Castelnuovo 9; adult/reduced €10/7; 9am-noon & 3-6pm Tue-Fri) unravels the town's industrial history, with early dyeing and printing equipment on display. At **A. Picci** (031 26 13 69; Via Vittorio Emanuele II 54; 3-7.30pm Mon, 9am-12.30pm & 3-7.30pm Tue-Sat) you can buy top-quality scarves, ties and fabrics for a fraction of the cost you'd pay elsewhere.

After wandering the medieval alleys of the historic centre take a stroll along **Passeggiata Lino Gelpi**, where you pass a series of waterfront mansions, finally arriving at **Villa Olmo** (www.grandimostrecomo.it; Via Cantoni 1; adult/reduced €10/8; 9am-8pm Tue-Thu, to 10pm Fri-Sun). Set grandly facing the lake, this Como landmark was built in 1728 by the Odescalchi family, related to Pope Innocent XI, and now hosts blockbuster art shows. During the summer the **Lido di Villa Olmo** (Via Per Cernobbio 2; 9am-7pm mid-May–Sep), an open-air swimming pool and lakeside bar, is open to the public.

On the other side of Como's marina, the **Funicolare Como-Brunate** (www.funicolarecomo.it; Piazza de Gasperi 4; one-way/return €2.80/5.10; 6am-10.30pm) whisks you uphill to the quiet village of **Brunate** for splendid views across the lake.

p119

Classic Trip

RICHARD I'ANSON/GETTY IMAGES ©

JEAN-PIERRE LESCOURRET/ALAMY ©

## WHY THIS IS A CLASSIC TRIP PAULA HARDY, AUTHOR

**Despite centuries of fame as a tourist destination, there's a timeless glamour to the Italian lakes, especially Lake Como with its mountainous amphitheatre of snow-capped Alps. One of the best ways to see it is to walk the old mule tracks. There are some easy walks with fabulous views around Brunate. Pick up a map showing the trails from the Como tourist office.**

Top: Villa Melzi D'Eril, Bellagio
Left: Palazzo Borromeo, Stresa
Right: Fisherman on Lake Como

M GEBICKI/GETTY IMAGES ©

**The Drive »** The 32km drive from Como to Bellagio along the SS583 is spectacular. The narrow road swoops and twists around the lake shore the entire way and rises up out of Como giving panoramic views over the lake. There are plenty of spots en route where you can pull over for photographs.

TRIP HIGHLIGHT

## 6 Bellagio

It's impossible not to be charmed by Bellagio's waterfront of bobbing boats, its maze of stone staircases, cypress groves and showy gardens.

**Villa Serbelloni** (☎031 95 15 55; Via Garibaldi 8; adult/child €8.50/4.50; ⏰tours 11.30am & 3.30pm Tue-Sun Apr-Oct) covers much of the promontory on which Bellagio sits. Although owned by the Rockefeller Foundation, you can still tour the gardens on a guided tour. Otherwise stroll the grounds of neoclassical **Villa Melzi D'Eril** (www.giardinidivillamelzi.it; Lungo Lario Manzoni; adult/child €6/4; ⏰9.30am-6.30pm Mar-Nov), which run right down to the lake and are adorned with classical statues couched in blushing azaleas.

**Barindelli** (☎338 211 0337; www.barindellitaxiboats.com; Piazza Mazzini) operates slick, mahogany cigarette boats in which you can tool around the headland for a sunset tour (€130, seats 10).

🛏 p119

**The Drive »** The best way to reach Tremezzo, without driving all the way around the bottom of the lake, is to take the ferry from Piazza Mazzini. One-way fares cost €2, but for sightseeing you may want to consider the one-day central lake ticket, covering Bellagio, Varenna, Tremezzo and Cadenabbia, for €12.

## 7 Tremezzo

Tremezzo is high on everyone's list for a visit to the 17th-century **Villa Carlotta** (☎0344 4 04 05; www.villacarlotta.it; Riva Garibaldi; adult/reduced €8.50/4.50; ⏰10am-4pm mid-Mar–Easter & Oct–mid-Nov, 9am-6pm Easter-Sep), whose botanic gardens are filled with orange trees knitted into pergolas and some of Europe's finest rhododendrons, azaleas and camellias. The villa, which is strung with paintings and fine alabaster-white sculptures (especially fine are those by Antonio Canova), takes its name from the Prussian princess who was given the palace in 1847 as a wedding present from her mother.

**The Drive »** As with the trip to Tremezzo, the best way to travel to Varenna is by ferry from Piazza Mazzini, in Bellagio.

LEOCH STUDIO/GETTY IMAGES ©

Varenna

## 8 Varenna

Wander the flower-laden pathway from Piazzale Martiri della Libertà to the gardens of **Villa Cipressi** (www.hotelvillacipressi.it; Via IV Novembre 22; adult/child €3/1.50; ⏰9am-7pm Mar-Oct), now a luxury hotel (singles €110 to €140, doubles €140 to €190), and, 100m further south, **Villa Monastero** (☎0341 29 54 50; www.villamonastero.eu; Via IV Novembre; adult/reduced €4/2; ⏰gardens 9am-7pm Mon-Thu, 9am-2pm Fri, house & gardens 2-7pm Fri, 9am-7pm Sat & Sun), a former convent turned into a vast residence by the Mornico family in the 17th century. In both cases, you can stroll through the verdant gardens admiring magnolias, camellias and exotic yuccas.

**The Drive »** Departing Bellagio, pick up the SS583, but this time head southeast towards Lecco down the other 'leg' of Lake Como. As with the stretch from Como to Bellagio, the road hugs the lake, offering spectacular views the whole 20km to Lecco. Once you reach Lecco head south out of town down Via Industriale and pick up the SS342 for the final 30km to Bergamo.

## 9 Bergamo

Although Milan's skyscrapers are visible on a clear day, historically Bergamo was more closely associated with Venice (Venezia). Hence the elegant Venetian-style architecture of **Piazza Vecchia**, considered by Le Corbusier to be 'the most beautiful square in Europe'. The **Palazzo della Ragione** (adult/reduced €5/3; ⏰10am-9pm Tue-Sun Jun-Sep, 9.30am-5.30pm Mon-Fri, 10am-6pm Sat & Sun Oct-Apr) was the seat of medieval city governance and is currently hosting a temporary exhibition of star-studded works by Botticelli, Bellini, Pisanello, Mantegna, Raphael and Canaletto from the **Accademia Carrara** (www.accademiacarrara.bergamo.it), which is under renovations until 2013.

Behind this secular core sits the **Piazza del Duomo**, with its modest baroque **cathedral** (⏰7.30-11.45am & 3-6.30pm). A great deal more interesting is the **Basilica di Santa Maria Maggiore** (⏰9am-12.30pm & 2.30-6pm Apr-Oct, to 5pm Mon-Fri, 9am-12.30pm & 2.30-6pm Sat, 9am-12.45pm & 3-6pm Sun Nov-Mar) next door. To its whirl of frescoed, Romanesque apses, begun in 1137, Gothic touches were added as was the Renaissance **Cappella Colleoni** (⏰9am-12.30pm & 2-6.30pm Mar-Oct, 9am-12.30pm & 2-4.30pm Tue-Sun Nov-Feb), the mausoleum-cum-chapel of the famous mercenary commander, Bartolomeo Colleoni (1696–1770). Demolishing an entire apse of the basilica, he commissioned Giovanni Antonio Amadeo to create a tomb that is now considered a masterpiece of Lombard art with its exuberant rococo frescoes by Giambattista Tiepolo.

✕ 🛏 p119

### SEAPLANES ON THE LAKE

For a touch of Hollywood glamour, check out **Aero Club Como** (www.lagomaggioreexpress.com), who has been sending seaplanes out over the lakes since 1930. The 30-minute flight to Bellagio from Como costs €140 for two people. Longer excursions over Lake Maggiore are also possible. In summer you need to reserve at least three days in advance.

# Eating & Sleeping

## Stresa 1

### Ristorante Il Vicoletto — Traditional Italian €€

(☎0323 93 21 02; www.ristoranteilvicoletto.com; Vicolo di Poncivo 3; meals €35-45; lunch & dinner Fri-Wed) Located a short walk uphill from the centre of Stresa, Il Vicoletto serves a short but commendable menu including lake trout, wild asparagus and risotto with radicchio and Taleggio cheese.

## Verbania 2

### Ristorante Milano — Modern Italian €€€

(☎0323 55 68 15; Corso Zanitelli 2; meals €50-60; lunch & dinner Wed-Sun, lunch Mon) Antique-filled Milano looks out over Isolino San Giovanni, where Toscanini spent his summers. The menu is seasonal, featuring fish from the lake and vegetables from the restaurant garden.

## Como 5

### Trattoria dei Combattenti — Trattoria €

(☎031 27 05 74; Via Balestra 5/9; meals €20; lunch & dinner Wed-Mon) Housed in the building of the Italian retired servicemen's association, this popular trattoria offers simple home-cooked dishes, including grilled meats, salad and seafood pasta.

### Ristorante Sociale — Traditional Italian €€

(☎031 26 40 42; www.ristorantesociale.it; Via Rodari 6; meals €25-30; lunch & dinner Wed-Mon) Once attached to the nearby theatre, the Sociale is a local institution. Dine upstairs beneath frescoes beside the outsized baroque fireplace. The menu features favourites such as risotto with chicory.

### Albergo Terminus — Hotel €€

(☎031 32 91 11; www.hotelterminus-como.it; Lungo Lario Trieste 14; s €145-195, d €150-240; P ❄ wifi) Converted from a 19th-century *palazzo* (mansion), the Terminus retains its turn-of-the-century glamour with art-nouveau architectural details and grand tapestries. Rooms continue the Liberty theme with soft-hued colours and Como fabrics.

## Bellagio 6

### Albergo Silvio — Hotel €€

(☎031 95 03 22; www.bellagiosilvio.com; Via Carcano 12; d €80-160; Mar–mid-Nov & Christmas week; P ❄ wifi pool) Located above the small fishing hamlet of Loppia, the Silvio offers contemporary lake-front rooms overlooking the 10th-century church of Santa Maria. The hotel restaurant with its outdoor terrace is also highly regarded (meals €30 to €50).

## Bergamo 9

### Roof Garden — Modern Italian €€€

(☎035 36 61 59; www.roofgardenrestaurant.it; Piazza della Repubblica 6, Città Bassa; meals €45-80) The rooftop restaurant of the Hotel San Marco is sexy and accomplished. Dine on creamed beans and sausage or veal with cardoncelli mushrooms and try not to be distracted by the wraparound views.

### Agnello d'Oro — Inn €

(☎035 24 98 83; www.agnellodoro.it; Via Gombito 22; s/d €63/100) Located on the corner of Piazza St Pancrazio, the Agnello d'Oro has 20 retro rooms (some with small balconies) and a heart-warming restaurant hung with copper pots.

***Limone sul Garda** Lovely lakeside vistas await*

# A Weekend at Lake Garda

*Poets, politicians, divas and dictators, they've all been drawn to glorious Lake Garda with mountains to the north, vine-clad hills to the south and a string of medieval towns encircling its shores.*

## TRIP HIGHLIGHTS

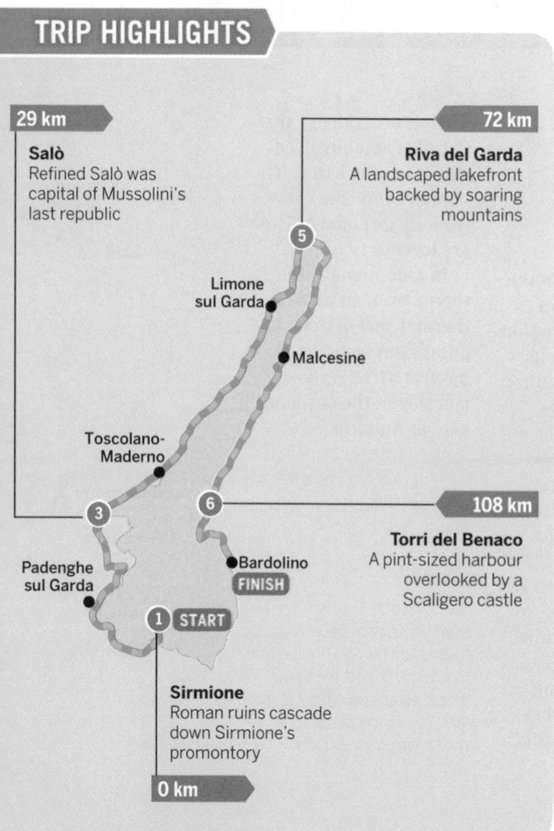


**4 DAYS**
**135KM / 84 MILES**

### GREAT FOR...

### BEST TIME TO GO

July for lake swimming and October for Bardolino's wine festival.

### ESSENTIAL PHOTO

Lakeside towns backed by mountains from aboard a boat.

### BEST FOR FAMILIES

Night swimming off pontoons floating along Riva's waterfront.

# 9 A Weekend at Lake Garda

At 370 sq km Lake Garda (Lago di Garda) is the largest of the Italian lakes, straddling the border between Lombardy and the Veneto. Vineyards, olive groves and citrus orchards range up the slopes and ensure the tables of Garda's trattorias are stocked with fine wines and oils. Boats buzz across the water and songbirds fill the crumbling terraces of Sirmione's Roman ruins. All you need now is a vintage Alfa Romeo to tool around the lakeside admiring the views.

TRIP HIGHLIGHT

## ❶ Sirmione

Over the centuries impossibly pretty Sirmione has drawn the likes of Catullus and Maria Callas to its banks. The village sits astride a slender peninsula that juts out into the lake and is occupied in large part by the **Grotte di Catullo** (Grotto of Catullus; ☎030 91 61 57; adult/reduced €4/2; ⏲8.30am-7pm Tue-Sat, 9am-2pm Sun Mar-Oct, 8.30am-2pm Tue-Sun Nov-Feb, museum to 7pm Tue-Sat), a misnomer for the ruins of an extensive Roman villa now comprising teetering stone arches and tumbledown walls. There's no evidence that Catullus actually lived here, but who cares? The wraparound lake views from its terraced hillside are legendary.

In true Roman style, there's even an offshore thermal spring that pumps out water at a natural 37°C. Wallow lakeside in the outdoor pool at **Aquaria** (www.termedisirmione.com; Piazza Don Angelo Piatti; pools €19-49; ⏲2-10pm Mon, 10am-10pm Tue-Sun Mar-Dec).

✕ p127

**The Drive »** The first 7km from Sirmione to Desenzano del Garda is on the SS572 lake road. Exit Sirmione past the Garda Village camp ground and at the first major roundabout turn right towards Desenzano.

## ② Desenzano del Garda

Known as the *porta del lago* (gateway to the lake), Desenzano may not be as pretty as other lakeside towns, but its ancient harbour, broad promenades and vibrant Piazza Matteotti make for pleasant wanderings. It is also a hub for summer nightlife.

Best of all are the mosaics in Desenzano's **Roman Villa** (030 914 35 47; Via Crocifisso 2; adult/reduced €2/1; 8.30am-7pm Mar-Oct, to 5pm Nov-Feb). Wooden walkways lead directly over vivid scenes of chariot-riding, grape-gathering cherubs.

Stretching north of Desenzano, the rolling hills of the Valtenesi are etched with vine trellises and olive groves,

### LINK YOUR TRIP

**7 Northern Cities**
A 30-minute drive down the A22 and A4 brings you to Verona and the cultural Northern Cities tour (p97).

**10 Roof of Italy**
Climb out of the lake basin on the SS240 to Rovereto for a dose of modern art and an epic drive across Europe's highest pass (p129).

Garda's Mediterranean microclimate ensuring ideal olive-growing conditions. **Frantoio Montecroce** (www.frantoiomontecroce.it; Viale Ettore Andreis 84) offers tutored oil tastings.

p127

**The Drive »** From Desenzano return to the SS572 and start to meander north right by the lake shore. The first 6km to Padenghe sul Garda are some of the most scenic on the lake, with cypresses and umbrella pines and clear views over the water.

TRIP HIGHLIGHT

## 3 Salò

Sedate and refined as Salò is today, in 1943 it was named the capital of the Social Republic of Italy as part of Mussolini's last-ditch efforts to organise Italian fascism in the face of advancing Allied forces. This episode, known as the Republic of Salò, saw more than 16 buildings turned into Mussolini's ministries and offices. Strolling between the sites is a surreal tour. The tourist office has an English-language booklet featuring significant locations.

Offshore you may spot the small, comma-shaped **Isola del Garda** (www.isoladelgarda.com; tours incl boat ride €24-30; ⏲Apr-Oct) crowned with neo-Gothic battlements and frothing with a luxuriant formal garden. It is the home of Contessa Cavazza and her family, who will host you on a two-hour guided tour of the villa's opulent rooms. Boats depart from Salò, Gardone Riviera, Garda and Sirmione.

p127

**The Drive »** Exit the medieval centre of Salò uphill on Via Umberto I and pick up the SS45bis heading north to Gardone. It's barely 7km along the narrow single carriageway, past old stone walls hiding lemon-coloured villas surrounded by luxuriant flora.

## 4 Gardone Riviera

In Gardone tour the home of Italy's most controversial poet, Gabriele d'Annunzio. Poet, soldier, hypochondriac and proto-fascist, d'Annunzio's home **Il Vittoriale degli Italiani** (☎0365 29 65 11; www.vittoriale.it; Piazza Vittoriale; gardens & museums adult/reduced €16/12; ⏲grounds 8.30am-8pm Apr-Sep, to 5pm Oct-Mar, museums to 7pm Apr-Sep, 9am-1pm & 2-5pm Oct-Mar) is as bombastic and extravagant as it is unsettling, and the decor certainly sheds light on the man. He retreated to Gardone in 1922, claiming that he wanted to escape the world that made him sick.

For something less oppressive visit the flower-filled oasis of **Fondazione André Heller** (☎336 410877; www.hellergarden.com; Via Roma 2; adult/child €9/5; ⏲9am-7pm Mar-Oct), designed in the 1990s by multimedia artist André Heller. Hidden among the greenery are 30 pieces of contemporary sculpture.

p127

**The Drive »** Exit Gardone northeast on Corso Zanardelli for a long, scenic 43km drive north. At Tignale and Limone sul Garda you'll pass the stone pillars of Garda's lemon-houses. The final 12km from Limone to Riva del Garda are extraordinary, passing through dynamite-

### TOP TIP: LAKE CRUISING

Fleets of ferries link many Lake Garda communities, providing a series of scenic mini-cruises. They're run by **Navigazione sul Lago di Garda** (www.navigazionelaghi.it), which publishes English-language timetables online. A one-day, unlimited travel ticket costs €25.80/13.40 per adult/child. A return fare for a single trip is €4.40.

Car ferries cross year-round from Toscolano-Maderno on the west bank to Torri del Benaco on the east bank.

**Sirmione** Waterfront views

blasted tunnels dramatic enough to make this the location for the opening chase scene in *Casino Royale*.

TRIP HIGHLIGHT

## 5 Riva del Garda

Even on a lake blessed by dramatic scenery, Riva del Garda still comes out on top. Encircled by towering rock faces and a looping landscaped waterfront, its appealing centre is a medley of grand architecture and wide squares. The town's strategic position was fought over for centuries and exhibits in the **Museo Civico** (Piazza Cesare Battisti 3; admission €2; ⏰10.30am-12.30pm & 1.30-6pm Tue-Sun Apr-Nov) reflect this turbulent past.

Riva makes a natural starting point for walks and bike rides, including trails around **Monte Rocchetta** (1575m), which looms over the northern end of the lake. Immediately south of the town is the shingle beach and landscaped park, cut throughout with a cycle path that extends 3km to neighbouring **Torbole**.

The other natural spectacle worth a trip is the **Cascata del Varone** (www.cascata-varone.com; admission €5.50; ⏰9am-7pm May-Aug, to 6pm Apr & Sep, to 5pm Mar & Oct), a 100m waterfall that thunders down the sheer limestone cliffs into a dripping gorge.

p127

**The Drive »** From Riva pick up the SS240 around Torbole and then turn south on the SS249. Lake views abound through columned 'windows' as you pass through mountain tunnels, and to the left Monte Baldo rises above the lake. A cable car runs to the summit from Malcesine, from where it's 22km to Torri del Benaco.

TRIP HIGHLIGHT

## 6 Torri del Benaco

Picturesque Torri del Benaco is one of the most appealing stops on the eastern bank. The 14th-century **Castello Scaligero** (Viale Fratelli Lavanda 2; adult/reduced €3/1; ⏲9.30am-12.30pm & 2.30-6pm Apr–mid-Jun & mid-Sep–Oct, 9.30am-1pm & 4.30-7.30pm mid-Jun–mid-Sep) overlooks a pint-sized harbour and packs a wealth of history into dozens of rooms, including exhibits on the lake's traditional industries of fishing, olive-oil production and lemon growing.

p127

**The Drive »** From the waterfront at Torri del Benaco it's a short 7km drive to Garda, around the headland. En route low stone walls or railings are all that stand between you and the water, while cypresses line front lawns to your left.

## 7 Garda

The bustling town of Garda lacks obvious charms, but it does boast the leafy headland of **Punta San Vigilio**, a gorgeous crescent bay backed by olive trees 3km to the north. The privately owned **Parco Baia delle Sirene** (www.parcobaiadellesirene; Punta San Vigilio; ⏲10am-7pm Apr-May, to 8pm Jun-Sep; 👪) has sun loungers and picnic tables beneath the trees; there's also a children's play area. Prices are seasonal and range from €5 to €12 per adult (€2 to €5 per child) per day.

The tiny headland is also the location of **Locanda San Vigilio** (☎045 725 41 90; www.locanda-sanvigilio.it; Punta San Vigilio; buffet €45; ⏲10am-5.30pm), with its excellent harbourside taverna. Book for one of the truly memorable candlelight buffets on Friday and Saturday.

**The Drive »** The final 5km drive to Bardolino, continuing on the SS249, gives you your final fill of big views. Over the short distance the road rises up, giving you lofty views over the water before dropping down amid olive groves into Bardolino.

## 8 Bardolino

More than 70 vineyards and wine cellars grace the gentle hills that roll east from Bardolino's shores, many within DOC and the even stricter DOCG regional quality-control classifications. They produce an impressive array of pink Chiaretto, ruby Classico, dry Superiore and young Novello.

One of the most atmospheric ways to savour their flavours is a tutored tasting at **Guerrieri Rizzardi** (☎045 721 00 28; www.guerrieri-rizzardi.com; Via Verdi 4; tastings €15; ⏲5pm Wed May-Oct). After a tour of the wine cellars, tastings take place in the kitchen garden, with tables laid out beside an orangery and a vineyard labyrinth.

Bardolino is at its most Bacchic during the **Festa dell'Uva e del Vino** in early October, when the town's waterfront fills with food and wine stands.

### DETOUR: LAGO DI LEDRO

**Start: 5 Riva del Garda**

From Riva take the SP37 and then the SS240 west into the mountains, past olive groves and vine-lined terraces. After 11km the road flattens and **Lago di Ledro** (www.valledileddro.com) comes into view. Only 2.5km long and 2km wide, this diminutive lake sits at an altitude of 650m and is set in a gorgeous valley beneath tree-covered mountains. **Molina di Ledro** is at the lake's eastern end, where thatched huts line up beside beaches and boat-hire pontoons.

# Eating & Sleeping

## Sirmione 1

**Ristorante La Rucola** Gardese €€€

(030 91 63 26; www.ristorantelarucola.it; Vicolo Strentelle 7; meals €60-75; Fri-Wed) Sirmione's most elegant restaurant combines a 1970s nightclub vibe with farmhouse chic. The food, however, is classic lake cooking featuring sea bass, prawns and numerous seasonal risottos.

## Desenzano del Garda 2

**La Cambusa** Bistrot €€

(342 1224813; www.allacambusabistrot.it; Via Canonica 12; meals €25-35; 10am-midnight) Located in an old butcher's shop, La Cambusa is earning itself some heartfelt accolades with home-brewed beer, top-notch salami and *aperitivo* (aperitif) platters with hand-cut Parmesan and Parma ham.

**Il Giardino Segreto** B&B €€

(030 917 22 94; www.relaisilgiardinosegreto.it; Via Curiel 2; d €95-140; P @) The Secret Garden has a boutique feel. Six double rooms feature vast beds, playful modern furnishings and works of art. Many have patios fronting the garden.

## Salò 3

**Osteria di Mezzo** Gardese €€

(0365 29 09 66; www.osteriadimezzo.it; Via Mezzo 10; meals €35-50; noon-11pm) Run by the Vanni family, this tiny, vaulted *osteria* (casual tavern) is much beloved by locals for its focus on Gardese ingredients and wines. Aside from lake fish such as coregone and salmerino, the menu features rabbit, lamb and wild boar.

**Villa Arcadio** Boutique Hotel €€

(0365 4 22 81; www.hotelvillaarcadio.it; Via Palazzina 2; d €95-140; P) Perched above Salò on the wooded hillside, this converted convent is the essence of lakeside glamour. Enjoy the vista of glassy lake and misty mountains from the panoramic pool, or retreat inside to frescoed rooms and ancient wood-beamed halls.

## Gardone Riviera 4

**Locanda Agli Angeli** Inn €€

(0365 2 09 91; www.agliangeli.com; Via Dosso 7; s €45-70, d €80-180; P) A delightful renovation has produced an 18th-century inn of old polished wood, gauzy curtain fabrics and bursts of lime, orange and aquamarine. The terrace has a compact pool and views across rooftops and the lake beyond. The restaurant serves classic Lake Garda cooking.

## Riva del Garda 5

**Osteria Le Servite** Osteria, Gardese €€

(0464 55 74 11; www.leservite.com; Via Passirone 68, Arco; 7-10.30pm Tue-Sun Apr-Sep, Thu-Sun only Oct-Mar) Drive a few kilometres inland from Riva's resort-style waterfront and you'll find a fascinating culinary hinterland. Amid Arco's vineyards Alessandro Manzana serves mimosa gnocchi, river fish and pork fillet with grape must. The wine list is accomplished, too.

**Villa Angelica** Villa €€

(0464 55 67 91; www.villaangelicariva.com; Via San Giacomo 48; d €85-130, q €130-180; P) Classified as one of Lake Garda's historic villas, the well-priced, handsome apartments at Villa Angelica seem almost too good to be true. Your hostess, Angelica, is happy to share the house's history with you or you can simply wander the English-style garden like Franz Kafka did when he came to stay.

## Torri del Benaco 6

**Albergo Gardesana** Hotel €€

(045 722 54 11; www.hotel-gardesana.com; Piazza Calderini 20; s €95-185, d €110-200; P @) The guest list at Gardesana has featured actors, writers, politicians and kings. Antiques fill the bedrooms, while the vine-fringed breakfast terrace has delightful harbour views.

***Bormio*** *Tour the icy land of 100 glaciers*

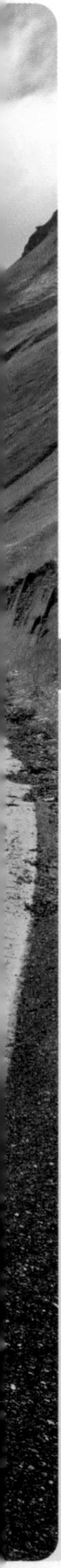

10

# Roof of Italy

*Traversing the Alps, from Lake Como through the Valtellina's vine-covered slopes and across the hair-raising Passo dello Stelvio to Merano, this is one of the north's most spectacular roads.*

## TRIP HIGHLIGHTS

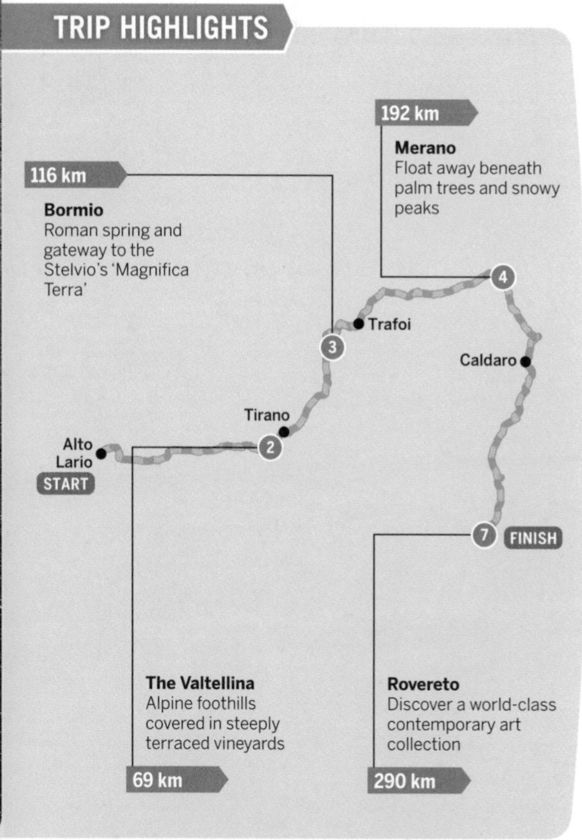

116 km
**Bormio**
Roman spring and gateway to the Stelvio's 'Magnifica Terra'

192 km
**Merano**
Float away beneath palm trees and snowy peaks

Trafoi
Caldaro
Tirano
Alto Lario START
FINISH

69 km
**The Valtellina**
Alpine foothills covered in steeply terraced vineyards

290 km
**Rovereto**
Discover a world-class contemporary art collection

**6 DAYS**
**290KM / 180 MILES**

**GREAT FOR...**

**BEST TIME TO GO**

June to September, when the Passo dello Stelvio is open.

Cloud-busting views on the Passo dello Stelvio.

Dipping in Merano's hot and cold spa pools amid mountain peaks.

# 10 Roof of Italy

Tracing the foothills of the Orobie Alps and the high passes of Parco Nazionale dello Stelvio, the borderlands of northern Italy offer up stunning wildernesses, stupendous scenery and warm welcomes in wooden farmhouses. Vineyards and orchards cloak the valleys of the Valtellina and Adige, while the region's historic cities – Merano, Trento and Rovereto – combine Austrian and Italian influences, creating a unique cultural and culinary melange.

## 1 Alto Lario

The towns of **Dongo**, **Gravedona** and **Sorico** once formed the independent republic of the Tre Pievi (Three Parishes) and were a hotbed of Cathar heresy. Now they're more popular with water-sports enthusiasts than Inquisitors. Lake Lario is another name for Lake Como (Lago di Como), so the area takes its name from being at the top *(alto)* of the lake. Gravedona, the largest of the three towns, sits on

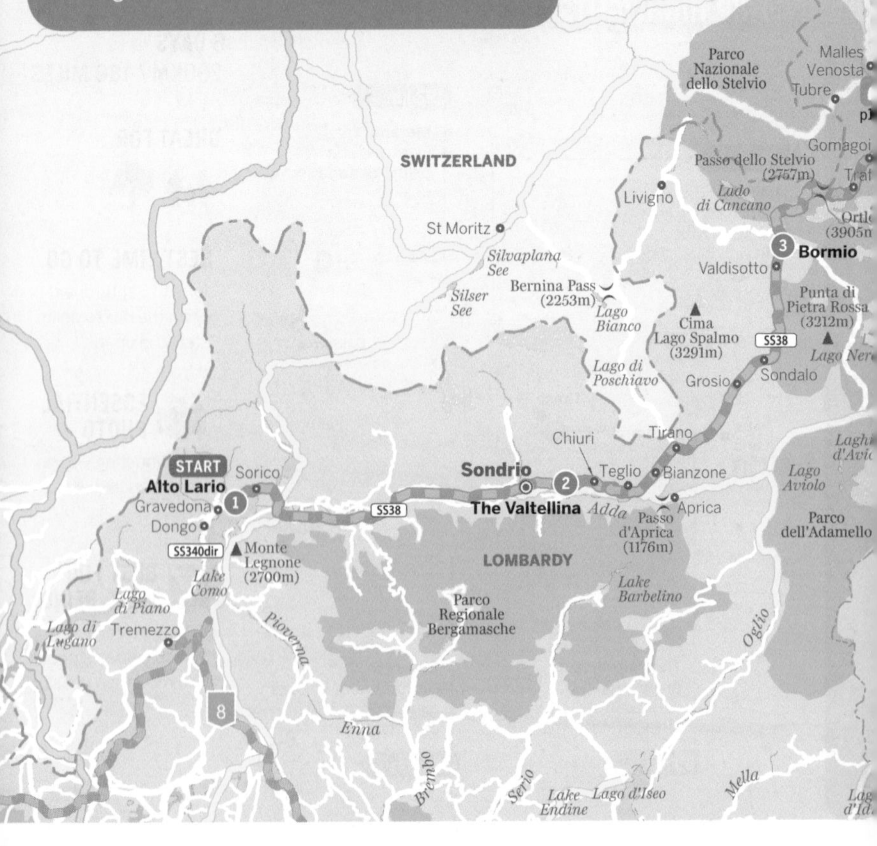

a gently curved bay with views across to Monte Legnone.

Up on the plateau at Peglio, **Chiesa di Sant'Eusebio** (⌚3-6pm Thu, Sat & Sun Jul-Sep) offers lake views and masterly frescoes by Como painter Giovan Mauro della Rovere, better known as Il Fiammenghino (Little Fleming). He sought refuge here after murdering a man and did penance painting the vivid *Last Judgement.*

Sorico, the most northerly of the three towns, guards the mouth of the river Mera, which flows into shallow **Lago di Mezzola**, once part of Lake Como and now a bird-breeding nature reserve.

✕ p135

**The Drive »** From Sorico take the SS340dir north. Cross over the waterway that connects Lake Como and Lago di Mezzola and continue until you hit a T-junction. Turn right, and at the roundabout turn left onto the SS38 towards Morbengo. Continue for a further 26km, chasing the Adda river all the way to Sondrio.

TRIP HIGHLIGHT

## 2 The Valtellina

The Valtellina cuts a broad swath down the Adda valley, where villages and vineyards hang precariously on the slopes of the Orobie Alps. The steep northern flank is carpeted by Nebbiolo grapes, which yield a light-red wine. Both body and alcohol content improve with altitude, so generations of Valtenesi built upwards, carrying the soil in woven baskets to high mountain terraces. Their rewards: a DOC regional quality-standard classification for Valtellina Superiore since 1968. In **Sondrio**, it's possible to visit the cellars of **Pellizzatti**

## LINK YOUR TRIP

### 8 The Graceful Italian Lakes

Take the scenic SS340dir to Tremezzo to tour Como's luxuriant gardens and Maggiore's Borromean palaces (p109).

### 12 Grande Strada delle Dolomiti

Descend into Bolzano from Castello Firmiano on the SS42 and head east into the Dolomites for mountain hikes and gourmet dinners (p145).

## TOP TIP: PASSO DELLO STELVIO

The high and hair-raising Passo dello Stelvio is only open from June to September, and is always subject to closures dependent on early or late snow falls. For the rest of the year, Bormio is best approached from Sondalo in Lombardy, or via Tubre into Switzerland to take the Munt la Schera tunnel to Livigno.



**Perego** (www.arpepe.com; Via Buon Consiglio 4), and in **Chiuri**, **Nino Negri** (www.ninonegri.it; Via Ghibellini 3).

The prettiest town in the valley is **Tirano**, where mule trains once came from Venice and Brescia, and which is now the departure point for the **Trenino Rosso del Bernina** (☎342 70 62 63; www.treninorosso.it; one-way/return €24.50/49), a gravity-defying rail track that traverses 196 bridges, crests the Bernina Pass (2253m) and crosses the Morteratsch glacier on the way to St Moritz in Switzerland.

p135

**The Drive »** From Tirano it is 37 scenic kilometres to the heady heights of Bormio. Continue northeast on the SS38, still tracking the Adda river and rising up through the terraces, past small hamlets such as Grosio and Sondalo and into the snow-capped mountains.

TRIP HIGHLIGHT

### 3 Bormio

Splendidly sited in a mountain basin at 1225m, Bormio was once the heart of a region dubbed Magnifica Terra. Most of the region's magnificent territory now lies within northern Italy's largest national park, the **Parco Nazionale dello Stelvio** (www.parks.it/parco.nazionale.stelvio), an icy land of 100 glaciers that includes one of Europe's largest, the **Ghiacciaio dei Forni**.

The Stelvio is largely the preserve of walkers, who come for the extensive network of well-organised mountain huts and marked trails – but there are a couple of well-serviced ski runs at **Solda** and the **Passo dello Stelvio** (2757m), both of which offer year-round skiing.

Back in Bormio's medieval centre, the **Bagni di Bormio** (www.bagnidibormio.it; Via Statale Stelvio; spa passes €41-45; ⏲10am-8pm, New Baths to 11pm Fri & Sat) was much loved by the likes of Pliny the Elder and Leonardo da Vinci. Hotel stays include unlimited spa access, but day passes are also available.

**The Drive »** The most difficult, and awe-inspiring, 96km is the spectacular road from Bormio to Merano, which crosses the cloud-covered Stelvio pass, 25km from Bormio. Approaching along the SS38, the road rises through a series of tight switchbacks, some with very steep gradients, and descends via equally alarming hairpin bends to quaint Trafoi on the other side. One of the highest roads in Europe, it is not for the faint-hearted. From Trafoi continue on the SS38 all the way to Merano.

TRIP HIGHLIGHT

### 4 Merano

Merano is where 19th-century Mitteleuropeans came to soothe their weary bones, do a 'grape' cure, and, perhaps, embark on a dalliance or two. The Hapsburg-era spa was the hot destination of its day and the city's therapeutic traditions have served it well in the new millennium, with the striking modern redevelopment of the **Terme Merano** (Therme Meran; ☎0473 25 20 00; www.thermemeran.it; Piazza Terme 1; 2hr bathing pass adult/child €12/8, all day €18/11; ⏲9am-10pm). Swim through the sluice towards 12 outdoor pools in summer and be met by a vision of palm-studded gardens and snow-topped mountains beyond.

You could also give over an entire day to the botanical gardens at

Merano

**Castel Trauttmansdorff** (www.trauttmansdorff.it; Via San Valentino 51a; garden & museum adult/child €10.80/7.90; ⏲9am-6pm Apr-Nov, to 11pm Fri summer), where exotic cacti and palms, beds of lilies, irises and tulips all cascade down the hillside surrounding a castle where Sissi (Empress Elisabeth) spent the summer.

 p135

**The Drive »** From Merano to Bolzano and the Castello Firmiano, the SS38 becomes a dual-lane autostrada, so the next 29km are easy motorway driving as you leave the high mountains behind you.

## 5 Castello Firmiano

Known as the 'Crown of Sigismund', the expansive walls and battlements of Castello Firmiano encircle the hilltop overlooking Bolzano and Appiano just like a princely coronet.

### DETOUR: MALLES VENOSTA

**Start: 3 Bormio**

Just north of Bormio on the scenic SS40 sits the old customs point of Malles Venosta. Aside from its handsome Gothic churches and historic centre, it sits just beneath the vast **Abbazia di Monte Maria** (☎0473 84 39 80; www.marienberg.it; Schlinig 1, Malles; admission €5; ⏲10am-4pm Mon-Sat), the highest Benedictine monastery in Europe. In the crypt are a series of superb Byzantine-Romanesque frescoes, which were only discovered in 1980. Their almost pristine condition makes them quite unique.

Fought over for 1000 years, it has long been a symbol of Tyrolean independence and now houses the **Messner Mountain Museum** (www.messner-mountain-museum.it; adult/reduced €9/7; ⌚10am-6pm Tue-Sun Mar-Nov), named after celebrated mountaineer Reinhold Messner. Exhibits explore humanity's relationship with the mountains while the inspiring design, involving hundreds of stairs, suggests shifting altitudes and uneven mountain terrain.

South of the castle stretches the **Weinstrasse** (www.suedtiroler-weinstrasse.it), a wine road winding through the Adige valley along the SP14 all the way to Trento. Producers line the route although the hub of the region is **Caldaro**.

**The Drive »** South of Bolzano the autostrada carves a straight line through the midst of the Adige valley. It's a fast, scenic route with the mountains overlapping in descending order in front of you. If you have more time, however, the preferred route is to pick up the SP14 from the castle to Caldaro and follow the wine route all the way to Magré (p135), where you can stop and taste some of the prized Adige wines.

## 6 Trento

During the tumultuous years of the Counter-Reformation, the Council of Trent convened here, dishing out far-reaching condemnations to uppity Protestants. Modern Trento is less preachy: quietly confident and easy to like. Frescoed streets fan out from the **Duomo** (⌚7am-noon & 2-8pm), which sits above a 6th-century temple and a **Paleo-Christian archaeological area** (admission €1.50).

On the opposite side of the square is the former bishop's residence, **Palazzo Pretoria** (☎0461 23 44 19; Piazza del Duomo 18; adult/reduced €4/2.50; ⌚9.30am-12.30pm & 2.30-6pm Wed-Mon), where illuminated manuscripts and paintings depict the Council of Trent.

Above it all, the mighty **Castello del Buonconsiglio** (www.buonconsiglio.it; Via Clesio 5; adult/reduced €8/5; ⌚10am-5pm Wed-Mon) is a reminder of the bloody history of these borderlands. During WWI, Italian patriot Cesare Battisti was held in the castle dungeon before being hanged by the Austrians as a traitor.

p135

**The Drive »** The final 30km drive south on the A22 leaves most of the majestic scenery behind, and the broad valley tapers out towards Rovereto.

TRIP HIGHLIGHT

## 7 Rovereto

In the winter of 1769, Leopold Mozart and his soon-to-be-famous musical son visited Rovereto. Those on a musical pilgrimage come to visit the **Church of San Marco** (Piazza St Marco; ⌚8.30am-noon & 2-7pm), where the 13-year-old Wolfgang wowed the Roveretini, and for the annual **Mozart Festival** (www.festivalmozartrovereto.com) in August.

The town that Mozart knew still has its tightly coiled streets, but it's the shock of the new that lures most to the **Museo di Arte Moderna e Contemporanea** (MART; http://english.mart.trento.it; Corso Bettini 43; adult/reduced €10/7; ⌚10am-6pm Tue-Thu, Sat & Sun, to 9pm Fri), one of Italy's best 20th-century art museums. Designed by Ticinese architect Mario Botta, it is a fitting home for some huge 20th-century works, including Warhol's *Four Marilyns* (1962), several Picassos and a clutch of contemporary art stars. Italian work is, naturally, well represented, with excellent pieces from Balla, Morandi, de Chirico, Fontana and Manzoni.

p135

# Eating & Sleeping

## Alto Lario ①

**Agriturismo Giacomino** Agriturismo €€

(☎0344 8 47 10; www.agriturismogiacomino.it; Via Fordeccia 42, Bugiallo, Sorico; meals €25-35; ⊙lunch daily, dinner on request) Situated at 1100m, Giacomino offers awe-inspiring views of Lago di Mezzola and five-course lunches full of farm products, including salami, rabbit, lamb and even wine from its own cellars. Reservations are essential.

## The Valtellina ②

**Altavilla** Valtellinese €€

(☎0342 72 03 55; www.altavilla.info; Via ai Monti 46, Bianzone; meals €30; ⊙Tue-Sun, daily in Aug; P) Anna Bertola's Alpine chalet is located amid the vineyards just north of Teglio. Expect expert wine recommendations to accompany traditional dishes such as *sciàtt* (buckwheat pancakes stuffed with Bitto cheese). Rooms are also available (singles €25 to €42, doubles €42 to €68).

**Osteria del Crotto** Osteria, Valtellinese €€

(☎0342 61 48 00; www.osteriadelcrotto.it; Via Pedemontana 22, Morbegno; meals €25-35) This *osteria* (casual tavern) serves Slow Food–authenticated products such as *violino di capra della Valchiavenna* (literally 'goat from the violin of the Valchiavenna'), a traditional salami sliced by resting it on the shoulder and shaving it like a violin player moving their bow.

## Merano ④

**Kallmünz** Gastronomic €€

(☎0473 21 29 17; www.kallmuenz.it; Piazza della Rena 12; degustation €40-50; ⊙Tue-Sun) With rendered walls and a beamed ceiling, the dining room here is elegant and simple. Great ingredients also shine: a venison tartare comes with baby herbs, pine nuts and a spritz of beet juice, and a pea and lettuce risotto is as vibrantly green as the valley itself.

**Hotel Aurora** Hotel €€

(☎0473 21 18 00; www.hotelaurora.bz; Passeggiata lungo Passirio 38; s €85-110, d €136-190; ❄📶) A family-run hotel working some fresh ideas in all-white rooms. The breakfast buffet includes *prosecco* and *kuglehof* (yeast cake), and entrance to the spa is included in room prices.

## Magré

**Paradeis** Winery €€

(☎0471 80 95 80; www.aloislageder.eu; Piazza Geltrude 5; ⊙10am-8pm, dining room noon-4pm Mon-Sat, to 11pm Thu) Take a seat at the communal table at Alois Lageder's biodynamic winery, for lunch or tasting. Whites – almost German in style, but shot through with the warmth of an Italian summer – are the money here.

## Trento ⑥

**Ai Tre Garofani** Contemporary, Trentino €€

(☎0461 23 75 43; Via Mazzini 33; meals €35-50; ⊙Tue-Sat) Young, creative and talented, the Linardis deliver a vibrant dining experience. Trust the wine recommendations – Niko is an internationally qualified sommelier.

**Elisa B&B** B&B €

(☎0461 92 21 33; www.bbelisa.com; Viale Rovereto 17; s/d €60/90; ❄📶) This is a true B&B, with three stylish rooms and a charming host who dispenses organic breakfasts (home-baked cakes, artisan cheese) and invaluable local tips.

## Rovereto ⑦

**Osteria del Pettirosso** Osteria, Wine Bar €

(www.osteriadelpettirosso.com; Corso Bettini 24; plates €2.50-12; ⊙Mon-Sat) There's a moody downstairs dining room, but most people come here for a platter of cheese (€7) or a couple of *crostone all lardo* (toasts with cured pork fat) and local wines by the glass.

**Courmayeur** *Transglacial views of Monte Bianco that will take your breath away*

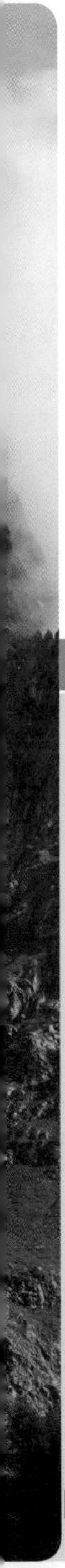

# Valle d'Aosta

*The Valle d'Aosta carves a deep and scenic path through the Alps to Monte Bianco. Explore an ancient, hybrid culture, sample Franco-Provençal food and eyeball epic peaks in cable cars.*

## TRIP HIGHLIGHTS

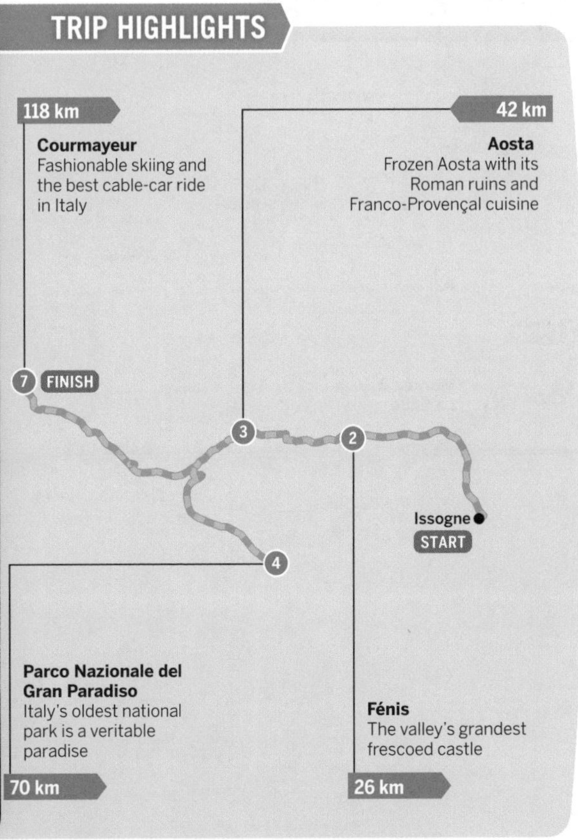

**118 km**
**Courmayeur**
Fashionable skiing and the best cable-car ride in Italy

**42 km**
**Aosta**
Frozen Aosta with its Roman ruins and Franco-Provençal cuisine

7 FINISH

Issogne START

**70 km**
**Parco Nazionale del Gran Paradiso**
Italy's oldest national park is a veritable paradise

**26 km**
**Fénis**
The valley's grandest frescoed castle

**5 DAYS**
**118KM / 73 MILES**

**GREAT FOR...**

**BEST TIME TO GO**

January to March for skiing; September for hiking.

**ESSENTIAL PHOTO**

Top-of-the-world views from the Funivie Monte Bianco.

**BEST FOR SKIING**

Courmayeur's slopes in the shadow of Monte Bianco.

# 11 Valle d'Aosta

Touring the Valle d'Aosta's castle-tipped peaks and glacial valley makes for one of Italy's most scenic drives. Courmayeur's fashion-parade of skiers hits the high slopes of Monte Bianco (Mont Blanc), while Valdostan farmers cultivate Alpine wines and ferment famous *fontina* cheeses in the pastures below. When the snow melts, the hiking in the Gran Paradiso park and along Aosta's high-altitude trails is even more sublime.

## 1 Issogne

Sitting on one of the only navigable routes over the Alps, the Valle d'Aosta's peaks are crowned with castles, each within view of the next, so messages could be transferred up and down the valley via flag signals.

Although many were little more than fortified barracks, as time progressed so their lordly inhabitants became more mindful of appearances. The **Castello d'Issogne** (☎0125 92 93 73; adult/reduced €5/3.50; ⏰9am-7pm

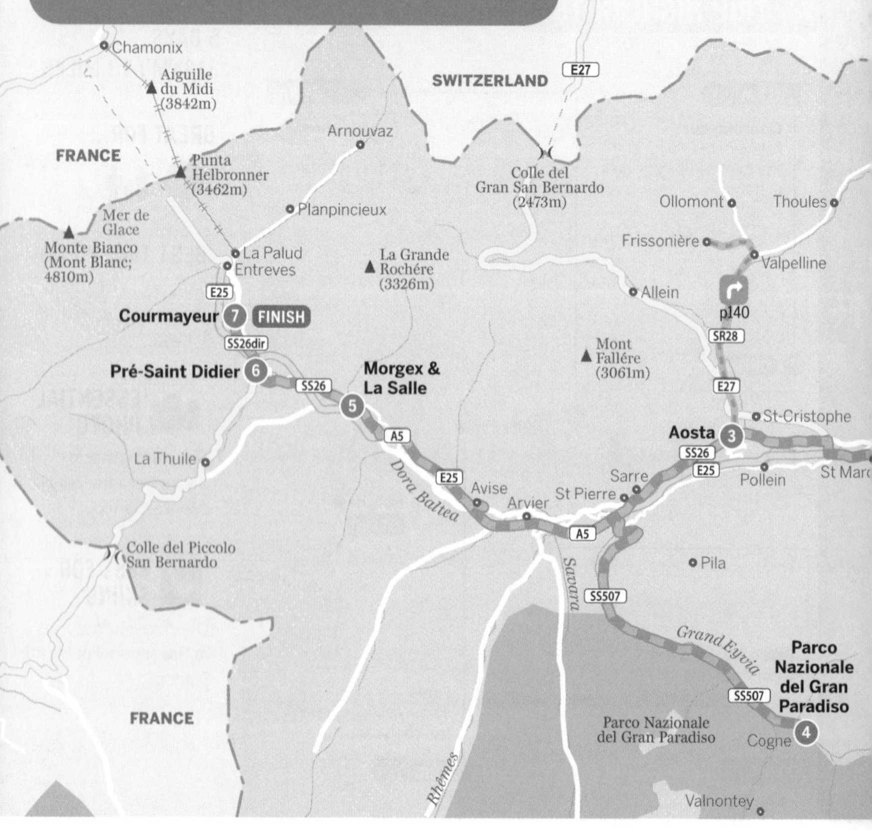

Mar-Sep, 10am-12.30pm & 1.30-5pm Thu-Tue Oct-Feb), for example, sitting on the right bank of the Dora Baltea river, is more of a seigniorial Renaissance residence, the interior decorated with rare Alpine frescoes. It looks quite different to the dour **Castello di Verrès** (adult/reduced €3/2; ⌚9am-6pm Mar-Sep, 10am-12.30pm & 1.30-5pm Fri-Wed Oct-Feb), located on the opposite bank, with which it was in constant conflict.

**The Drive »** From Issogne it's a 26km drive along the A5 autostrada to Fénis. The peaks of the lower Alps are already visible and frame your route. After Montjovet duck through a series of tunnels as you sweep westwards into the valley. Take the exit for Nus and follow signs for the castle.

TRIP HIGHLIGHT

## 2 Fénis

The finest castle in the Valle d'Aosta is without a doubt the magnificently restored **Castello di Fénis** (adult/reduced €5/3.50; ⌚9am-7pm Mar-Sep, 10am-12.30pm & 1.30-5pm Wed-Mon Oct-Feb), owned by the powerful Challant clan from 1242 onwards. It features rich frescoes, including an impressive etching of St George slaying a fiery dragon. The castle is laid out in a pentagonal shape with square and cylindrical turrets lording it over the lush chestnut forests. It was never really used as a defensive post, but served as a plush residence for the Challants until 1716. The on-site museum allows access to a weaponry display, the kitchens, the battlements, the former residential quarters and the frescoed chapel.

**The Drive »** Aosta is just 16km from the Castello di Fénis. Rejoin the A5/E25 for 8km through pretty mountainous forests. Then exit towards Aosta Est onto the E27 for 1.2km, and after you pass through the toll



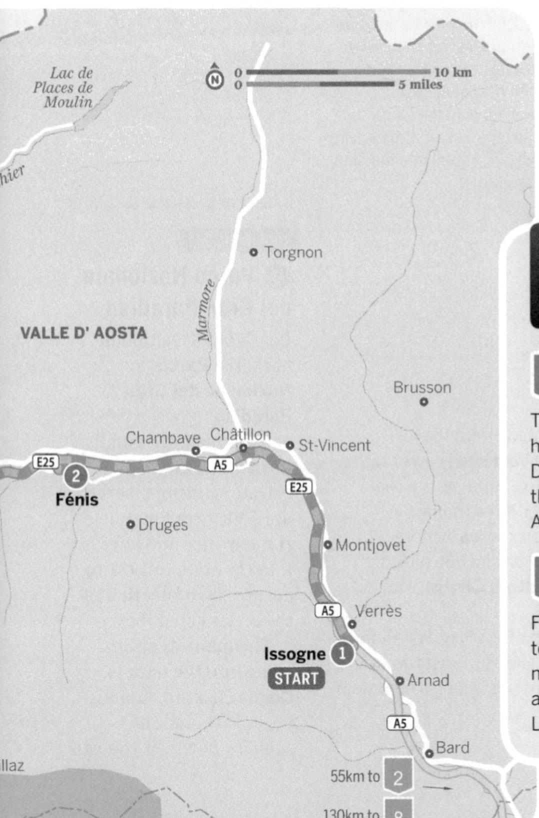


### LINK YOUR TRIP

**2 Savoy Palace Circuit**

The Gran Paradiso was the hunting preserve of the Dukes of Savoy; pick up their trail in Turin, down the A5 from Issogne (p55).

**8 The Graceful Italian Lakes**

From Alpine peaks to a Mediterranean microclimate, take the A5 and A4 from Issogne to Lago d'Orta (p109).

booths follow signs for Aosta Centro, which is a further 4km.

TRIP HIGHLIGHT

## 3 Aosta

Jagged Alpine peaks rise like marble cathedrals above the town of Aosta, a once-important Roman settlement that has sprawled rather untidily across the valley floor since the opening of the Monte Bianco tunnel in the 1960s. But its 2000-year-old centre still harbours Roman relics, such as the **Arco di Augusto** (Piazza Arco di Augusto), the **Roman bridge**, spanning the Buthier river since the 1st century, and the **Porta Praetoria**, the main gate to the Roman city. Even the **Roman theatre** (Via Porta Praetoria; ⏲9am-7pm Sep-Jun, to 8pm Jul & Aug) remains in use as a venue for summer concerts.

Otherwise, more Challant-commissioned artworks can be seen in the **Chiesa di Sant'Orso** (Via Sant'Orso; ⏲9am-7pm), which dates back to the 10th century.

For skiing and hiking on the slopes above, ascend the **Aosta-Pila cable car** (one-way/return €3/5; ⏲8am-12.15pm & 2-5pm, to 6pm Jun-Aug) to the 1800m-high resort of **Pila**.

✕ 🛏 p143

**The Drive »** Leave Aosta heading westwards for the next scenic 26km to Cogne. You'll pick up the Viale Piccolo San Bernardino first for a couple of kilometres and then merge with the SS26. After about 3km turn left onto the SS507 and start the beautiful, mountain-hugging ascent into the Gran Paradiso.

### DETOUR: VALPELLINE

**Start: 3 Aosta**

Aosta's signature cheese is made from the full-cream, unpasteurised milk of Valdostan cows that have grazed on pastures up to 2700m above sea level, before being matured for three months in underground rock tunnels. You can learn more about the history, 'terroir' and production of Aostan cheeses at the **Valpelline Visitors Centre** (www.fontinacoop.com; Frissonière; ⏲8.30am-12.30pm & 2.30-6.30pm Mon-Fri, 9am-noon & 3-6pm Sat & Sun). Follow the SR28 for 7km north to Valpelline, turn east towards Ollomont and after 1.5km turn west along a mountain road to Frissonière.

EOIN CLARKE/GETTY IMAGES ©

TRIP HIGHLIGHT

## 4 Parco Nazionale del Gran Paradiso

Italy's oldest national park, the **Parco Nazionale del Gran Paradiso** (www.parks.it), is aptly named. Originally it was the Savoy's own private hunting reserve until Vittorio Emanuele II made nice and gave it to the state in 1922 to ensure the protection of the endangered ibex.

The main stepping stone into the park is **Cogne** (1534m), famous for its lace-making, samples of which you can

**Courmayeur** The slopes of Val Veny

buy at **Le Marché Aux Puces** (Rue Grand Paradis 4; ⏱Thu-Tue). Easy walks in the park are possible, such as the 3km stroll to the village of **Lillaz** on trail 23, where there is a geological park and a waterfall that drops 150m. Trails 22 and 23 will get you to the village of **Valnontey**, where you can visit the **Giardino Alpino Paradisa** (adult/child €3/1.50; ⏱10am-5.30pm Jun–mid-Sep, to 6.30pm Jul & Aug), an Alpine garden displaying mountain flora and rare butterflies.

p143

**The Drive »** The longest drive on the tour is 42km to Morgex and La Salle. The first 20km involve retracing your route down the SS507 out of the mountains. When you reach the bottom follow signs to rejoin the A5/E25 autostrada in the direction of Monte Bianco. From here it's 18km to Morgex through the forested valley.

## 5 Morgex & La Salle

The ruined towers of **Châtelard**, which guard the road over the Piccolo San Bernardo pass, also cast a shadow over Europe's highest vineyards strung out between the two communes of Morgex and La Salle. The wines from these Alpine vines, produced almost exclusively from the Prié Blanc grape grown between 900m and 1200m, is light and fruity with overtones of mountain herbs and freshly cut hay.

Given the extremes of temperature at this altitude (some vines run almost to the snow line), vintners employ a unique system of cultivation called *pergola bassa* (low-level arbours), where vines are planted low to the ground to protect them. Since 1983 the Aostan government has sought to preserve these ancient traditions by setting up the cooperative **La Cave du Vin Blanc Morgex et de la Salle** (www.caveduvinblanc.com; Chemin des Iles 31, La Ruine; ⌚10am-noon & 3.30-6.30pm Mon, Tue & Thu-Sat), which processes the grapes from the 90 or so local small-holdings. Aosta's **tourist office** (Piazza Chanoux 2, Aosta; ⌚9am-6.30pm) has an English-language booklet with information on individual cellars and the cooperative.

**The Drive »** From either La Salle or Morgex descend through the vineyards and rejoin the SS26 for the short 7km drive to Pré-Saint Didier. The road passes under the A5 and then wriggles alongside the river Thuile all the way to Pré.

## 6 Pré-Saint Didier

Bubbling at a natural 37°C from the mountains' depths, where the river Thuile forces its way through a narrow gorge into the Dora valley, the thermal waters at **Terme di Pré-St-Didier** (www.termedipre.it; Allée des Thermes; admission €42-48; ⌚9.30am-9pm Sun-Thu, 8.30am-11pm Fri-Sat) have been a source of therapeutic treatment since the bath-loving Romans were in town. In addition to saunas, whirlpools and toning waterfalls there's an indoor-outdoor thermal pool. It's lit by candles and torches on Saturday nights, when it is spectacular amid the snow and stars.

**The Drive »** The scenic drive to Courmayeur is on the SS26dir. Cross over the river Thuile in Pré and head westwards with the towering snow-capped peaks of the high passes in front of you. They're an awesome sight, especially in spring when they're framed by the deepest green conifers.

TRIP HIGHLIGHT

## 7 Courmayeur

Flush up against France and linked by a dramatic cable-car ride to its cross-border cousin in Chamonix, Courmayeur has grafted upmarket ski facilities onto an ancient Roman base. Its pièce de résistance is lofty **Monte Bianco**, western Europe's highest mountain, 4810m of solid rock and ice that rises like an impregnable wall above the Valle d'Aosta. Ride the **Funivie Monte Bianco** (www.montebianco.com; return trip from La Palud €38; ⌚8.30am-12.40pm & 2-4.30pm) for transglacial views that will take your breath away.

First stop is the 2173m-high midstation **Pavillon du Mt Fréty** (return €16), where there's a restaurant and the **Mt Fréty Nature Oasis** (admission €2; ⌚9.30am-6pm Jul-Sep). At the top of the ridge is **Punta Helbronner** (3462m). From Punta Helbronner another cable car (late May to late September) takes you on a spectacular 5km ride across the Italian border to the **Aiguille du Midi** (3842m) in France, from where the world's highest cable car transports you into Chamonix. The journey from Courmayeur to Chamonix costs €50, and includes a bus back through the Mont Blanc tunnel. It's worth every penny.

p143

### SKIING MONTE BIANCO

Courmayeur offers some extraordinary skiing in the shadow of Monte Bianco. The two main ski areas – the **Plan Checrouit** and **Pre de Pascal** – are interlinked by 100km of runs. Three lifts leave from the valley floor, one from **Courmayeur** itself, one from the village of **Dolonne** and one from nearby **Val Veny**. They are run by **Funivie Courmayeur Mont Blanc** (www.courmayeur-montblanc.com).

# Eating & Sleeping

## Aosta 3

**Vecchia Aosta** Valdostan €€
(☎0165 36 11 86; www.vecchiaaosta.it; Piazza Porte Pretoriane 4; set menu €30-35; ⏲lunch & dinner Tue-Sat, lunch Sun) Grafted onto a section of the old Roman wall, Vecchia Aosta's setting is sublime. Try the spiced beef with cloves and cinnamon and the Geispi, a local liqueur made of wildflowers.

**Il Vecchio Ristoro** Gastronomic €€€
(☎0165 3 32 38; www.ristorantevecchio ristoro.it; Via Tourneuve 4; meals €50, menu degustazione €80; ⏲lunch & dinner Tue-Sat, dinner Mon) Originating from the Valtellina, Alfio Fascendini knows a thing or two about good food and wine. Sample the chestnut bread, the saffron-creamed pearl barley with crispy artichokes and the smoked fillet of bream.

**Hotel Milleluci** Luxury Hotel €€
(☎0165 4 42 74; www.hotelmilleluci.com; Loc Porossan 15; s €120-150, d €170-210; P ❄ @ ≋) Old wooden skis, claw-foot baths, indoor and outdoor pools, a sauna and gym make for a fabulous stay at this family-run farmhouse set on the hillside above Aosta.

## Parco Nazionale del Gran Paradiso 4

**Lou Ressignon** Valdostan €€
(☎0165 7 40 34; www.louressignon.it; Via des Mines 23, Cogne; meals €28-40; ⏲lunch & dinner Tue-Sun) In a wood-panelled dining room with red curtains bunched at the windows, David and Elizabeth Allera keep Valdostan traditions alive, serving bowls of belly-filling *seupetta á la cogneintze*, a dish of rice and toasted bread slathered in *fontina* cheese. They also offer five well-priced chalet rooms (doubles €75 to €100).

**Hotel Ristorante Petit Dahu** Traditional Italian €€
(☎0165 7 41 46; www.hotelpetitdahu.com; Valnontey; restaurant menu €35; ⏲closed May & Oct; P) Straddling two traditional stone-and-wood buildings, this friendly spot has a wonderful restaurant that prepares rustic dishes using wild Alpine herbs. It also has rooms (singles €36 to €50, doubles €72 to €100).

**Hotel Bellevue** Luxury Hotel €€€
(☎0165 7 48 25; www.hotelbellevue.it; Rue Grand Paradis 22, Cogne; d €210-320, 2-person chalet €250-340; ⏲mid-Dec–mid-Oct; P ≋) Overlooking meadows, this green-shuttered mountain hideaway evokes its 1920s origins with romantic canopied timber 'cabin beds'. Its four restaurants include a Michelin-starred affair and a cheese restaurant with cheese from the family's own cellar.

## Courmayeur 7

**La Terraza** International €€
(Via Circonvalazione 73; meals €35-45; ⏲lunch & dinner) Serves the full gamut of pizzas, steaks and après-ski nosh. True to the local spirit there are also plenty of Valdostan dishes, including polenta, spicy sausage and fondue.

**La Chaumière** Italian €€€
(Località Planchecrouit 15; ⏲lunch) Set on the slopes above Courmayeur, within walking distance of the cable car, is the fabulous sun-kissed terrace of La Chaumière. Views straight down the Aosta valley are accompanied by superlative polenta and 38 carefully-sourced wines.

**Auberge de la Maison** Chalet €€
(☎0165 86 98 11; www.aubergemaison.it; Via Passerin d'Entreves 16, Entreves; s €125-180, d €140-230; P ᯤ) Overlooking the Courmayeur valley, this *auberge* (inn) is located in the village of Entreves. Crackling fires welcome you into warmly traditional Alpine rooms, where majolica stoves and wooden beds await.

***Dolomites** Dazzling, million-dollar views from Corvara, in the Alta Badia*

Classic Trip

# Grande Strada delle Dolomiti

12

*The Dolomites are one of the most beautiful mountain ranges in the world. Devotees come for skiing in winter, hiking and rock climbing in spring and summer, and harvest festivals in autumn.*

## TRIP HIGHLIGHTS



**7–10 DAYS**
**195KM / 121 MILES**

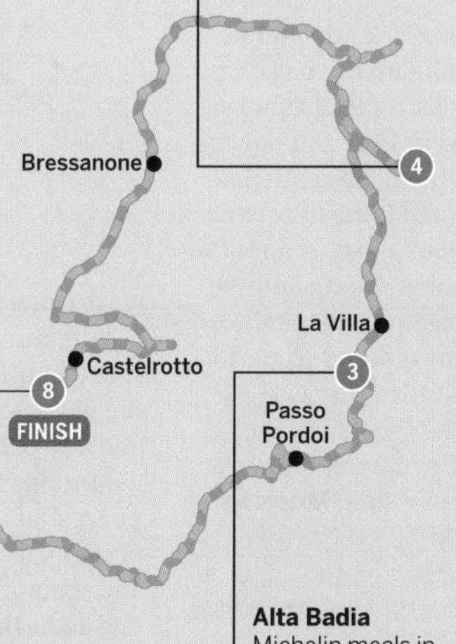

### GREAT FOR...

### BEST TIME TO GO

December for Christmas markets and skiing; June for spring flowers.

### ESSENTIAL PHOTO

The humpbacked Marmolada with a foreground of mountain flowers.

### BEST FOR OUTDOORS

The villages of Alta Badia and the beautiful Lago di Braies.

Classic Trip

# 12 Grande Strada delle Dolomiti

Ranging across the South Tyrol, Alto Adige and Veneto, the Dolomites (Dolomiti) combine Austrian and Italian influences with the local Ladin culture. On this grand road trip *(grande strada)* your hosts may wear lederhosen, cure ham in their chimneys and use sleighs to travel from village to village. More recently a new generation of eco-chic hotels, cutting-edge spas and Michelin-starred restaurants have started grabbing the headlines, but overall these mountain peaks remain very low key.

TRIP HIGHLIGHT

## 1 Bolzano

Once a stop on the coach route between Italy and the flourishing Austro-Hungarian Empire, Bolzano has been a long-time conduit between cultures. The city's fine museums include the **Museo Archeologico dell'Alto Adige** (☎0471 32 01 00; www.iceman.it; Via Museo 43; adult/reduced €9/7; ⏲10am-6pm Tue-Sun), where the mummified remains of the 5300-year-old iceman, Ötzi, are on display. He was found 3200m up the melting glacier on Hauslabjoch Pass in 1991, but how he got there, 52 centuries before alpinism became a serious sport, is a matter of some debate and the museum explores the many mooted scenarios.

At the other end of the spectrum, the city's contemporary art museum, **Museion** (☎0471 22 34 13; www.museion.it; Via Dante 2; adult/reduced €6/3.50, Thu evening free; ⏲10am-6pm Tue-Sun, to 10pm Thu), is housed in a huge multifaceted glass cube, a surprising architectural assertion that beautifully vignettes the old-town rooftops and surrounding mountains from within. There's an impressive permanent collection, and temporary shows highlight the local art scene's ongoing dialogue

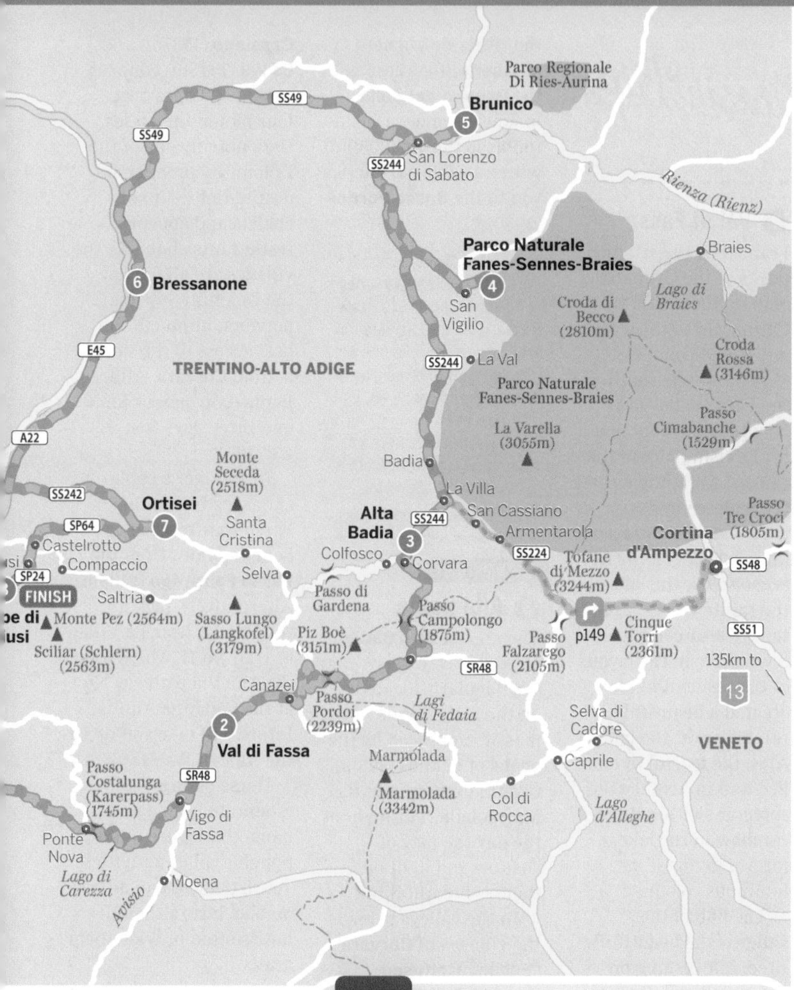

Parco Regionale Di Ries-Aurina
SS49
Brunico
5
SS49
SS244
San Lorenzo di Sabato
Rienza (Rienz)
Parco Naturale Fanes-Sennes-Braies
Braies
6
Bressanone
4
San Vigilio
Lago di Braies
Croda di Becco (2810m)
Croda Rossa (3146m)
E45
TRENTINO-ALTO ADIGE
SS244
La Val
Parco Naturale Fanes-Sennes-Braies
Passo Cimabanche (1529m)
La Varella (3055m)
A22
Monte Seceda (2518m)
Badia
SS242
Ortisei
La Villa
Passo Tre Croci (1805m)
Alta Badia
SS244
San Cassiano
SP64
7
Santa Cristina
3
Armentarola
Cortina d'Ampezzo
Castelrotto
Colfosco
SS224
Tofane di Mezzo (3244m)
SS48
Compaccio
Corvara
SP24
Selva
FINISH
Saltria
Passo di Gardena
Passo Campolongo (1875m)
Cinque Torri (2361m)
SS51
Monte Pez (2564m)
Sasso Lungo (Langkofel) (3179m)
Piz Boè (3151m)
Passo Falzarego (2105m)
p149
Sciliar (Schlern) (2563m)
SR48
135km to
13
Canazei
Passo Pordoi (2239m)
Lagi di Fedaia
Selva di Cadore
2
Val di Fassa
VENETO
Passo Costalunga (Karerpass) (1745m)
Marmolada
Caprile
SR48
Marmolada (3342m)
Col di Rocca
Lago d'Alleghe
Vigo di Fassa
Ponte Nova
Lago di Carezza
Moena
Avisio

with Austria and Germany.

p155

**The Drive »** Exit Bolzano on the SS241 to the Val di Fassa. The road is the start of a long assent, the first section through a steep-sided canyon. At Ponte Nova the first peaks of the Dolomites come into view and after 26km Lago di Carezza is visible on your right.

## LINK YOUR TRIP

### 9 A Weekend at Lake Garda

Tool down the A22 to Lake Garda and visit the vineyards and olive groves around its shores (p121).

### 13 A Venetian Sojourn

Drop down from Cortina d'Ampezzo on the SS51 and SS50 for a tour of Venetian palaces and frescoes (p157).

## 2 Val di Fassa

Framed by the stirring peaks of the Gruppo del Sella to the north, the Catinaccio to the west and the Marmolada (3342m) to the southeast, the Fassa Valley is a beautiful introduction to the rising mountain ranges. Amid the forests, the iridescent blue-green **Lago di Carezza** is known locally as *de lec ergobando* ('the lake of the rainbow'), as legend tells of a sorcerer who, trying to win the favour of the resident nymph, created a beautiful rainbow over the lake. Alas, the fearful nymph fled and in his fury the sorcerer shattered the rainbow in the lake, forever giving it its luminous colour.

The hub of the valley is the beautifully sited, but verging on overdeveloped, **Canazei** and, to a lesser extent, the riverside village of **Moena**. To access the **Gruppo del Sella** mountain range ascend to **Passo Pordoi** (2239m), where a cable car carries you to the **Sasso Pordoi** (2950m).

**The Drive »** From Lago di Carezza it's 38km up a series of rapid switchbacks to Passo Pordoi. From the lofty summit, you'll have a view over the 33 hairpin bends that you'll be descending on the SR48. It's only 7km, but it's slow going and the views over meadows and villages are superb. At Arabba bear left on the SS244 for Corvara.

TRIP HIGHLIGHT

## 3 Alta Badia

The area of **Alta Badia** (www.altabadia.org) is spectacularly located on the Sella Ronda massif, embraced by the peaks of Pelmo (3168m), Civetta (3218m) and the Marmolada. Throughout the day the play of shadow and light on them is breathtaking.

In the valleys below, the villages of **Corvara** (1568m), **Colfosco** (1645m), **La Villa** (1433m), **Badia** (1324m), **San Cassiano** (1537m) and **La Val** (1348m) connect 130km of slopes over four mountain passes. Undoubtedly one of the Dolomites' premier ski destinations – luxury chalets and gourmet restaurants abound – the villages are all part of the Dolomiti Superski network, although the best access to the slopes is from Corvara. Alta Badia-only passes for one/three days cost €37/107.

In summer a cable car ascends into the Parco Naturale Fanes-Sennes-Braies from the **Passo Falzarego** (2105m). Alternatively, pick up trail No 12, near La Villa, or trail No 11, which joins the Alta Via pathway No 1 at the Capanna Alpina. Either will take you up to the Alpe di Fanes.

Horse-riding, mountain biking and hang-gliding are other popular valley activities. Tourist offices can advise on bike hire, although hotels often provide them gratis.

p155

**The Drive »** From Corvara the 27km to San Vigilio, the unofficial HQ of the Fanes-Sennes-Braies park, is a pleasant, easy drive down the SS244. Chalets dot the hillsides and Alpine cows graze in the valleys, making for an idyllic scene. After 23km turn right on Via Longega for San Vigilio.

### TOP TIP: SKI PASS

The **Dolomiti Superski** (www.dolomitisuperski.com) ski pass gives access to more than 1900km of pistes and 450 lifts spread over 12 resorts. Adult passes cost from €42/116/205 for one/three/six days.

TRIP HIGHLIGHT

## 4 Parco Naturale Fanes-Sennes-Braies

Hidden behind a wall of rocks northeast of Corvara is the Parco Naturale Fanes-Sennes-Braies, a 25,680 hectare windswept plain, potent with Ladin legends that have resonated over the centuries, inspiring JRR Tolkien's Middle Earth in *Lord of the Rings*. Not surprisingly, the valley and the high Fanes plateau, with its sculpted ridges and buttress towers of rock, are considered among the most evocative places in the Dolomites and have transfixed artists and poets for centuries. Wordsworth considered it a 'region of the Heavens' and architect Le Corbusier called the rocky pinnacles 'the most beautiful architecture in the world'.

East down the Val Pusteria is the mystical **Lago di Braies**, a glassy lake set within an amphitheatre of stone. Crouched at its southern edge is 'Gate Mountain', **Sas dla Porta**, once thought to hide a gateway to the underworld. A wooden platform stretches out into the lake for those brave enough to swim in its chilling waters, otherwise stroll the banks and ponder legends of lost worlds.

### DETOUR: CORTINA D'AMPEZZO

**Start: 3 Alta Badia**

Thirty-four winding kilometres in the shadow of **Tofane di Mezzo** (3244m) from La Villa lies pricey, icy Cortina d'Ampezzo, the Italian supermodel of ski resorts. Sitting in a crescent-shaped glacial valley surrounded by wooded slopes, Cortina is undeniably beautiful, gaining international fame in the '60s and '70s when Elizabeth Taylor and Henry Fonda came to town to film *Ash Wednesday*. Unapologetically Italian in feel, ladies in fur coats *passeggiata* (stroll) along the Corso with their pampered pooches.

Book a table on the terrace at **Il Meloncino** (0436 44 32; www.ilmeloncino.it; Locale Rumerlo 1; meals €60; Wed-Mon) for local specialities as exquisite as the Alpine views.

**The Drive »** Head back down the hill from San Vigilio to the SS244 and take a right for Brunico, 17km north. As you descend the valley the scenery, while still bucolic, is less dramatic. At picturesque San Lorenzo di Sabato you'll cross the milky Rio di Pusteria as you enter Brunico.

## 5 Brunico

The Val Pusteria's big smoke, Brunico, gets a bad rap from those who've only driven through its unremarkable main drag. The quintessentially Tyrolean historic centre, is, however, delightful.

Right by the town gate is **Acherer Patisserie & Blumen** (0474 41 00 30; www.acherer.com; via Centrale; 8am-7pm Mon-Fri, to 5pm Sat & Sun), creator and purveyor of the region's best apple strudel and Sachertorte. The young owner reopened his grandfather's former bakery after apprenticing in Vienna. His inventive chocolates and seasonal preserves have won accolades from gourmet bible *Gambero Rosso*.

On the outskirts of town, visit local wool manufacturer **Moessmer** (www.moessmer.it; Via Walther von der Vogelweide Str 6) for top-quality cashmere and Tyrolean tweeds from its outlet shop.

**The Drive »** Exit Brunico onto the main SS49/E66 autostrada and follow the winding Rio di Pusteria river up the valley to Bressanone. After 21km you'll pass the frescoed Castello di Rodengo high up on your left, before dropping down through

Classic Trip

ANDREW BAIN/GETTY IMAGES ©

CLÉMENT PHILIPPE/ARTERRA PICTURE LIBRARY/GETTY IMAGES ©

## WHY THIS IS A CLASSIC TRIP

PAULA HARDY, AUTHOR

It's hard to overstate the incredible natural beauty of the Dolomites. The shape, colours and contours of the mountains are endlessly varied in the moody pink, purple and grey light. Walking the *alta vie* (high ways) you honestly feel like Heidi. I'll never forget sitting down at Gostner Schwaige (p155) and being presented with a creamy broth poured into a bowl of bread on a bed of hay, surrounded by still-fragrant wildflowers.

Top: Cyclist near Brunico
Left: Bressanone
Right: Mountain road in the Alta Badia

MATTEO COLOMBO/GETTY IMAGES ©

the vineyards of Varna into Bressanone.

## 6 Bressanone

Beautiful Bressanone (Brixen), with its palace of the prince-bishops and illustrious history, is the artistic and cultural capital of the Val Pusteria.

The first **cathedral** (Piazza del Duomo; 7am-noon & 2-6pm) was built here in the 10th century by the Bishop of Säben. Though rebuilt in the 18th century along baroque lines, it retains its fabulous 12th-century cloister, the cross-vaults decorated with superb 15th-century frescoes. Bressanone's prince-bishops obviously had an eye for art, and the **Hofburg** (www.hofburg.it; Piazza Palazzo Vescovile 2; adult/reduced €3.50/free; 10am-5pm Tue-Sun), their Renaissance *palazzo* (mansion), was similarly decorated in lavish style. Amid the noble apartments you'll find treasures from the Middle Ages and a collection of *presepi* (wooden nativity scenes).

p155

**The Drive »** From Bressanone you'll rejoin the main A22 autostrada south towards Modena. It winds through forested valleys for 20km, past Castello di Velturno on your right and above the river Isarco. Exit for the Val Gardena onto the SS242 for the scenic 15km climb to Ortisei at 1236m.

### 7 Ortisei

Ortisei is the main hub of the Val Gardena and the Alpe di Siusi mountain region. The valley's historical isolation has ensured the survival of many traditions. Like the Alta Badia and Val di Fassa, this is one of only five valleys where Ladin is a majority tongue, while the villages of Ortisei (1236m), **Santa Cristina** (1428m) and **Selva** (1563m) are characterised by folksy architecture and a profusion of woodcarving shops. Ortisei's **Museum de Gherdëina** (☎0471 79 75 54; www.museumgherdeina.it; Via Rezia 83; adult/reduced €6/4; ⊙10am-noon & 2-6pm Tue-Fri, Mon in summer) has a particularly beautiful collection of wooden toys and sculptures, as does the local church, **St Ulrich**.

From the centre of Ortisei a high-speed cable car ascends the slopes of Alpe di Siusi, Europe's largest high-altitude Alpine meadow. To the northeast, another cable car ascends to **Monte Seceda** (2518m) with unforgettable views of the **Gruppo di Odle**, a cathedral-like series of mountain spires. From Seceda, trail No

GLENN VAN DER KNIJFF/GETTY IMAGES ©

**Ortisei** With views of the towering Gruppo di Odle

2A passes through sloping pastures dotted with wooden *malghe* (shepherds' huts).

Afterwards descend for traditional après-ski at the five-star **Hotel Adler** (www.adler-dolomiti.com), which has been serving up cocktails since 1810.

p155

**The Drive »** The 15km drive to Siusi is staggeringly beautiful. Take the SS242 back towards the autostrada but after 1.2km veer left onto the SP64. Views of the rocky peaks surround you as you pass quaint shepherds' huts. At 1060m you'll pass through Castelrotto with its onion-domed church, from where you take the SP24 for the final 10km.

TRIP HIGHLIGHT

## 8 Alpe di Siusi

There are few more beautiful juxtapositions than the undulating green pastures of the Alpe di Siusi – Europe's largest plateau – ending dramatically at the base of the Sciliar Mountains. To the southeast lies the Catinaccio range, its German name 'Rosengarten' – an apt description of the eerie pink hue given off by the dolomite rock at sunset. Signposted by their onion-domed churches, the villages that dot the valleys – including **Castelrotto** (Kastelruth), **Fié allo Sciliar** (Völs am Schlern) and **Siusi** – are unexpectedly sophisticated.

Part of the Dolomiti Superski network (see p148), the gentle slopes of the Alpe di Siusi are even better hiking terrain, and average stamina will get you to the **Rifugio Bolzano** (www.schlernhaus.it; ⏲Jun-Oct), one of the Alps' oldest mountain huts, which rests at 2457m, just under **Monte Pez** (2564m). Take the **Panorama chairlift** (one-way/return €3.50/5) from Compaccio to the Alpenhotel, followed by paths S, No 5 and No 1.

Horses are also a big part of local life and culture, and there's nothing more picturesque than a local chestnut Haflinger pony galloping across these endless pastures. **Gstatschhof Ponyhof** (☎0471 72 78 14; www.gstatschhof.com; Via Alpe di Siusi 39) offers accommodation and summer programs.

p155

### LOCAL KNOWLEDGE: WALK THE HIGH PASSES

The Dolomites' *alta vie* – literally high ways – are high-altitude paths, designed for experienced walkers, but most not requiring mountaineering skill or equipment. From mid-June to mid-September, a network of mountain huts offering food and accommodation line the route. Descriptions of each route can be found at www.dolomiti-altevie.it.

**Alta Via No 1** Lago di Braies to Belluno, north to south

**Alta Via No 2** Bressanone to Feltre, passing through Odle, the mythical Ladin kingdom

**Alta Via No 3** Villabassa to Longarone

**Alta Via No 4** San Candido to Pieve di Cadore

# Eating & Sleeping

## Bolzano 1

**Kaiserkron** Modern Italian €€€

(0471 30 91 61; www.kaiserkron.bz; Piazza della Mostra 2; meals €40-50; Mon-Sat) Robert Weiser serves a short and original menu and an accomplished Italian wine list in scenic Piazza della Mostra. Dishes such as veal tenderloin with truffles on a bed of turnips are superbly prepared.

## Alta Badia 3

**Prè de Costa** Ladin €€€

(0471 84 94 43; www.predecosta.it; Str Pre de Costa 20, Armentarola; meals €100; 7-9.30pm Mon-Sat) Housed in an old barn surrounded by a wide meadow and the Armentarola forest, Prè de Costa serves Ladin cuisine, prepared by owner Mrs Herta. Many dishes, such as the sweet pumpkin ravioli, are heritage recipes.

**Stüa de Michil** Ladin €€€

(0471 83 10 00; www.hotel-laperla.it; Col Alt 105, Corvara; meals €100; 7-9.30pm Mon-Sat) Strewn with Alpine antiques, the farmhouse kitchen of the Hotel La Perla is ridiculously atmospheric. Beautifully presented dishes rework Ladin or Tyrolean traditions and utilise biodynamic ingredients.

**Lagacio** Apartment Hotel €€

(0471 84 95 03; www.lagacio.com; Strada Micurá de Rü 48, San Cassiano; apt €146-290; ) This residence hotel has young, friendly staff and stylishly pared-back apartments with balconies. Attention to detail is keen: kitchens come with WMF-branded gadgets and espresso machines.

## Bressanone 6

**Restaurant Finsterwirt** Tyrolean €€€

(0472 83 53 43; www.finsterwirt.com; Domgasse 3, Vicolo del Duomo; meals €40-60; lunch Tue-Sun Aug–mid-Jun) Housed in one of the oldest buildings in Bressanone, Finsterwirt is an institution. For nearly a decade chef and owner Herman Mayr has been serving imaginative Tyrolean cuisine. Menu highlights include rare strawberry spinach and mountain artichokes.

## Ortisei 7

**Hotel am Stetteneck** Hotel €€

(0471 79 65 63; www.stetteneck.com; Via Rezia 14; d €88-190; ) This elegant hotel dates from 1913 (during WWI Italian troops were bivouacked here) and is right in the centre of town. Come for graceful service, and lovely village and mountain views from big bay windows. Weekly stays only in winter.

## Alpe di Siusi 8

**Gostner Schwaige** Mountain Refuge €

(1930m; footpath No 3 from Compaccio; meals €15-25; Jun-Oct & Dec-Apr) Chef Franz Mulser gives new meaning to the tag 'locally sourced' at his mountain refuge. The butter and cheese come from the barn next door, and herbs from the garden outside. Boards of salami, steaming broth and slow-cooked stews are the order of the day.

**Chalet Gerard** Chalet €€€

(0471 79 52 74; www.chalet-gerard.com; Plan de Gralba, Selva Val Gardena; half-board s €105-145, d €180-240; ) A remote modern chalet with panoramic views, architect-designed fire spots, a steam room and the option to ski-in. The restaurant is both romantic – all pine and candlelight – and highly regarded.

## **Venice** *A water world brimming with history and romance*

JOSEPH SPANTI

Classic Trip

# A Venetian Sojourn

*Pinch yourself, and you might expect to wake from this dream of pink palaces, teal waters and golden domes. Instead, you're in the Veneto, where gondoliers call Ooeee! and water laps at your feet.*

## TRIP HIGHLIGHTS

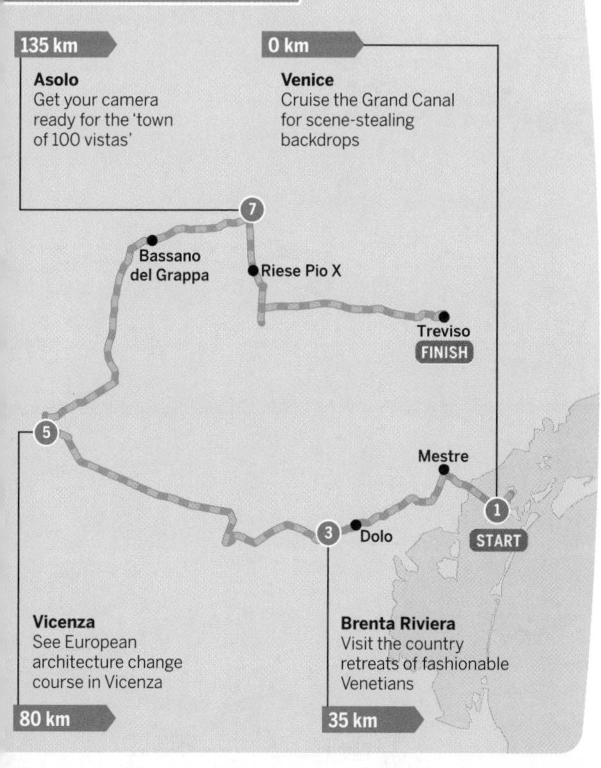

**0 km**
**Venice**
Cruise the Grand Canal for scene-stealing backdrops

**35 km**
**Brenta Riviera**
Visit the country retreats of fashionable Venetians

**80 km**
**Vicenza**
See European architecture change course in Vicenza

**135 km**
**Asolo**
Get your camera ready for the 'town of 100 vistas'

1 START – Mestre – Dolo – 3 – 5 – Bassano del Grappa – 7 – Riese Pio X – Treviso FINISH

**4–5 DAYS**
**186KM / 115 MILES**

**GREAT FOR...**

**BEST TIME TO GO**

January to June for snow-covered gondolas, Carnival and the Biennale.

**ESSENTIAL PHOTO**

The Ponte di Rialto from a Grand Canal perspective.

From the avant-garde in Venice to Tiepolo frescoes in Palladian villas.

Classic Trip

# 13 A Venetian Sojourn

Scan the Veneto coastline and you might spot signs of modern life – beach resorts, malls, traffic. But look closer and you'll catch the waft of fresh espresso from Piazza San Marco's 250-year-old cafes, faded villas on the Brenta Riviera and masterpieces everywhere: Titians in Venice (Venezia), Palladios in Vicenza and Giottos in Padua (Padova). This calls for a toast with bubbly local *prosecco* – so raise your glass to *la bea vita* (the good life).

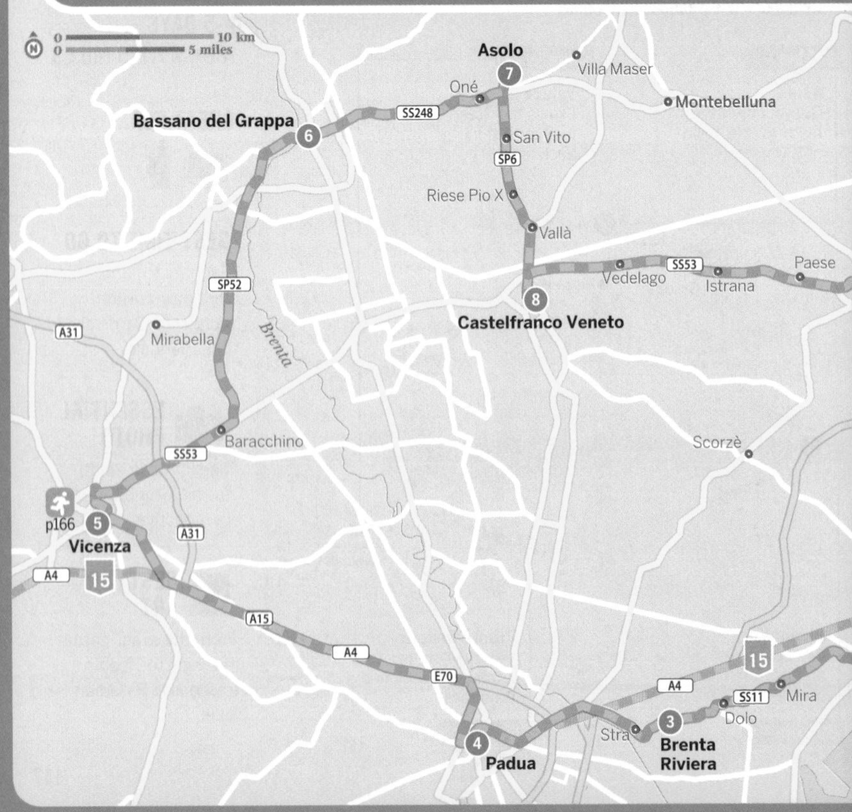

TRIP HIGHLIGHT

## 1 Venice

Take the No 1 *vaporetto* (passenger ferry; €6.50) down the **Grand Canal** for scene-stealing backdrops featured in four James Bond films. It starts with controversy at the **Ponte di Calatrava**, a luminous glass-and-steel bridge that cost triple the original €4-million estimate. Ahead are castle-like **Fondaco dei Turchi**, the historic Turkish trading house, and **Ca d'Oro**, a 1430 filigree Gothic marvel.

Points of Venetian pride include the **Pescaria**, where fishmongers have been slinging lagoon crab for 600 years, before the marble marvel of the **Ponte di Rialto**. If you're feeling peckish, jump ashore for a gourmet food tour with our leg stretcher (p52).

The next two canal bends could cause architectural whiplash, with Renaissance **Palazzo Grimani**, followed by **Palazzo Grassi** (www.palazzograssi.it; Campo San Samuele 3231; adult/reduced €15/10; 10am-7pm Wed-Mon), site of contemporary-art sensations between Biennales, and Baldassare Longhena's baroque jewel box **Ca' Rezzonico** (www.museiciviciveneziani.it; Fondamenta Rezzonico 3136; adult/reduced €8/5.50; 10am-6pm Wed-Mon Apr-Oct, to 5pm Nov-Mar).

Finally, stone lions flank the **Peggy Guggenheim Collection** (www.guggenheim-venice.it; Palazzo Venier dei Leoni 704; adult/reduced €12/7; 10am-6pm Wed-Mon), where the American heiress collected ideas, lovers and art. It's situated just before the dramatic dome of Longhena's **Chiesa di Santa Maria della Salute** comes into view.

p165

**The Drive »** The first leg of this journey is by boat rather than car. Take *vaporetto* No 41, the Circular line, to Murano. Nos 5 and 13 also head here.

## 2 Murano

Woe betide the glassblower with wanderlust: Murano's trade secrets were so jealously guarded that any glass-worker who left the city was accused of treason and subject to assassination. Today, glass artisans ply their trade at workshops along Murano's **Fondamenta dei Vetrai**, marked by

### LINK YOUR TRIP

**14 Trieste to Tarvisio**
Look eastwards down the A4 to Trieste and the borderlands with Slovenia, as many Venetians have done before you (p169).

**15 World Heritage Wonders**
From the wonders of Venice to Unesco's list of World Heritage Sites, continue down the A4 from Vicenza to Verona (p181).

'Fornace' (Furnace) signs.

If you're not in the market for an enormous chandelier shaped like an escaping lagoon monster, then make your way to the **Museum of Glass** (www.museiciviciveneziani.it; Fondamenta Giustinian 8; adult/reduced €8/5.50; ⏰10am-6pm Thu-Tue Apr-Oct, to 5pm Nov-Mar), which has been showcasing Murano's glass-making prowess since 1861.

**The Drive »** Ironically the first 8km of the drive, from Venice to the Brenta Canal's most romantic villa, is the least attractive part of this route, which takes you through the industrial wastelands of Mestre along the SS11. For Villa Pisani and Villa Foscarini Rossi continue a further 19km on the gradually more scenic Via Nazionale through Mira and Dolo.

TRIP HIGHLIGHT

## 3 Brenta Riviera

Every 13 June for 300 years, summer officially kicked off with a traffic jam along the Grand Canal, as a flotilla of fashionable Venetians headed to their villas along the Brenta Riviera. Eighty villas still strike elegant poses, although private ownership and privacy hedges leave much to the imagination. Just four of them are open to the public as museums.

The most romantic of the four is the Palladio-designed, 1555–60 **Villa Foscari** (www.lamalcontenta.com; Via dei Turisti 9, Malcontenta; adult/reduced €10/8; ⏰9am-noon Tue & Sat May-Oct), also known as 'La Malcontenta' for the grand dame of the Foscari clan allegedly exiled here for adultery. Further down river, at Stra, **Villa Pisani Nazionale** (www.villapisani.beniculturali.it; Via Doge Pisani 7; adult/reduced €10/7.50, grounds only €7.50/5; ⏰9am-5pm Tue-Sun, to 8pm Apr-Sep) provides a Versailles-like reminder with its 114 rooms, vast gardens and reflecting pools.

Well-heeled Venetians wouldn't dream of decamping to the Brenta without their favourite cobblers, sparking a local tradition of high-end shoemaking. Their art is commemorated with a Shoemakers' Museum in **Villa Foscarini Rossi** (www.villafoscarini.it; Via Doge Pisani 1/2, Stra; admission €5; ⏰9am-1pm & 2.30-6pm Mon-Fri, 2.30-6pm Sat & Sun Apr-Oct, 9am-1pm Mon-Fri Nov-Mar).

p165

**The Drive »** From Stra it is a short 16km drive through the Padovan periphery into Padua. Leave Stra northwest on Via Venezia, cross beneath the A4 autostrada and follow the road round to merge with the Tangenziale Nord into Padua.

## 4 Padua

The Brenta Canal once ran right through Padua, 40km west of Venice. It made things a lot more convenient for Padua-bound Venetians when the city came under Venetian dominion in 1405. Venetian governors set up house in the triple-decker, Gothic **Palazzo della Ragione** (Piazza delle Erbe; adult/reduced €4/2; ⏰9am-7pm Tue-Sun, to 6pm Nov-Jan), its

### TOP TIP: CRUISING THE VENETIAN RIVIERA

You can travel the entire length of the Brenta Canal on **Il Burchiello** (☎049 820 69 10; www.ilburchiello.it; full-day adult €71-84, reduced €56, half-day adult/reduced €51/40), a luxury barge that lets you watch 50 villas drift by from velvet couches. Full-day cruises leave from Venice's Stazione Maritima (Tuesday, Thursday and Saturday) or from Padua (Wednesday, Friday and Sunday).

vast main hall frescoed by Giotto acolytes Giusto de' Menabuoi and Nicolò Mireto.

One illustrious Venetian, general Erasmo da Narni (aka Gattamelata or 'Honeyed Cat'), is commemorated with a bronze equestrian statue in front of the epic **Basilica di Sant'Antonio** (www.basilicadelsanto.org; Piazza del Santo; ⌚6.30am-7.45pm, to 6.45pm Nov-Mar). It was cast in 1453, and was the first life-size casting since antiquity. Not far from Gattamelata is the **Oratorio di San Giorgio** (Piazza del Santo; admission €4; ⌚9am-12.30pm & 2.30-5pm, to 7pm Apr-Sep), where Titian's 1511 portrait of St Anthony shows him calmly reattaching his own foot.

By now it will be clear that Padua's place in the history of art is a distinguished one. The presence of the university at **Palazzo Bo** attracted big names such as Giotto, Fra Filippo Lippi, Donatello and even Mantegna. Padua was also the birthplace of Palladio, and Antonio Canova sculpted his first marble here for the **Prato della Valle**. See the original in the **Musei Civici agli Eremitani** (Piazza Eremitani 8; museum adult/reduced/under 6yr €10/8/free, free with Scrovegni Chapel; ⌚9am-7pm Tue-Sun), along with Giotto's heavenly vision in the **Scrovegni Chapel** (www.cappelladegliscrovegni.it; Giardini dell'Arena; adult/reduced €13/8; ⌚9am-7pm, by reservation only).

## LOCAL KNOWLEDGE: THE MUSIC OF VENICE

Musician and director Gianantonio de Vincenzo says 'To enjoy concerts, first you have to find them – but our idea with **Venezia Suona** (www.veneziasuona.it) is to have wonderful concerts find people wherever they are. We've invited international musicians to play inside boats, at deserted-island army barracks, even on top of the Tronchetto parking garage. That's the ugliest place in Venice, but for one afternoon, it was glorious.'

✕ p165

**The Drive »** Leave Padua following signs for Verona and the A4 autostrada for the 42km drive northwest to Vicenza. Although the A4 is heavily trafficked, as you leave Padua behind you the road becomes more scenic and you'll spy the Euganean hills to the south.

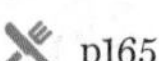

TRIP HIGHLIGHT

### 5 Vicenza

When Andrea Palladio moved from Padua to Vicenza he began to produce some extraordinary buildings marrying sophistication and rustic simplicity, reverent classicism and bold innovation. Stretch your legs on our Palladio walk for a quick, but astonishing, summary of his finest works (p166). His showstopper, **La Rotonda** (www.villalarotonda.it; Via della Rotonda 45; admission villa/gardens €10/5; ⌚gardens 10am-noon & 3-6pm Tue-Sun, villa Wed & Sat only, mid-Mar–mid-Nov), sits on a hill overlooking the city, its namesake dome and identical colonnaded facades giving it the ultimate classical proportions.

Walk up the narrow path opposite to **Villa Valmarana 'ai Nani'** (www.villavalmarana.com; Stradella dei Nani 8; admission €8; ⌚10am-noon & 3-6pm Tue-Sun Apr-Oct, 10am-noon & 2.30-5pm Sat & Sun Nov-Mar), which is nicknamed for the 17 dwarfs ('ai Nani') who guard the garden walls. In 1757 the entire interior was redecorated with frescoes by Giambattista Tiepolo and his son Giandomenico.

🛏 p165

**The Drive »** Pushing away from the autostrada, northwards towards Bassano del Grappa, the scenery becomes decidedly rural, passing through vineyards, cornfields and small towns. Drive 7km northeast on the SS53 and just past Baracchino turn left onto the SP52 for the final 14km to Bassano del Grappa.

Classic Trip

## WHY THIS IS A CLASSIC TRIP

PAULA HARDY, AUTHOR

**This trip is a fantastic combination of grand-slam sites and delightful out-of-the-way surprises. Venice's marble palaces and Giotto's groundbreaking frescoes in the Scrovegni Chapel are understandably world famous, but who knows about the 1500 pairs of historic shoes in Villa Foscarini Rossi or the floor-to-ceiling frescoes at Villa Valmarana and Villa Maser? They are quite wonderful, and what's more you'll often have them all to yourself.**

Top: Treviso district
Left: *Castelfranco Madonna* by Giorgione, Castelfranco Veneto
Right: Bassano del Grappa

CHROMORANGE/GETTY IMAGES ©

## 6 Bassano del Grappa

Bassano del Grappa sits with charming simplicity on the banks of the river Brenta as it winds its way free from Alpine foothills. It is broached by the **Ponte degli Alpini**, Palladio's 1569 covered bridge. Fragile as it seems it is cleverly designed to withstand the rush of spring meltwaters from Monte Grappa. It's always been critical in times of war: Napoleon bivouacked here for many months and in the Great War hundreds of soldiers died on the slopes of Monte Grappa, where Ernest Hemingway drove his ambulance and came to town after the conflict to write *A Farewell to Arms*.

The town is also famous for its after-dinner firewater, grappa, which was invented here. At the **Poli Museo della Grappa** (www.poligrappa.com; Via Gamba 6; admission free; 9am-7.30pm) you can explore four centuries of production and enjoy a free tasting.

**The Drive »** The 18km drive along the SS248 from Bassano to Asolo passes through small towns and large, flat fields. Just past Oné you'll enter the lower reaches of Asolo; turn left at the sign and climb the cypress-clad hillside to the historic centre. For Villa Maser continue a further 5km on the SS248.

TRIP HIGHLIGHT

### 7 Asolo

East of Bassano rises Asolo, known as the 'town of 100 vistas' for its panoramic hillside location. It was once the haunt of the Romans and a personal gift from Venice to Caterina, 15th-century queen of Cyprus, in exchange for her abdication. A historic hit with writers, poet Robert Browning bought a house here and named his last work *Asolando* (1889). Try to catch the **antiques market**, held every second Sunday of the month.

Beneath Asolo's forested hilltop Palladio and Veronese conspired to create the Veneto's finest monument to *la bea vita* at **Villa Maser** (www.villadimaser.it; adult/reduced €6/5; ⌚10am-6pm Apr-Jun, Sep & Oct, Tue, Thu, Sat & Sun Nov-Mar, Jul & Aug). Palladio set the arcaded villa into a verdant hillside, while inside Veronese imagined an Arcadian idyll in his floor-to-ceiling trompe l'oeil frescoes.

✕ p165

**The Drive ››** Descend from Asolo's sylvan heights and zigzag across the SS248 onto the SP6 towards Castelfranco Veneto for a 20km drive south through the small towns of San Vito, Riese Pio X and Vallà.

### 8 Castelfranco Veneto

Giorgio Barbarelli da Castelfranco (aka Giorgione) was one of the great masters of the High Renaissance, and one of its most mysterious. Born in Castelfranco he was a contemporary of Titian but an early death from the plague in 1510 left an adoring public with just six acclaimed canvases. Like Titian, with whom he worked on the frescoes of Fondaco dei Tedeschi in Venice, he is credited with revolutionising Renaissance painting, freeing it from its linear constraints and using a refined chiaroscuro technique called *sfumato* ('smokey') to blur hard lines and enhance the emotional quality of the colour, light and perspective.

Luckily for Castelfranco, one of his few surviving works, an altarpiece known as *Castelfranco Madonna*, still hangs in the Cappella Costanza in the **Duomo** (Vicolo del Christo 10; ⌚9am-noon Mon-Fri). More of the Giorgione school of work can be viewed in the **Casa di Giorgione** (www.museocasagiorgione.it; Piazza San Liberale; adult/reduced €5/3; ⌚10am-12.30pm & 3-6.30pm Tue-Sat, 10am-7pm Sun).

**The Drive ››** At Castelfranco Veneto you're back on the SS53 again. This time heading 27km further east towards Treviso. Pass through Vedelago and on through flat, flat fields of corn to Istrana, Paese and then Treviso.

### 9 Treviso

Totally outdone by supermodel *La Serenissima*, Treviso seems becalmed beyond the tourist mayhem, its quiet canals, weeping willows and frescoed facades the backdrop to another midsized Italian town. So why drop in? Well, Treviso has made a handsome contribution to human happiness, giving us De' Longhi appliances, Pinarello bicycles, *radicchio Trevisano* (red radicchio in season from December through February) and Italy's favourite dessert, tiramisu. You can trace its provenance back to **Antico Ristorante alle Beccherie** (☎0422 54 08 71; Piazza Ancilotto 1; ⌚lunch Tue-Sun), where the coffee-soaked dessert was allegedly designed as a pick-me-up for city prostitutes.

You can also cycle along the river Sile and gaze on Titian's *Annunciation* in the **Duomo** (Piazza del Duomo; ⌚9am-noon & 3.30-6.30pm), but the best reason to come to Treviso is to shop and eat. What better way to end a tour of the Veneto?

p165

# Eating & Sleeping

## Venice 1

**Venissa** — Modern Venetian €€€
(☎041 527 22 81; www.venissa.it; Fondamenta Santa Caterina 3, Mazzorbo; ⏲ noon-3pm & 7-9.30pm Tue-Sun) The stars (including the Michelin variety) are aligning over Venissa in Mazzorbo, the garden island where anything grows – and you can practically eat the landscape in Paola Budel's bowl of breadcrumb gnocchi, bobbing in a broth of fennel and asparagus.

**Oltre Il Giardino** — B&B €€€
(☎041 275 00 15; www.oltreilgiardino-venezia.com; Fondamenta Contarini, San Polo 2542; d €150-350; ❄ @) Originally home to Alma Mahler, widow of Austrian composer Gustav, this 1920s country house brims with historic charm and modern comforts: marquetry composer's desks, flat-screen TVs and Bulgari bath products.

## Brenta Riviera 3

**Da Conte** — Modern Italian €
(☎041 47 95 71; Via Caltana 133, Mira; meals €10-15; ⏲ dinner Tue-Sat) An unlikely bastion of sophistication lodged practically underneath an overpass, Da Conte has one of the best wine lists in the region, and offers creative takes on classic lagoon cuisine, such as roasted quail.

## Padua 4

**Godenda** — Wine Bar €€
(☎049 877 41 92; www.godenda.it; Via Squarcione 4/6; meals €30-50; ⏲10am-3pm & 7pm-1am Mon-Sat, closed Aug) The menu changes with the seasons at this elegant wine bar, with creative takes on old Venetian classics, such as a sublime monkfish with fava beans and house-made pasta sprinkled with jerked horse meat.

## Vicenza 5

**Relais Ca' Muse** — Design Hotel €€
(☎0444 37 64 43; www.camuse.it; Via Valle 62, Sovizzo; d from €140; P ❄ @ 🛜 ≋) Impossible to categorise, this gallery/hotel/social experiment in an old stone farmhouse is well worth the 15-minute drive from Vicenza for its serene rooms, remarkable and racy collection of contemporary art and well-tended grounds.

## Asolo 7

**Villa Cipriani** — Hotel Restaurant €€€
(☎0423 52 34 11; www.villaciprianiasolo.com; Via Canova 298; meals €60; ⏲12.30-2.30pm & 8-10.30pm) The Ciprianis behind this Renaissance villa are the same as those in Venice, and they are just the latest in a long line of illustrious owners, including the Guinnesses, Galantis and poet Robert Browning. Now you, too, can enjoy the perfumed garden and dine overlooking cypress-cloaked Asolo.

## Treviso 9

**Antico Morer** — Seafood €€
(☎0423 52 34 11; www.ristoranteanticomorer.com; Via Jacopo Riccati 28; meals €35-40; ⏲12.30-2.30pm & 8-10.30pm) Dine beneath the mulberry tree, after which the restaurant takes its name, on the finest seafood in Treviso, including the grand raw platter, which Gaetano selects at the market every day.

**Maison Matilda** — B&B €€€
(☎0422 58 22 12; www.maisonmatilda.com; Via Jacopo Riccati 44; d €190-350; P 🛜) This darkly beautiful town house is the perfect display of contemporary Italian design, from its Carrara marble bathrooms and deco bedrooms to its sleek modernist furniture.

# STRETCH YOUR LEGS VICENZA

**Start/Finish** Teatro Olimpico

**Distance** 3km

**Duration** 1½ hours

When Palladio escaped an oppressive employer in his native Padua, few knew the humble stonecutter would transform not only his adoptive city of Vicenza, but also the history of European architecture. It's no wonder Vicenza has been declared one grand Unesco World Heritage Site.

Take this walk on Trip

13



## Teatro Olimpico

Palladio's **Teatro Olimpico** (www.olimpico.vicenza.it; Piazza Matteotti 11; combined ticket with Museo Civico adult/reduced €8.50/6.50; ⏲9am-5pm Tue-Sun), which he began in 1580, was inspired by Roman amphitheatres. Vincenzo Scamozzi finished the theatre, adding a stage set modelled on the ancient Greek city of Thebes; check online for opera, jazz and classical performances. The ticket also gets you into the Museo Civico.

**The Walk ››** Pick up the main Corso Palladio and walk southwest. Then turn right up Contrà Santa Corona, and proceed past the red-brick Dominican church. Shortly afterwards you'll arrive at the Gallerie di Palazzo Leoni Montanari on your left.

## Gallerie di Palazzo Leoni Montanari

Outside it may look like a bank, but a treasure beyond accountants' imagining awaits inside the **Gallerie di Palazzo Leoni Montanari** (www.palazzomontanari.com; Contrà Santa Corona 25; adult/reduced €5/4; ⏲10am-6pm Tue-Sun). Grand salons are adorned with Canaletto's lagoon landscapes and Pietro Longhi 18th-century society satires. Up another flight, 400 Russian icons are spotlit in darkened galleries.

**The Walk ››** Retrace your steps to Corso Palladio and walk its length, lined with mansions and notable buildings. Turn right up Via Fogazzaro and after a short distance arrive in Piazza San Lorenzo.

## Tempio di San Lorenzo

Not everything in Vicenza is Palladian, not least the **Tempio di San Lorenzo** (Piazza San Lorenzo). In the Middle Ages Franciscan friars tended to the sick here and guarded the relics of St Lawrence. Now the facade is a Gothic extravagance. Sadly much of the interior decoration was damaged when Napoleon's troops set up barracks here, although the flower-filled 14th-century cloister remains.

**The Walk ››** Make your way back to Corso Palladio via Contrà Cordenons and turn right. A short walk further west will bring you to the end

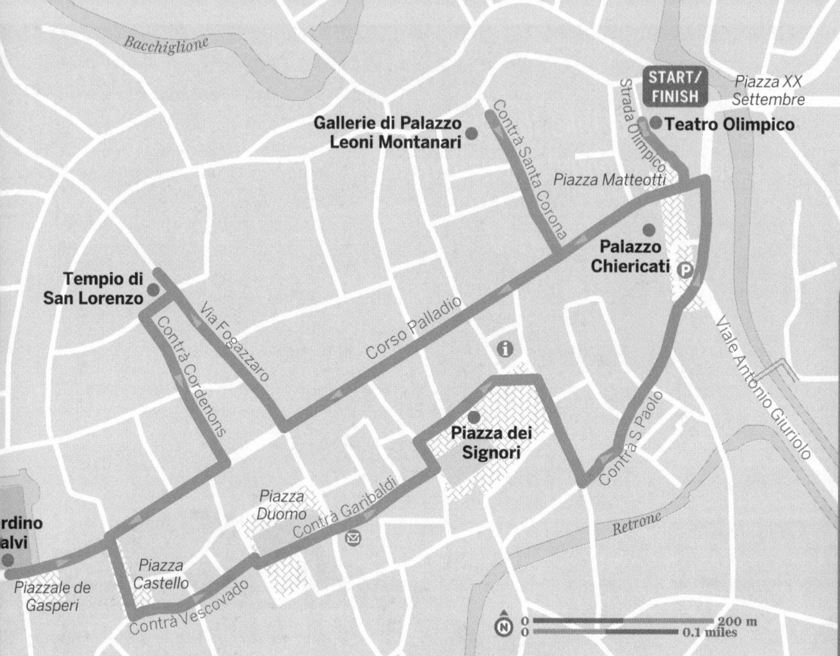


of the Corso in front of Torrione di Porta Castello. Pass under it to the gardens.

## Giardino Salvi

Just beyond the city walls, Luigi Valmarana commissioned the **Giardino Salvi** (Corso S Felice) as a meeting place for intellectuals and academics. Silver firs, Himalayan cedars and tulip trees line its neatly tended lawns, which sit between two Palladian lodges: the **Loggia Longhena**, built by Baldassare Longhena, and the **Loggia Valmarana**, a Doric temple, attributed to a student of Andrea Palladio.

**The Walk »** Head south, through morning market stalls, out of Piazza Castello on Contrà Vescovado. After a few steps you'll pass through Piazza Duomo and continue along Contrà Garibaldi until you reach Piazza dei Signori.

## Piazza dei Signori

The heart of historic Vicenza is Piazza dei Signori, where Palladio lightens the mood of government buildings with his trademark play of light and shadow. Dazzling white Piovene stone arches frame shady double arcades in the **Basilica Palladiana**. Across the piazza, white stone and stucco grace the exposed red-brick colonnade of the 1571-designed **Loggia del Capitaniato**.

**The Walk »** From Piazza dei Signori head south and pick up Contrà S Paolo, which bears left (northeast) back to Piazza Matteotti.

## Palazzo Chiericati

Built in 1550, Palazzo Chiericati is one of Palladio's finest buildings and now houses the **Museo Civico** (www.museicivicivicenza.it; Piazza Matteotti 37/39; combined ticket with Teatro Olimpico adult/reduced €8.50/6.50; ⌚9am-5pm Tue-Sun). The frescoed ground floor includes the Sala dal Firmamento (Salon of the Skies), with Domenico Brusasorci's ceiling fresco of Diana galloping across the sky to meet the sun.

**The Walk »** Exit the *palazzo* onto Piazza Matteotti and you'll see the Teatro Olimpico to your left at the end of the square.

**Collio** Take the high road across this mountainous terrain

CARLO ZUSTOVI/GETTY IMAGES ©

# Trieste to Tarvisio

*Meander the borderlands from Trieste to Tarvisio and you'll find an amazing reserve of historical sights amid the Alpine hillsides. So kick back with the locals and toast this curious corner of Italy.*

## TRIP HIGHLIGHTS

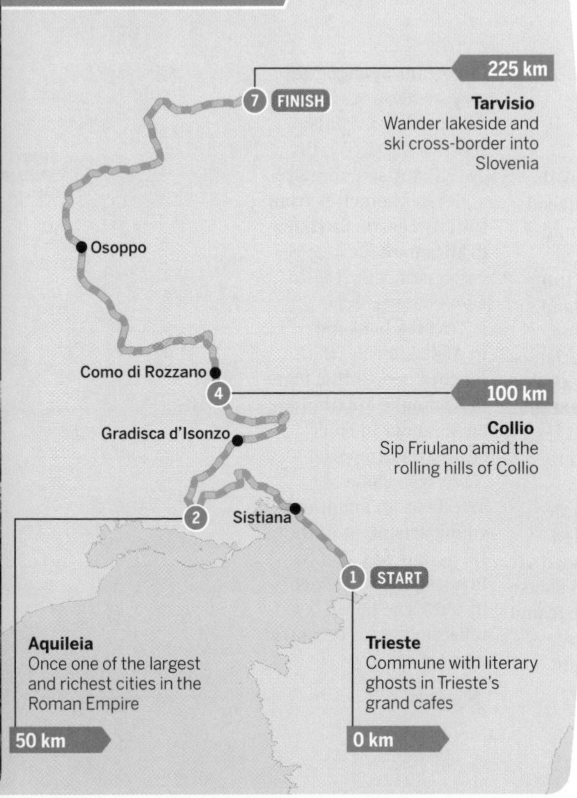

7 FINISH
225 km
**Tarvisio**
Wander lakeside and ski cross-border into Slovenia

Osoppo

Como di Rozzano

4
100 km
**Collio**
Sip Friulano amid the rolling hills of Collio

Gradisca d'Isonzo

2
Sistiana

1 START

**Aquileia**
Once one of the largest and richest cities in the Roman Empire
50 km

**Trieste**
Commune with literary ghosts in Trieste's grand cafes
0 km

**7 DAYS**
**225KM / 140 MILES**

### GREAT FOR...

### BEST TIME TO GO

May to October for fine weather and the grape harvest.

### ESSENTIAL PHOTO

Mosaic sea monsters and songbirds at Aquileia.

### BEST CULTURE

A true borderland: multilingual, multicultural and historically fascinating.

# 14 Trieste to Tarvisio

With its triple-barrelled moniker, Friuli Venezia Giulia's multicultural nature should come as no surprise on this tour of the region. Starting in the capital Trieste, the home of Habsburg princes and for centuries Austria's seaside salon, climb the steep plateau to Cividale, the city of Julius Caesar, eavesdrop on multilingual gossip in Gorizia, drink Hungarian-style Tocai in Collio and end in the Giulie Alps where you can ski into Slovenia.

TRIP HIGHLIGHT

### 1 Trieste

From as long ago as the 1300s, Trieste has faced east. It flourished under Habsburg patronage between 1382 and 1918, attracting writers and philosophers such as Thomas Mann and James Joyce to the busy cafes on **Piazza dell Unità d'Italia**, where they enjoyed the city's fluid character where Latin, Slavic, Jewish and Germanic culture intermingled.

The neighbourhood of **Borgo Teresiano** reflects this cultural melange and on Via San Francesco d'Assisi you can tour Trieste's nationally important **Synagogue** (www.triestebraica.it; Via San Francesco d'Assisi 19; admission €3.50; guided tours 10am, 11am & noon Sun).

Seven kilometres from the city centre, **Castello di Miramare** (www.castello-miramare.it; adult/reduced €6/4; 9am-6.30pm) is Trieste's bookend to Austrian rule, the fanciful neo-Gothic home of Archduke Maximilian, commander in chief of Austria's Imperial Navy, who came to Trieste as an ambitious young aristocrat in the 1850s and was shot by firing squad in Mexico in 1867. The house is a reflection of his eccentric wanderlust.

p175

AUSTRIA
Villach
E55
Arnoldstein
Tarvisio
7
FINISH
A23
Laghi di Fusine
Krajnska Gora
Vršič Pass (1611m)
Sella Nevea
Chiusaforte
Monte Canin (2587m)
Mt Triglav (2864m)
Bovec
Lake Bohinj
Ukanc
Ribčev Laz
Kobarid
Mt Vogel (1922m)
Tolmin
Most na Soči
Ronchis
Cividale del Friuli
San Leonardo
5
SS54
SLOVENIA
SS356
Como di Rozzano
Soča
Nova Gorica
Collio
4
San Lorenzo Isontino
Cormòns
3
Gorizia
SS56
Natisone
Ajdovščina
Palmanova
Gradisca d'Isonzo
Cervignano del Fruli
SS351
Redipuglia
A4
Monfalcone
SS352
2
Aquileia
Sistiana
SS14
Isonzo
Laguna di Grado
Sežana
Villa Opicina
Golfo di Trieste
Grado
Trieste
1
START
E61
Muggia
Adriatic Sea
Izola
Koper
E751
Portorož
CROATIA

**The Drive »** Head northwest out of Trieste along Viale Miramare (SS14), where you'll keep sea views to your left for almost 20km. At Sistiana join the A4 (towards Venice) for 18km to Redipuglia. Then exit southwest towards Papariano and Aquileia for the final 16km through rural farmland.

TRIP HIGHLIGHT

## 2 Aquileia

Colonised by Rome in 181 BC, Aquileia was one of the largest and richest cities of the empire. Levelled by Attila's Huns in AD 452, the city's inhabitants fled south and west where they founded Grado and then Venice. A smaller town rose in its place in the early Middle Ages with the construction of the present **basilica** (Piazza Capitolo; admission free;

### LINK YOUR TRIP

#### 12 Grande Strada delle Dolomiti

Just after Osoppo exit the A23 for Tolmezzo and weave your way along the SS52 to Cortina d'Ampezzo and the Dolomites beyond (p145).

#### 13 A Venetian Sojourn

From Aquileia hop onto the A4 for a fast ride down to the Venetian lagoon, where golden domes and frescoed palaces await (p157).

9am-6pm Mon-Sat, 10-11.15am Sun), which is carpeted with one of the largest and most spectacular Roman-era mosaics in the world.

Beyond the basilica explore the scattered ruins of the **Porto Fluviale**, the old port, and the standing columns of the ancient **Forum** on Via Giulia Augusta. Then visit the **Museo Archeologico Nazionale** (Via Roma 1; adult/reduced €4/2; 8.30am-7.30pm Tue-Sun) for one of Italy's most important collections of Roman artefacts.

 p175

**The Drive »** Exit Aquileia north on the SS352 and after 3km veer off northeast onto the SS351 through open farmland towards Gradisca d'Isonzo. Then cross the broad Isonzo river before merging with Via Raccordo Villese-Gorizia after 10km. Drive a further 15km before exiting on the SS55 into Gorizia.

### 3 Gorizia

An often-contested border zone and the scene of some of the most bitter fighting of WWI's eastern front, Gorizia was, most recently, an Iron Curtain checkpoint. Its crumbling fences and watchtowers can still be seen on **Piazza Transalpina**, which since 2007 has marked the Slovenian border.

For a salutary lesson in its bloody past visit the imposing **castello** (Borgo Castello 36; adult/child €3/free; 9.30am-1pm & 3-7.30pm Tue-Sun Apr-Oct, 9.30am-6pm Tue-Sun Nov-Mar) and the **Museo della Grande Guerra** (adult/child €3.50/free; 9am-7pm Tue-Sun), which charts the tragic story of WWI, when Gorizia sat on the Italian-Austrian frontline.

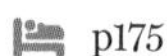 p175

**The Drive »** The short 14km trip to Cormòns is a very pretty rural drive. Exit Gorizia westwards on Via Udine and then turn off northwards on the SS56 at San Lorenzo Isontino. From here it's a 7km drive through vineyards to Cormòns.

TRIP HIGHLIGHT

### 4 Collio

Famed for its winemakers and country restaurants, the Collio produces some of the finest, mineral-rich white wines in Italy from local varietals such as Friulano, Malvasia Istriana and Ribolla Gialla. The area's vineyards are arranged like a quilt around the town of **Cormòns**, where the local wine shop, **Enoteca di Cormòns** (0481 63 03 71; www.enoteca-cormons.it; Piazza XXIV Maggio 21; 11am-10pm Wed-Mon), offers tastings with platters of Montasio cheese.

Even in high season, it is easy to drop in to dozens of family-run wineries and taste rare vintages with vintners such as **Renato Keber** (0481 63 98 44; www.renatokeber.com; Località Zegla 15). Larger vineyards, offering international export, are **Venica & Venica** (0481 6 12 64; www.venica.it; Località Cerò 8, Dolegna del Collio).

If you feel peckish, drop into **La Subida** (0481 6 05 31; www.lasubida.it; Località Monte, Cormòns; meals €30-50; lunch & dinner Sat & Sun,

**TOP TIP: SKI PASSES**

Multiday passes (two/four/six days from €44/80/114) enable you to ski in Italy, Slovenia and Austria, on the slopes of Sella Nevea, Tarvisio, Zoncolan, Bovec, Krajnska Gora and Arnoldstein.

The Monte Canin ski lift is free to Friuli Venezia Giulia Card holders; this regional discount card entitles card holders to discounts on multiday passes and equipment hire. **Promotur** (0428 65 39 15; www.promotur.org; Camporosso, Tarvisio) sells passes at each of the resorts and they cost €15/20 for 48/72 hours.

WESTEND61/GETTY IMAGES ©

**Aquileia** Take in the picturesque surrounds by bike

dinner Mon, Thu & Fri), where border-crossing dishes and ingredients bring the landscape to the plate.

p175

**The Drive »** The next 16km to Cividale del Friuli are the most scenic on the trip. Rolling northwards from Cormòns on a country lane through the vineyards on the SS356, you'll pass through small villages such as Como di Rozzano, where Perusini offers tastings and farmhouse accommodation.

## 5 Cividale del Friuli

Founded by Julius Caesar in 50 BC as Forum de Lulii (ultimately 'Friuli'), Cividale's picturesque stone streets are worth a morning's quiet contemplation. Splitting the town in two is the **Ponte del Diavolo** (Devil's Bridge), its central arch supported by a huge rock said to have been thrown into the river by the devil.

Cividale's most important sight is the **Tempietto Longobardo** (Borgo Brossano; adult/reduced €6/4; ⌚9.30am-12.30pm & 3-5pm, to 6.30pm summer). Dating from the 8th century AD, its frescoes and ancient Lombard woodwork are both unusual and extremely moving. Your ticket also gives you access to the **Museo Cristiano** (Piazza del Duomo; ⌚10am-1pm & 3-6pm Wed-Sun) in the cathedral, where you can see the 8th-century, stone Altar of Ratchis.

**The Drive »** Wend your way out of Cividale across the Natisone river on Via Fiore dei Liberti. To your right you'll get a great view of the Ponte del Diavolo. Then take a hard left onto Viale Udine, which becomes the SS54 and carries you 18km to Udine.

## 6 Udine

While reluctantly ceding its premier

## DETOUR: SAN DANIELE DEL FRIULI

**Start: 6 Udine**

Just northwest of Udine, on the SS463, San Daniele del Friuli sits in an undulating landscape. Its 8000 inhabitants prepare Friuli's greatest gastronomic export, the dark, exquisitely sweet Prosciutto di San Daniele. Salt is the only method of preservation allowed and the 27 *prosciuttifici* (ham-curing plants) in the town are safeguarded by EU regulations. Try it at Ai Bintars (p175).

In August, the town holds the Aria di Festa, a four-day festival of open house tours and tastings. For a list of *prosciuttifici* that are open year-round, see the **tourist office** (☎0432 94 07 65; Piazza Pellegrino 4; ⏰9am-1pm & 2-6pm Mon-Fri, 11am-1pm & 4.30-6.30pm Sat & Sun).

status to Trieste in the 1950s, Udine remains the spiritual, and gastronomic, capital of Friuli. At the heart of its walled medieval centre sits the **Piazza della Libertà**, dubbed the most beautiful Venetian square on the mainland.

Other Venetian echoes can be seen in the shimmering Tiepolo frescoes in the **cathedral** (admission free; ⏰9am-noon & 4-6pm Tue-Sat, 4-6pm Sun) and the **Oratorio della Purità** (Piazza del Duomo), open for guided tours only. The *Assumption* on the ceiling was one of Giambattista's very first commissions, while the eight biblical scenes in chiaroscuro are by his son Giandomenico. For more Tiepolos and rare views of the city framed by the Alps beyond, walk up the hill to the **castle**. Local legend has it that when Attila the Hun plundered Aquileia in AD 452, he ordered his soldiers to build the hill from where he could witness its destruction. Now it houses the **Galleria d'Arte Antica** (☎0432 27 15 91; adult/child €3/1.50, Sun morning free; ⏰9.30am-12.30pm & 3-6pm Tue-Sun).

✕ 🛏 p175

**The Drive »** From Udine join the A23 all the way to Tarvisio. The first 30km continue through the same low-lying rural landscape, with the forested slopes of the Carnic Alps coming into sharp perspective at Osoppo. Here you'll cross the Tagliamento river and sweep eastwards into the Giulie Alps for the remaining 70km to Tarvisio.

TRIP HIGHLIGHT

### 7 Tarvisio

Wedged into the Val Canale between the Giulie and eastern Carnic Alps, Tarvisio is just 7km short of the Austrian border and 11km from Slovenia.

Despite its modest elevations, this is the snowiest (and coldest) pocket in the whole Alpine region, with heavy snowfalls not uncommon into May. The main ski centres are at Tarvisio, with a good open 4km run that promises breathtaking views, and 60km of cross-country tracks; and at **Sella Nevea** (www.sellanevea.net). Sella Nevea is linked to Bovec in Slovenia. In summer the hiking, caving, canoeing and windsurfing are all good, especially around the **Laghi di Fusine** (Fusine Lakes).

🛏 p175

# Eating & Sleeping

## Trieste 1

### Caffè Tommaseo — Cafe €

(www.caffetommaseo.com; Riva III Novembre; meals €22; 8am-12.30am) Virtually unchanged since its 1830 opening, the richly moulded ceilings, primrose-yellow walls and Viennese mirrors here couldn't be more evocative.

## Aquileia 2

### Taberna Marciani Aquileia — Tavern €

(www.tabernamarciani.com; Via Roma 10; meals €10-15; daily) The bearded crew holding up the bar might look, and act, like they are in a touring band, but they're more likely archaeologists from the nearby dig. Popular for plates of local meats and cheese and good wine by the glass.

## Gorizia 3

### Palazzo Lantieri — Palazzo €€

(0481 53 32 84; www.palazzo-lantieri.com; Piazza Sant'Antonio 6; s €100, d €140-150, apt €200-220; P) Owned by the Lantieris since 1450, this enormous *palazzo* (mansion) forms part of Gorizia's defensive walls and was originally moated. Grand, antique-filled rooms creak with history and overlook a Persian-style garden.

## Collio 4

### Terra e Vini — Winery €€

(0481 6 00 28; www.terraevini.it; meals €28-55; Via XXIV Maggio, Brazzano di Cormons; lunch Tue-Sun, dinner Tue-Sat) The Felluga family is Friulian wine royalty. Their 19th-century *osteria* (casual tavern) looks over the plantings. Feast on tripe on Thursdays, salt cod on Fridays and Gorizia asparagus or goose any day of the week.

### Perusini — Agriturismo €€

(0432 67 50 18; www.perusini.com; Via del Torrione 13, Località Gramogliano; 1-bedroom apt €75-95, 2-bedroom apt €140-160; P) Make yourself at home amid the vines on the Perusini estate. Sympathetically renovated farm buildings now offer a range of self-catering accommodation. At the weekend, dine overlooking the valley in the estate's restaurant, **Al Postiglione** (0432 75 90 22; Fri-Sun).

## Udine 6

### Trattoria ai Frati — Trattoria, Friulian €€

(0432 50 69 26; Piazzetta Antonini 5; meals €25-30; Mon-Sat) An old-style eatery on a cobbled cul-de-sac where you can expect such local specialities as *frico* (cheese-and-potato omelette) and pumpkin gnocchi with smoked ricotta.

### Next Hotel Clocchiatti — Design Hotel €€

(0432 50 50 47; www.hotelclocchiatti.it; Via Cividale 29; s €60-150, d €80-220; P) Two properties, one location: older style (cheaper) rooms are in the original villa, while the contemporary annexe lines up around a pool and outdoor bar. Fresh cakes, Mariage Frères teas and attentive service make breakfast special.

## San Daniele del Friuli

### Ai Bintars — Italian €

(0432 95 73 22; www.aibintars.com; Via Trento Trieste 67; mains €15-25; Fri-Tue; P) No menu, no fuss, no kerbside appeal, Ai Bintars simply serves the best prosciutto and salami alongside small plates of marinated vegetables, local cheeses and generous hunks of bread.

## Tarvisio 7

### Hotel Edelhof — Chalet €€

(0428 4 00 81; www.hoteledelhof.com; Via Armando Diaz 13; s €70-85, d €100-140; P) With its oak-panelled rooms, traditional folk art and furnishings and warm majolica oven heating up the dining room, the Edelhof has an authentic Heidi vibe and a basement spa.

# Central Italy

**AS FLORENCE'S RENAISSANCE SKYLINE FADES INTO THE BACKGROUND THE OPEN ROAD BECKONS.** Motoring through Tuscany's voluptuous, wine-rich hills is one of Italy's great driving experiences and one of the many on offer in this fascinating part of the country.

To the north of Tuscany, Emilia-Romagna is a mecca for foodies, its handsome medieval towns supplying many of Italy's most revered delicacies. Travel to Italy's green, rural heart where you'll come across artistic treasures by Renaissance heroes, ancient Roman ruins and Etruscan tombs.

And all the while the road leads inexorably, often tortuously, towards Rome, the Eternal City.

**Val d'Orcia** This Unesco-listed area boasts sublime landscapes (Trip 22, 23)
DOUGLAS PEARSON/GETTY IMAGES ©

# Central Italy

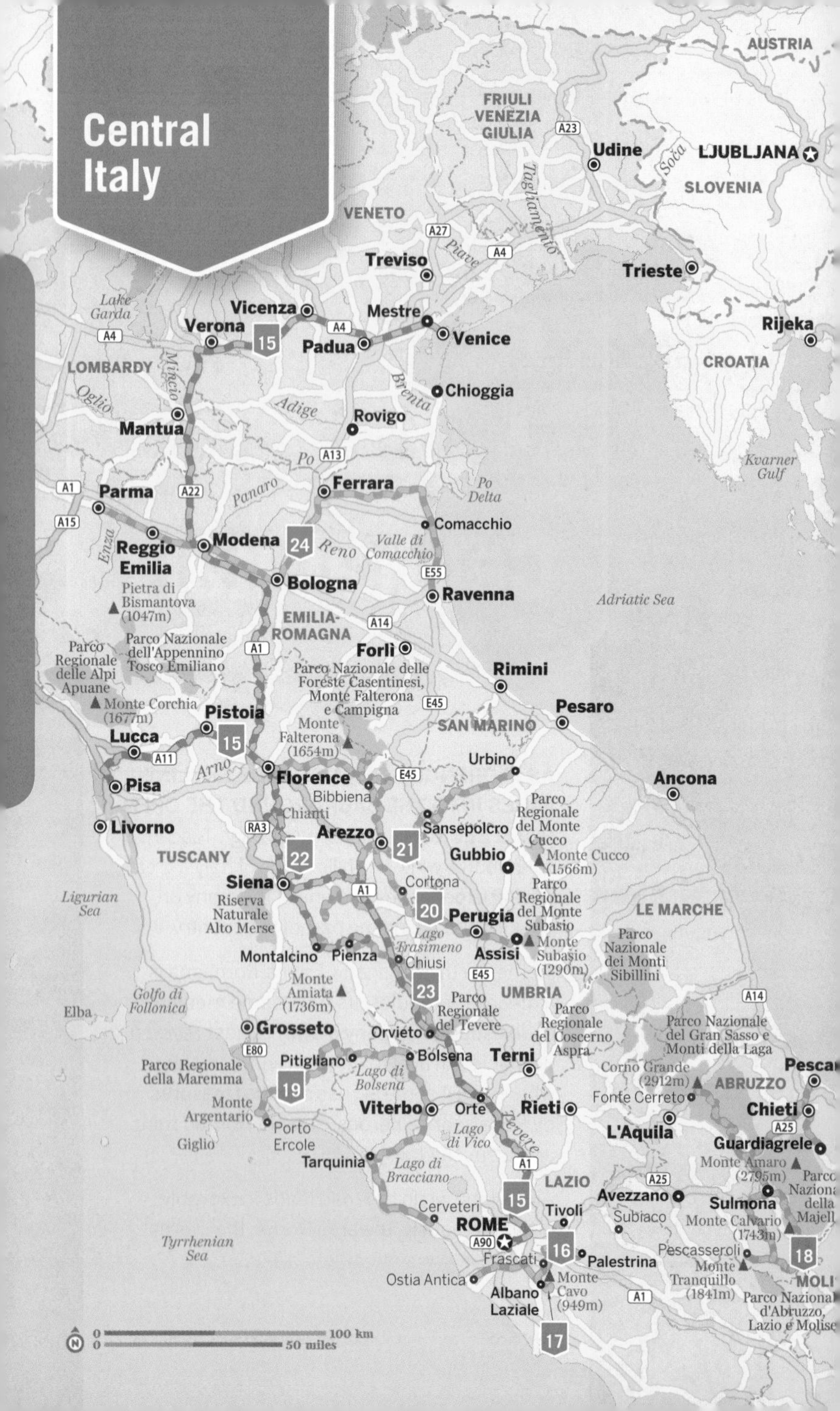

AUSTRIA
FRIULI VENEZIA GIULIA
A23
Udine
LJUBLJANA
Soča
SLOVENIA
Tagliamento
VENETO
A27
Piave
A4
Treviso
Trieste
Lake Garda
Vicenza
Mestre
A4
Verona
15
Padua
Venice
Rijeka
A4
LOMBARDY
Mincio
CROATIA
Brenta
Chioggia
Oglio
Adige
Rovigo
Mantua
Po
A13
Kvarner Gulf
A1
Parma
A22
Panaro
Ferrara
Po Delta
A15
Comacchio
Enza
Reggio Emilia
Modena
24
Reno
Valle di Comacchio
E55
Bologna
Ravenna
Pietra di Bismantova (1047m)
Adriatic Sea
EMILIA-ROMAGNA
A14
Parco Nazionale dell'Appennino Tosco Emiliano
Parco Regionale delle Alpi Apuane
A1
Forlì
Parco Nazionale delle Foreste Casentinesi, Monte Falterona e Campigna
Rimini
Monte Corchia (1677m)
E45
Pesaro
Pistoia
Monte Falterona (1654m)
SAN MARINO
Lucca
15
A11
Urbino
Arno
Florence
E45
Ancona
Pisa
Bibbiena
Parco Regionale del Monte Cucco
Chianti
Livorno
RA3
Sansepolcro
Arezzo
21
TUSCANY
22
Gubbio
Monte Cucco (1566m)
Siena
A1
Cortona
Parco Regionale del Monte Subasio
Ligurian Sea
Riserva Naturale Alto Merse
20
Perugia
LE MARCHE
Lago Trasimeno
Monte Subasio (1290m)
Parco Nazionale dei Monti Sibillini
Montalcino
Pienza
Chiusi
Assisi
E45
Monte Amiata (1736m)
23
UMBRIA
Golfo di Follonica
Parco Regionale del Tevere
Parco Regionale del Coscerno Aspra
A14
Elba
Parco Nazionale del Gran Sasso e Monti della Laga
Grosseto
Orvieto
E80
Bolsena
Terni
Pitigliano
Lago di Bolsena
Corno Grande (2912m)
ABRUZZO
Pescara
Parco Regionale della Maremma
19
Fonte Cerreto
Monte Argentario
Viterbo
Orte
Rieti
Chieti
Tevere
L'Aquila
A25
Porto Ercole
Lago di Vico
Giglio
Guardiagrele
Tarquinia
A1
Monte Amaro (2795m)
Lago di Bracciano
LAZIO
A25
Parco Nazionale della Majella
15
Avezzano
Sulmona
Cerveteri
Tivoli
Subiaco
Monte Calvario (1743m)
ROME
A90
16
Pescasseroli
18
Tyrrhenian Sea
Frascati
Palestrina
Monte Tranquillo (1841m)
MOLISE
Ostia Antica
Monte Cavo (949m)
Albano Laziale
A1
Parco Nazionale d'Abruzzo, Lazio e Molise
17
0 — 100 km
0 — 50 miles
N

*Classic Trip*

**15 World Heritage Wonders 14 Days** From Rome to Venice, discover the Unesco-listed treasures of Italy's art cities. (p181)

**16 Roaming Around Rome 3 Days** Trawl through ancient ruins and hilltop towns in Rome's fascinating hinterland. (p193)

**17 Castelli Romani 2–3 Days** Escape to the verdant hills and volcanic lakes south of Rome. (p201)

**18 Abruzzo's Wild Landscapes 6 Days** Immerse yourself in glorious, untamed nature in Abruzzo's magnificent national parks. (p209)

**19 Etruscan Tuscany & Lazio 3–4 Days** Explore Etruscan tombs and frescoed treasures. (p217)

**20 Monasteries of Tuscany & Umbria 5 Days** Remote sanctuaries, frescoed monasteries and rugged forests. (p225)

**21 Piero della Francesca Trail 7 Days** This classic art trail reveals Renaissance masterpieces and unspoiled Apennine landscapes. (p233)

*Classic Trip*

**22 Tuscan Wine Tour 4 Days** Red wine fuels this jaunt around historic Chianti vineyards and Tuscan cellars. (p243)

**23 Tuscan Landscapes 3–4 Days** From Siena to Orvieto, this trip traverses Tuscany's most scenic landscapes. (p253)

**24 Foodie Emilia-Romagna 7 Days** Enjoy local delicacies and elegant medieval architecture in Emilia-Romagna's gastro cities. (p261)

### Necropolis Tarquinia

The Etruscan tombs at Tarquinia's Unesco-listed Necropolis are a remarkable sight, yet they rarely attract big crowds. Visit on Trip 19

### Santo Stefano di Sessanio

It's a thrilling drive up to this *borgo* (medieval town) in Abruzzo's Parco Nazionale del Gran Sasso e Monti della Laga on Trip 18

### Palazzo Ducale, Urbino

The palatial residence of an art-loving Renaissance aristocrat dominates Urbino's charming historic centre on Trip 21

### Ostia Antica

Overshadowed by the more famous ruins in Rome, one of central Italy's most compelling archaeological sites is visited on Trip 16

### Montalcino

Crowned by a 14th-century fort, this hilltop town is home to one of Italy's top red wines. Indulge yourself on Trip 22

**Roman Forum** *Explore the once-beating heart of the ancient city*

Classic Trip

# World Heritage Wonders

15

*From Rome to Venice, this tour of Unesco World Heritage Sites takes in some of Italy's greatest hits, including the Colosseum and the Leaning Tower of Pisa, and some lesser-known treasures.*

## TRIP HIGHLIGHTS

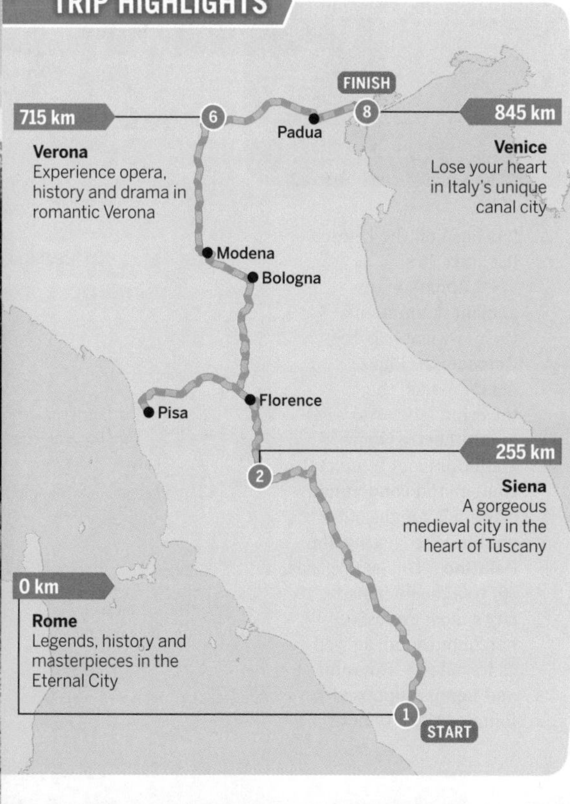

FINISH

715 km

6

Padua

8

845 km

**Verona**
Experience opera, history and drama in romantic Verona

**Venice**
Lose your heart in Italy's unique canal city

Modena

Bologna

Pisa

Florence

255 km

2

**Siena**
A gorgeous medieval city in the heart of Tuscany

0 km

**Rome**
Legends, history and masterpieces in the Eternal City

1

START

**14 DAYS**
**845KM / 525 MILES**

### GREAT FOR...

### BEST TIME TO GO

April, May and September for ideal sightseeing weather and local produce.

### ESSENTIAL PHOTO

Roman Forum from the Palatino.

### BEST FOR RENAISSANCE ART

Florence's Galleria degli Uffizi.

Classic Trip

# 15 World Heritage Wonders

Topping the Unesco charts with 47 World Heritage Sites, Italy offers the full gamut, ranging from historic city centres and man-made masterpieces to snow-capped mountains and areas of outstanding natural beauty. This trip through central and northern Italy touches on the country's unparalleled artistic and architectural legacy, taking in ancient Roman ruins, priceless Renaissance paintings, great cathedrals and, to cap it all off, Venice's unique canal-scape.

TRIP HIGHLIGHT

### 1 Rome

An epic, monumental metropolis, Italy's capital is a city of thrilling beauty and high drama. Its historic centre which, according to Unesco, boasts 'some of the major monuments of antiquity', has been a World Heritage Site since 1980, and the **Vatican**, technically a separate state but in reality located within the city limits of Rome (Roma), has been on the Unesco list since 1984.

Of Rome's many ancient monuments, the most iconic is the **Colosseum** (Piazza del Colosseo), the towering 1st-century-AD amphitheatre where gladiators met in mortal combat and condemned criminals fought off wild beasts. Nearby, the **Palatino** (Via di San Gregorio 30) was the ancient city's most exclusive neighbourhood, as well as its oldest – Romulus and Remus supposedly founded the city here

in 753 BC. From the Palatino, you can descend to the skeletal ruins of the **Roman Forum** (Largo della Salara Vecchia), the once-beating heart of the ancient city. All three sights are covered by a single ticket (adult/ reduced €12/7.50) and are open from 8.30am to one hour before sunset.

To complete your tour of classical wonders search out the **Pantheon** (Piazza della Rotonda; admission free; ⌚8.30am-7.30pm Mon-Sat, 9am-6pm Sun), the best preserved of Rome's ancient monuments. One of the most influential buildings in the world, this domed temple, now church, is an extraordinary sight with its martial portico and soaring interior.

p190

**19 Etruscan Tuscany & Lazio**

From Rome take the A12 autostrada up to Cerveteri and connect with this tour of ancient Etruscan treasures (p217).

**22 Tuscan Wine Tour**

From Florence head south to Tuscany's Chianti wine country to indulge in some wine tasting at the area's historic vineyards (p243).

**The Drive »** The easiest route to Siena, about three hours' away, is via the A1 autostrada. Join this from the Rome ring road, the GRA (Grande Raccordo Anulare), and head north, past Orvieto's dramatic cliff-top cathedral, to the Valdichiano exit. Take this and follow for Siena.

TRIP HIGHLIGHT

## 2 Siena

Siena is one of Italy's most enchanting medieval towns. Its walled centre, a beautifully preserved warren of dark lanes, Gothic *palazzi* (mansions) and pretty piazzas, is centred on **Piazza del Campo** (known as Il Campo), the sloping shell-shaped square that stages the city's annual horse race, Il Palio.

On the piazza, the 102m-high **Torre del Mangia** (admission €8; ⌚10am-7pm Mar–mid-Oct, to 4pm mid-Oct–Feb) soars above the Gothic **Palazzo Pubblico** (Palazzo Comunale), home to the city's finest art museum, the **Museo Civico** (adult/reduced €8/4.50; ⌚10am-7pm). Of Siena's churches, the one to see is the 13th-century **Duomo** (Piazza del Duomo; admission €3; ⌚10.30am-6.30pm Mon-Sat, 1.30-5.30pm Sun), one of Italy's greatest Gothic churches. Highlights include the remarkable white, green and red facade, and, inside, the magnificent inlaid marble floor that illustrates historical and biblical stories.

✕ 🛏 p190

**The Drive »** There are two alternatives to get to Florence. The quickest, which is via the fast RA3 Siena–Firenze Raccordo, takes about 1½ hours. But if you have the time, we recommend the scenic SR222, which snakes through the Chianti wine country, passing through quintessential hilltop towns and vine-laden slopes. Reckon on at least 2½ hours for this route.

## 3 Florence

Cradle of the Renaissance and home of Michelangelo,

### WORLD HERITAGE SITES

With 47 World Heritage Sites, Italy has more than any other country. But what exactly is a World Heritage Site? Basically it's anywhere that Unesco's World Heritage Committee decides is of 'outstanding universal value' and inscribes on the World Heritage List. It could be a natural wonder such as the Great Barrier Reef in Australia or a man-made icon such as New York's Statue of Liberty, a historic city centre or a great work of art or architecture.

The list was set up in 1972 and has since grown to include 962 sites from 157 countries. Italy first got in on the act in 1979 when it successfully nominated its first entry – the prehistoric rock drawings of the Valcamonica valley in northeastern Lombardy. The inscription process requires sites to be nominated by a country and then independently evaluated. If they pass scrutiny and meet at least one of 10 selection criteria, they get the green light at the World Heritage Committee's annual meeting. Once on the list, sites qualify for management support and access to the World Heritage Fund.

Italian nominations have generally fared well and since Rome's historic centre and the Chiesa di Santa Maria delle Grazie in Milan were inscribed in 1980, many of the nation's greatest attractions have made it onto the list – the historic centres of Florence, Naples, Siena and San Gimignano; the cities of Venice, Verona and Ferrara; the archaeological sites of Pompeii, Paestum and Agrigento; as well as natural beauties such as the Amalfi Coast, Aeolian Islands, Dolomites and Tuscany's Val d'Orcia.

Machiavelli and the Medici, Florence (Firenze) is magnetic, romantic, unique and busy. A couple of days is not long here but it's enough for a breathless introduction to the city's top sights.

Towering above the medieval skyline, the **Duomo** (Piazza del Duomo; 10am-5pm Mon-Wed & Fri, to 4.30pm Thu, to 4.45pm Sat, 1.30-4.45pm Sun) dominates the city centre with its famous red-tiled dome and striking facade. A short hop away, **Piazza della Signoria** opens onto the sculpture-filled **Loggia dei Lanzi** and the **Torre d'Arnolfo** above **Palazzo Vecchio** (www.museicivicifiorentini.it; Piazza della Signoria; adult/reduced €6.50/4.50; 9am-7pm Fri-Wed, to 2pm Thu), Florence's lavish City Hall.

Next to the *palazzo*, the **Galleria degli Uffizi** (Uffizi Gallery; www.uffizi.firenze.it; Piazza degli Uffizi 6; adult/reduced €6.50/3.25, plus exhibition supplement; 8.15am-6.50pm Tue-Sun) houses one of the world's great art collections, including works by Botticelli, Leonardo da Vinci, Michelangelo, Raphael and many other Renaissance maestros. For more on the historic centre, flip to our walking tour (p240).

 p190

**The Drive »** From Florence it's about 1½ hours to Pisa along the A11 autostrada. At the end of the motorway, after the toll booth, head left onto Via Aurelia (SS1) and follow signs to Pisa centro.

## 4 Pisa

Once a maritime republic to rival Genoa and Venice, Pisa now owes its fame to an architectural project gone horribly wrong. The **Leaning Tower of Pisa** (Torre Pendente) is an extraordinary sight and one of Italy's most photographed monuments. The tower, originally erected as a *campanile* (bell tower) from the late 12th century, is one of three Romanesque buildings on the immaculate lawns of **Piazza dei Miracoli** (also known as Campo dei Miracoli or Piazza del Duomo).

The candy-striped **Duomo** (10am-6pm), begun in 1063, has a graceful tiered facade and cavernous interior, while to its west, the cupcake-like **Battistero** (Baptistery; 8am-8pm Apr-Oct, 10am-5pm Nov-Mar) is something of an architectural hybrid, with a Pisan-Romanesque lower section and a Gothic upper level and dome.

p191

### DETOUR: SAN GIMIGNANO

**Start: 2 Siena**

Dubbed the medieval Manhattan thanks to its 15 11th-century towers, San Gimignano is a classic hilltop town and an easy detour from Siena.

From the car park next to Porta San Giovanni, it's a short walk up to **Palazzo Comunale** (Piazza del Duomo; admission €5; 9.30am-7pm Apr-Sep, 10am-5.30pm Oct-Mar), which houses the town's art gallery, the **Pinacoteca**, and tallest tower, the **Torre Grossa**. Nearby, the Romanesque basilica, known as the **Collegiata** (Piazza del Duomo; adult/child €3.50/1.50; 10am-7.10pm Mon-Fri, to 5.10pm Sat, 12.30-7.10pm Sun, closed 2nd half of Nov & Jan), boasts some remarkable Ghirlandaio frescoes.

Before leaving town, be sure to sample the local Vernaccia wine at the **Museo del Vino** (Wine Museum; Parco della Rocca; admission free, tastings 4/6 wines €6/10; 11.30am-6.30pm) next to the Rocca (fortress).

San Gimignano is about 40km northwest of Siena. Head for Florence until Poggibonsi and then pick up the SS429.

Classic Trip

MATTES REN/HEMIS.FR/GETTY IMAGES ©

MARK HORN/GETTY IMAGES ©

## WHY THIS IS A CLASSIC TRIP

DUNCAN GARWOOD, AUTHOR

**Every one of the towns and cities on this drive is special. The great treasures of Rome, Florence and Venice are amazing but, for me, it's the lesser-known highlights that make this such an incredible trip – Modena's stunning Romanesque cathedral, the Scrovegni Chapel in Padua, and Verona's gorgeous medieval centre.**

Top: Pisa's Piazza dei Miracoli
Left: Cheese shop, Modena
Right: Saffron fields with San Gimignano in the distance

FILIPPO MONTEFORTE/AFP/GETTY IMAGES ©

**The Drive »** It's a 2½-hour drive up to Modena from Pisa. Head back towards Florence on the A11 and then pick up the A1 to Bologna. Continue as the road twists and falls through the wooded Apennines before flattening out near Bologna. Exit at Modena Sud (Modena South) and follow for the centro.



## 5 Modena

One of Italy's top foodie towns, Modena boasts a stunning medieval centre and a trio of Unesco-listed sights. First up is the gorgeous **cathedral** (Corso Duomo; ⌚6.30am-12.30pm & 3.30-7pm), which is widely considered to be Italy's finest Romanesque church. Features to look out for include the Gothic rose window and a series of bas-reliefs depicting scenes from Genesis.

Nearby, the 13th-century **Torre Ghirlandina** (Piazza Torre; admission €2; ⌚9.30am-12.30pm & 3-7pm Sat & Sun Apr-Oct), an 87m-high tower topped by a Gothic spire, was named after Seville's Giralda bell tower by exiled Spanish Jews in the early 16th century. The last of the Unesco threesome is **Piazza Grande**, just south of the cathedral. The city's focal square, this is flanked by the porticoed Palazzo Comunale, Modena's elegant town hall.

✖ 🛏 p191

**The Drive »** From Modena reckon on about 1¼ hours to Verona, via the A1 and A22 autostradas. Follow the A22 as it traverses the flat Po valley plain, passing the medieval town of Mantua (Mantova; worth a quick break) before connecting with the A4. Turn off at Verona Sud and follow signs for the town centre.



TRIP HIGHLIGHT

## 6 Verona

A World Heritage Site since 2000, Verona's historic centre is a beautiful compilation of architectural styles and inspiring buildings. Chief among these is its stunning Roman amphitheatre, known as the **Arena** (045 800 32 04; www.arena.it; Piazza Brà; adult/reduced €6/4.50; 1.30-7.30pm Mon, 8.30am-7.30pm Tue-Sun). Dating to the 1st century AD, this is Italy's third-largest amphitheatre after the Colosseum and Capua amphitheatre, and although it can no longer seat 30,000, it still draws sizeable crowds to its opera and music concerts.

From the Arena, it's an easy walk to the river Adige and **Castelvecchio** (Corso Castelvecchio 2; adult/reduced €6/4.50; 1.30-7.30pm Mon, 8.30am-7.30pm Tue-Sun), Verona's picturesque castle and top art museum. Like many of the city's outstanding monuments, this was built during the 14th-century reign of the tyrannical della Scala (Scaligeri) family, whose eye-catching Gothic tombs, the **Arche Scaligere** (Via Arche Scaligere), stand near elegant Piazza dei Signori.

p191

**The Drive »** To Padua it's about an hour from Verona on the A4 Venice autostrada. Exit at Padova Ovest (Padua West) and join the SP47 after the toll booth. Follow this until you see, after a road bridge, a turn-off signposted to the centro.

## 7 Padua

Travellers to Padua (Padova) usually make a beeline for the city's main attraction, the **Scrovegni Chapel** (049 201 00 20; www.cappelladegliscrovegni.it; Giardini dell'Arena; adult/reduced €13/6; 9am-7pm by reservation), but there's more to Padua than Giotto frescoes and it's actually the **Orto Botanico** (www.ortobotanico.unipd.it; Via dell'Orto Botanico; adult/reduced €4/3; 9am-1pm & 3-7pm Apr-Oct, 9am-1pm Mon-Sat Nov-Mar) that represents Padua on Unesco's list of World Heritage Sites. The oldest botanical garden in the world, this dates to 1545 when a group of medical students planted some rare plants in order to study their medicinal properties. A short walk from the garden, Padua's vast **Basilica di Sant'Antonio** (www.basilicadelsanto.org; Piazza del Santo; 6.20am-7.45pm) is a major pilgrimage destination, attracting thousands of visitors a year who pay homage to St Anthony, the city's patron saint, who is buried here.

p191

**The Drive »** Traffic permitting, it's about 45 minutes from Padua to Venice, along the A4. Pass through industrial Mestre and over the Ponte della Libertà lagoon bridge to the car park on Piazzale Roma.

TRIP HIGHLIGHT

## 8 Venice

The end of the road, quite literally, is Venice (Venezia). Of the city's many must-sees the most famous are on Piazza San Marco, including the **Basilica di San Marco** (www.basilicasanmarco.it; Piazza San Marco; 9.45am-5pm Mon-Sat, 2-4pm Sun), Venice's great showpiece church. Built originally to house the bones of St Mark, it's a truly awe-inspiring vision with its spangled spires, Byzantine domes, luminous mosaics and lavish marble work. For a bird's-eye view, head to the nearby **campanile** (bell tower; adult/child €8/4; 9am-7pm, to 3.45pm Nov-Easter).

Adjacent to the basilica, the **Palazzo Ducale** (Piazzetta di San

Marco; adult/reduced €16/8; ⏲9am-7pm) was the official residence of Venice's doges (ruling dukes) from the 9th century. Inside, its lavishly decorated chambers harbour some seriously heavyweight art, including Tintoretto's gigantic *Paradiso* (Paradise) in the Sala del Maggiore Consiglio. Connecting the palace to the city dungeons, the **Ponte dei Sospiri** (Bridge of Sighs) was named after the sighs that prisoners – including Casanova – emitted en route from court to cell. For a gastronomic taste of the city, try our walking tour (p52).

✕ 🛏 p191

## ITALIAN ART & ARCHITECTURE

### The Ancients

In pre-Roman times, the Greeks built theatres and proportionally perfect temples in their southern colonies at Agrigento, Syracuse and Paestum, whilst the Etruscans concentrated on funerary art, creating elaborate tombs at Tarquinia and Cerveteri. Coming in their wake, the Romans specialised in roads, aqueducts and monumental amphitheatres such as the Colosseum and Verona's Arena.

### Romanesque

With the advent of Christianity in the 4th century, basilicas began to spring up, many with glittering Byzantine-style mosaics. The Romanesque period (c 1050–1200) saw the construction of fortified monasteries and robust, bulky churches such as Bari's Basilica di San Nicola and Modena's cathedral. Pisa's striking *duomo* (cathedral) displays a characteristic Tuscan variation on the style.

### Gothic

Gothic architecture, epic in scale and typically embellished by gargoyles, pinnacles and statues, took on a more classical form in Italy. Assisi's Basilica di San Francesco is an outstanding early example, but for the full-blown Italian Gothic style check out the cathedrals in Florence, Venice, Siena and Orvieto.

### Renaissance

From quiet beginnings in 14th-century Florence, the Renaissance erupted across Italy before spreading across Europe. In Italy, painters such as Giotto, Botticelli, Leonardo da Vinci and Raphael led the way, while architects Brunelleschi and Bramante rewrote the rule books with their beautifully proportioned basilicas. All-rounder Michelangelo worked his way into immortality, producing masterpieces such as *David* and the Sistine Chapel frescoes.

### Baroque

Dominating the 17th century, the extravagant baroque style found fertile soil in Italy. Witness the Roman works of Gian Lorenzo Bernini and Francesco Borromini, Lecce's flamboyant *centro storico* (historic centre) and the magical baroque towns of southeastern Sicily.

### Neoclassicism

Signalling a return to sober classical lines, neoclassicism majored in the late 18th and early 19th centuries. Signature works include Caserta's Palazzo Reale and La Scala opera house in Milan. In artistic terms, the most famous Italian exponent was Antonio Canova.

# Eating & Sleeping



## Rome 1

**Trattoria Monti** Traditional Italian €€
(06 446 65 73; Via di San Vito 13a; meals €45; lunch & dinner Tue-Sat, lunch Sun) An intimate, arched restaurant specialising in regional cooking from Le Marche. Expect exemplary game stews, pungent truffles and *pecorino di fossa* (sheep's cheese aged in caves), as well as wonderful fried starters such as *olive ascolane* (meat-stuffed olives). Book for dinner.

**Casa Coppelle** Modern Italian €€
(06 6889 1707; www.casacoppelle.it; Piazza delle Coppelle 49; meals €35) Exposed brick walls, books, flowers and subdued lighting set the stage for wonderful French-inspired food at this intimate, romantic restaurant near the Pantheon.

**La Piccola Maison** B&B €€
(06 4201 6331; www.lapiccolamaison.com; Via dei Cappuccini 30; d €70-200; ) The excellent Piccola Maison has a great location close to Via Veneto, pleasingly plain rooms decorated with contemporary flair, and thoughtful staff. It's a great deal.

## Siena 2

**Enoteca I Terzi** Modern Italian €€
(0577 4 43 29; www.enotecaiterzi.it; Via dei Termini 7; meals €39; 11am-1am Mon-Sat) Close to the Campo, this classy modern *enoteca* (wine bar) is a favourite with local office workers, who linger over light-as-air fried *baccalà* (cod), delicate handmade pasta, flavoursome risotto and succulent grilled meats.

**Campo Regio Relais** Boutique Hotel €€€
(0577 22 20 73; www.camporegio.com; Via della Sapienza 25; d €190-250; ) Siena's most charming hotel has six individually decorated and luxuriously equipped rooms. In summer, breakfast is served on a terrace, which has a sensational view of the *duomo*.

## Florence 3

**L'Osteria di Giovanni** Traditional Tuscan €€
(055 28 48 97; www.osteriadigiovanni.it; Via del Moro 22; meals €45; lunch & dinner Fri-Mon, dinner Tue-Thu) It's not the decor or eclectic choice of wall art that stands out at this friendly neighbourhood eatery. It's the cuisine, staunchly Tuscan and stunningly creative. Think chickpea soup with octopus or pear- and ricotta-stuffed *tortelli* (ravioli) bathed in a leek-and-almond cream.

**Trattoria Cibrèo** Trattoria €€
(Via dei Macci 122r; meals €35; 12.50-2.30pm & 6.50-11.15pm Tue-Sat Sep-Jul) Resist the queues and dine at this popular trattoria for a taste of authentic Tuscan cuisine – perhaps a simple plate of polenta, followed by homemade sausages, beans in a spicy tomato sauce and braised celery. No reservations, no credit cards, no coffee and arrive early to snag a table.

**Hotel L'Orologio** Design Hotel €€€
(055 27 73 80; www.hotelorologioflorence.com; Piazza di Santa Maria Novella 24; d €178-450) The type of seductive, super-stylish address James Bond would feel at home in, this elegant hotel showcases the owner's luxury wristwatch collection, with four stars, five floors, 54 rooms named after watches, and clocks pretty much everywhere you look.

## Pisa 4

**Sottobosco** Cafe €

(www.sottoboscocafe.it; Piazza San Paolo all'Orto; lunches €15; 10am-midnight Tue-Fri, noon-1am Sat, 7pm-midnight Sun) What a tourist-free breath of fresh air this creative cafe is! Tuck into a sugary ring doughnut and cappuccino at a glass-topped table filled with artists' crayons perhaps, or a collection of buttons. Lunch dishes (salads, pies and pasta) are simple and homemade, and come dusk, jazz bands play or DJs spin tunes.

## Modena 5

**Hosteria Giusti** Gastronomic €€€

(059 22 25 33; www.hosteriagiusti.it; Vicolo Squallore 46; meals €70; 12.30-2pm Tue-Sat) US celebrity-chef Mario Batelli is one of the many fans of this illustrious Modena *osteria* (casual tavern). An unassuming place, it specialises in regional fare such as *tortelloni di ricotta e zucca* (pasta stuffed with ricotta and pumpkin) and *zampone* (pigs' trotters).

**Hotel Cervetta 5** Hotel €€

(059 23 84 47; www.hotelcervetta5.com; Via Cervetta 5; d/tr €120/155; ) A smart option in the historic centre, adjacent to Piazza Grande, with quasi-boutique facilities, clean, modern bathrooms and the latest in TV technology. Fruity breakfasts and wi-fi are included; garage parking (€15) isn't.

## Verona 6

**Pintxos Bistrot** Gastronomic €€€

(045 59 42 87; www.ristorantealcristo.it; Piazzetta Pescheria 6; meals €40-60; lunch & dinner Tue-Sun) This airy bistro offers an excitingly eclectic menu mixing Italian pasta, Catalan cheeses and hams, and small-plate dishes perfumed with exotic ingredients such as lemon grass and tamarind.

## Padua 7

**Godenda** Modern Italian €€

(049 877 41 92; www.godenda.it; Via Squarcione 4/6; meals €30-50; 10am-3pm & 7pm-1am Mon-Sat, closed Aug) Though hidden under an ancient portico, this foodie favourite manages to be airy and modern. The seasonal menu features creative takes on old Venetian classics such as monkfish with fava beans and homemade pasta with jerked horse meat. Reservations recommended.

## Venice 8

**All'Arco** Traditional Venetian €

(Calle dell'Arco 436; cicheti €1.50-4; noon-8.30pm Mon-Sat Apr-Jun & Sep, to 3.30pm Oct-Mar, closed Jul & Aug) Popular with locals, this tiny *osteria* serves Venice's best *cicheti* (Venetian tapas) – think wild asparagus wrapped in roast beef with grainy mustard followed by Dolomite strawberries and aged balsamic vinegar.

**Anice Stellato** Traditional Venetian €€

(041 72 07 44; Fondamenta della Sensa 3272; meals €25-40; noon-2pm & 7.30-11pm Wed-Sun) If finding this friendly place in the little-visited historic Jewish Ghetto seems like an adventure, wait until dinner arrives: herb-encrusted lamb chops, homemade ravioli and lightly fried *moeche* (soft-shelled crab) gobbled whole. Tin lamps and recycled paper place-mats on communal tables keep the focus on local food and local company – all memorable. Book ahead.

**Novecento** Boutique Hotel €€

(041 241 37 65; www.novecento.biz; Calle del Dose 2683/84; d €130-260) A colourful choice with nine bohemian-chic rooms, a garden for leisurely breakfast and the occasional in-house art exhibition.

***Ostia Antica*** *Imagine life in the 4th century BC at these evocative ruins*

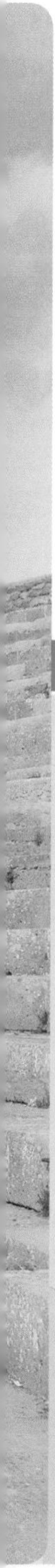

# Roaming Around Rome 16

*Rome's little-explored hinterland is a real eye-opener, with verdant scenery and thrilling cultural treasures – haunting ancient ruins, hilltop villas and landscaped Renaissance gardens.*

## TRIP HIGHLIGHTS

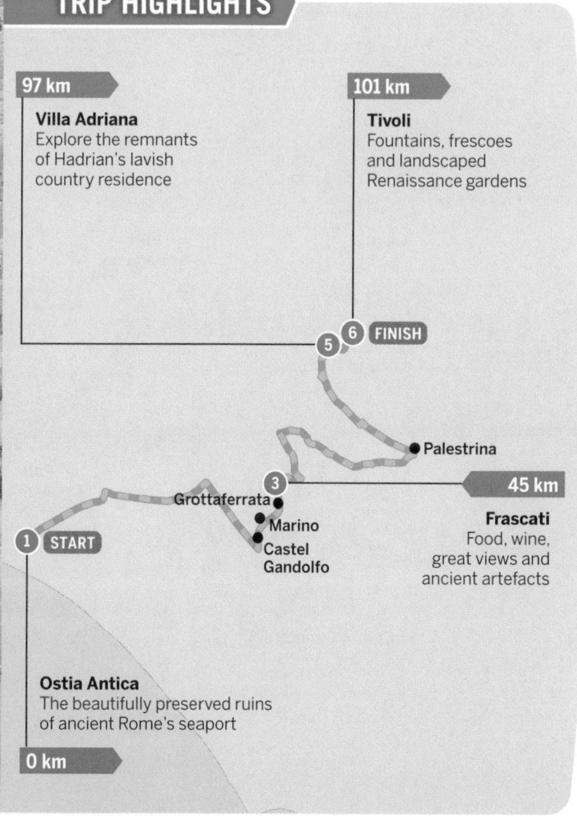

97 km
**Villa Adriana**
Explore the remnants of Hadrian's lavish country residence

101 km
**Tivoli**
Fountains, frescoes and landscaped Renaissance gardens

6 FINISH
5
Palestrina
3
45 km
Grottaferrata
Marino
Castel Gandolfo
1 START

**Frascati**
Food, wine, great views and ancient artefacts

**Ostia Antica**
The beautifully preserved ruins of ancient Rome's seaport

0 km

### 3 DAYS 101KM / 62 MILES

### GREAT FOR...

### BEST TIME TO GO

Spring's good for the ancient sites, early summer for romantic views.

### ESSENTIAL PHOTO

Fountains at Tivoli's Villa d'Este.

### BEST FOR WINE BUFFS

Frascati's traditional cellars.

# 16 Roaming Around Rome

While Rome (Roma) hogs the limelight, the area around the capital makes for an absorbing drive with its wealth of historic sights. Headline acts include the remarkably well-preserved ruins of ancient Rome's port at Ostia Antica, and Emperor Hadrian's vast palace complex at Tivoli. Tivoli is one of several hilltop towns that feature on this trip, along with the wine town of Frascati and the papal retreat of Castel Gandolfo.

TRIP HIGHLIGHT

## 1 Ostia Antica

The remarkably well-preserved ruins of Ostia Antica, ancient Rome's main seaport, form one of Italy's most compelling and under-appreciated archaeological sites. The city was founded in the 4th century BC at the mouth of the Tiber and developed into a major port with a population of around 100,000. Decline came in the 5th century when barbarian invasions and

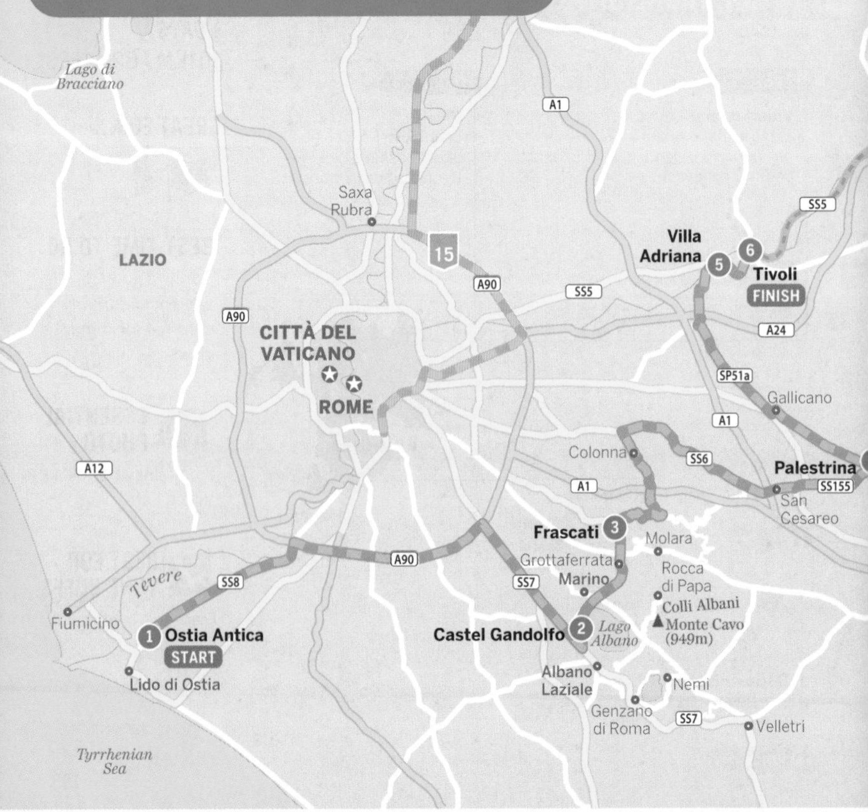

an outbreak of malaria led to its abandonment and slow burial in river silt, thanks to which it has survived so well.

The **Scavi Archeologici di Ostia Antica** (Ruins of Ostia Antica; www.ostiaantica.net; Viale dei Romagnoli 717; adult/reduced €6.50/3.25; 8.30am-7pm Tue-Sun Apr-Oct, to 6pm Nov-Feb, to 5pm Mar) are spread out and you'll need a few hours to do them justice. The main thoroughfare, the **Decumanus Maximus**, leads from the city's entrance (the Porta Romana) to highlights such as the **Terme di Nettuno** (Baths of Neptune), whose floor features a famous mosaic of Neptune driving his seahorse chariot. Next door, the steeply stacked **amphitheatre** was built by Agrippa and later enlarged to hold 3000 people. Behind the theatre, the **Piazzale delle Corporazioni** (Forum of the Corporations) housed Ostia's merchant guilds and is decorated with well-preserved mosaics. Further towards Porta Marina, the **Thermopolium** is an ancient cafe complete with a bar and fresco advertising the bill of fare.

p199

**The Drive »** Head back towards Rome and take the Grande Raccordo Anulare (GRA) for Naples. Exit at the Ciampino Airport turn-off and continue up Via Appia (SS7), until you come to traffic lights halfway up a long climb. Make a left turn to Lago Albano and follow this road up under the towering umbrella pines to Castel Gandolfo at the top. All told, it takes about 35 minutes.

## 2 Castel Gandolfo

One of the prettiest towns in the Castelli Romani, an area of wooded wine-rich hills just south of Rome, Castel Gandolfo makes for a memorable stop. It's not a big place but what it lacks in size it makes up for in atmosphere and on a warm summer's evening there's no better place for a romantic tête-à-tête. Action is centred on **Piazza della Libertà**, a refined baroque square overlooked by the **Palazzo Pontificio** (closed to visitors), the pope's impressive summer residence. But a stop here is not so much about sightseeing as lapping up the gorgeous views over Lago Albano and enjoying a leisurely alfresco meal.

p199

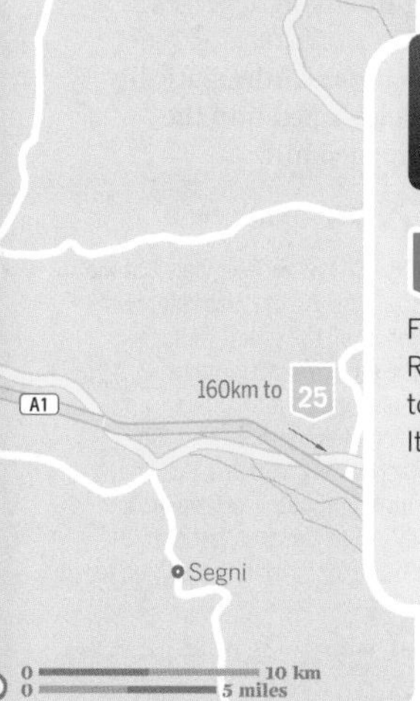

### LINK YOUR TRIP

#### 15 World Heritage Wonders

From Ostia Antica head into Rome along Via Ostiense to join up with this tour of Italy's greatest hits (p181).

#### 25 Shadow of Vesuvius

Take the A1 autostrada from near Frascati and head down to Naples (Napoli), the starting point for this exploration of Vesuvius, Pompeii and other classic sites (p273).

RENE MATTES/HEMIS/CORBIS ©

**The Drive »** To Frascati, it's a pretty straightforward 20-minute drive. From Castel Gandolfo follow the road for Marino, enjoying glimpses of the lake off to your right, and then Grottaferrata. Here you'll come to a roundabout. Take the third exit and Frascati is 4km further on.

TRIP HIGHLIGHT

## 3 Frascati

Best known for its crisp white wine, Frascati is a popular day-trip destination. On hot summer weekends Romans pile into town to hang out in the elegant historic centre and fill up on *porchetta* (herb-roasted pork) and local wine. You can follow suit by filling up from the food stalls on **Piazza del Mercato** or searching out the traditional *cantinas* (originally wine and olive-oil cellars, now informal restaurants) that pepper the centre's narrow lanes. Once you've explored the town and admired the sweeping views from the tree-lined avenue at the bottom of Piazza Marconi, head up to **Villa Aldobrandini**. Designed by Giacomo della Porta and built by Carlo Maderno, this regal 16th-century villa sits haughtily above town in a stunning hillside position. The villa itself is closed to the public but you can visit the impressive early baroque **gardens** (Via Cardinal Massai 18; admission free; ⌚9am-6pm Mon-Fri) dramatically landscaped into the wooded hill.

✕ 🛏 p199

**The Drive »** Take Viale Catone from the top of Piazza Marconi, following the green signs for the autostrada. Continue, passing through Colonna, until soon afterwards you hit the fast-flowing SS6 (Via Casilina). Turn right onto the Casilina and after San Cesareo, left onto the SS155 for a twisting climb up to

**Tivoli** Avenue of the Hundred Fountains at Villa d'Este

Palestrina. Plan on about half an hour from Frascati.

## 4 Palestrina

The pretty town of Palestrina stands on the slopes of Monte Ginestro, one of the foothills of the Apennines. In ancient times Praeneste, as it was then known, was a favourite summer retreat for wealthy Romans and the site of a much-revered temple dedicated to the goddess of fortune. Little remains intact of the 2nd-century-BC **Santuario della Fortuna Primigenia**, but much of what is now the historic centre was built over its six giant terraces. Nowadays, the town's main act is the fantastic **Museo Archeologico Nazionale di Palestrina** (Piazza della Cortina; admission €5; ⏲9am-8pm), housed in the 17th-century **Palazzo Colonna Barberini**. Highlights of the museum's collection include the wonderful 'Capitoline Triad', a marble sculpture of Jupiter, Juno and Minerva; and a spectacular 2nd-century-BC mosaic showing the flooding of the Nile, an incredibly rich depiction of daily life in ancient Egypt.

✕ p199

**The Drive »** It takes just over half an hour to get to Villa Adriana. Exit Palestrina and head northwest towards Gallicano. Here, follow the signs to Tivoli, continuing past the shrubbery and under the Castello di Passerano until you see Villa Adriana signposted a few kilometres short of Tivoli.

TRIP HIGHLIGHT

## 5 Villa Adriana

Emperor Hadrian's sprawling 1st-century summer residence, **Villa Adriana** (☎06 3996 7900; adult/reduced €8/4, parking €2;

9am-7pm, last admission 5.30pm) was one of ancient Rome's grandest properties, lavish even by the decadent standards of the day. Hadrian personally designed much of the complex, taking inspiration from buildings he'd seen around the world. The **pecile**, a large porticoed pool, was a reproduction of a building in Athens, and the **canopo** is a copy of the sanctuary of Serapis near Alexandria – its long canal of water was originally surrounded by Egyptian statues, representing the Nile.

To the east of the *pecile* is Hadrian's private retreat, the **Teatro Marittimo**. Built on an island in an artificial pool, it was originally a mini-villa accessible only by swing bridges, which the emperor would have raised when he felt like a dip. There are also nymphaeums, temples and barracks, and a museum with the latest discoveries from ongoing excavations (often closed).

**The Drive »** Pick up Via Tiburtina (SS5), the main Rome–Tivoli road, and head up to Tivoli centro. It's a short, steep, twisting climb up to the town centre that should take about 15 minutes.

TRIP HIGHLIGHT

## 6 Tivoli

Tivoli's elevated historic centre is an attractive, if often busy, spot. Its main attraction is the Unesco-protected **Villa d'Este** (www.villadestetivoli.info; Piazza Trento; adult/reduced €8/4; 8.30am-1hr before sunset Tue-Sun), a one-time Benedictine convent that Lucrezia Borgia's son, Cardinal Ippolito d'Este, transformed into a pleasure palace in 1550. From 1865 to 1886 it was home to Franz Liszt and inspired his compositions *To the Cypresses of the Villa d'Este* and *The Fountains of the Villa d'Este*.

The villa's rich mannerist frescoes merit a glance, but it's the **garden** that you're here for: water-spouting gargoyles and elaborate avenues lined with deep-green, knotty cypresses and extravagant fountains. Highlights include the **Fountain of the Organ**, an extravagant baroque ensemble that uses water pressure to play music through a concealed organ, and the 130m-long **Avenue of the Hundred Fountains**, which joins the Fountain of Tivoli to the Fountain of Rome.

p199

### DETOUR: SUBIACO

**Start: 6 Tivoli**

Remote-feeling and dramatic, Subiaco is well worth the trip to see its two breathtaking Benedictine monasteries. The **Monastery of St Benedict** (admission free; 9am-12.30pm & 3-6pm) is carved into the rock over the cave where St Benedict holed up for three years to meditate and pray. Apart from its stunning setting, described by Petrarch as 'the edge of Paradise', it's adorned with rich 13th- to 15th-century frescoes.

Halfway down the hill from St Benedict is the **Monastery of St Scholastica** (9.30am-12.30pm & 3.30-7pm), the only one of the 13 monasteries built by St Benedict still standing in the Valley of the Amiene. If you decide to stay, its **Foresteria** (07 748 55 69; www.benedettini-subiaco.org; per person B&B €37) is a great place to spend a contemplative night. But book ahead, as Benedictine clergy from around the world often make the pilgrimage here to work in the monastery's famous **library** and **archive**. There's also a restaurant offering set menus for €19 and €27.

# Eating & Sleeping

## Ostia Antica ❶

**Ristorante Cipriani** — Traditional Roman **€€**

(☎06 5635 2956; Via del Forno 11; meals €30; ⊙closed Wed & dinner Sun) Dig into classic Roman dishes such as *pasta alla gricia* (with lardons and onion) or *cacio e pepe* (pasta with salty pecorino cheese and black pepper) while seated on a cobbled street near Ostia's 15th-century castle.

**Ristorante Monumento** — Traditional Roman **€€**

(☎06 565 00 21; Piazza Umberto I 8; meals €30; ⊙Tue-Sun) A former favourite of film director Federico Fellini, this historic restaurant is a reliable choice, specialising in homemade pasta and fresh seafood.

## Castel Gandolfo ❷

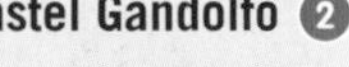

**Antico Ristorante Pagnanelli Dal 1882** — Gastronomic **€€€**

(☎06 936 00 04; www.pagnanelli.it; Via Antonio Gramsci 4; meals €70; ⊙closed Tue winter) One of the top restaurants in the Castelli Romani, this is a romantic choice. Housed in a blushing red villa half-drowned in cascading foliage, it offers superlative food and memorable views over Lago Albano.

## Frascati ❸

**Vie dei Canti** — Wine Bar **€**

(☎940 1 04 13; Via D'Estouteville 3; meals €25; ⊙7.30pm-midnight Mon-Sat) A rustic *enoteca* (wine bar) tucked away down a cobbled alleyway. Its softly lit, wood-lined interior is a lovely setting to sip on local wine accompanied by platters of delicious cheese, cured meats and *crostone* (toasted bread).

**Cacciani** — Hotel **€**

(☎06 940 19 91; www.cacciani.it; Via Armando Diaz 13; d €75-100; ❄ ☎) This decent three-star offers comfortable, understated rooms, most with views down to Rome. Its **restaurant** (☎06 942 03 78; meals €55; ⊙Tue-Sat) is one of the best in town, serving a mix of classic Roman dishes and creative modern fare.

## Palestrina ❹

**Albergo Ristorante Stella** — Restaurant **€€**

(☎06 953 81 72; Piazza della Liberazione 3; meals €30) Right in the heart of the action, this is a basic no-frills restaurant-hotel near the cathedral. It sports a weary 1960s look but dishes such as *pappardelle alla lepre* (egg-noodle pasta with hare and tomato sauce) hit the mark, and the rooms (doubles €70), while nothing special, do the job.

## Tivoli ❻

**Sibilla** — Modern Italian **€€€**

(☎0774 33 52 81; www.ristorantesibilla.com; Via della Sibilla 50; meals €50; ⊙May-Sep) Serving creative modern takes on traditional Roman cuisine, this impressive restaurant has a glorious setting overlooked by two ruined temples and overlooking the slopes of Villa Gregoriana. But it's not all show – the food lives up to the view and is less expensive than you might expect.

**Trattoria del Falcone** — Trattoria **€€**

(☎0774 31 23 58; Via del Trevio 34; meals €30; ⊙Wed-Mon) Popular with both tourists and locals, this lively trattoria has been dishing up classic pasta dishes since 1918.

***Castel Gandolfo*** *Wander past Palazzo Pontificio, the pope's summer residence*

CRAIG BUCHANAN/ALAMY ©

# Castelli Romani

17

*Take in Roman ruins, elegant hilltop towns and languid lakeside lunches on this gentle drive through a pretty pocket of wooded hills and volcanic lakes on Rome's southern doorstep.*

## TRIP HIGHLIGHTS

0 km

**Frascati**
Explore the historic centre of this elegant wine town

1 Frascati START

4

20 km

**Lago Albano**
Beautiful volcanic lake in a plunging green amphitheatre

5

Albano Laziale

6

Nemi FINISH

Genzano di Roma

**Castel Gandolfo**
Feast on fine views and the romantic atmosphere

22 km

**Ariccia**
Famous for its hearty traditional eateries

26 km

**2–3 DAYS**
**40KM / 25 MILES**

**GREAT FOR...**

**BEST TIME TO GO**

Spring and early summer for great colours, clear views and alfresco dining.

**ESSENTIAL PHOTO**

Lago Albano from Castel Gandolfo.

**BEST FOR FOODIES**

Ariccia's *fraschette* (rustic eateries).

# 17 Castelli Romani

For millennia the Colli Albani (Alban hills) and their 13 towns – known collectively as the Castelli Romani – have provided Romans with a cool summer refuge and still today they flock here to enjoy the lovely scenery and local flavours. This tour takes in the area's highlights, including the elegant wine town of Frascati, and Castel Gandolfo, the charming hilltop *borgo* (medieval town) where the pope has his summer residence.

TRIP HIGHLIGHT

## 1 Frascati

Frascati is a charming town offering hazy views over Rome (Roma), as well as delicious food and wine. Its main sight is the **Museo Tuscolano** (☎06 941 71 95; Piazza Marconi 6; admission €3; ⏲10am-6pm Tue-Fri, to 7pm Sat & Sun), which displays artfully lit ancient Roman artefacts in the converted stables of **Villa Aldobrandini** (the big 16th-century villa that you see looming over Piazza Marconi). Once you've finished in the museum, and admired the ornate baroque facade of the 17th-century **Cattedrale di San Pietro** (Piazza San Pietro), take some time to explore the centre's elegant shop-lined streets, swoon over the views, and feast on the local Castelli food. To get into the swing, pick up a *panino con porchetta* (sandwich filled with herb-roasted pork) from one of the stands on **Piazza del Mercato**, or head to a traditional *cantina* (cellar-cum-trattoria) for *porchetta*, olives, salami and cheese accompanied by jugs of local white wine.

✕ 🛏 p207

**The Drive »** From Frascati, it's about 15 minutes to Tuscolo. Head towards Marino until a set of traffic lights on Via Anagnina.

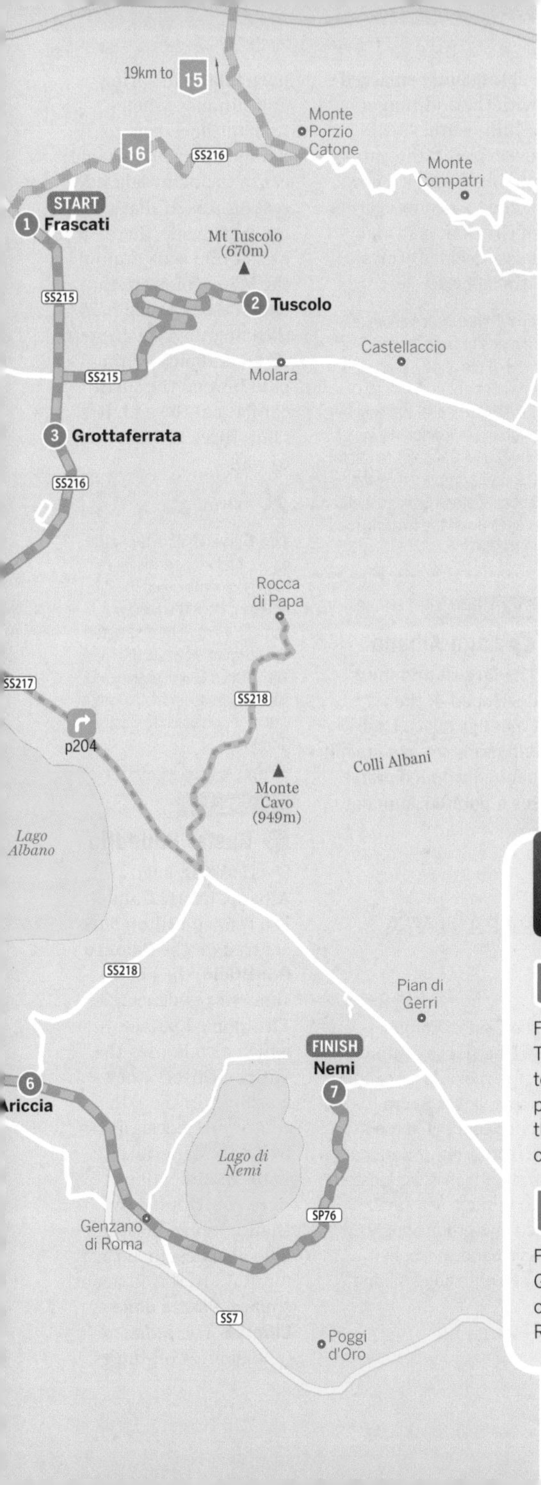

Go left towards Rocca Priora, and then, after a kilometre or so, you'll see Tuscolo signposted off to the left. From here the road climbs up past green fields, hedgerows and pine trees to the site at the top.

## 2 Tuscolo

The ruins of the ancient town of **Tusculum** are dotted around the grassy summit of Mt Tuscolo (670m). A Latin settlement dating to the early Iron Age, Tusculum was an important Roman town – Cicero had a villa nearby – and later a medieval stronghold until it was destroyed by a Roman army in 1191. Little remains of the city today except a small amphitheatre, a crumbling villa and a small stretch of road

## LINK YOUR TRIP

### 15 World Heritage Wonders

From Frascati, follow Via Tuscolana for about 20km to central Rome, the starting point for this epic drive through Italy's headline cities (p181).

### 16 Roaming Around Rome

From Frascati or Castel Gandolfo, pick up this tour of classic sights around Rome (p193).

leading up to the site, but it's an atmospheric spot for a picnic and the views are wonderful.

**The Drive »** Double back the way you came to the main Frascati–Marino road and, at the traffic lights, head left towards Marino. Continue and then take a right turn opposite Ristorante Pezzetta onto Via Piave. Follow it to the bottom, turn right and continue until you see cobbled Corso del Popolo on the left. From Tuscolo it's about 20 minutes.

### 3 Grottaferrata

Well-to-do Grottaferrata is worth a stop for its fortified abbey, the **Monastero Esarchico di Santa Maria di Grottaferrata** (Corso del Popolo 128; 7am-12.30pm & 3.30pm-1hr before sunset), aka the Abbazia Greca di San Nilo. Founded in 1004 and subsequently enlarged with the addition of a 13th-century bell tower and 15th-century fortifications, it's now home to a congregation of Greek monks and has a decidedly mystic atmosphere.

**The Drive »** It's about 20 minutes to Lago Albano. Skirt around the abbey, keeping it on your right, to Via degli Ulivi. Take this, then, at the end, turn right and follow for Marino and Castel Gandolfo. In Castel Gandolfo, drop a left by the Antico Ristorante Pagnanelli and plunge down the twisting road to the lake.

TRIP HIGHLIGHT

### 4 Lago Albano

The largest and most developed of the Castelli's lakes, Lago Albano is set in a steeply banked wooded crater. It's a popular hangout, particularly in spring and summer, when Romans flock here to parade up and down and eat in the many lakeside restaurants. If that's not your scene, there's a great 11km **walk** around the lake – follow to the end of the lakeside road (keeping the lake on your right) and pick up the path beyond the small car park at the end. It takes three to 3½ hours to walk.

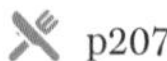
p207

**The Drive »** With the water on your left, follow the lakeside road and continue up the hill, doubling back the way you came. Try not to be distracted by the great views as the road, Via Antonio Gramsci, ascends steadily, crossing the railway line as it curves up to Castel Gandolfo.

TRIP HIGHLIGHT

### 5 Castel Gandolfo

Overlooking Lago Albano, Castel Gandolfo is a refined hilltop *borgo* centred on the **Palazzo Pontificio**, the pope's summer residence. This domed palace, which also houses the Vatican Observatory, was built in the 17th century to a design by Carlo Maderno. Later modifications were contributed by Gian Lorenzo Bernini, who also designed the fountain in the adjacent square, **Piazza della Libertà**. The *palazzo* (mansion) is off-limits

## DETOUR: ROCCA DI PAPA & VIA SACRA

**Start: 3 Grottaferrata**

The second-highest town in the Castelli Romani, **Rocca di Papa** cascades down the slopes of **Monte Cavo** (949m). It has an attractive medieval core but the main reason to pass by is to walk **Via Sacra**, an ancient Roman road that once connected the Appian Way (Via Appia Antica) with a temple on the summit of Monte Cavo. The road, which is signposted from the top of town, winds up through a wooded hill to the summit, now marked by a group of ugly antennae. En route, you'll pass a panoramic point, the only place where you can see both Lago Albano and Lago di Nemi.

Rocca di Papa is on the SS218.

MARCO SCATAGLINI/ALAMY ©

Grottaferrata

## ARICCIA'S GRAVITY DEFYING ROAD

Weird but true. On a stretch of the SS218 between Rocca di Papa and Ariccia, the road dips down before rising again, forming a shallow V shape. If you stop your car here, on the downhill section, and take the hand brake off, the car rolls backwards, apparently uphill. Similarly, if you pour water on the road, it drains upwards. The reason why remains a mystery. Some claim it's an optical illusion, that the road is a so-called gravity hill, where what appears to be a descent is in fact a gentle upward rise. Others believe it's the result of a gravitational anomaly caused by magnetic forces arising from the area's volcanic innards. Try it and see what you think; it's about 2km from the centre of Ariccia, a few hundred metres from the roundabout that connects the SS218 with the SS217 Via dei Laghi. But be careful, as it's quite a fast stretch of road.

to the public but still attracts hordes of tourists, particularly on summer Sundays when the pope delivers the weekly Angelus here.

There are no great must-sees in town but it's a lovely place for a relaxed stroll, and the views over the lake are ravishing.

p207

**The Drive »** From Castel Gandolfo follow the SS216 down to Albano Laziale. Once in Albano, head left through the town centre, along Via Appia (SS7). If the centre's closed to traffic follow the one-way system around and pick up Via Appia a bit further down. Continue along Via Appia, past the park and over the bridge to Ariccia.

TRIP HIGHLIGHT

### 6 Ariccia

Ariccia is something of a gastronomic hot spot, famous for its *porchetta* and popular **fraschette** (rustic, *osteria*-style eateries). Its second claim to fame is **Palazzo Chigi** (www.palazzochigiariccia.it; Piazza di Corte 14; 10am-1.30pm & 3.30-7pm Sat & Sun), a 17th-century palace designed by Gian Lorenzo Bernini for the Chigi family. Luchino Visconti filmed interior shots for *Il Gattopardo* (1963) here and parts of the palace are open for visits, including, in summer, the surrounding Parco Chigi.

p207

**The Drive »** To get to Nemi town from Ariccia, continue up Via Appia to Genzano di Roma and follow the signs along the SP76. But to get to Lago di Nemi, go left under the white 'Genzano' sign and follow the road down to a roundabout. Take the last exit onto Via Diana and continue down to the lake, about five minutes away.

### 7 Nemi

Perched on a crater's edge high above **Lago di Nemi**, Nemi is a pretty town, popular with day-tripping Romans who come here in summer to taste the local wild strawberries. In town you can enjoy great views over the lake, but to get down to its verdant shores you'll have to backtrack and descend from Genzano.

In ancient times, the lake was the centre of a cult to the goddess Diana and a favourite holiday spot of the emperor Caligula. These days it's home to a small museum – the **Museo delle Navi Romani** (06 939 80 40; Via Diana 15; admission €3; 9am-7pm Mon-Sat, to 1pm Sun) – which displays scale models of two ancient Roman boats that were found in the lake in 1932.

p207

# Eating & Sleeping

## Frascati 1

**Cacciani** Traditional Italian €€€
(06 942 03 78; www.cacciani.it; Via Armando Diaz 13; meals €55; Tue-Sat) One of the top restaurants in the Castelli Romani, Cacciani is a Frascati institution. The menu offers some modern creative dishes but it's the regional staples such as spaghetti *cacio e pepe* (with pecorino cheese and pepper) that really stand out. There's also a weighty wine list and a lovely terrace with twinkling views of Rome.

**Hosteria San Rocco** Traditional Roman €€
(06 9428 2786; Via Cadorna 1; lunch & dinner) To try a typical *osteria* (casual tavern) search out 'Da Trinco' as it's called by locals, and dine on scrumptious antipasti and traditional pasta dishes such as spaghetti *alla gricia* (with pancetta and cheese).

**Cacciani** Hotel €
(06 940 19 91; www.cacciani.it; Via Armando Diaz 13; d €75-100; ) The hotel of the Cacciani restaurant. Rooms are simple but comfortable enough and most have views down to Rome.

## Lago Albano 4

**La Quintessa** Modern Italian €€
(06 938 02 00 29; Via Spiaggia del Lago 20, Castel Gandolfo; meals €40) With fantastic views over the lake, this place boasts a chic design that wouldn't seem out of place in central Rome. It's not just looks, though; the food lives up to the setting, with classic Roman dishes, good pizza and much more besides.

## Castel Gandolfo 5

**Antico Ristorante Pagnanelli Dal 1882** Gastronomic €€€
(06 936 00 04; www.pagnanelli.it; Via Antonio Gramsci 4; meals €70; closed Tue winter) A local landmark, this refined restaurant offers sophisticated food and romantic lakeside views. The panoramic terrace is the place to book, but wherever you end up you'll enjoy top-class seafood and creative meat dishes.

**Hotel Pagnanelli Lucia** Hotel €€
(06 936 14 22; www.albergopagnanelli.it; Via Antonio Gramsci 2; d from €100) A modest two-star hotel perched high above Lago Albano. The simple, airy rooms have rustic wrought-iron beds and lovely lake views.

## Ariccia 6

**Osteria da Angelo** Traditional Italian €
(06 933 17 77; www.osteriadaangelo.it; Via dell'Uccelliera 24; fixed menu €12-25; closed Wed lunch) One of Ariccia's oldest *fraschette*, this is an excellent choice for a characteristic Castelli meal. Don't expect frills, just wooden benches, plastic cups, fresh local wine and lots of hearty food – *porchetta*, cured hams, olives, robust pastas and slabs of grilled meat.

## Nemi 7

**Trattoria la Sirena del Lago** Trattoria €€
(06 936 80 20; Via del Plebiscito 26; meals €30) At this cliff-top favourite, the local game and trout are excellent and the local wine refreshing. In season, try the wild strawberries, a famous Nemi speciality.

**Santo Stefano di Sessanio** *Enjoy sweeping panoramas in this remote village*

TOM MACKIE/ALAMY ©

# Abruzzo's Wild Landscapes

18

*This stunning mountain region offers superb driving and spectacular scenery. Roads snake through silent valleys and stone-clad villages, over highland plains and past thick forests.*

## TRIP HIGHLIGHTS

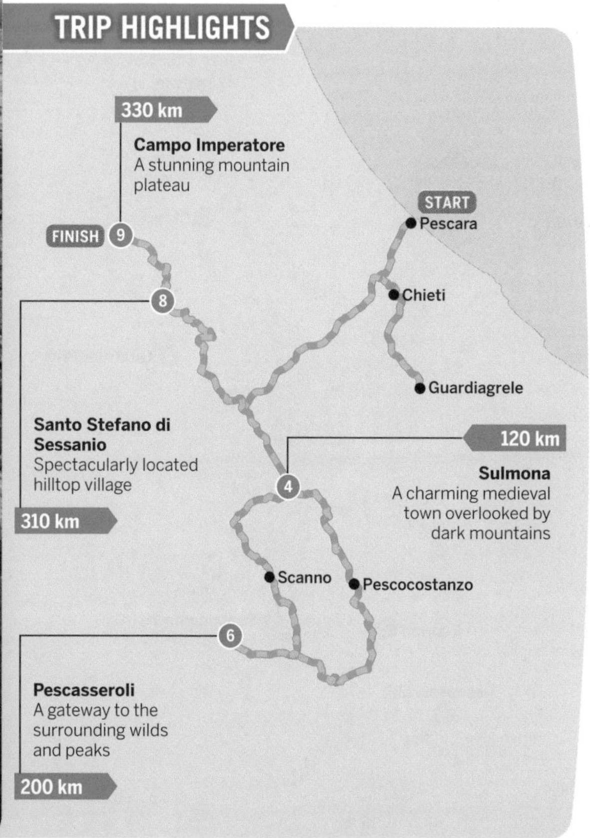

START Pescara

Chieti

Guardiagrele

120 km
**Sulmona**
A charming medieval town overlooked by dark mountains

Scanno

Pescocostanzo

200 km
**Pescasseroli**
A gateway to the surrounding wilds and peaks

310 km
**Santo Stefano di Sessanio**
Spectacularly located hilltop village

330 km
**Campo Imperatore**
A stunning mountain plateau

FINISH

**6 DAYS**
**330KM / 205 MILES**

**GREAT FOR...**

**BEST TIME TO GO**

June, July and September for perfect weather and clear views.

**ESSENTIAL PHOTO**

Corno Grande from Campo Imperatore.

**BEST FOR HIKING**

The hills around Pescasseroli.

# 18 Abruzzo's Wild Landscapes

Although little more than an hour's drive from Rome (Roma), Abruzzo is largely unknown to foreign visitors. Yet with its thrilling mountain scenery and rural, back-country charm, it's ideal for a road trip. This route takes in the best of the region's three national parks, winding over great green hills and past ancient beech woods populated by wolves and bears, as stark snow-capped summits shimmer in the distance. Cultural gems also await, such as the charming medieval town of Sulmona.

### 1 Pescara

Before heading into the wild interior spend a day relaxing on the beach in Pescara, Abruzzo's largest city. Action centres on the animated seafront although there are a couple of small museums worth a look – the **Museo delle Genti d'Abruzzo** (www.gentidabruzzo.it; Via delle Caserme 24; adult/reduced €6/3; ⌚9am-1pm Mon-Sat & 4-7pm Sat & Sun Sep-Jun, 10am-1pm Mon-Fri & 9.30pm-12.30am Thu, Fri & Sat Jul & Aug), which illustrates

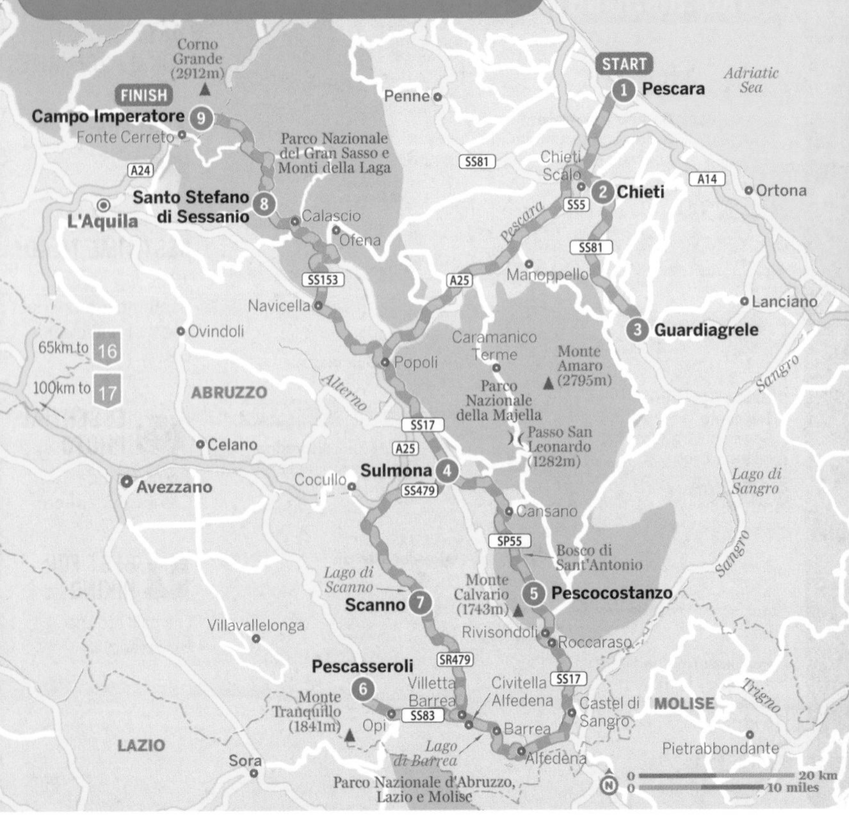

local rural culture, and the **Museo Casa Natale Gabriele D'Annunzio** (Corso Manthonè 116; admission free or with exhibition supplement; 9am-1pm Mon-Fri & 3.30-5.30pm Tue & Thu), birthplace of controversial fascist poet Gabriele D'Annunzio.

 p215

**The Drive »** From central Pescara it's about half an hour to Chieti. Follow the green signs to the autostrada, which direct you onto the Raccordo Pescara-Chieti, a fast-moving dual carriageway that runs past factories and warehouses towards the distant mountains. Exit for Chieti and follow signs for Chieti centro and then the Civetta and Museo Archeologico Nazionale.

**LINK YOUR TRIP**

**16 Roaming Around Rome**

From Fonte Cerreto take the A24 for about 105km southwest to Tivoli, one of the gems in Rome's fascinating hinterland (p193).

**17 Castelli Romani**

Pick up the A24 near Fonte Cerreto and continue for 140km southwest to Frascati, and a tour of the wine-rich Castelli Romani (p201).

**TOP TIP: ARRIVING IN SULMONA**

Try to time your arrival in Sulmona between 1.30pm and 5.30pm, when traffic restrictions are lifted and you can drive into the historic centre. It makes getting to your hotel much easier.

## 2 Chieti

Overlooking the Aterno valley, hilltop Chieti dates back to pre-Roman times, as you'll discover in its two archaeology museums. The most important of these is the **Museo Archeologico Nazionale dell'Abruzzo** (www.archeoabruzzo.beniculturali.it; Villa Comunale; adult/reduced €4/2; 9am-8pm Tue-Sat, to 7pm Sun), home to the 6th-century-BC *Warrior of Capestrano*, the most important pre-Roman find in central Italy and a much-publicised regional icon. Uphill from the museum, the **Complesso Archeologico la Civitella** (www.lacivitella.it; Via Pianell; adult/reduced €4/2; 9am-8pm Mon-Sat, to 7pm Sun) is built around a Roman amphitheatre.

**The Drive »** Descend from Chieti's centre until you see signs for Guardiagrele and the SS81 off to the left. The road twists and turns slowly for the first few kilometres but eventually broadens out and becomes quicker as it runs past woods and vineyards up to Guardiagrele, about 26km (40 minutes) away.

## 3 Guardiagrele

Dubbed 'Abruzzo's terrace' by poet Gabriele D'Annunzio, this ancient *borgo* (medieval town) on the eastern flank of the **Parco Nazionale della Majella** (www.parcomajella.it) commands sweeping views. Admire these and the striking **Chiesa di Santa Maria Maggiore** (Piazza di Santa Maria Maggiore) with its 14th-century arched portico and austere Romanesque facade.

p215

**The Drive »** To Sulmona it's about two hours from Guardiagrele. Double back to Chieti on the SS81, then follow signs for the autostrada towards L'Aquila and then the SS5 to Chieti Scalo and Manoppello. Pass through Popoli and continue on the SS17 until you see Sulmona signposted about 18km on.

TRIP HIGHLIGHT

## 4 Sulmona

Overlooked by the grey Morrone massif, Sulmona is an atmospheric medieval town famous for its *confetti* (sweets traditionally given to guests at Italian weddings). Action is focused on **Corso Ovidio**, named after local boy Ovid, and **Piazza Garibaldi**, a striking piazza accessed through a 13th-century **aqueduct**. Here on the square, you can peruse religious and contemporary art at the **Polo Culturale Santa Chiara** (admission €3; ⏲9am-1pm & 3.30-7.30pm Tue-Sun).

At the other end of Corso Ovidio, **Palazzo dell'Annunziata** (Corso Ovidio) sits above a 1st-century-BC Roman villa, the **Domus di Arianna**. Upstairs, a **museum** (admission free; ⏲9am-1pm & 3.30-7.30pm) has a small collection of archaeological items.

p215

**The Drive »** The 50-minute run over to Pescocostanzo takes you through some beautiful mountain terrain, via the Bosco di Sant'Antonio (ideal for a picnic). From Sulmona head towards Cansano and follow the road as it ascends the increasingly rocky landscape. At Cansano take the SP55 for Pescocostanzo.

ALBRECHT WEISSER/IMAGE BROKER/ALAMY ©

## 5 Pescocostanzo

Surrounded by lush highland meadows, Pescocostanzo (elevation 1400m) is a characteristic hilltop town whose historical core has changed little in over 500 years. Of particular note is the **Collegiata di Santa Maria del Colle**, an atmospheric Romanesque church with a lavish baroque interior. Nearby, **Piazza del Municipio** is flanked by a number of impressive *palazzi* (mansions), including **Palazzo Comunale** with its distinctive clock tower, and **Palazzo Fanzago**, designed by the great baroque architect Cosimo Fanzago in 1624.

History apart, Pescocostanzo also offers skiing on **Monte Calvario** and summer hiking in the **Bosco di Sant'Antonio**.

**The Drive »** Reckon on about 75 minutes to Pescasseroli. Continue past Rivisondoli to the SS17, then turn south (left) towards Roccaraso. After Castel di Sangro head right onto the SS83. This beautiful road swoops and dips its way through Alfedena, Barrea, past the artificial Lago di Barrea, and

**Parco Nazionale del Gran Sasso e Monti della Laga** Views of Corno Grande in the distance

on to Villetta Barrea, Opi and Pescasseroli.

TRIP HIGHLIGHT

## 6 Pescasseroli

Deep in the heart of the Marsican mountains, Pescasseroli is the main centre of the **Parco Nazionale d'Abruzzo, Lazio e Molise** (www.parcoabruzzo.it), the oldest and most popular of Abruzzo's national parks. Hiking opportunities abound with clearly marked paths for all levels and in winter there's popular downhill skiing. If you're travelling with kids, you can see bears at the **Centro Visita** (Via Colli dell'Oro; adult/child €6/4; ⌚10am-1.30pm & 3-6.30pm; 👪) and learn about wolves in Civitella Alfedena at the **Centro Lupo** (Wolf Centre; admission €3; ⌚10am-1pm & 3-6.30pm).

🛏 p215

**The Drive »** To Scanno it takes about an hour. Double back to Villetta Barrea and turn left onto the SR479. Wind your way up through a pine forest and past grassy slopes to the Passo Godi at about 1500m, from where the road starts its slow, tortuous descent to Scanno.

## ABRUZZO WILDLIFE

Abruzzo's three national parks – Parco Nazionale del Gran Sasso e Monti della Laga; Parco Nazionale della Majella; and Parco Nazionale d'Abruzzo, Lazio e Molise – are home to thousands of animal species. Most famous of all is the Marsican brown bear, of which there are an estimated 40 in the Parco Nazionale d'Abruzzo, Lazio e Molise. Apennine wolves also prowl the deep woods, sometimes emerging in winter when thick snow forces them to approach villages in search of food. Other notable animals include the Abruzzi chamois and red deer, and, overhead, golden eagles and peregrine hawks.

### 7 Scanno

A tangle of steep alleyways and sturdy, grey-stone houses, picture-pretty Scanno is an atmospheric *borgo* known for its finely worked filigree gold jewellery. Explore the pint-sized historic centre and then head down to Lago di Scanno – a couple of kilometres out of town on the road to Sulmona – for a cool lakeside drink.

 p215

**The Drive »** This two-hour leg can be broken up by overnighting in Sulmona (p211), 31km from Scanno through the breathtaking Gole di Sagittario. From Sulmona pick up the SS17 to Popoli and then follow signs for L'Aquila, climbing steadily to Navicella. Here, take the SS153 towards Pescara. Exit for Ofena and climb the snaking road past Calascio and on to Santo Stefano di Sessanio.

TRIP HIGHLIGHT

### 8 Santo Stefano di Sessanio

If you really want to get away from it all, you can't get much more remote than this picturesque village high in the **Parco Nazionale del Gran Sasso e Monti della Laga** (www.gransassolagapark.it). Once a 16th-century Medici stronghold, it suffered damage in the 2009 earthquake and many of its stone buildings are now under scaffolding. That said, it's still a memorable experience to explore its steeply sloping streets and enjoy the great panoramas. For information, ask at the helpful **Centro Visite** (www.centrovisitesantostefanodisessanio.it; Piazza Municipio; ⌚10am-1pm & 2-6pm Tue-Sun).

p215

**The Drive »** From Santo Stefano, Campo Imperatore is signposted as 13km. It's actually more like 20km (20 minutes), but you'll forget about such things as the awesome scenery unfolds ahead of you. Just follow the road and its continuation, the SS17bis, and admire the views.

TRIP HIGHLIGHT

### 9 Campo Imperatore

The high point – quite literally – of this trip is the highland plain known as Campo Imperatore (average elevation 1800m). Often referred to as 'Italy's Little Tibet', this magnificent grassy plateau provides spectacular views of **Corno Grande** (2912m), the highest mountain in the Apennines. But as daunting as it might appear, the Corno Grande is not an especially arduous climb, and the 9km *via normale* (normal route) from the Hotel Campo Imperatore is one of the area's most popular trekking routes.

From Campo Imperatore, signs direct you down to **Fonte Cerreto**, a small cluster of hotels set around a *funivia* (cable car) station, and the nearby A24 autostrada.

# Eating & Sleeping

## Pescara 1

### Osteria La Lumaca — Osteria €€

(085 451 08 80; www.osterialalumaca.com; Via delle Caserme 51; lunch menu €8-15, meals €35; lunch & dinner Mon-Fri, dinner Sat) They take their food seriously at this warm wood-panelled restaurant. Particularly outstanding are the cured meats and Abruzzo lamb. The fixed-price lunch menus are excellent value.

### Hotel Alba — Hotel €

(085 38 91 45; www.hotelalba.pescara.it; Via Michelangelo Forti 14; d €75-120; P) Conveniently located near Pescara's pedestrian-only central strip, this is a cheerful three-star place. Rooms vary but the best sport polished wood, firm beds and plenty of sunlight. Garage parking costs €10.

## Guardiagrele 3

### Antichi Sapori — Sandwich Shop €

(www.saporidiabruzzo.com; Via Tripio 135; panino €2; 8am-1pm & 5-8pm Tue-Sat, 8am-1pm Sun) An old-fashioned deli in the historic centre, this is a great place for a doorstopper *panino* (filled bread) and regional delicacies – honey, marinated vegetables and local red wine.

## Sulmona 4

### Hosteria dell'Arco — Trattoria €

(0864 21 05 53; Via M D'Eramo 20; meals €20-25; lunch & dinner Tue-Sat, lunch Mon) With its laid-back atmosphere and rustic surroundings, this is the archetypal family-run trattoria. Dine on superb local food, starting with a fabulous antipasto spread followed by delicious char-grilled meats.

### Albergo Ristorante Stella — Hotel €

(0864 5 26 53; www.hasr.it; Via Panfilo Mazara 18; d from €70; ) A bright little three-star in the *centro storico* (historic centre). Rooms are modern and comfortable with parquet floors, hard beds and plenty of sunshine. Discounts are available for stays of more than one night.

## Pescasseroli 6

### Hotel La Conca — Hotel €

(0863 91 05 62; www.hotelconca.it; Via Vicenne; d €65-100, half-board per person €55-75; ) Just off Pescasseroli's main drag, this unpretentious chalet-style three-star has spacious rooms decorated in modest country style with blond-wood beds and traditional woollen bedspreads.

## Scanno 7

### Ristorante Gli Archetti — Traditional Italian €€

(0864 7 46 45; www.gliarchetti.it; Via Silla 8; meals €35-40; closed Tue winter) Housed in the cellar of a noble *palazzo*, this rustic restaurant is a great place to taste traditional Abruzzese cooking. Dishes, which include homemade pastas and local meats, make much use of regional ingredients such as pecorino from Scanno, saffron from Navelli, and fresh mountain vegetables. Reservations recommended.

## Santo Stefano di Sessanio 8

### Sextantio — Hotel €€

(0862 89 91 12; www.sextantio.it; Via Principe Umberto; r from €100; ) This enchanting *albergo diffuso* (diffused hotel) has 27 rooms scattered throughout the village. These marry traditional handmade blankets and rustic furniture with under-floor heating, mood lighting and divinely deep bathtubs. The hotel's restaurant, **Locanda Sotto gli Archi** (tasting menu €50; dinner daily, lunch by reservation), serves quality regional fare.

**Bolsena**
*A 13th-century fortress dominates the skyline*

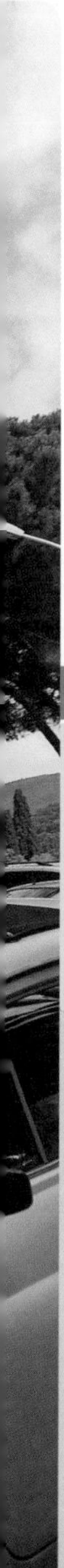

# Etruscan Tuscany & Lazio

*From Tuscan seascapes and rugged hilltop towns to tufa-carved tombs and raunchy frescoes, this tour takes you into the heart of ancient Etruria, the land the Etruscans once called home.*

## TRIP HIGHLIGHTS

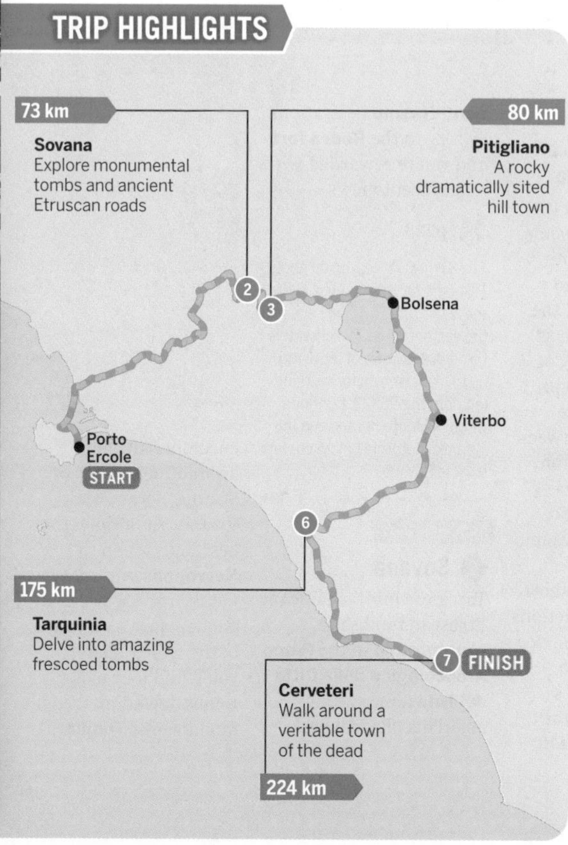

73 km
**Sovana**
Explore monumental tombs and ancient Etruscan roads

80 km
**Pitigliano**
A rocky dramatically sited hill town

Bolsena

Viterbo

Porto Ercole
START

175 km
**Tarquinia**
Delve into amazing frescoed tombs

FINISH

**Cerveteri**
Walk around a veritable town of the dead
224 km

**3–4 DAYS**
**224KM / 139 MILES**

**GREAT FOR...**

**BEST TIME TO GO**

Early summer is good for sightseeing and the sea.

Pitigliano rising out of the rock.

Etruscan trails around Sovana and Pitigliano.

# 19 Etruscan Tuscany & Lazio

Long before Rome came into existence, the Etruscans had forged a great civilisation in the pitted, rugged hills of southern Tuscany, Umbria and northern Lazio. This trip leads through these little-known parts of the country, opening the window onto dramatic natural scenery and spectacular Etruscan treasures. From Tuscany's pock-marked peaks to the haunting tombs that litter Lazio's soft green slopes, it's a beguiling ride.

## 1 Porto Ercole, Monte Argentario

To warm you up for the road ahead, spend some time exploring Monte Argentario, a rugged promontory just off the southern Tuscan coast. The more appealing of its two towns is Porto Ercole, an attractive harbour nestled between three Spanish forts on the promontory's less-crowded eastern side. This is where Caravaggio died in 1610, and although it's fairly short on traditional attractions its hillside *centro storico* (historic centre) is a charming place for a stroll. Continue to the top, past the **Chiesa di Sant'Erasmo** (Piazza Santa Barbara) to the **Rocca fort** and you're rewarded with magnificent views.

p223

**The Drive »** Reckon on about 1¾ hours for this first leg. Cross the water over to Albinia and join the eastbound SS74. Follow this through expanses of farmland up to Manciano, before turning left onto the SS322. Continue through Montemerano and the Terme di Saturnia before curving back to Sovana.

TRIP HIGHLIGHT

## 2 Sovana

Tuscany's most significant Etruscan tombs are concentrated in the **Parco Archeologico della Città del Tufa** (www.leviecave.it), an archaeological park encompassing land around the villages of Sovana, Sorano and Vitozza. At Sovana, the best finds are in the **Necropolis** (admission €5; 10am-7pm Tue-Sun late Mar-Nov), just 1.5km west of the village. Here you'll find four major tombs, including the monumental **Tomba**

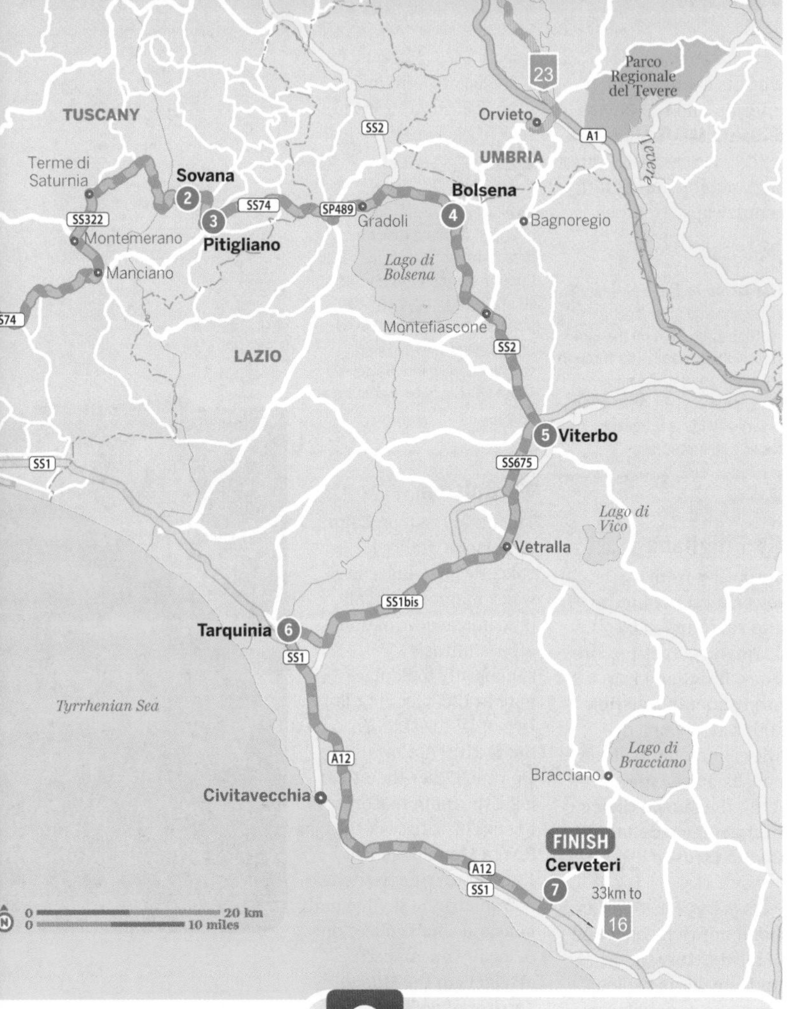


**Ildebranda**, with traces of carved columns and stairs, as well as two stretches of original Etruscan road – **Via del Cavone** and **Via Cava di Poggio Prisca**.

The village itself boasts a pretty main street and two beautiful Romanesque churches – the **Duomo** (daily

## LINK YOUR TRIP

### 16 Roaming Around Rome

At Cerveteri, pick up the A12 autostrada and continue south 45km, via Fiumicino, to Ostia Antica, Rome's very own Pompeii (p193).

### 23 Tuscan Landscapes

From Bolsena, take the SS2 Via Cassia 65km north to San Quirico d'Orcia, one of the gems in Tuscany's stunning Val d'Orcia (p253).

summer, Sat & Sun rest of yr), with its austere vaulted interior, and the **Chiesa di Santa Maria Maggiore** (daily summer, Sat & Sun rest of yr), notable for its 16th-century apse frescoes.

 p223

**The Drive »** Head east out of Sovana and after a couple of kilometres go right on the SP46. This winding road twists through scorched open peaks and occasional pockets of woodland as it descends to Pitigliano, about 10 minutes away.

---

TRIP HIGHLIGHT

## 3 Pitigliano

Sprouting from a towering tufa outcrop and surrounded by dramatic gorges on three sides, Pitigliano is a lovely knot of twisting stairways, cobbled alleys and quaint stone houses. In the middle of it all, the **Museo Civico Archeologico della Civiltà Etrusca** (Piazza della Fortezza; adult/child €3/2; 10am-5pm Thu-Mon) has a small but rich collection of local Etruscan finds, including some huge *bucchero* (black earthenware pottery) dating from the 6th century BC.

The town also has an interesting Jewish history – at one point it was dubbed 'Little Jerusalem' – which you can find out about at **La Piccola Gerusalemme** (www.lapiccolagerusalemme.it; Vicolo Manin 30; adult/reduced €4/3; 10am-1pm & 2.30-6pm Sun-Fri Apr-Sep, 10am-12.30pm & 3-5.30pm Sun-Fri Oct-Mar).

p223

**The Drive »** Head east on the SS74 until the road forks. Bear right for Gradoli and follow through the increasingly lush countryside until you hit the fast-flowing SS2 (Via Cassia). Go right and skirt the lake's northern banks into Bolsena. All told it should take about half an hour.

---

## 4 Bolsena

The main town on **Lago di Bolsena**, Italy's largest volcanic lake, Bolsena was a major medieval pilgrimage destination after a miracle supposedly took place here in 1263, leading Pope Urban IV to establish the festival of Corpus Domini. Other than the lake, the main reason to stop by is to visit the **Rocca Monaldeschi**, a 13th-century fortress that dominates the skyline and houses a small collection of locally unearthed artefacts in the **Museo Territorial del Lago di Bolsena** (Piazza Monaldeschi 1; adult/reduced €5/3.50; 10am-1pm & 4-9pm Tue-Sun Jun-Sep, shorter hrs rest of yr).

**The Drive »** It's a straightforward 50-minute drive to Viterbo along the SS2. This takes you down Lago di Bolsena's eastern side, past orchards, vineyards and olive groves through the medieval town of Montefiascone and on to Viterbo.

---

## 5 Viterbo

Founded by the Etruscans and eventually taken over by Rome (Roma), Viterbo was an important medieval centre, and in the 13th century became the residence of the popes. Its Etruscan past is chronicled at the **Museo Nazionale Etrusco** (Piazza della Rocca; admission €6;

Pitigliano

⌚8.30am-7.30pm Tue-Sun), one of several interesting sights in the walled *centro storico*. To the south, the Renaissance **Piazza del Plebiscito** is overlooked by **Palazzo dei Priori** (Piazza del Plebiscito; admission free; ⌚9am-1pm & 3-7pm), Viterbo's city hall, which boasts some fine 16th-century frescoes. Southwest of here, **Piazza San Lorenzo** was the medieval city's religious heart, where cardinals came to vote for their popes and pray in the 12th-century **Cattedrale di San Lorenzo**.

Next door, the **Museo del Colle del Duomo** (adult/reduced incl guided visit to Palazzo dei Papi, Sala del Conclave & Loggia €7/5;⌚10am-1pm & 3-8pm Tue-Sun, to 6pm winter) displays a small collection of religious artefacts, including a reliquary said to contain the chin (!) of John the Baptist. The adjacent **Palazzo dei Papi** was built in the 13th century to entice the papacy away from Rome. Its main feature is the **Sala del Conclave**, an impressive hall where five popes were elected.

p223

**The Drive »** Exit Viterbo and pick up the SS675 heading towards Rome. Continue on this fast dual carriageway until the turn-off for SS2 (Via Cassia). Take this and continue to Vetralla, where you should go right onto the SS1bis (Via Aurelia bis) and continue on to Tarquinia. Allow 50 minutes all told.

TRIP HIGHLIGHT

## 6 Tarquinia

The pick of Lazio's Etruscan towns, Tarquinia is a gem. Its highlight is the 7th-century-BC **Necropolis** (Via Ripagretta; adult/child €6/3, incl museum €8/4; ⌚8.30am-1hr before sunset Tue-Sun), one of Italy's most important Etruscan sites. Some 6000 tombs have been excavated here since 1489, of which 20 are open to the public, including the **Tomba della Caccia e della Pesca**, the richly decorated **Tomba dei Leopardi**, and the **Tomba della Fustigazione** with its erotic depiction of ancient S&M.

In the *centro storico,* the **Museo Nazionale Tarquiniense** (Piazza Cavour; adult/child €6/3, incl Necropolis €8/4; ⌚8.30am-7.30pm Tue-Sun) is a delightful museum, showcasing some wonderful Etruscan artefacts, including a breathtaking terracotta frieze of winged horses (the Cavalli Alati).

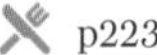 p223

**The Drive »** The easiest way to Cerveteri, about 45 minutes away, is by the A12 autostrada. Take this towards Rome/Civitavecchia and exit at the Cerveteri/Ladispoli turn-off. After the toll booth, head left into town.

TRIP HIGHLIGHT

## 7 Cerveteri

Cerveteri, or Kysry to the Etruscans and Caere to Latin-speakers, was one of the most important commercial centres in the Mediterranean from the 7th to the 5th century BC. The main sight is the Unesco-listed **Necropoli di Banditaccia** (Via del Necropoli; adult/reduced €6/3, incl museum €8/4; ⌚8.30am-1hr before sunset) just outside town. This 10-hectare site is laid out like a town of the dead, with streets, squares and terraces of *tumuli* (circular tomb structures cut into the earth and capped with turf). Some of the major tombs, including the 6th-century-BC **Tomba dei Rilievi**, are decorated with painted reliefs.

Back in Cerveteri, the **Museo Nazionale di Cerveteri** (Piazza Santa Maria; adult/reduced €6/3, incl Necropolis €8/4; ⌚8.30am-7.30pm Tue-Sun) displays treasures from the tombs.

 p223

### THE ETRUSCANS

Of the many Italic tribes that emerged from the Stone Age, the Etruscans left the most enduring mark. By the 7th century BC their city-states – places such as Caere (modern-day Cerveteri), Tarquinii (Tarquinia), Veii (Veio), Perusia (Perugia), Volaterrae (Volterra) and Arretium (Arezzo) – were the dominant forces in central Italy.

Debate rages about their origins – Roman historian Herodotus claimed they came to Italy from Asia Minor to escape famine – but what is not disputed is that they gave rise to a sophisticated society based on agriculture, trade and mineral mining. They were skilled architects, and although little remains of their buildings, archaeologists have found evidence of aqueducts, bridges and sewers, as well as temples. In artistic terms, they were known for their jewellery and tomb decoration, producing elaborate stone sarcophagi and bright, vivid frescoes.

For much of their existence, they were rivals of the Greeks, who had colonised much of southern Italy from the 8th century BC, but in the end it was the Romans who finally conquered them. In 396 BC they lost the key town of Veii, and by the 2nd century BC they and their land had largely been incorporated into the rapidly expanding Roman Republic.

# Eating & Sleeping

## Porto Ercole, Monte Argentario 1

**Il Pellicano** Gastronomic €€€

(0564 83 81 11; www.pellicanohotel.com; Località Lo Sbarcatello; set menu €125; dinner Apr-Oct) Proud possessor of two Michelin stars, this classy restaurant at the five-star hotel of the same name specialises in seafood and has two outdoor terraces with spectacular views. There's also a less-expensive poolside grill and bar here.

## Sovana 2

**La Tavernetta** Trattoria €

(Via del Pretorio 3; pizzas €4-6, meals €22; daily summer, Wed-Mon rest of yr) Serving traditional local dishes all day and pizzas from its wood-fired oven at night, this casual eatery is a safe choice for a simple meal.

## Pitigliano 3

**Il Tufo Allegro** Traditional Italian €

(0564 61 61 92; Vicolo della Costituzione 5; 3-course menus €22-24; closed Tue & Wed lunch) The aromas emanating from the kitchen door should be enough to draw you down to the cavernous dining room, which is carved out of tufa foundations. The chef is known for his *menù Goym* (Gentiles menu), which features Jewish-influenced dishes such as *buglione d'agnello* (lamb soup with tomato and bread).

**Le Camere del Ceccottino** Pensione €

(0564 61 49 26; Via Roma 159; r €80-100; ) This sparkling *pensione* (guesthouse) offers an excellent location near the *duomo* and well-equipped rooms (satellite TV, tea-and-coffee-making facilities, comfortable beds). Opt for the superior or prestige room if possible, as the standard versions are slightly cramped. No breakfast.

## Viterbo 5

**Ristorante Tre Re** Trattoria €€

(0761 30 46 19; Via Gattesco 3; meals €35; Fri-Wed) This historical trattoria dishes up steaming plates of tasty local specialities and seasonally driven dishes. None is more typical than the *pollo alla viterbese*, excellent roast chicken stuffed with spiced potato and green olives.

**Tuscia Hotel** Hotel €

(0761 34 44 00; www.tusciahotel.com; Via Cairoli 41; d €62-82; P ) The best of the city's midrange options, this central, spick-and-span three-star is leagues ahead of the competition in cleanliness and comfort. The rooms are large, light and kitted out with satellite TV. There's also a sunny roof terrace and private garage (€8).

## Tarquinia 6

**Ristorante Arcadia** Traditional Italian €€

(0766 85 55 01; Via Mazzini 6; meals €30; Tue-Sun) In a side street adjacent to the Museo Nazionale Tarquiniense, this friendly restaurant serves up excellent pasta and juicy grilled meats.

## Cerveteri 7

**Antica Locanda le Ginestre** Traditional Italian €€

(06 994 06 72; Piazza Santa Maria 5; meals €35; Tue-Sun) This top-notch family-run restaurant offers delicious food prepared with organically grown local produce and served in an elegant dining room or flower-filled courtyard. Book ahead.

***Assisi*** *Admire glorious frescoes at Basilica di San Francesco*

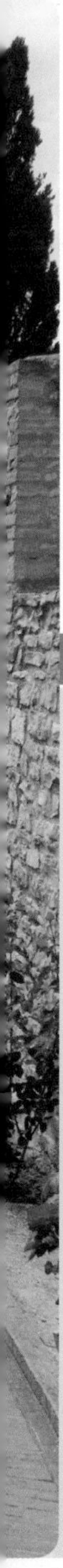

# Monasteries of Tuscany & Umbria

*This trip takes in world-famous basilicas, remote hermitages and secluded sanctuaries as it leads from Assisi to medieval monasteries in the windswept woodlands of eastern Tuscany.*

## TRIP HIGHLIGHTS

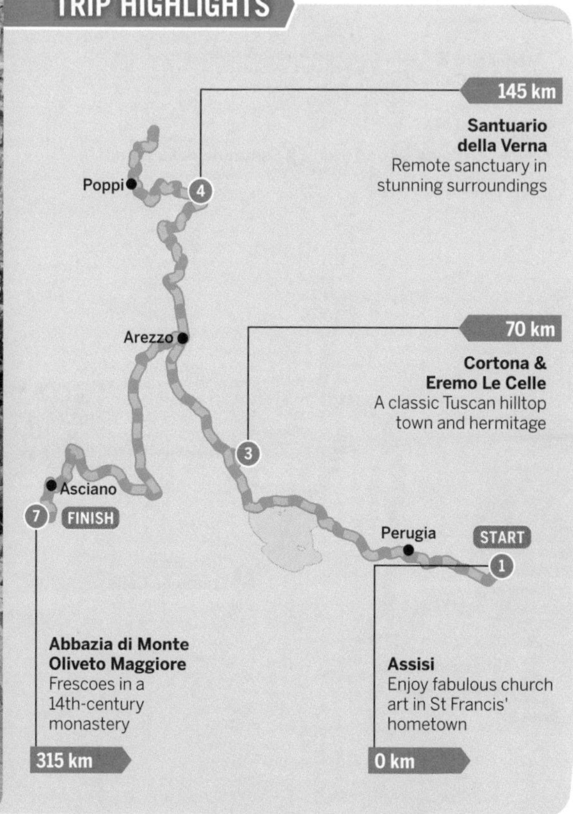

**145 km**

**Santuario della Verna**
Remote sanctuary in stunning surroundings

Poppi
4

Arezzo

**70 km**

**Cortona & Eremo Le Celle**
A classic Tuscan hilltop town and hermitage

3

Asciano
7 FINISH

Perugia
START
1

**Abbazia di Monte Oliveto Maggiore**
Frescoes in a 14th-century monastery

**315 km**

**Assisi**
Enjoy fabulous church art in St Francis' hometown

**0 km**

**5 DAYS**
**315KM / 196 MILES**

**GREAT FOR...**

**BEST TIME TO GO**

Summer and early autumn are best for monastic visits.

The towered castle at Poppi.

The forests around the Santuario della Verna.

# 20 Monasteries of Tuscany & Umbria

Away from the crowds and bright lights, an austere 11th-century monastery sits in silence surrounded by forest and rocky mountainsides. Welcome to the Monastero & Sacro Eremo di Camaldoli, one of the remote, art-rich monasteries that you'll discover on this tour of central Umbria and Tuscany's northeastern Casentino region. Most people don't venture up here, but with its ancient forests and dark peaks, it makes for a gripping drive.

TRIP HIGHLIGHT

## 1 Assisi

Birthplace of St Francis, this medieval hilltop town is a major destination for millions of pilgrims. Its biggest drawcard is the **Basilica di San Francesco** (Piazza di San Francesco), which comprises two gloriously frescoed churches – the Gothic **upper church** (⌚8.30am-6.45pm Easter-Nov, to 5.45pm Dec-Easter), which was built between 1230 and 1253 and features superb frescoes by Giotto

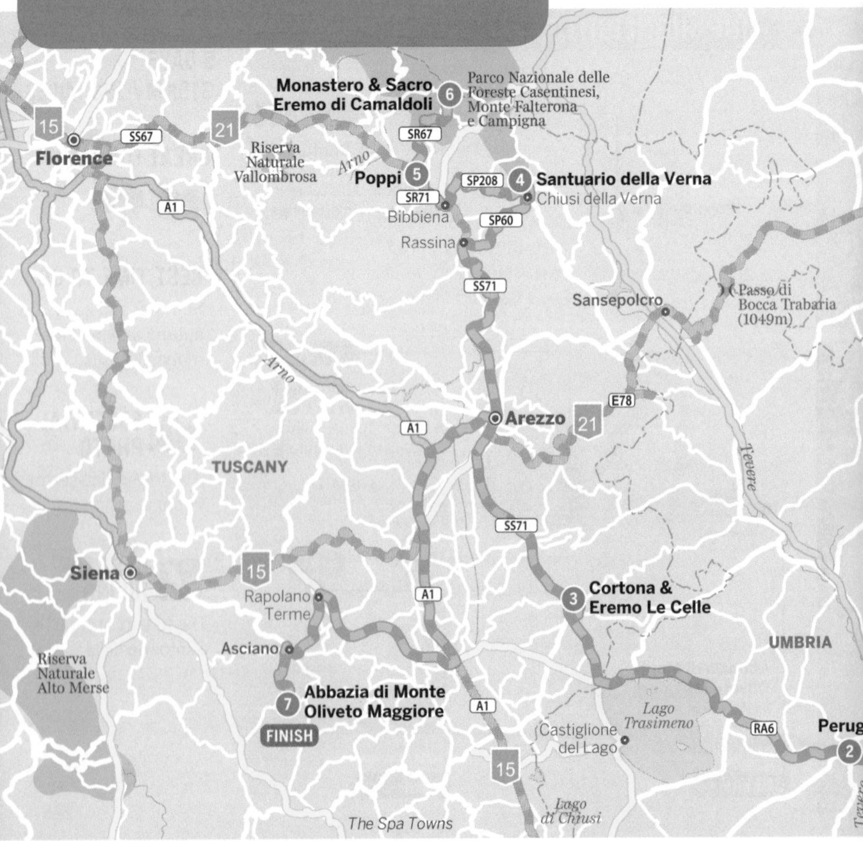

and works by Cimabue and Pietro Cavallini, and the dimly lit **lower church** (6am-6.45pm Easter-Nov, to 5.45pm Dec-Easter), with frescoes by Simone Martini, Cimabue and Pietro Lorenzetti.

At the other end of the *centro storico* (historic centre), the 13th-century **Basilica di Santa Chiara** (Piazza Santa Chiara; 6.30am-noon & 2-7pm) is the last resting place of St Clare, a contemporary of St Francis and founder of the Order of the Poor Ladies, aka the Poor Clares.

p231

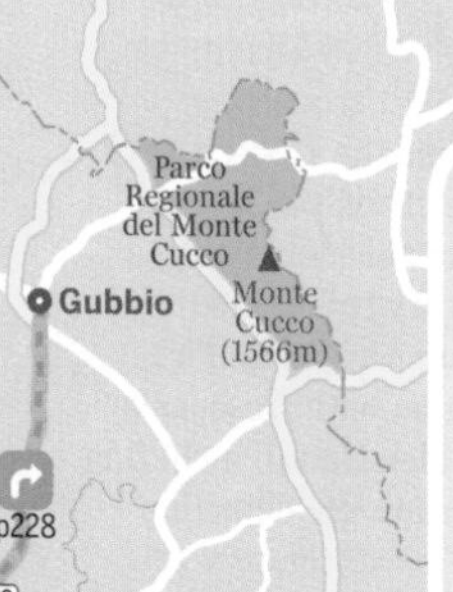


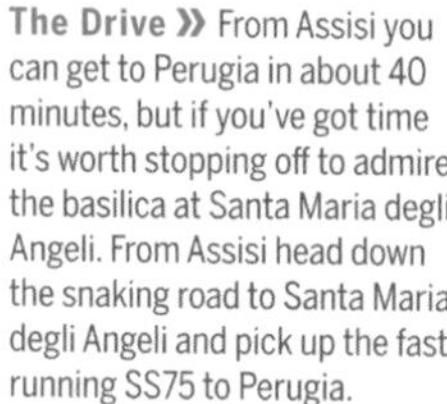

**The Drive »** From Assisi you can get to Perugia in about 40 minutes, but if you've got time it's worth stopping off to admire the basilica at Santa Maria degli Angeli. From Assisi head down the snaking road to Santa Maria degli Angeli and pick up the fast-running SS75 to Perugia.

## 2 Perugia

With its hilltop medieval centre and international student population, Perugia is as close as Umbria gets to a heaving metropolis – which isn't all that close. Action is focused on the main strip, **Corso Vannucci**, and **Piazza IV Novembre**, home to the austere 14th-century **Cattedrale di San Lorenzo** (Piazza IV Novembre; 10am-12.30pm & 3-5.30pm Tue-Sun) with its unfinished two-tone facade.

Over the square, the 13th-century **Palazzo dei Priori** houses Perugia's best museums, including the **Galleria Nazionale dell'Umbria** (Corso Vannucci 19; adult/reduced €6.50/3.25; 8.30am-7.30pm Tue-Sun), with a collection containing works by local heroes Perugino and Pinturicchio. Close to the *palazzo* (mansion), the impressive **Nobile Collegio del Cambio** (Exchange Hall; Corso Vannucci 25; adult/reduced €4.50/2.60; 9am-12.30pm & 2.30-5.30pm Mon-Sat, 9am-1pm Sun) also has some wonderful frescoes by Perugino.

p231

**The Drive »** From Perugia it's just under an hour's drive to Cortona. Pick up the RA6 Raccordo Autostradale Bettolle-Perugia and head west, skirting Lago Trasimeno before joining the northbound SS71 at the lake's northwestern corner. From there the pace slackens as the road cuts through vineyards and sunflower fields up to Cortona.

TRIP HIGHLIGHT

## 3 Cortona & Eremo Le Celle

A stunning hilltop town, and setting for the film *Under the Tuscan Sun*, Cortona has a remarkable artistic pedigree. Fra' Angelico

### LINK YOUR TRIP

**15 World Heritage Wonders**

From the Abbazia di Monte Oliveto Maggiore, head 30km north to Siena, one of the stars of this classic trip (p181).

**21 Piero della Francesca Trail**

Push north from Cortona to Arezzo and join up with this art-based trail that runs from Urbino to Florence (p233).

lived and worked here in the late 14th century, and fellow artists Luca Signorelli and Pietro da Cortona were both born within its walls – all three are represented in the excellent **Museo Diocesano** (Piazza del Duomo 1; adult/child €5/3; ⌚10am-7pm Tue-Sun).

Three kilometres north of town in dense woodland, the Franciscan hermitage called **Eremo Le Celle** (www.lecelle.it; Strada dei Cappuccini 1) sits next to a picturesque stream. It's a wonderfully tranquil spot, disturbed only by the bells calling the resident friars to mass in the cave-like **Chiesa Cella di San Francesco**.

p231

**The Drive »** The 1¾-hour drive to the Santuario della Verna takes you deep into the heart of the Casentino hills. From Cortona head north on the SS71. About 25km beyond Arezzo, in Rassina, follow signs right and continue up the densely wooded slopes to Chiusi della Verna. The sanctuary is about 3km above Chiusi.

TRIP HIGHLIGHT

## 4 Santuario della Verna

St Francis of Assisi is said to have received the stigmata at the **Santuario della Verna** (www.santuariolaverna.org, in Italian; ⌚6.30am-7.30pm winter, to 10pm summer) on the southeastern edge of the **Parco Nazionale delle Foreste Casentinesi, Monte Falterona e Campigna** (www.parcoforestecasentinesi.it). The sanctuary, which is dramatically positioned on a windswept mountainside, harbours some fine works by Andrea della Robbia, including ceramics in the **basilica** and a magnificent *Crucifixion* in the **Cappella delle Stimmate** (⌚8am-5pm winter, to 7pm summer), the 13th-century chapel built on the spot where the saint supposedly received the stigmata.

**The Drive »** Allow about 40 minutes to Poppi from the sanctuary. The first leg, along the SP208, winds through the lush tree-covered mountains to Bibbiena, from where it's an easy 5km north on the SR71. You'll know you're near when you see Poppi's castle up on your left.

## 5 Poppi

Perched high above the Arno plain, Poppi is crowned by **Castello dei Conti Guidi** (www.buonconte.com, in Italian; Piazza Repubblica 1; adult/child €5/4; ⌚10am-7pm daily mid-May–Oct, shorter hr rest of yr). Inside the 13th-century structure, you'll find a fairy-tale courtyard, a library full of medieval manuscripts, and a chapel with frescoes by Taddeo Gaddi, including a gruesome depiction of *Herod's Feast* with a dancing Salome and headless John the Baptist.

p231

### DETOUR: GUBBIO

**Start: 2 Perugia**

Stacked on the steep slopes of an Umbrian mountainside, the medieval town of Gubbio is well worth a visit. Highlights include **Piazza Grande**, with grandstand views over the surrounding countryside, and the **Museo Civico** (Palazzo dei Consoli; Piazza Grande; adult/reduced €5/2.50; ⌚10am-1pm & 3-6pm), where you'll find Gubbio's most famous treasures – the Eugubian Tablets. Dating to between 300 BC and 100 BC, these bronze tablets are the best existing examples of ancient Umbrian script.

For a change of scene, and yet more views, take the **Funivia** (ticket €5; ⌚9am-7pm daily summer, shorter hr rest of yr) up to the Basilica di Sant'Ubaldo high above up on Monte Ingino.

Gubbio is just over an hour's drive northeast of Perugia on the SS298.

**Abbazia di Monte Oliveto Maggiore**

## ST FRANCIS OF ASSISI

Born in Assisi in 1181, the son of a wealthy merchant, Giovanni Francesco di Bernardone spent his youth carousing. However, following a holy vision in his early 20s, he decided to give up his possessions in order to live a humble, 'primitive' life in imitation of Christ, preaching and helping the poor. He travelled widely around Italy (and beyond) performing miracles (curing the sick, communicating with animals) and setting up monasteries until his death in 1226. He was canonised two years later.

Today, various places claim links with St Francis (San Francesco), including Gubbio where he supposedly brokered a deal between the townsfolk and a man-eating wolf, and Rome where he was given permission by Pope Innocent III to found the Franciscan order at the Basilica di San Giovanni in Laterano.



**The Drive »** Camaldoli is about 14km from Poppi. Take SR67 (Via Camaldoli) and follow it up through the forest until you come to a fork in the road – the hermitage is uphill to the right; the monastery is downhill to the left.

### 6 Monastero & Sacro Eremo di Camaldoli

The 11th-century **Monastero & Sacro Eremo di Camaldoli** (www.monasterodicamaldoli.it) sits immersed in thick forest on the southern fringes of the Parco Nazionale delle Foreste Casentinesi, Monte Falterona e Campigna. Home to about 20 Benedictine monks, it boasts some wonderful art: in the monastery's **church** you'll find three paintings by Vasari: *Deposition from the Cross; Virgin with Child, St John the Baptist and St Girolamo;* and a Nativity*;* while at the hermitage, the small church harbours an exquisite altarpiece by Andrea della Robbia.

For a souvenir, pop into the 16th-century **pharmacy** (⌚9am-12.30pm & 2.30-6pm) and pick up soap, perfumes and other items made by the resident monks.

**The Drive »** From the Monastero, it's a 2¼-hour haul down to the Abbazia di Monte Oliveto Maggiore, 10km south of Asciano. From Camaldoli double back to the SS71 and head south for Arezzo and the A1. Come off the autostrada at the Valdichiana exit and follow for Siena until the Rapolano Terme turn-off. Take this and continue on to Asciano and the Abbazia.

TRIP HIGHLIGHT

### 7 Abbazia di Monte Oliveto Maggiore

Dating to the late 14th century, the red-brick **Abbazia di Monte Oliveto Maggiore** (www.monteolivetomaggiore.it; admission free, library donation requested; ⌚9.15am-noon & 3.15-5pm Mon-Sat, 9am-12.30pm Sun) is still a retreat for Benedictine monks who live the contemplative life while tending vines and olives and studying in one of Italy's most important medieval libraries. For visitors, the highlight is the Great Cloister's magnificent **fresco series**, painted by Luca Signorelli and Il Sodoma, illustrating the life of St Benedict. You can also visit the church, frescoed refectory, magnificent 16th-century library, pharmacy and chapter house.

# Eating & Sleeping

## Assisi ①

### Trattoria Pallotta — Traditional Italian €€

(☎075 81 26 49; Vicolo della Volta Pinta; meals from €25; Wed-Mon) Head through the Volta Pinta (Painted Vault) off Piazza del Comune into this gorgeous setting of vaulted brick walls and wood-beamed ceilings. They serve all the Umbrian classics here, as well as a less traditional vegetarian menu.

### Hotel Alexander — Hotel €€

(☎0758 1 61 90; www.hotelalexanderassisi.it; Piazza Chiesa Nuova 6; d €80-140; ) In a central location by the Chiesa Nuova, this comfortable hotel has nine rooms decorated in a restrained modern style. Their size varies, so if possible get one on the top floor, which is huge and has great views.

## Perugia ②

### Ristorante Nànà — Traditional Italian €€

(☎075 573 35 71; Corso Cavour 202; meals €35; Mon-Sat) This excellent family-run restaurant serves rustic dishes in a refined *nuovo* style, such as *ravioli di patate e tartufo su crema di broccoli* (potato and truffle ravioli on a bed of creamed broccoli).

### Primavera Minihotel — Hotel €

(☎075 572 16 57; www.primaveraminihotel.it; Via Vincioli 8; d €70-100; @) This central hotel, run by a dedicated English- and French-speaking mother-daughter team, is a great find, tucked in a quiet corner. The magnificent views complement the bright and airy rooms. Breakfast costs €3 to €8.

## Cortona & Eremo Le Celle ③

### La Bucaccia — Traditional Italian €€

(☎0575 60 60 39; www.labucaccia.it; Via Ghibellina 17; meals €35) Set in a medieval stable that was incorporated into a Renaissance *palazzo*, this is an atmospheric and enjoyable option for characteristic Tuscan fare. The four-course set menu is particularly good value.

### Casa Chilenne — B&B €€

(☎0575 60 33 20; www.casachilenne.com; Via Nazionale 65; s/d €85/110; @) Run by American-born Jeanette and her Cortonese husband Luciano, this wonderfully welcoming B&B has it all – a central location, comfortable rooms, a lavish breakfast spread and keen prices.

## Poppi ⑤

### L'Antica Cantina — Traditional Italian €€

(☎0575 52 98 44; www.anticacantina.com; Via Lapucci 2; set menus €30; closed Mon, Tue lunch & all Jan) An old-fashioned vaulted dining space located on a side street off Via Cesare Battisti, 'The Old Cantina' is Poppi's best eatery. It offers set three-course menus and genial service.

### Borgo Corsignano — Boutique Hotel €€

(☎0575 50 02 94; www.borgocorsignano.it; Località Corsignano; d €100-130; P@) Occupying a medieval village that was once home to Camaldoli monks, this gorgeous country hotel is a five-minute drive from Poppi. It offers self-contained apartments and a wealth of facilities, including two swimming pools, a wellness centre, a *cantinetta* (small wine cellar) and sculpture-filled gardens.

**Arezzo** *Time your visit for a medieval festival*

# Piero della Francesca Trail

*Follow in the footsteps of the Renaissance painter Piero della Francesca as you wind your way from the medieval centre of Urbino to Florence, stopping en route to admire his greatest works.*

## TRIP HIGHLIGHTS

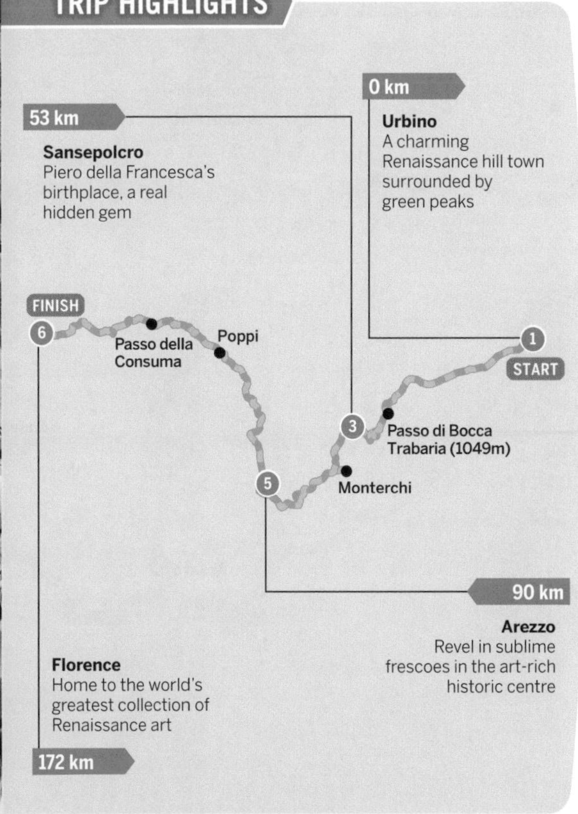

**0 km**
**Urbino**
A charming Renaissance hill town surrounded by green peaks

**53 km**
**Sansepolcro**
Piero della Francesca's birthplace, a real hidden gem

**90 km**
**Arezzo**
Revel in sublime frescoes in the art-rich historic centre

**172 km**
**Florence**
Home to the world's greatest collection of Renaissance art

FINISH 6 · Passo della Consuma · Poppi · 5 · Monterchi · 3 · Passo di Bocca Trabaria (1049m) · 1 START

**7 DAYS**
**172KM / 107 MILES**

**GREAT FOR...**

**BEST TIME TO GO**

June to September for summer pageantry.

**ESSENTIAL PHOTO**

Views from the Passo della Consuma.

**BEST FOR FILM BUFFS**

Arezzo's Piazza Grande, a location for scenes in *La vita è bella*.

# 21 Piero della Francesca Trail

The Piero della Francesca trail was first advocated by the British author Aldous Huxley in *The Best Picture,* a 1925 essay he wrote in praise of della Francesca's *Resurrezione* (Resurrection). The roads have improved since Huxley's day but the trail remains a labour of love for art fans as it leads through dramatic Apennine scenery, over mountain passes and onto bustling medieval towns, culminating in Italy's revered Renaissance city, Florence (Firenze).

TRIP HIGHLIGHT

### 1 Urbino

Hidden away in hilly Le Marche, the charming town of Urbino was a key player in the Renaissance art world. Its ruler, the Duca Federico da Montefeltro, was a major patron and many of the top artists and intellectuals of the day spent time here at his behest. Piero della Francesca arrived in 1469 and, along with a crack team of artists and architects, worked

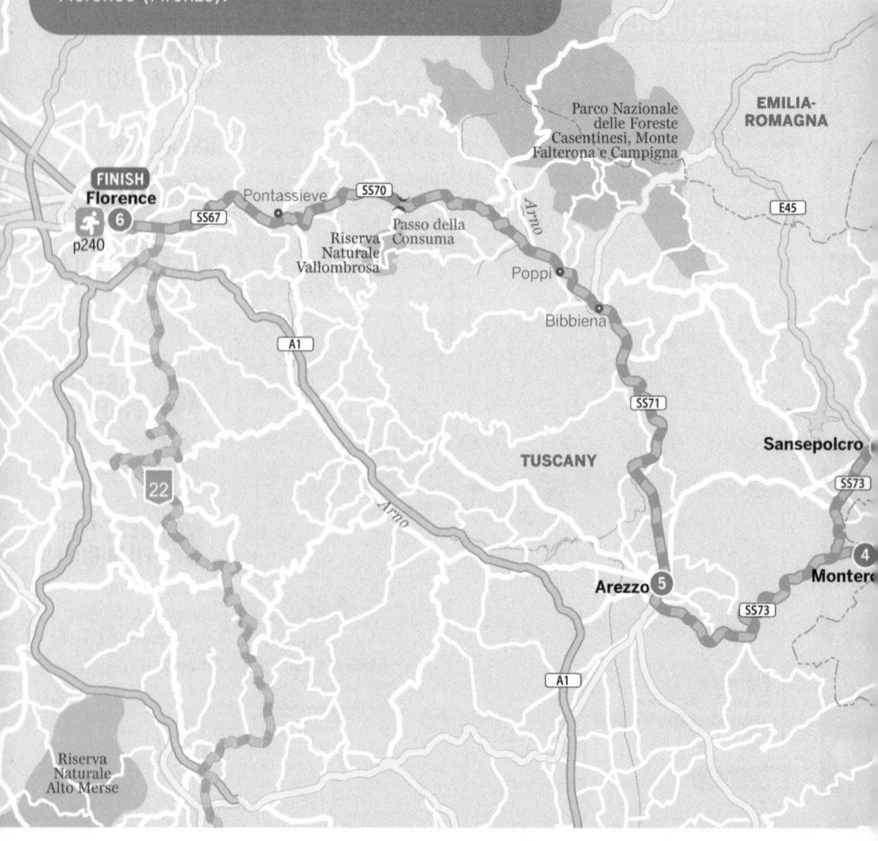

on the duke's palatial residence, the **Palazzo Ducale** (☎199 151123; www.palazzoducaleurbino.it; Piazza Duca Federico; adult/reduced €5/2.50; ⏲8.30am-2pm Mon, to 7.15pm Tue-Sun). This magnificent palace now houses the Galleria Nazionale delle Marche and its rich collection of Renaissance paintings, including Piero della Francesca's great *Flagellazione di Cristo* (Flagellation of Christ).

A short walk away, you can pay homage to Urbino's greatest son at the **Casa Natale di Raffaello** (Via Raffaello 57; adult/reduced €3/1; ⏲9am-1pm & 3-7pm Mon-Sat, 10am-1pm Sun Mar-Oct, 9am-2pm Mon-Sat, 10am-1pm Sun Nov-Feb), the house where superstar painter Raphael was born in 1483.

p239

**The Drive »** The 50km (1½-hour) drive up to the Passo di Bocca Trabaria involves hundreds of hairpin bends and tortuous climbing as it traverses a magnificent swath of Apennine mountains. From Urbino pick up the SS73bis and head through Montesoffio and Urbania before climbing up to the pass.

## 2 Passo di Bocca Trabaria

The Bocca Trabaria mountain pass (1049m) divides the Valtiberina (Tiber Valley), on the Urbino side, from the upper Valle del Metauro (Metauro Valley). It's a spectacular spot, well worth a quick pause, with sweeping views over the Apennines and several hiking trails heading into the surrounding mountains.

**The Drive »** Allow about half an hour for the 20km descent from Bocca Trabaria to Sansepolcro. For the first 15km or so the winding road plunges down the valley slopes to San Giustino, from where it's an easy hop northwest to Sansepolcro on the SS3bis.

### LINK YOUR TRIP

**22 Tuscan Wine Tour**
From Florence head south on the SR222 to the Castello di Verrazzano, one of the historic Chianti vineyards on this classic wine tour (p243).

**24 Foodie Emilia-Romagna**
Head 125km north from Urbino via the A14 autostrada to connect with Ravenna and this tasty trip through Emilia-Romagna (p261).

TRIP HIGHLIGHT

## 3 Sansepolcro

Birthplace of Piero della Francesca and home to three of his great works, Sansepolcro is an authentic hidden gem. Its unspoiled historic centre is littered with *palazzi* (mansions) and churches harbouring great works of art, including the 14th-century **Cattedrale di San Giovanni Evangelista** (Via Giacomo Matteotti 4; 8.30am-12.30pm & 3-7pm), which contains an *Ascension* by Perugino. The highlight, though, is the **Museo Civico** (www.museocivicosansepolcro.it; Via Aggiunti 65; adult/reduced €8/5; 9.30am-1.30pm & 2.30-7pm), whose small but top-notch collection boasts three Piero della Francesca masterpieces: *Resurrezione* (Resurrection; c 1460), the *Madonna della Misericordia* (c 1455–60) and *Saint Julian* (1455–58).

p239

**The Drive »** Head southwest from Sansepolcro along the SS73 following signs for Arezzo. After roughly 12km of easy driving through pleasant green countryside, turn left onto the SP221 and continue for 3km to Monterchi. It takes about 25 minutes.

## 4 Monterchi

This unassuming village boasts one of Piero della Francesca's best-loved works, the *Madonna del Parto* (Pregnant Madonna, c 1460). Housed in its own museum, the **Museo della Madonna del Parto** (Via della Reglia 1; adult/reduced €3.50/2; 9am-1pm & 2-7pm), it depicts a heavily pregnant Madonna wearing a simple blue gown and standing in a tent, flanked by two angels who hold back the tent's curtains as a framing device. In a nice touch, pregnant women get free entry to the museum.

**The Drive »** Double back the way you came and turn left onto the quick-running SS73. The road, which opens to four lanes in certain tracts, snakes its way through thickly wooded hills up to Arezzo.

TRIP HIGHLIGHT

## 5 Arezzo

The biggest town in eastern Tuscany, Arezzo has a distinguished cultural history. Petrarch and art historian Giorgio Vasari were both born here, and, between 1452 and 1466, Piero della Francesca painted one of his greatest works, the *Leggenda della Vera Croce* (Legend of the True Cross) fresco cycle in the **Basilica di San**

***Leggenda della Vera Croce*** Piero della Francesca's fresco cycle is in Arezzo's Basilica di San Francesco

**Francesco's Cappella Bacci** (Piazza San Francesco; adult/reduced €8/5; ⌚9am-6.30pm Mon-Fri, 9am-5.30pm Sat, 1-5.30pm Sun).

Once you've seen that, take time to admire the magnificent Romanesque facade of the **Pieve di Santa Maria** (Corso Italia 7; ⌚8.30am-12.30pm & 3-7pm) en route to the **Cattedrale di San Donato** (Piazza Duomo; ⌚7am-12.30pm & 3-6.30pm) and yet another della Francesca fresco – the exquisite *Mary Magdalene* (c 1460).

Film buffs should also stop by **Piazza Grande**, where scenes were filmed for Roberto Benigni's *La vita è bella* (Life is Beautiful), and where the city celebrates its big annual festival, the **Joust of the Saracino**, on the third Saturday in June and first Sunday in September.

p239

## PIERO DELLA FRANCESCA

Though many details about his life are hazy, it's believed that Piero della Francesca was born around 1420 in Sansepolcro and died in 1492. Trained as a painter from the age of 15, his distinctive use of perspective, mastery of light and skilful synthesis of form and colour set him apart from his artistic contemporaries. His most famous works are the *Leggenda della Vera Croce* (Legend of the True Cross) in Arezzo, and *Resurrezione* (Resurrection) in Sansepolcro, but he is most fondly remembered for his luminous *Madonna del Parto* (Pregnant Madonna) in Monterchi.

## THE RENAISSANCE

Bridging the gap between the Middle Ages and the modern world, the Renaissance *(il Rinascimento)* emerged in 14th-century Florence and quickly spread throughout Italy.

### The Early Days

Giotto di Bondone (1267–1337) is generally considered the first great Renaissance artist, and with his exploration of perspective and a new interest in realistic portraiture, he inspired artists such as Lorenzo Ghiberti (1378–1455) and Donatello (c 1382–1466). In architectural terms, the key man was Filippo Brunelleschi (1377–1446), whose dome on Florence's Duomo was one of the era's blockbuster achievements. Of the following generation, Sandro Botticelli (c 1444–1510) was a major player and his *Birth of Venus* (c 1485) was one of the most successful attempts to resolve the great conundrum of the age – how to give a painting both a realistic perspective and a harmonious composition.

### The High Renaissance

By the early 16th century, the focus had shifted to Rome and Venice. Leading the way in Rome was Donato Bramante (1444–1514), whose classical architectural style greatly influenced the Veneto-born Andrea Palladio (1508–80). One of Bramante's great rivals was Michelangelo Buonarotti (1475–1564), whose legendary genius was behind the Sistine Chapel frescoes, the dome over St Peter's Basilica, and the *David* sculpture. Other headline acts included Leonardo da Vinci (1452–1519), who developed a painting technique (sfumato) enabling him to modulate his contours using colour; and Raphael (1483–1520), who more than any other painter mastered the art of depicting large groups of people in a realistic and harmonious way.

**The Drive »** The quickest route to Florence is via the A1 autostrada, but you'll enjoy the scenery more if you follow the SS71 up the Casentino valley and on to the medieval castle town of Poppi. At Poppi pick up the SS70 to tackle the heavily forested Passo della Consuma (1050m) and descend to Pontassieve and the SS67 into Florence. Allow about 2¾ hours.

TRIP HIGHLIGHT

## 6 Florence

The last port of call is Florence, the city where the Renaissance kicked off in the late 14th century. Paying the way was the Medici family, who sponsored the great artists of the day and whose collection today graces the **Galleria degli Uffizi** (Uffizi Gallery; www.uffizi.firenze.it; Piazza degli Uffizi 6; adult/EU concession €6.50/3.25, plus possible exhibition supplement; ⏲8.15am-6.50pm Tue-Sun). Here you can admire Piero della Francesca's famous portrait of the red-robed *Duke and Duchess of Urbino* (1465–1472) alongside works by Renaissance giants, from Giotto and Cimabue to Botticelli, Leonardo da Vinci, Raphael and Titian.

Elsewhere in town, you'll find spiritually uplifting works by Fra' Angelico in the wonderful **Museo di San Marco** (Piazza San Marco 1; adult/reduced €4/2; ⏲8.15am-1.50pm Mon-Fri, to 4.50pm Sat & Sun, closed 1st, 3rd, 5th Sun & 2nd & 4th Mon of month), and superb frescoes by Masaccio, Masolino da Panicale and Filippino Lippi at the **Cappella Brancacci** (☎055 238 21 95; Piazza del Carmine 44; admission €6; ⏲10am-5pm Mon & Wed-Sat, 1-5pm Sun, booking necessary), over the river in the Basilica di Santa Maria del Carmine.

For a walking tour of the city, see p240.

✕ 🛏 p239

# Eating & Sleeping

## Urbino 1

**La Trattoria del Leone** Trattoria €

(0722 32 98 94; Via Cesare Battisti 5; meals €24; dinner daily, lunch Sat & Sun) This unassuming city-centre trattoria just off the main square specialises in inventive regional cuisine, so expect plenty of salamis and cheese, earthy roast meats and full-blooded red wines.

**Albergo Italia** Hotel €€

(0722 27 01; www.albergo-italia-urbino.it; Corso Garibaldi 32; s €50-70, d €80-120; ) Set behind the Palazzo Ducale, the Italia could not be better positioned. Modern but well designed, the multistorey building is restfully quiet while offering all the amenities of a business hotel. In warmer months, take breakfast on the balcony.

## Sansepolcro 3

**Ristorante Da Ventura** Traditional Italian €

(0575 74 25 60; www.albergodaventura.it; Via Aggiunti 30; meals €25; closed Mon & dinner Sun) A fabulous eatery known locally for its huge joints of roasted meat. For vegetarians there are generous plates of homemade pasta served with truffles or fresh porcini mushrooms. Upstairs, you can bunk down in a simple B&B (singles/doubles €45/65, half-board per person €50).

## Arezzo 5

**La Torre di Gnicche** Traditional Italian €€

(0575 35 20 35; Piaggia San Martino 8; meals €28; closed Wed & 2 weeks in Jan) Just off Piazza Grande, this is a fine restaurant specialising in traditional local dishes. Its soups are delicious – in summer try *pappa al pomodoro* (a thick bread and tomato soup), in winter *ribollita* (a 'reboiled' bean, vegetable and bread soup with black cabbage).

**Graziella Patio Hotel** Boutique Hotel €€€

(0575 40 19 62; www.hotelpatio.it; Via Cavour 23; d €165-250, ste €250-320; P) Each of the 10 themed rooms in Arezzo's most characterful hotel is dedicated to one of Bruce Chatwin's travel books and decorated accordingly. Request 'Utz' – it's the nicest. Valet parking is available.

## Florence 

**Trattoria Mario** Tuscan €

(www.trattoriamario.com; Via Rosina 2; meals €15-25; noon-3.30pm Mon-Sat, closed 3 weeks Aug) Get here at noon to ensure a stool around a shared table at this noisy, busy, fabulous trattoria. Monday and Thursday are tripe days, Friday is fish, and Saturday sees local Florentines flock here for a brilliantly blue *bistecca alla fiorentina* (T-bone steak). No advance reservations; no credit cards.

**Hotel Torre Guelfa** Historic Hotel €€

(055 239 63 38; www.hoteltorreguelfa.com; Borgo SS Apostoli 8; d from €100; ) If you want to kip in a genuine Florentine *palazzo* without breaking the bank, this well-appointed hotel is the address. Scale its 13th-century tower for a sundowner overlooking Florence and you'll be blown away. A couple of its spacious rooms share the same staggering panorama.

# STRETCH YOUR LEGS FLORENCE

**Start/Finish** Galleria dell'Accademia

**Distance** 2.5km

**Duration** One day

To get the best out of Florence (Firenze), leave your car and head into the city's historic centre on foot. This tour provides a great introduction to the city, passing through its headlining piazzas, basilicas and galleries.

**Take this walk on Trips**

## Galleria dell'Accademia

Before heading into the heart of the historic centre, take time to salute Florence's fabled poster boy. Michelangelo's *David* (1504), arguably the most famous sculpture in the Western world, stands in all his naked glory in the **Galleria dell'Accademia** (www.uffizi.firenze.it; Via Ricasoli 60; adult/reduced €6.50/3.25; ⌚8.15am-6.50pm Tue-Sun). He originally guarded Palazzo Vecchio but was moved here in 1873.

**The Walk ››** From the gallery, head south along Via Ricasoli, past the Carabé gelateria, down to Via de' Pucci. Turn right, skirting past Palazzo Pucci, as you continue on to Piazza San Lorenzo.

## Basilica di San Lorenzo

A fine example of Renaissance architecture, the **Basilica di San Lorenzo** (Piazza San Lorenzo; admission €3.50; ⌚10am-5.30pm Mon-Sat) is best known for its Brunelleschi-designed **Sagrestia Vecchia** (Old Sacristy). Around the corner, at the rear of the basilica, the **Cappelle Medicee** (Medici Chapels; Piazza Madonna degli Aldobrandini; adult/reduced €6/3; ⌚8.15am-1.50pm Tue-Sat, 2nd & 4th Mon & 1st, 3rd & 5th Sun of month) has some exquisite Michelangelo sculptures.

**The Walk ››** From Piazza Madonna degli Aldobrandini, head down Via de' Conti and its continuation Via F Zanetti to Via de' Cerretani. Hang a left and soon you'll see Piazza del Duomo ahead.

## Duomo

Florence's 14th-century **Duomo** (Piazza del Duomo; ⌚10am-5pm Mon-Wed & Fri, to 4.30pm Thu, to 4.45pm Sat, 1.30-4.45pm Sun) is the city's most iconic landmark with its pink, white and green marble facade and red-tiled **dome** (admission €8; ⌚8.30am-7pm Mon-Fri, to 5pm Sat). Nearby, you can climb the **campanile** (bell tower; admission €6; ⌚8.30am-7pm daily) and admire the bas-reliefs on the 11th-century **Battistero** (Piazza di San Giovanni; admission €5; ⌚11.15am-7pm Mon-Sat, 8.30am-2pm 1st Sat of month & Sun).

**The Walk ››** It's a straightforward 400m or so down Via dei Calzaiuoli to Piazza della Signoria.

## Piazza della Signoria

This lovely cafe-lined piazza is overlooked by the **Torre d'Arnolfo** (9am-9pm Fri-Wed & 9am-2pm Thu Apr-Sep, 10am-5pm Fri-Wed & 9am-2pm Thu Oct-Mar), the high point of **Palazzo Vecchio** (www.museicivicifiorentini.it; Piazza della Signoria; adult/reduced €6.50/4.50; 9am-7pm Fri-Wed, to 2pm Thu), Florence's medieval City Hall. It still houses the mayor's office but you can visit its lavish apartments.

**The Walk »** To get to the Galleria degli Uffizi takes a matter of seconds, although we can't vouch for how long it'll take to get inside. The gallery is just off the piazza's southeastern corner, in a grey porticoed palazzo.

## Galleria degli Uffizi

The **Galleria degli Uffizi** (Uffizi Gallery; www.uffizi.firenze.it; Piazza degli Uffizi 6; adult/EU concession €6.50/3.25, plus possible exhibition supplement; 8.15am-6.50pm Tue-Sun) boasts one of Italy's greatest art collections, bequeathed to Florence in 1743 by the Medici family on condition that it never leave the city. The highlight is the stash of Renaissance art, including Botticelli's *La nascita di Venere* (Birth of Venus), Leonardo da Vinci's *Annunciazione* (Annunciation) and Michelangelo's *Tondo doni* (Holy Family).

**The Walk »** Pick up Via Lambertesca, over the way from the gallery entrance, and follow it to Via Por Santa Maria. Go left and it's a short hop to the river.

## Ponte Vecchio

Ponte Vecchio, Florence's celebrated bridge, has twinkled with the wares of jewellers since the 16th century when Ferdinando I de' Medici ordered them here to replace the often malodorous presence of the town butchers, who were wont to toss unwanted leftovers into the river. The bridge as it stands was built in 1345 and was the only one in Florence saved from destruction by the retreating Germans in 1944.

**The Walk »** To get back to the Galleria dell'Accademia, pick up bus C1 from Lungarno Generale Diaz and head up to Piazza San Marco.

**Panzano in Chianti** *Wet your whistle in Italy's famed wine country*

CEPHAS PICTURE LIBRARY/ALAMY ©

Classic Trip

# Tuscan Wine Tour

22

*Tuscany has its fair share of highlights, but few can match the indulgence of a drive through its wine country – an intoxicating blend of scenery, acclaimed restaurants and ruby-red wine.*

## TRIP HIGHLIGHTS

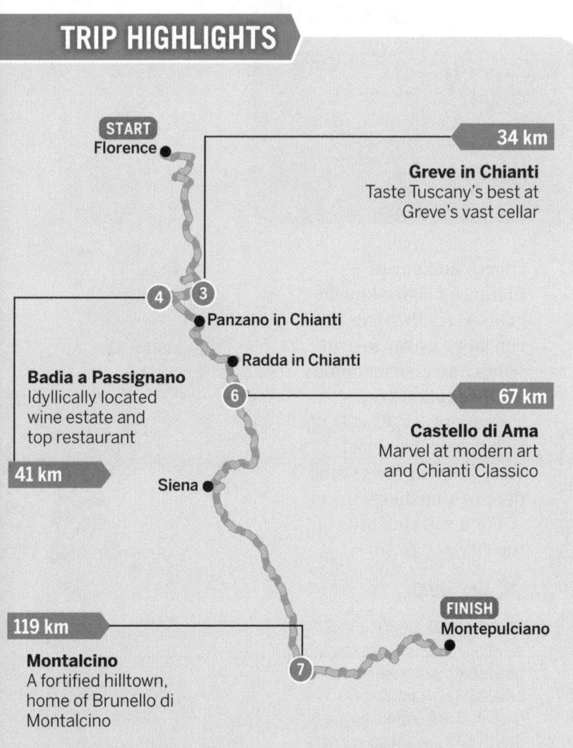


**4 DAYS**
**185KM / 115 MILES**

**GREAT FOR...**

**BEST TIME TO GO**

Autumn for earthy hues and the grape harvest.

**ESSENTIAL PHOTO**

Panoramas from Montalcino's Fortezza.

**BEST FOR GOURMETS**

Tuscan *bistecca* (steak) in Panzano in Chianti.

Classic Trip

# 22 Tuscan Wine Tour

Meandering through Tuscany's bucolic wine districts, this classic Chianti tour offers a taste of life in the slow lane. Once out of Florence (Firenze), you'll find yourself on quiet back roads driving through wooded hills and immaculate vineyards, stopping off at wine estates and hilltop towns to sample the local vintages. En route, you'll enjoy soul-stirring scenery, farmhouse food and some captivating Renaissance towns.

## 1 Florence

Whet your appetite for the road ahead with a one-day cooking course at the **Food & Wine Academy** (☎055 012 39 94; www.florencecookingclasses.com; Via de' Lamberti 1; course with lunch €79), one of Florence's many cookery schools. Once you're done at the stove, sneak out to visit the **Chiesa e Museo di Orsanmichele** (Via dell'Arte della Lana; admission free; church 10am-5pm daily, museum 10am-5pm Mon), an inspirational 14th-century church and one of Florence's lesser-known gems. Over the river, you can stock up on Tuscan wines and gourmet foods at **Obsequium** (www.obsequium.it; Borgo San Jacopo 17-39r), a well-stocked wine shop on the ground floor of a medieval tower.

For a walking tour of the city, see p240.

p251

**The Drive »** From Florence it's about an hour to Verrazzano. Head south along the scenic SR222 (Via Chiantigiana) towards Greve. When you get to Greti, you'll see a shop selling wine from the Castello di Verrazzano and, just before it, a right turn up to the castle.

## ❷ Castello di Verrazzano

Some 26km south of Florence, the **Castello di Verrazzano** (☎055 85 42 43; www.verrazzano.com) lords it over a 220-hectare estate where Chianti Classico, Vin Santo, grappa, honey, olive oil and balsamic vinegar are produced. In a previous life, the castle was home to Giovanni di Verrazzano (1485–1528), an adventurer who explored the North American coast and is commemorated in New York by the Verrazano-Narrows bridge linking Staten Island to Brooklyn.

### LINK YOUR TRIP

**21 Piero della Francesca Trail**

Instead of heading into Chianti wine country from Florence, join this trail of revered Renaissance frescoes (p233).

**24 Foodie Emilia-Romagna**

From Florence, continue 120km north on the A1 to Bologna and a tour of Emilia-Romagna's great food towns (p261).

At the Castello, you can choose from a range of guided tours, including a Classic Wine Tour (1½ hours; adult €14; 10am and 3pm Monday to Friday) and Wine & Food Experience (three hours, adult €52; noon Monday to Friday), which includes lunch with the estate wines. Book ahead.

**The Drive »** From the Castello it's a simple 10-minute drive to Greve in Chianti. Double back to the SR222 in Greti, turn right and follow for about 3km.

TRIP HIGHLIGHT

## 3 Greve in Chianti

The main town in the Chianti Fiorentino, the northernmost of the two Chianti districts, Greve in Chianti has been an important wine centre for centuries. The history of its traditional winemaking industry is lovingly illustrated at the **Museo del Vino** (☎055 854 62 75; www.museovino.it; Piazza Nino Tirinnanzi 10; adult/reduced €5/4; ⏰11am-5pm Mon & Wed-Sat mid-Mar–mid-Oct), one of three local enterprises run by the Bencistà Falorni family. Their main family business is the **Antica Macelleria Falorni** (www.bencistafalorni.it; Piazza Matteotti 71; ⏰8am-7.30pm Mon-Sat, 10am-1pm Sun), an atmospheric butcher's shop that they established in the early 18th century and which specialises in delicious picnic-perfect *finocchiona briciolona* (pork salami made with fennel seeds and Chianti wine). They also run **Le Cantine di Greve in Chianti** (www.lecantine.it; Piazza delle Cantine 2; ⏰10am-7pm), the town's top cellar, where you can sample all sorts of local wines.

**The Drive »** From Greve turn off the main through road, Viale Giovanni di Verrazzano, near the Esso petrol station, and head up towards Montefioralle. Continue on as the road climbs past olive groves and through woods to Badia a Passignano, about 15 minutes away.

TRIP HIGHLIGHT

## 4 Badia a Passignano

Encircled by cypress trees and surrounded by swaths of olive groves and vineyards, the 11th-century **Badia a Passignano** (Passignano Abbey; ☎055 807 12 78; www.osteriadipassignano.com) sits at the heart of a historic wine estate. It's owned by the Antinoris, one of Tuscany's oldest and most prestigious winemaking families, and offers a range of gastro visits and tours. Guided cellar tours, vineyard visits and cookery courses require a minimum of four people and prior booking, but you can taste and purchase wines and olive oil at **La Bottega** (⏰10am-6.30pm Mon-Sat), the estate's wine shop, without a reservation.

✕ 🛏 p251

**The Drive »** From Badia a Passignano, double back towards Greve and pick up the signposted SP118 for a pleasant 3km drive along the narrow tree-shaded road to Panzano.

## 5 Panzano in Chianti

The quiet medieval town of Panzano is an essential stop on any gourmet's tour of Tuscany. Here you

### TOP TIP: DRIVING IN CHIANTI

To cut down on driving stress, purchase a copy of *Le strade del Gallo Nero* (€2), a useful map that shows major and secondary roads and has a comprehensive list of wine estates. It's available at Greve in Chianti's **tourist office** (☎055 854 62 99; www.comune.greve-in-chianti.fi.it/ps/s/info-turismo; Piazza Matteotti 11; ⏰10am-1pm & 3-7pm Apr-Nov).

## TUSCAN REDS

Something of a viticultural powerhouse, Tuscany excites wine buffs with its myriad of full-bodied, highly respected reds. Like all Italian wines, these are classified according to strict guidelines, with the best denominated *Denominazione di Origine Controllata e Garantita* (DOCG), followed by *Denominazione di Origine Controllata* (DOC) and *Indicazione di Geografica Tipica* (IGT).

### Chianti

Cheery, full and dry, contemporary Chianti gets the thumbs up from wine critics. Produced in seven subzones from Sangiovese and a mix of other grape varieties, Chianti Classico is the best known, with its Gallo Nero (Black Cockerel) emblem that once symbolised the medieval Chianti League. Young, fun Chianti Colli Senesi from the Siena hills is the largest subzone; Chianti delle Colline Pisane is light and soft in style; and Chianti Rùfina comes from the hills east of Florence.

### Brunello di Montalcino

Brunello is up there at the top with Italy's most prized wines. The product of Sangiovese grapes, it must spend at least two years ageing in oak. It is intense and complex with an ethereal fragrance, and is best paired with game, wild boar and roasts. Brunello grape rejects go into Rosso di Montalcino, Brunello's substantially cheaper but wholly drinkable kid sister.

### Vino Nobile di Montepulciano

Prugnolo Gentile grapes (a clone of Sangiovese) form the backbone of the distinguished Vino Nobile di Montepulciano. Its intense but delicate nose and dry, vaguely tannic taste make it the perfect companion to red meat and mature cheese.

### Super Tuscans

Developed in the 1970s, the Super Tuscans are wines that fall outside the traditional classification categories. As a result they are often made with a combination of local and imported grape varieties, such as Merlot and Cabernet. Sassacaia, Solaia, Bolgheri, Tignanello and Luce are all super-hot Super Tuscans.



can stock up on meaty picnic fare at the **Antica Macelleria Cecchini** (www.dariocecchini.com; Via XX Luglio 11; ⌚9am-4pm Mon-Thu & Sun, to 6pm Fri & Sat), a celebrated butcher's shop run by the poetry-spouting guru of Tuscan meat, Dario Cecchini. Alternatively, you can eat at one of his three eateries: the **Officina della Bistecca** (☎055 85 21 76; set menu €50; ⌚dinner 8pm Tue, Fri & Sat, lunch 1pm Sun), which serves a simple set menu based on *bistecca*; **Solociccia** (☎055 85 27 27; set menu €30; ⌚dinner 7pm & 9pm Thu, Fri & Sat, lunch 1pm Sun), where guests share a communal table to sample meat dishes other than *bistecca*; and **Dario Doc** (light menu €20; ⌚lunch Mon-Sat), a casual daytime eatery. Book ahead for the Officina and Solociccia.

**The Drive »** From Panzano, it's about 20 minutes to the Castello di Ama. Strike south on the SR222 towards Radda in Chianti, enjoying views off to the right as you wend your way through the green countryside. At Croce, just beyond Radda, turn left and head towards Lecchi and San Sano. The Castello di Ama is signposted after a further 7km.

Classic Trip

ARMIN FABER/BON APPETIT/ALAMY ©

JILL HUNTER/ALAMY ©

## LOCAL KNOWLEDGE
### CATERINA BENCISTÀ FALORNI, GREVE IN CHIANTI

**I'm the ninth generation of the Bencistà Falorni family, which founded the Antica Macelleria Falorni in 1729 in the main square of Greve in Chianti. I like Chianti in September and October, when the grapes are harvested and the sunlight on the hills is beautiful. My favourite drive? From Greve in Chianti to Castellina, with each curve in the road unfolding breathtaking views.**

Top: Wine cellar, Castello di Ama
Left: Dario Cecchini, butcher and restaurateur, Panzano in Chianti
Right: Vineyard, Castelnuovo dell'Abate

DIGFOTO/GETTY IMAGES ©

TRIP HIGHLIGHT

## 6 Castello di Ama

To indulge in some contemporary-art appreciation between wine tastings, make for the **Castello di Ama** (☎0577 74 60 31; www.castellodiama.com; guided tours €10, with wine & oil tasting €35; ⏲10am-4pm Tue-Sat Apr-Oct) near Lecchi. The highly regarded Castello di Ama estate produces a fine Chianti Classico and has an original sculpture park showcasing 12 site-specific works by artists including Louise Bourgeois, Chen Zhen, Anish Kapoor, Kendell Geers and Daniel Buren. Book ahead.

**The Drive »** Reckon on about 1½ hours to Montalcino from the Castello. Double back to the SP408 and head south to Lecchi and then on towards Siena. Skirt around the east of Siena and pick up the SR2 (Via Cassia) to Buonconvento and hilltop Montalcino, off to the right of the main road.

TRIP HIGHLIGHT

## 7 Montalcino

Montalcino, a pretty medieval town perched above the Val d'Orcia, is home to one of Italy's great wines, Brunello di Montalcino (and the more modest, but still very palatable, Rosso di Montalcino). There are plenty of *enoteche* (wine bars) where you can taste and buy, including one in the **Fortezza** (Piazzale Fortezza; adult/child €4/2; ⏲9am-6pm Tue-Sun), the 14th-century fortress that dominates the town's skyline.

For a historical insight into the town's winemaking past, head to the **Museo del Brunello** (www.museodelbrunello.it, in Italian; Fattoria dei Barbi, Podernovaccio; adult/reduced €4/2; ⏲11am-6pm), a small museum off the road to the Abbazia di Sant'Antimo.

p251

**The Drive ››** From Montalcino, head downhill and then, after about 8km, turn onto the SR2. At San Quirico d'Orcia pick up the SP146, a fabulously scenic road that weaves along the Val d'Orcia through rolling green hills, past the pretty town of Pienza, to Montepulciano. Allow about an hour.

## ❽ Montepulciano

Set atop a narrow ridge of volcanic rock, the Renaissance centre of Montepulciano produces the celebrated red wine Vino Nobile. For a drop, head up the main street, called in stages Via di Gracciano nel Corso, Via di Voltaia del Corso and Via dell'Opio nel Corso, to the **Cantine Contucci** (www.contucci.it; Via del Teatro 1; admission free, fee for tastings; ⏲8.30am-12.30pm & 2.30-6pm Mon-Fri, from 9.30am Sat & Sun), housed underneath the *palazzo* (mansion) of the same name. A second cellar, the **Cantina de' Ricci** (☎0578 75 71 66; www.dericci.it; Via Collazzi 7; tasting €6, light lunch plus tasting & guided visit €10; ⏲10.30am-1.30pm & 3.30-7.30pm), occupies a grotto-like space underneath **Palazzo Ricci** near **Piazza Grande**, the town's highest point.

p251

### WINE TASTING GOES HIGH TECH

One of Tuscany's biggest cellars, the Cantine di Greve in Chianti stocks more than 2000 labels, of which 140 are available for tasting. It's a lovely, brick-arched place, but wine tasting here is a very modern experience, thanks to a sophisticated wine-dispensing system that preserves wine in an open bottle for up to three weeks and allows tasters to serve themselves by the glass. The way it works at the Cantine is that you buy a prepaid wine card costing €10 to €25 from the central bar, stick it into one of the many taps and out trickles your tipple of choice. Any unused credit is then refunded when you return the card.

### DETOUR: ABBAZIA DI SANT'ANTIMO

**Start: ❼ Montalcino**

The striking Romanesque **Abbazia di Sant'Antimo** (www.antimo.it; Castelnuovo dell'Abate; admission free; ⏲10.15am-12.30pm & 3-6.30pm Mon-Sat, 9.15-10.45am & 3-6pm Sun) lies in an isolated valley just below the village of Castelnuovo dell'Abate, 10.5km from Montalcino.

According to tradition, Charlemagne founded the original monastery in 781. The exterior, built in pale travertine stone, is simple but for the stone carvings, which include various fantastical animals. Inside, study the capitals of the columns lining the nave, especially the one representing Daniel in the lions' den.

Music lovers should try to time their visit to coincide with the daily services, which include Gregorian chants. Check the website for times.

# Eating & Sleeping

## Florence 1

### Il Santo Bevitore — Tuscan €€

(055 21 12 64; www.ilsantobevitore.com; Via di Santo Spirito 64-66r; meals €35; lunch & dinner Sep-Jul) A much raved about address, this restaurant is an understated ode to stylish dining with a cavernous whitewashed, wood- and bottle-lined interior. The menu is a creative reinvention of seasonal classics, and different for lunch and dinner. Reservations recommended.

### Palazzo Guadagni Hotel — Hotel €€

(055 265 83 76; www.palazzoguadagni.com; Piazza Santo Spirito 9; d €100-170; ) Above a buzzing summertime square, this 16th-century Renaissance palace is a wonderfully romantic place to stay. The spacious rooms tastefully mix old and new, and there's a dreamy loggia terrace.

## Badia a Passignano 4

### Osteria di Passignano — Gastronomic €€€

(055 807 12 78; www.osteriadipassignano.com; Via di Passignano 33; meals €75; lunch & dinner Mon-Sat) This elegant dining room is one of Tuscany's most impressive restaurants. The delectable food utilises local produce and is decidedly Tuscan in inspiration, but its execution is refined rather than rustic.

### Fattoria di Rignana — Agriturismo €€

(055 85 20 65; www.rignana.it; Rignana; d from €100; P @ ) This old farmstead and noble villa near Badia a Passignano has the lot – a historic setting, glorious views, a large swimming pool and walking access to a decent local *cantina*. Rooms are available in the 17th-century villa or adjoining *fattoria* (farmhouse).

## Montalcino 7

### Ristorante di Poggio Antico — Modern Italian €€€

(0577 84 92 00; www.poggioantico.com; meals from €50; lunch & dinner Tue-Sun, closed lunch Sun Nov-Mar) Located 4.5km outside town on the road to Grosseto, the Poggio Antico vineyard makes award-winning wines, conducts tastings (€22 for five wines) and free tours, and has one of the area's best restaurants.

### Hotel Vecchia Oliviera — Hotel €€

(0577 84 60 28; www.vecchiaoliviera.com; Via Landi 1; d €120-190; P ) Just beside the Porta Cerbaia, this former olive mill has been tastefully restored and converted into a stylish small hotel. Each of the 11 rooms is individually decorated and the superiors come with a view and jacuzzi.

## Montepulciano 8

### Enoteca a Gambe di Gatto — Traditional Italian €€

(0578 75 74 31; Via dell'Opio nel Corso 34; meals €34; closed Wed & Jan-Easter) This relaxed, intimate restaurant serves delicious Tuscan fare. The daily menu fluctuates wildly, depending on market offerings, and meals start with a complimentary tasting of wine and olive oil.

### Locanda San Francesco — Boutique Hotel €€€

(0578 75 87 25; www.locandasanfrancesco.it; Piazza San Francesco 5; r €180-215; P @ ) Four handsome rooms (two with magnificent views) and an elegantly furnished lounge await at this luxury hotel.

***Montepulciano*** *Amble past churches and mansions in this delightful hill town*

GUY EDWARDES/GETTY IMAGES ©

# Tuscan Landscapes

# 23

*Rolling hills capped by medieval towns, golden wheat fields and snaking lines of cypress trees – immerse yourself in Tuscan scenery on this trip through the region's southern stretches.*

## TRIP HIGHLIGHTS

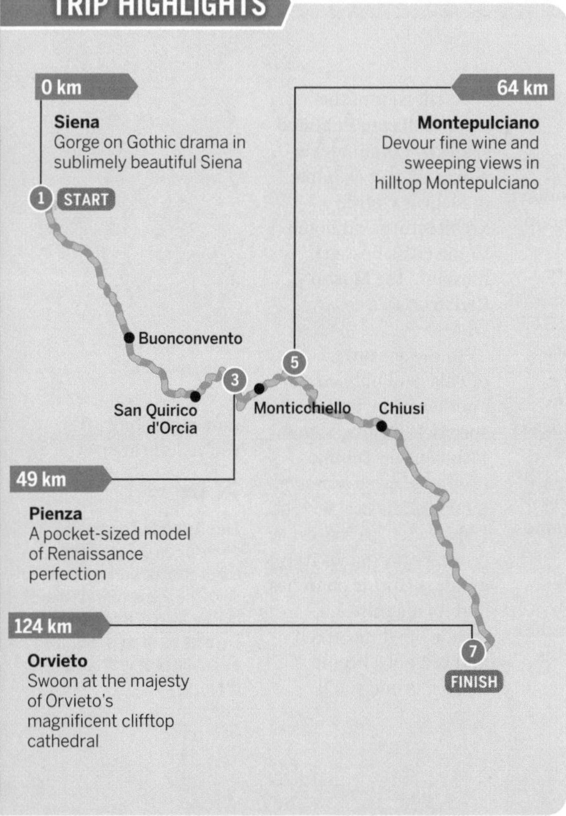

**3–4 DAYS**
**124KM / 77 MILES**

**GREAT FOR...**

**BEST TIME TO GO**

May to September for blue skies and fab photos.

**ESSENTIAL PHOTO**

The Val d'Orcia between San Quirico d'Orcia and Pienza.

**BEST FOR RENAISSANCE ARCHITECTURE**

Montepulciano's historic centre.

# 23 Tuscan Landscapes

Ever since medieval pilgrims discovered Tuscany en route from Canterbury to Rome, the region has been captivating travellers. This trip strikes south from Siena, running through the Crete Senesi, an area of clay hills scored by deep ravines, to the Unesco-listed Val d'Orcia, whose soothing hills and billowing plains are punctuated by delightful Renaissance towns. The end of the road is Orvieto, home to one of Italy's most feted Gothic cathedrals.

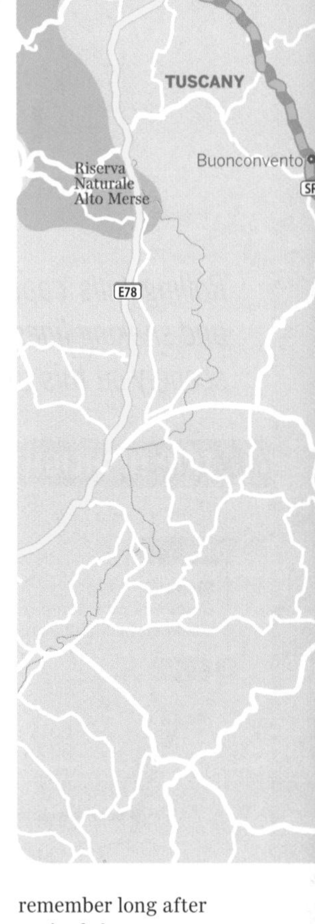

## 1 Siena

With its medieval *palazzi* (mansions) and humbling Gothic architecture, Siena's historic centre is a sight to compare with any in Tuscany. To admire it from above, climb to the top of the **Torre del Mangia** (admission €8; ⏲10am-7pm Mar–mid-Oct, to 4pm mid-Oct–Feb), the slender 14th-century tower that rises above **Piazza del Campo**, and look down on a sea of red-tiled roofs and, beyond, to the green, undulating countryside that awaits you on this trip.

At the foot of the tower, **Palazzo Pubblico** (Palazzo Comunale) is a magnificent example of Sienese Gothic architecture and home to the city's best art museum, the **Museo Civico** (adult/reduced €8/4.50; ⏲10am-7pm).

To the southwest of Palazzo Pubblico, another inspiring spectacle awaits. Siena's 13th-century **Duomo** (Piazza del Duomo; admission €3; ⏲10.30am-8pm Mon-Sat, 1.30-6pm Sun Jun-Aug, shorter hr rest of yr) is one of Italy's greatest Gothic churches, and its magnificent facade of white, green and red polychrome marble is one you'll remember long after you've left town.

✕ 🛏 p241

**The Drive »** The first leg down to San Quirico d'Orcia, about an hour's drive, takes you down the scenic SR2 via the market town of Buonconvento. En route you'll pass cultivated fields and swaths of curvaceous green plains.

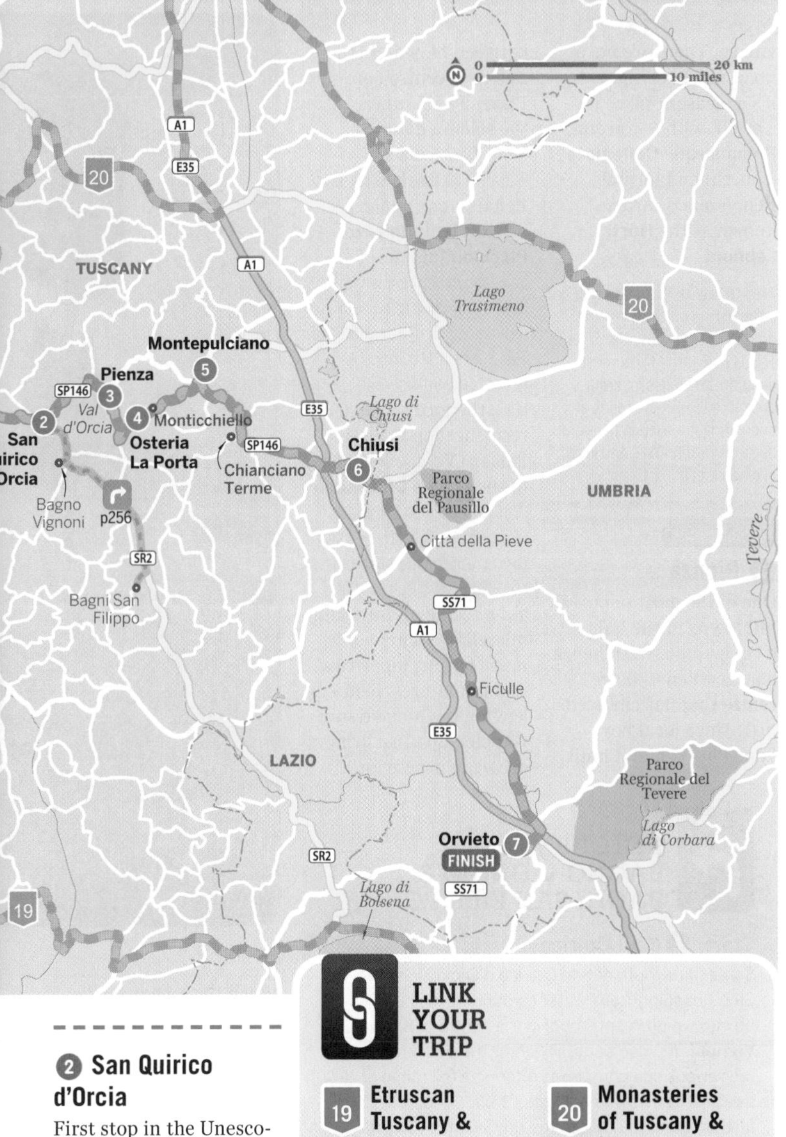


## ❷ San Quirico d'Orcia

First stop in the Unesco-protected Val d'Orcia is San Quirico d'Orcia. A fortified medieval town and one-time stopover on the Via Francigena pilgrim route between Canterbury and Rome, it's now a lovely, low-key

### LINK YOUR TRIP

#### 19 Etruscan Tuscany & Lazio

From Orvieto, continue 45km south on the SS71 to Viterbo and join up with this Etruscan treasure hunt (p217).

#### 20 Monasteries of Tuscany & Umbria

Head southeast from Siena along the SP438 to the Abbazia di Monte Oliveto Maggiore to tour monasteries (p225).

village. There are no great must-see sights but it's a pleasant place for a stroll, with a graceful Romanesque **Collegiata** (church) and formal Renaissance gardens known as the **Horti Leononi**.

**The Drive »** From San Quirico d'Orcia it's a quick 15-minute drive to Pienza along the SP146. This is one of the trip's most beautiful stretches, offering unfettered views over seas of undulating grasslands peppered by stone farmhouses and lines of elegant cypress trees.

TRIP HIGHLIGHT

## 3 Pienza

One of the most popular hill towns in the Val d'Orcia, pint-sized Pienza boasts a Renaissance centre that has changed little since local boy Pope Pius II had it built between 1459 and 1462. Action is centred on Piazza Pio II, where the solemn **duomo** (8.30am-1pm & 2.15-6.30pm) is flanked by two Renaissance *palazzi* – on the right, **Palazzo Piccolomini** (www.palazzopiccolominipienza.it; 30min guided tours adult/reduced €7/5; 10am-6.30pm Tue-Sun mid-Mar–mid-Oct, to 4.30pm mid-Oct–mid-Mar), the former papal residence; on the left, Palazzo Vescovile, home to the **Museo Diocesano** (Corso Rossellino 30; adult/reduced €4.10/2.60; 10am-1pm & 3-6pm Wed-Mon mid-Mar–Nov, Sat & Sun only Dec–mid-Mar) and an intriguing miscellany of artworks, manuscripts, tapestries and miniatures. Before leaving town make sure you pick up some local *pecorino* cheese for which the area is justly famous.

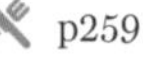 p259

**The Drive »** From Pienza strike south on the SP18 and head into the heart of the countryside, enjoying more bucolic scenery as you go. After 6km or so you'll see a sign to Monticchiello off to the left. Take this and continue for another 4km.

CORNELIA DOERR/GETTY IMAGES ©

### DETOUR: BAGNO VIGNONI & BAGNI SAN FILIPPO

**Start: 2 San Quirico d'Orcia**

Some 5km south of San Quirico d'Orcia along the SR2, hot sulphurous water (around 49°C) bubbles up into a picturesque pool in the centre of **Bagno Vignoni**. You can't actually enter the pool but there are various spa complexes offering a full range of treatments. For free hot-water frolics continue 15km further along the SR2 to the tiny village of **Bagni San Filippo**, where there are thermal cascades in an open-air reserve. You'll find these just uphill from Hotel le Terme – follow a sign marked 'Fosso Bianco' down a lane for about 150m to limestone outcrops and you'll come to a set of warm, tumbling cascades that get more spectacular the further downhill you walk. It's a pleasant if slightly whiffy spot for a picnic.

**Pienza** Cypress trees line the road

## 4 Osteria La Porta

A 15-minute drive southeast from Pienza brings you to **Monticchiello**, a sleepy medieval hilltop village. Just inside the main gate, the highly regarded **Osteria La Porta** (☎0578 75 51 63; Via del Piano 3; meals €40; ⏰Fri-Wed) has a small terrace with panoramic views of the Val d'Orcia and a reputation for food and service that behoves a reservation, even in low season. The fixed menu at lunchtime offers great value, and *spuntini* (snacks) such as bruschetta, olives and cheese plates are served outside usual meal hours.

**The Drive »** Take the SP88 and follow it as it ploughs on through fields and light woodland to the main SP146. Go left and continue past orderly vineyards and olive groves up to San Biagio and 2km further on to Montepulciano. All told it's about 20 minutes.

TRIP HIGHLIGHT

## 5 Montepulciano

Famous for its Vino Nobile wine, Montepulciano is a steeply stacked hill town harbouring a wealth of *palazzi* and fine buildings, as well as grandstand views over the Val di Chiana and Val d'Orcia. The main street, aka the Corso, climbs steeply, passing **Caffè Poliziano**, which has been operating since 1868, as it leads to the **Cantine Contucci** (www.contucci.it; Via del Teatro 1; admission free, fee for tastings; 8.30am-12.30pm & 2.30-6pm Mon-Fri, from 9.30am Sat & Sun), one of two historic wine cellars in town. Nearby **Piazza Grande** is flanked by the 14th-century **Palazzo Comunale** (access to panoramic terrace €2; 9am-6pm Mon-Sat) and late-16th-century **duomo** (9am-noon & 4-7pm).

 p259

**The Drive »** Reckon on about 40 minutes to cover the 25km to Chiusi. From Montepulciano head southeast along the SP146 to Chianciano Terme, a popular spa town. Continue on towards the A1 autostrada, and Chiusi is just on the other side of the highway.

## 6 Chiusi

Once an important Etruscan centre, Chiusi is now a sleepy country town. Its main attractions are the Etruscan tombs dotted around the surrounding countryside, two of which are included in the ticket price of the **Museo Archeologico Nazionale** (0578 20 17 77; Via Porsenna 93; adult/reduced €4/2; 9am-8pm). In town, you can go underground in the **Labirinto di Porsenna** (Museo della Cattedrale, Piazza Duomo; admission €3; 9.45am-12.45pm & 4-6.30pm Jun-Oct, shorter hr rest of yr), a series of tunnels dating to Etruscan times that formed part of the town's water supply system.

**The Drive »** You have two choices for Orvieto. The quick route is on the A1 autostrada (about 45 minutes), but it's a more interesting drive along the SS71 (1½ hours). This passes through Città della Pieve, birthplace of the painter Perugino, and Ficulle, known since Roman times for its artisans.

TRIP HIGHLIGHT

## 7 Orvieto

Over the regional border in Umbria, the precariously perched town of Orvieto boasts one of Italy's finest Gothic cathedrals. The **Cattedrale di Orvieto** (www.opsm.it; Piazza Duomo; admission €2, incl Cappella di San Brizio €3; 9.30am-7.30pm Apr-Oct, 9.30am-1pm & 2.30-5pm Nov-Mar) took 30 years to plan and three centuries to complete. Work began in 1290, originally to a Romanesque design, but as construction proceeded, Gothic features were incorporated into the structure. Highlights include the richly coloured facade, and, in the **Cappella di San Brizio**, Luca Signorelli's fresco cycle *The Last Judgement*.

Across the piazza from the cathedral, the **Museo Claudio Faina e Civico** (www.museofaina.it; Piazza Duomo 29; adult/reduced €8/5; 9.30am-6pm Apr-Sep, 10am-5pm Tue-Sun Oct-Mar) houses an important collection of Etruscan archaeological artefacts.

p259

### THE PALIO

Siena's Palio is one of Italy's most spectacular annual events. Dating from the Middle Ages, it comprises a series of colourful pageants and a wild horse race on 2 July and 16 August. Ten of Siena's 17 *contrade* (town districts) compete for the coveted *palio* (silk banner).

From about 5pm, representatives from each *contrada* parade around the Campo in historical costume, all bearing their individual banners. Then, at 7.45pm in July and 7pm in August, the race gets the green light. For scarcely one exhilarating minute, the 10 horses and their bareback riders tear three times around the temporarily constructed dirt racetrack with a speed and violence that makes spectators' hair stand on end.

# Eating & Sleeping

## Siena 1

**Morbidi** Deli €

(Via Banchi di Sopra 75; 9am-8pm Mon-Sat) Local gastronomes come here to stock up on cheese, cured meats and imported delicacies. If you're self-catering you can join them, but make sure you also investigate the downstairs lunch buffet (from 12.30pm to 2.30pm), which offers fantastic value.

**Campo Regio Relais** Boutique Hotel €€€

(0577 22 20 73; www.camporegio.com; Via della Sapienza 25; d €190-250; ) Siena's most charming hotel has six individually decorated and luxuriously equipped rooms. In summer, breakfast is served on a terrace, which has a sensational view of the *duomo*.

## Pienza 3

**Osteria Sette di Vino** Osteria €

(0578 74 90 92; Piazza di Spagna 1; soups €6, bruschetta €3, cheese plates €6; Thu-Tue) Grab one of the piazza tables and sit down to earthy Tuscan dishes such as *zuppa di pane e fagioli* (bread and white-bean soup) and *pecorino con lardo* (grilled *pecorino* cheese with *lardo* – cured strips of back fat). Cash only; no coffee.

## Montepulciano 5

**Osteria Acquacheta** Osteria €

(0578 71 70 86; www.acquacheta.eu; Via del Teatro 22; meals €19; closed Tue) Hugely popular with locals and tourists alike, this bustling place specialises in *bistecca alla fiorentina* (chargrilled T-bone steak), which comes to the table in huge, lightly seared and exceptionally flavoursome slabs. Book ahead.

**La Grotta** Traditional Italian €€

(0578 75 74 79; www.lagrottamontepulciano.it; Via San Biagio 15; 6-course set menu €48; Thu-Tue) On the road to Chiusi, La Grotta has elegant dining rooms and a gorgeous courtyard garden that's perfect for summer dining. The food is simple but delicious, and service is exemplary.

**Locanda San Francesco** Boutique Hotel €€€

(0578 75 87 25; www.locandasanfrancesco.it; Piazza San Francesco 5; r €180-215; P ) Four handsome rooms (two with magnificent views) and an elegantly furnished lounge await at this luxury establishment.

## Orvieto 7

**Ristorante I Sette Consoli** Modern Italian €€

(0763 34 39 11; Piazza Sant'Angelo 1/a; meals €45; Thu-Tue) With its inventive, artfully presented dishes, such as guinea fowl stuffed with chestnuts, this top restaurant gets foodies flocking in all the way from Rome and Milan. In good weather, try to get a seat in the garden. Reservations recommended for dinner.

**Hotel Maitani** Hotel €€

(0763 34 20 11; www.hotelmaitani.com; Via Lorenzo Maitani 5; d €126, breakfast €10; P ) Every detail is covered, from a travel-sized toothbrush and toothpaste in each room to chocolates (Perugino, of course) on your pillow. Rooms, several of which have cathedral or countryside views, are pin-drop quiet, as they come with not one but two double-glazed windows.

***Parma*** *Don't leave before sampling the ham*

# Foodie Emilia-Romagna 24

*Experience the best of 'cucina italiana' on this tour of Italy's culinary heartland. Great food and wine besides, you'll also come across artistic treasures and medieval cities at every turn.*

## TRIP HIGHLIGHTS

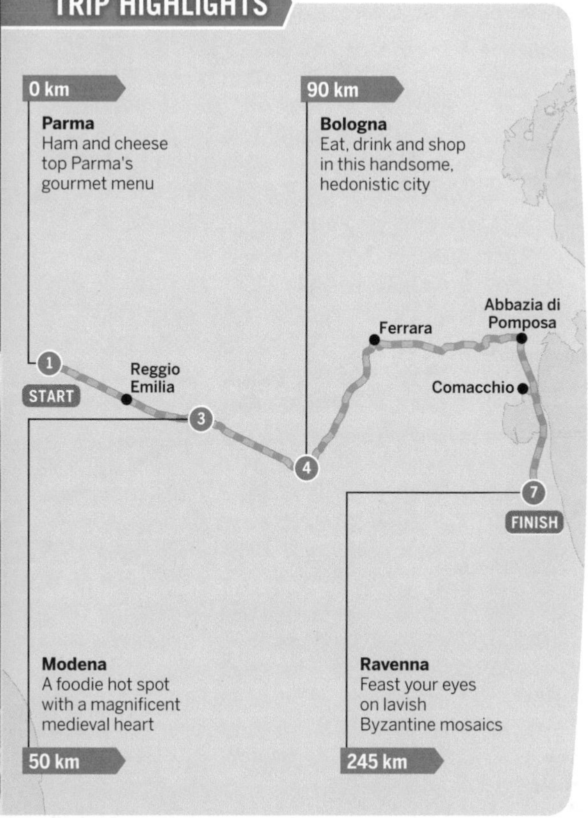

**0 km**
**Parma**
Ham and cheese top Parma's gourmet menu

**90 km**
**Bologna**
Eat, drink and shop in this handsome, hedonistic city

Ferrara
Abbazia di Pomposa
Reggio Emilia
Comacchio
START
FINISH

**Modena**
A foodie hot spot with a magnificent medieval heart
**50 km**

**Ravenna**
Feast your eyes on lavish Byzantine mosaics
**245 km**

**7 DAYS**
**245KM / 152 MILES**

**GREAT FOR...**

**BEST TIME TO GO**

Autumn is ideal for fresh seasonal produce.

**ESSENTIAL PHOTO**

Food stalls and delis in Bologna's Quadrilatero district.

**BEST FOR ART LOVERS**

Ravenna's sparkling mosaics.

# 24 Foodie Emilia-Romagna

Sandwiched between Tuscany and the Veneto, Emilia-Romagna is a foodie's dream destination. Many of Italy's signature dishes originated here, and its regional specialities are revered across the country. This tasty trip takes in the region's main culinary centres of Parma, Modena and Bologna, as well as the charming Renaissance town of Ferrara, and art-rich Ravenna, celebrated for its glorious Byzantine mosaics.

TRIP HIGHLIGHT

## 1 Parma

Handsome and prosperous, Parma is one of Italy's culinary hot spots, producing the country's finest ham *(prosciutto di Parma)* and its most revered cheese *(parmigiano reggiano)*. To stock up on these, as well as local Lambrusco wines and other regional delicacies, head to the **Salumeria Garibaldi** (Via Garibaldi 42; ⌚8am-8pm Mon-Sat), a

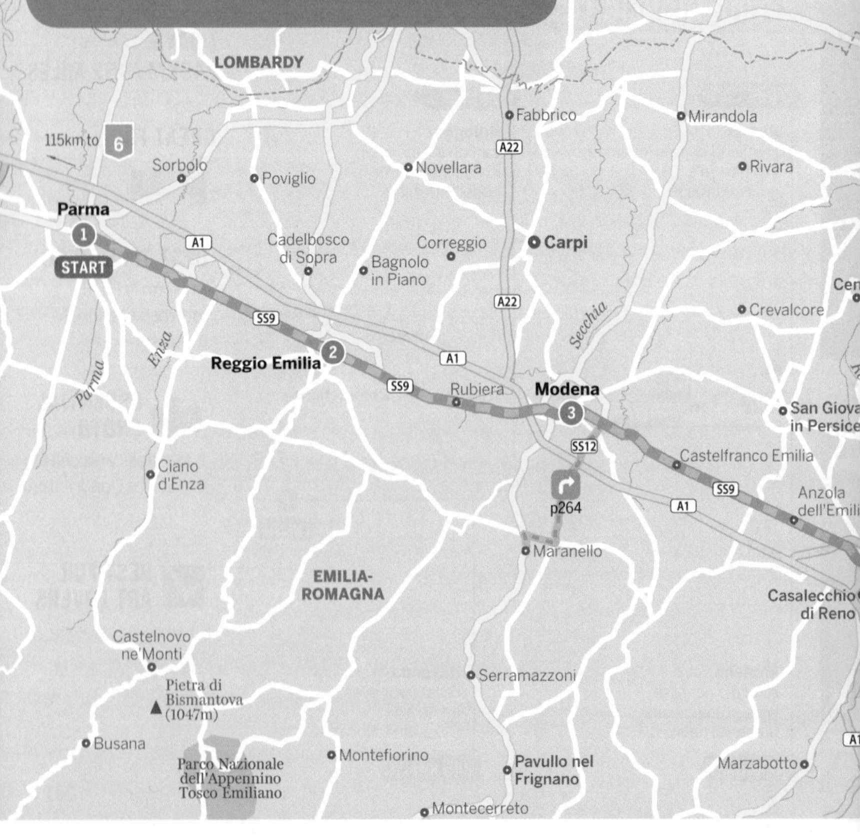

divine deli in the historic centre.

Once you've fed your appetite, feed your soul at the city's 12th-century **duomo** (Piazza del Duomo; 9am-12.30pm & 3-7pm), with its classic Lombard-Romanesque facade and ornate baroque interior. Nearby, the octagonal **Battistero** (Piazza del Duomo; admission €6; 9am-12.30pm & 3-6.45pm) displays a hybrid Romanesque-Gothic look in pink and white marble. Parma's main art collection, which includes works by locals Parmigianino and Correggio alongside paintings by Fra' Angelico, El Greco and a piece attributed to Leonardo da Vinci, are in the **Galleria Nazionale** (admission €6; 8.30am-2pm Tue-Sun), one of several museums in the monumental **Palazzo della Pilotta** (Piazza della Pace).

p267

**The Drive »** From Parma, it's a straightforward 50-minute drive southeast on the SS9

## LINK YOUR TRIP

**6 Cinematic Cinque Terre**

From Parma head 120km along the A15 autostrada to La Spezia, gateway to the spectacular Cinque Terre coastline (p87).

**7 Northern Cities**

From Ferrara take the A13 autostrada for 80km to Padua, home of one of Italy's great Renaissance masterpieces (p97).

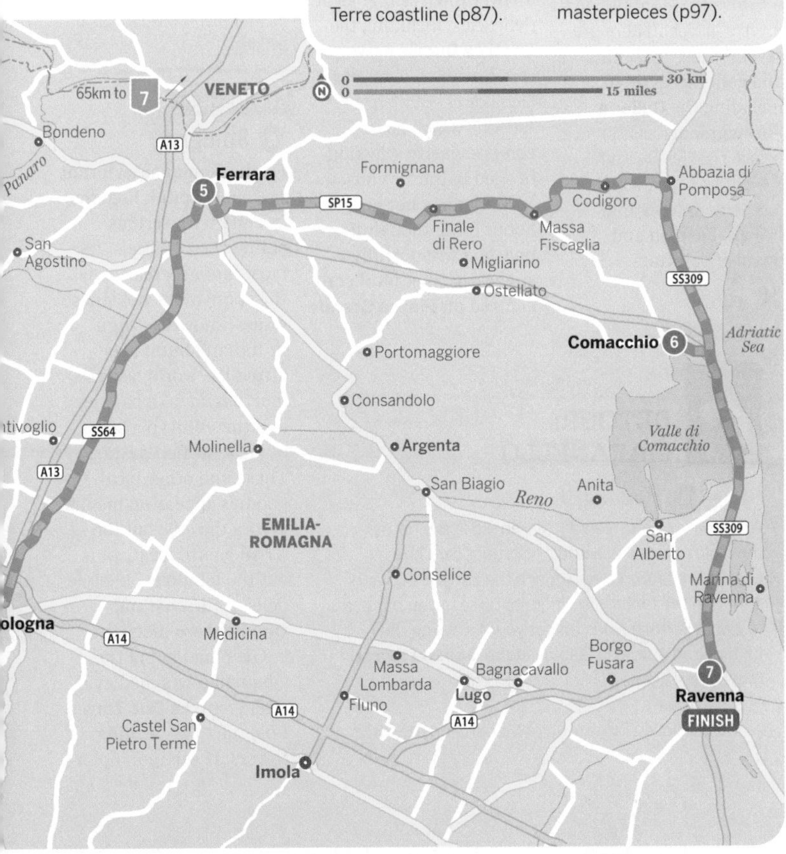

65km to 7
VENETO
0 30 km
0 15 miles
Bondeno
A13
Panaro
Ferrara 5
Formignana
SP15
Codigoro
Abbazia di Pomposa
Finale di Rero
Massa Fiscaglia
San Agostino
Migliarino
Ostellato
SS309
Comacchio 6
Adriatic Sea
Portomaggiore
Consandolo
tivoglio
SS64
Molinella
Argenta
Valle di Comacchio
A13
San Biagio
Reno
Anita
EMILIA-ROMAGNA
San Alberto
SS309
Conselice
Marina di Ravenna
ologna
A14
Medicina
Borgo Fusara
Massa Lombarda
Bagnacavallo
Fluno
Lugo
7 Ravenna
FINISH
A14
A14
Castel San Pietro Terme
Imola

(Via Emilia) through fairly uninspiring flat farmland to Reggio Emilia. If you're in a hurry, the quicker A1 autostrada covers the same route.

## 2 Reggio Emilia

Genteel Reggio Emilia puts the *reggiano* in *parmigiano reggiano* (Parmesan cheese). Apart from its cheese, the city is best known as the birthplace of the Italian flag – the famous red, white and green tricolour – whose history is chronicled at the **Museo del Tricolore** (Piazza Prampolini; admission free; ⌚9am-noon Tue-Fri, 10am-1pm & 4-7pm Sat-Sun). There are several other museums and galleries in town, including the **Galleria Parmeggiani** (Corso Cairoli 1; ⌚9am-noon Tue-Fri, 10am-1pm & 4-7pm Sat & Sun), which has some interesting Italian, Flemish and Spanish paintings.

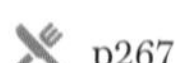 p267

**The Drive »** The run down to Modena takes about an hour on the SS9. The scenery is much like the first leg from Parma – flat fields, petrol stations, agricultural buildings and the occasional stone farmhouse. At Modena head for the *centro*.

TRIP HIGHLIGHT

## 3 Modena

Modena is one of Italy's great gastro centres, the creative force behind *aceto balsamico* (balsamic vinegar), *zamponi* (pig's trotters), *cotechino* (stuffed pork sausage) and sparkling Lambrusco wines. You'll find shops all over town selling local delicacies, including the **Enoteca Ducale** (www.enotecaducale.it; Corso Vittorio Emanuele 15; ⌚9am-7pm Tue-Sun), which has a comprehensive selection of aged balsamic vinegars.

Modena is not just about food, though. It boasts a wonderfully suggestive medieval core, centred on **Piazza Grande** and the **cathedral** (Corso Duomo; ⌚6.30am-12.30pm & 3.30-7pm), considered by many to be the finest Romanesque church in Italy. Inseparable from the cathedral is the early-13th-century tower, the **Torre Ghirlandina** (Piazza Torre; admission €2; ⌚9.30am-12.30pm & 3-7pm Sat & Sun Apr-Oct).

 p267

**The Drive »** From Modena take the SS9 southeast to Bologna. It's only about 40km away but traffic is often heavy and it can take up to 1¼ hours to get there. In Bologna the centre is closed to most traffic, so if you're staying downtown contact your hotel to ask about parking.

TRIP HIGHLIGHT

## 4 Bologna

Emilia-Romagna's vibrant regional capital, Bologna is a city with serious culinary credentials. Its most famous creation is the eponymous bolognese sauce (known as *ragù* in Italian), but it also gifted the world lasagne, *mortadella* (aka baloney) and tortellini (pockets of meat-stuffed pasta). These and other local goodies appear on menus across the city, but for a real gastro treat, sniff out the fabulous old-style delis in the bustling **Quadrilatero** district.

Overshadowing the Quadrilatero's medieval streets are **Le Due Torri**, Bologna's two leaning towers. If vertigo's not a

### DETOUR: MARANELLO

**Start: 3 Modena**

A mecca for petrol heads, Maranello is the home town of Ferrari. The world's sportiest cars have been manufactured here since the early 1940s and although the factory is off-limits (unless you happen to own a Ferrari), you can get your fix ogling the flaming red autos on display at the **Galleria Ferrari** (www.galleria.ferrari.com; Via Ferrari 43; adult/reduced €13/9; ⌚9.30am-7pm).

Maranello is 17km south of Modena on the SS12.

STUART KELLY/ALAMY ©

**Modena** Via Emilia

problem, you can climb the taller of the two, the 97.6m-high **Torre degli Asinelli** (admission €3; 9am-6pm), and survey the historic centre from on high. The big barn-like structure you'll see to the northwest is the **Basilica di San Petronio** (Piazza Maggiore; 7.45am-1pm & 3-6pm), the world's fifth-largest basilica, which lords over **Piazza**

## VIA EMILIA

For the first half of this trip, from Parma to Bologna, you'll be following the region's most famous road, the ruler-straight Via Emilia. Built by the Romans in the 2nd century BC, it ran for 206km through the Po river valley connecting the region's main cities – Placentia (Piacenza), Parma, Regium (Reggio Emilia), Mutina (Modena), Bononia (Bologna) and Ariminum (Rimini). Within decades of completion it had opened up Italy's fertile northern hinterland to economic expansion, and converted the rich river plain into the empire's proverbial breadbasket – a position it still enjoys today.

**Maggiore**, Bologna's striking showpiece square. Also on the piazza is the **Palazzo Comunale** (Town Hall), home to a couple of interesting art museums.

 p267

**The Drive »** Head north out of Bologna along Via Stalingrado and follow the SS64. This leads through orderly farmland and neat villages to Ferrara, about 1½ hours away. In Ferrara, turn left after the river and head for the *centro storico* (historic centre) car park on Via Darsena.

## 5 Ferrara

Ferrara was once the seat of the powerful Este family (1260–1598) and although it is often bypassed by travellers, it's an attractive place with an austere Renaissance cityscape and compact historic centre. In food terms, specialities include the town's uniquely shaped bread, known as *coppia ferrarese,* and *cappellacci di zucca* (hat-shaped pasta stuffed with squash, herbs and nutmeg).

The town centre, which is easily explored on foot, is focused on **Castello Estense** (Viale Cavour; adult/reduced €8/6.50; 9.30am-5.30pm), a martial 14th-century castle complete with moat and drawbridge. Linked to the castle by an elevated passageway is the 13th-century crenulated **Palazzo Municipale**, now largely occupied by administrative offices. Opposite, Ferrara's pink-and-white, 12th-century **duomo** (Piazza Cattedrale; 7.30am-noon & 3-6.30pm Mon-Sat, 7.30am-12.30pm & 3.30-7.30pm Sun) sports a graphic three-tier facade, combining Romanesque and Gothic styles.

 p267

**The Drive »** Head east out of Ferrara on the SP15 and continue on the straight road past immaculate vineyards onto the tiny village of Massa Fiscaglia. Bear left here and continue on to Codigoro and the Abbazia di Pomposa (well worth a quick stop). From the abbey it's a straight 20-minute run down the SS309 to Comacchio.

## 6 Comacchio

Resembling a mini-Venice with its canals and brick bridges, Comacchio is the main centre in the Po Delta (Foci del Po). This area of dense pine forests and extensive wetlands, much of it protected in the **Parco del Delta del Po** (www.parcodeltapo.it), offers superlative birdwatching and excellent cycling. Foodies can try the prized local speciality, eel, which is served with great relish at the many restaurants and trattorias on Comacchio's canals.

**The Drive »** From Comacchio, Ravenna is only an hour's drive away, 40km south on the SS309. The road spears down a narrow strip of land between a lagoon and the Adriatic coast, but you won't see much water thanks to lengthy curtains of verdant trees and heavy foliage.

TRIP HIGHLIGHT

## 7 Ravenna

No tour of Emilia-Romagna would be complete without a stop at Ravenna to see its remarkable Unesco-protected mosaics. Relics of the city's golden age as capital of the Western Roman and Byzantine Empires, they are described by Dante in his *Divine Comedy,* much of which he wrote here.

The mosaics are spread over five sites – **Basilica di San Vitale** (Via Fiandrini), **Mausoleo di Galla Placidia** (Via Fiandrini), **Basilica di Sant'Apollinare Nuovo** (Via di Roma), **Museo Arcivescovile** (Piazza Arcivescovado) and **Battistero Neoniano** (Via Battistero) – all of which have the same opening hours and are covered by a single **ticket** (adult/reduced €9.50/8.50; 9am-7pm). Outside town you'll find more mosaics at the **Basilica di Sant'Apollinare in Classe** (Via Romea Sud, Classe; adult/reduced €5/2.50; 8.30am-7.30pm Mon-Sat, 1-7.30pm Sun).

For more info, and to check seasonal opening hours (those listed here are for April to September), visit www.ravennamosaici.it.

p267

# Eating & Sleeping

## Parma 1

**La Greppia** Gastronomic €€€

(☎0521 23 36 86; Via Garibaldi 39a; meals from €45) La Greppia is hallowed ground for the kind of gourmands who know their *ragù* from their bolognese. Sticking tradition and modernity in the same blender, it comes up with Parmesan mousse, pear poached in wine, and plenty more surprises. Service is impeccable.

**Century Hotel** Hotel €€

(☎0521 03 98 00; www.centuryhotel.it; Piazzale dalla Chiesa 5a; d €120; P ❄ 📶) Hotels next to train stations are often scruffy abodes designed for economically minded fly-by-nighters, but the trussed-up Century bucks the trend, offering slick four-star amenities at three-star prices.

## Reggio Emilia 2

**Trattoria da Penna** Traditional Italian €

(Via dell'Aquila 6a; meals €25; ⏲lunch daily, dinner Wed-Sun) With its colourful, funky decor and jazzy soundtrack, this bright eatery offers hearty fare. Expect local cheese and cured hams, regional pastas and filling meat dishes.

## Modena 3

**Ristorante da Danilo** Traditional Italian €€

(Via Coltellini 29-31; meals €25-30; ⏲Mon-Sat) Head to Danilo's traditional dining room to feast on antipasti of salami, *pecorino* (sheep's-milk cheese) and fig marmalade; *secondos* (second courses) of *bollito misto* (mixed boiled meats); and risottos.

## Bologna 4

**Drogheria della Rosa** Traditional Italian €€

(☎051 22 25 29; www.drogheriadellarosa.it; Via Cartoleria 10; meals €35-40; ⏲lunch & dinner) With its wooden shelves, and apothecaries' jars and bottles, it's not difficult to picture this place as the pharmacy that it once was. Nowadays it's a charming, high-end trattoria specialising in Bolognese classics such as tortellini and steak with balsamic vinegar.

**Il Convento dei Fiori di Seta** Boutique Hotel €€

(☎051 27 20 39; www.silkflowersnunnery.com; Via Orfeo 34; r €130-270; ❄) A chic boutique hotel housed in a 14th-century convent. Religious-inspired frescoes sit alongside Mapplethorpe-style flower photos and snazzy modern light fixtures; beds come with linen sheets, and bathrooms feature cool mosaic tiles.

## Ferrara 5

**Osteria del Ghetto** Osteria €€

(☎0532 76 49 36; www.osteriadelghetto.it; Via Vittoria 26; meals €25-30; ⏲Wed-Mon) An understated jewel amid the winding streets of Ferrara's old Jewish ghetto. Head through the nondescript downstairs bar to the bright upstairs dining room for a delightful meal of fresh fish and Ferrara staples such as *cappellacci di zucca*.

## Ravenna 7

**Osteria La Mariola** Modern Italian €€

(☎0544 20 14 45; Via P Costa 1; meals €35-40) Housed in a 16th-century *palazzo*, La Mariola is a handsome choice, comprising a restaurant and *enoteca* (wine bar). Food is a shade more artistic than the usual homespun fare and there's a wine list that will satisfy most amateur buffs.

**Albergo Cappello** Boutique Hotel €€€

(☎0544 21 98 13; www.albergocappello.it; Via IV Novembre 41; d €180-260; P ❄ 📶) Colour-themed rooms at this finely coiffed hotel set Murano glass chandeliers, original 15th-century frescoes and coffered ceilings against modern fixtures and flat-screen TVs. There's also an excellent restaurant and wine bar attached.

400 m

# Southern Italy

**NATURE ITSELF SEEMS A LITTLE WILDER IN SOUTHERN ITALY**, where a single landscape can encompass smoking volcanoes, fertile green valleys, steep sea cliffs and cobalt seas. Italy's greatest hits may lie further to north, but the south may actually tug harder at the heartstrings, with its friendly and voluble people, piquant culinary traditions, wild backcountry and splendorous, palm-fanned cities.

With the exception of Naples' notorious traffic, this is also perfect driving country. Naples, Vesuvius and the Amalfi Coast are Grand Tour musts. But lesser-known routes reward for their pure surprise factor, from Cilento's pristine coast to the ski slopes of Sicily's Madonie Mountains.

**Aeolian Islands** Views across cobalt seas from Lipari to Vulcano (Trip 35)
JEAN-PIERRE DEGAS/HEMIS/CORBIS ©

# Southern Italy

**34** **Into the Madonie Mountains 3–5 Days**
Escape from Sicily's coast into this hiker's rugged paradise. (p357)

**35** **Sicilian Island Hop 7 Days**
After climbing smouldering Etna, strike out for the Aeolian's volcanic mysteries. (p365)

**36** **Sicilian Baroque 5 Days**
Gawk at the sumptuous cities and towns of Sicily's scenic southeast. (p373)

**37** **Emerald Coast 5–7 Days**
See why the Aga Khan bet his fortune on this splendid stretch of Sardinia. (p381)

**38** **Historic Sardinia 7 Days**
Cross Sardinia's wild interior in search of the island's Bronze Age past. (p389)

## DON'T MISS

### Vietri sul Mare

Bring back a piece of the Amalfi Coast from this seaside idyll, renowned for its bright-hued ceramics, on Trip 27

### Capo Palinuro

Hike this rocky promontory for gorgeous views of the Cilento coast, followed by a snorkel in its cobalt waters, on Trip 28

### Matera

Visit Matera, where ancient cave dwellings are transformed into wine bars and boutique sleeps, on Trip 31

### Hotel Ristorante Pomieri

At this lonely inn, mountain-grown ingredients are transmuted into unforgettable meals, on Trip 34

### Monte Fossa delle Felci

Pack a picnic starring the prized local Malvasia wine, then climb Salina's highest peak for dazzling views on Trip 35

***Pompeii** Walk among ruins in the presence of powerful Mt Vesuvius*

Classic Trip

# Shadow of Vesuvius

25

*Beginning in the tumult that is Naples, this trip winds around the Bay of Naples to the ruins of Pompeii and Herculaneum to seaside Sorrento – even daring the slopes of Vesuvius itself.*

## TRIP HIGHLIGHTS

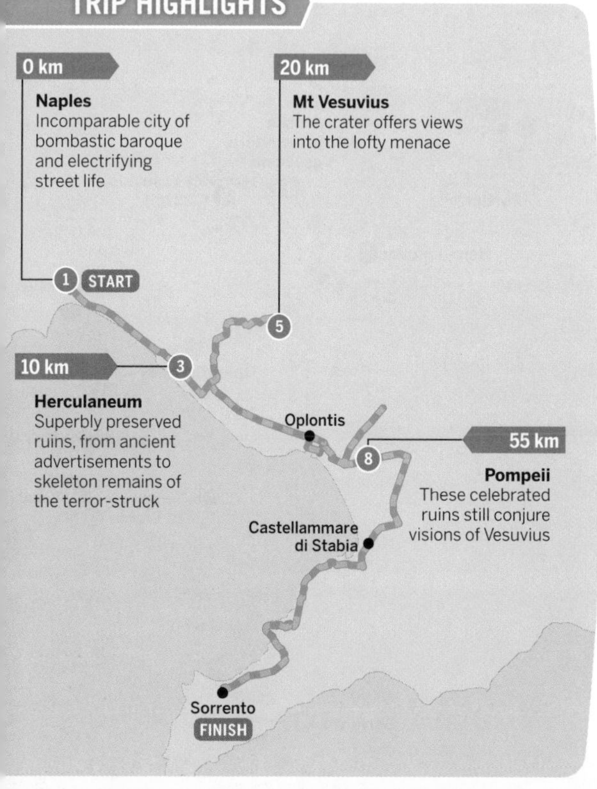

0 km
**Naples**
Incomparable city of bombastic baroque and electrifying street life

20 km
**Mt Vesuvius**
The crater offers views into the lofty menace

10 km
**Herculaneum**
Superbly preserved ruins, from ancient advertisements to skeleton remains of the terror-struck

55 km
**Pompeii**
These celebrated ruins still conjure visions of Vesuvius

1 START
5
3
Oplontis
8
Castellammare di Stabia
Sorrento
FINISH

**2–3 DAYS**
**90KM / 56 MILES**

### GREAT FOR...

### BEST TIME TO GO

Spring and autumn for best weather; December for stunning Christmas displays.

### ESSENTIAL PHOTO

Capture Vesuvius' brooding majesty from Naples' waterfront.

### BEST FOR HISTORY

Relive history amid Herculaneum's ruins.

Classic Trip

# 25 Shadow of Vesuvius

This trip begins in Naples (Napoli), a city that rumbles with contradictions – grimy streets hit palm-fringed boulevards; crumbling facades mask golden baroque ballrooms. Rounding the Bay of Naples and the dense urban sprawl, you quickly reach some of the world's most spectacular Roman ruins including Pompeii and Herculaneum, as well as lesser-known jewels, from salubrious ancient villas to Portici's royal getaway. Above it all looms Vesuvius' dark beauty.

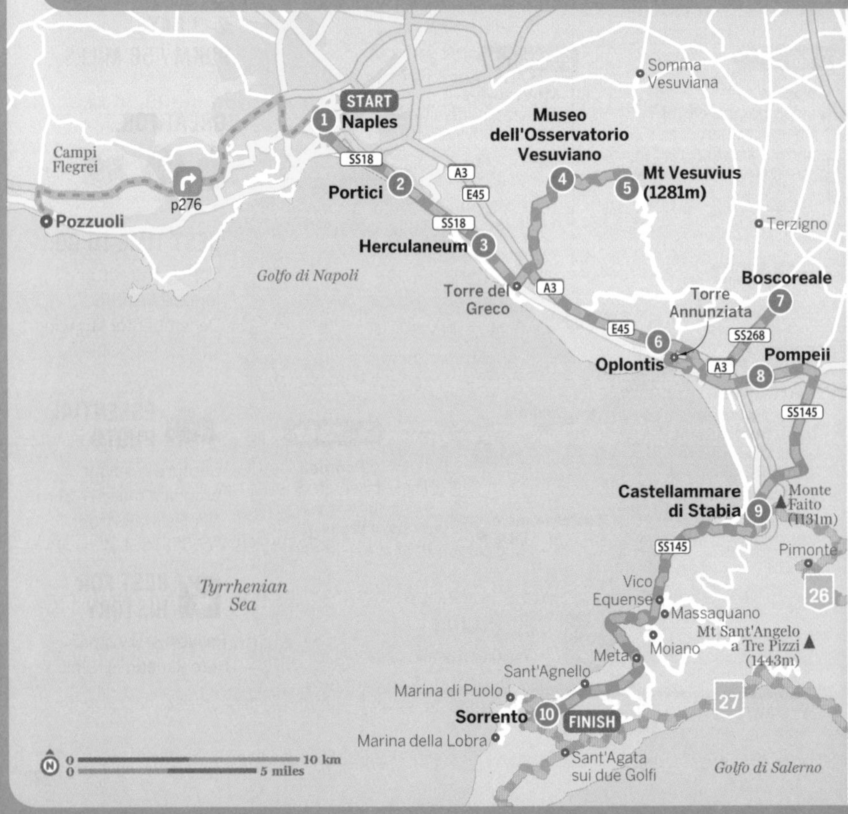

TRIP HIGHLIGHT

### 1 Naples

Italy's most misunderstood city is also one of its finest – an exhilarating mess of bombastic baroque churches, bellowing baristas and electrifying street life. Contradiction is the catchphrase here. It's a place where anarchy, pollution and crime sidle up to lavish palaces, mighty museums and aristocratic tailors.

The Unesco-listed *centro storico* (historic city centre) is an intoxicating warren of streets packed with ancient churches, citrus-filled cloisters and first-rate pizzerias. It's here, under the washing lines, that you'll find classic Neapolitan street life – overloaded Vespas hurtling through cobbled alleyways and clued-up *casalinghe* (homemakers) bullying market vendors. Move towards the sea and the cityscape opens up. Imperious palaces flank show-off squares where Gucci-clad shoppers strut their stuff, then lunch in chandeliered cafes. This is Royal Naples, the Naples of the Bourbons that so impressed the 18th-century grand tourists.

To buff up for Pompeii and Herculaneum, head to the **Museo Archeologico Nazionale** (081 44 01 66; Piazza Museo Nazionale 19; admission €6.50; 9am-7.30pm Wed-Mon). With one of the world's finest collections of Graeco-Roman artefacts, it stars a small but stunning collection of mosaics, mostly from Pompeii, plus a room full of ancient erotica.

p281

**The Drive »** A straight 8km drive along the SS18 provides an easy journey from central Naples straight to the Palazzo Reale di Portici – if the other drivers behave, of course.

**LINK YOUR TRIP**

**26 Southern Larder**

From Sorrento, you can embark on this culinary adventure along the Amalfi Coast and the Golfo di Salerno, where mozzarella rules the roost (p283).

**27 Amalfi Coast**

Sorrento kicks off this week-long adventure of hairpin turns and vertical landscapes amid the world's most glamorous stretch of coastline (p291).

### 2 Portici

The town of Portici lies at the foot of Mt Vesuvius and had to be rebuilt in the wake of its ruin by the 1631 eruption. Charles III of Spain, king of Naples and Sicily, erected his stately royal **palace** (Via Università 101; irregular) here between 1738 and 1748. After the fall of the Bourbons and Italy's unification in 1860, the palace found new life as the Portici botanic gardens and the Royal Higher School of Agriculture. Today, the exquisite botanic gardens are operated by the University of Naples Federico II.

**The Drive »** The entrance to the ruins of Herculaneum lie just down the street, a few hundred metres down the SS18.

TRIP HIGHLIGHT

### 3 Herculaneum

Superbly conserved, the ruins of ancient **Herculaneum** (081 732 43 38; www.pompeiisites.org; Corso Resina 6; adult/EU 18-25yr/EU under 18yr & over 65yr €11/5.50/free, combined ticket incl Pompeii, Oplontis, Stabiae & Boscoreale €20/10/free; 8.30am-7.30pm Apr-Oct, to 5pm Nov-Mar, last entry 90min before closing) are smaller, less daunting and easier to navigate than Pompeii. They also include some of the area's richest archaeological finds, from ancient advertisements and mosaics to carbonised furniture and skeletons of people who died cowering in terror.

Destroyed by an earthquake in AD 63, Herculaneum was completely submerged in the AD 79 eruption of Mt Vesuvius. However, because it was much closer to the volcano than Pompeii, it drowned in a sea of mud, essentially fossilising the town and ensuring that even delicate items were discovered remarkably well preserved.

Look out for the **Casa d'Argo**, a well-preserved example of a Roman noble family's house, complete with porticoed garden and *triclinium* (dining area). **Casa dei Cervi** (House of the Deer) is an imposing example of a Roman nobleman's villa, with two stories ranged around a central courtyard and animated with murals and still-life paintings. And don't miss the 1st-century-AD **Terme Suburbane** (Suburban Baths; closed for restoration at writing), with deep pools, stucco friezes and bas-reliefs looking down upon marble seats and floors.

p281

**The Drive »** The museum is only 10km from Herculaneum. Keep heading down the SS18 until you reach the centre of Torre del Greco, where you will turn right on Via Vittorio Veneto, which will quickly turn into Via Guglielmo Marconi. Follow the signs as you wind your way up the lower elevations of Mt Vesuvius, and the Bay of Naples comes into view.

## DETOUR: CAMPI FLEGREI

**Start: 1 Naples**

Stretching west of Posillipo Hill to the Tyrrhenian Sea, the oft-overlooked Campi Flegrei (Phlegrean Fields) counterbalances its ugly urban sprawl with steamy active craters, lush volcanic hillsides and priceless ancient ruins. While its Greek settlements are Italy's oldest, its Monte Nuovo is Europe's youngest mountain. It's not every week that a mountain just appears on the scene. At 8pm on 29 September 1538, a crack appeared in the earth near the ancient Roman settlement of Tripergole, spewing out a violent concoction of pumice, fire and smoke over six days. By the end of the week, Pozzuoli had a new 134m-tall neighbour.

Today, Europe's newest mountain is a lush and peaceful nature reserve. Before exploring the Campi Flegrei, stop at the helpful **tourist office** (☎081 526 66 39; Piazza Giacomo Matteotti 1a; ⏰9am-1pm & 4-7.30pm daily Jun-Sep, 9am-2pm & 2.30-3.40pm Mon-Fri Oct-May) in Pozzuoli to pick up tourist information and maps of the area, and purchase a €4 cumulative ticket that covers most of the key archaeological sites.

## 4 Museo dell'Osservatorio Vesuviano

Halfway up Mt Vesuvius, this **museum** (Museum of the Vesuvian Observatory; (☎081 610 84 83; www.ov.ingv.it; Via dell'Osservatorio 14, Ercolano; admission free; ⏰9am-2pm Mon-Fri, 10am-2pm Sat & Sun) contains an interesting array of artefacts telling the history of 2000 years of Vesuvius-watching. Founded in 1841 to monitor Vesuvius' moods, it is the oldest volcanic observatory in the world. To this day, scientists are still constantly monitoring the active volcanoes at Vesuvius, Campi Flegrei and Ischia.

**The Drive »** It's many more hairpin turns as you make your way along the same road almost to Vesuvius' crater, about 7km away. Views across the Bay of Naples and Campania are magnificent.

TRIP HIGHLIGHT

## 5 Mt Vesuvius

Since exploding into history in AD 79, Vesuvius has blown its top more than 30 times. The most devastating of these was in 1631, and the most recent was in 1944. It is the only volcano on the European mainland to have erupted within the last hundred years. What redeems this lofty menace is the spectacular view from its **crater** (adult/reduced/under 8yr €6.50/4.50/free; ⌚9am-6pm Jul & Aug, to 5pm Apr-Jun, to 4pm Mar & Oct, to 3pm Nov-Feb, ticket office closes 1hr before the crater) – a breathtaking panorama that takes in sprawling city, sparkling islands, and the Monti Picentini, part of the Apennine mountains.

The end of the road is the summit car park and the ticket office. From here, a relatively easy 860m path leads up to the summit (allow 35 minutes), best tackled in sneakers and with a jacket in tow (it can be chilly up top, even in summer). When the weather is bad the summit path is shut and bus departures are suspended.

**The Drive »** The first part of this 21km stretch heads back down Vesuvius the same way you came up. Head all the way down to the A3 highway, turn left onto it and head southeast. The villas of Oplontis are just off the Torre Annunziata exit.

**Mosaics from Pompeii** Located in the Museo Archeologico Nazionale in Naples

## 6 Oplontis

Buried beneath the unappealing streets of modern-day Torre Annunziata, Oplontis was once a seafront suburb under the administrative control of Pompeii. First discovered in the 18th century, only two of its houses have been unearthed, and only one, **Villa Poppaea** (www.pompeiisites.org; Via dei Sepolcri, Torre Annunziata; admission €5.50; ⌚8.30am-5pm), is open to the public. This villa is a magnificent example of an *otium* villa (a residential building used for rest and recreation), and may once have belonged to Emperor Nero's second wife.

**The Drive »** This brief 5km jaunt has you once again heading south on the SS18 to SS268 (Via Settetermini), which leads through scruffy Neapolitan suburbs to the Antiquarium di Boscareale.

### VESUVIAN WINES

Vesuvian wine has been relished since ancient times. The rare combination of rich volcanic soil and a favourable microclimate created by its slopes make the territory one of Italy's most interesting viticultural areas. Lacryma Christi (literally 'tears of Christ') is the name of perhaps the most celebrated wine produced on the slopes of Mt Vesuvius. Other prized vintages include Piedirosso, Aglianico and Greco del Vesuvio.

Classic Trip

DRIENDL GROUP/GETTY IMAGES ©

KEVEN OSBORNE/FOX FOTOS/GETTY IMAGES ©

## WHY THIS IS A CLASSIC TRIP
### ROBERT LANDON, AUTHOR

**After two millennia, the explosion of Mt Vesuvius is still fresh in our collective imaginations. On this trip you not only wander among the ruins of Roman cities frozen in time by the eruption, but actually glimpse into the infamous crater itself. And of course the trip kicks off in the sublime madness of Naples, an unruly and beautiful city unlike any other in Italy.**

Top: Vico Equense with Mt Vesuvius in the distance
Left: Hikers ascend Mt Vesuvius
Right: Ruins at Campi Flegrei

GREG ELMS/GETTY IMAGES ©



## 7 Boscoreale

Inaugurated in 1991, the **Antiquarium di Boscoreale** (www.pompeiisites.org; Via Settetermini 15; admission €5.50; 8.30am-5pm, to 6pm Apr-Oct) is a modern museum dedicated to life before the AD 79 eruption. Located on the lower slopes of Vesuvius, it holds a treasure trove of artefacts from Pompeii, Herculaneum and the surrounding region.

**The Drive »** Head straight back down the SS268 for about 4km all the way back to the SS18, which will take you through about 2km of scruffy suburbs right up next to the ruins of Pompeii.

TRIP HIGHLIGHT

## 8 Pompeii

Nothing piques human curiosity like a mass catastrophe, and few beat the ruins of **Pompeii** (081 857 53 47; www.pompeiisites.org; entrances at Porta Marina & Piazza Anfiteatro; admission €11; 8.30am-7.30pm Apr-Oct, last entry 6pm, to 5pm Nov-Mar, last entry 3.30pm), a stark reminder of Vesuvius' malign forces.

Of Pompeii's original 66 hectares, 44 have now been excavated. However, expect a noticeable lack of clear signage, areas cordoned off for no apparent reason, and the odd stray dog.

Audio guides (€6.50) are a sensible investment, and a good guidebook will help – try the €10 *Pompeii* published by Electa Napoli. To do justice to the site, allow at least three hours.

Highlights include the site's main entrance at **Porta Marina**, the most impressive of the seven gates that punctuated the ancient town walls. Just outside the wall is the impressive **Terme Suburbane**. These baths are famed for the risqué frescoes in the *apodyterium* (changing room). Immediately on the right as you enter Porta Marina is the 1st-century-BC **Tempio di Venere** (Temple of Venus), formerly one of the town's most opulent temples. The **Tempio di Apollo** (Temple of Apollo) is the oldest and most important of Pompeii's religious buildings, dating to the 2nd century BC. And the **Villa dei Misteri**, one of the most complete structures left standing in Pompeii, contains the remarkable fresco *Dionysiac Frieze*. One of the world's largest ancient paintings, it depicts the initiation of a bride-to-be into the cult of Dionysus, the Greek god of wine.

✕ p281

**The Drive »** The 9km trip from Pompeii begins heading south along the SS145 (Corso Italia). It will take you through a mixture of suburbs and small farms. Ahead, you will see the mountains of the Amalfi Coast rear up. The ancient villas of Stabiae are just east of Corso Italia, off Via Giuseppe Cosenza.

## 9 Castellammare di Stabia

South of Oplontis in modern-day Castellammare di Stabia, Stabiae was once a popular resort for wealthy Romans. It stood on the slopes of the Varano hill overlooking the entire Bay of Naples, and according to ancient historian Pliny it was lined for miles with extravagant villas. You can visit two **villas** (www.pompeiisites.org; Via Passeggiata Archeologica; admission free; ⏲8.30am-6pm): the 1st-century-BC Villa Arianna and the larger Villa San Marco, said to measure more than 11,000 sq m.

**The Drive »** This trip is a bit longer, at 21km, than the last few. Head back to the SS145, which will soon head over to the coast. Enjoy beautiful views over the Bay of Naples as you wind your way past Vico Equense, Meta and Piano di Sorrento to Sorrento.

## 10 Sorrento

For an unabashed tourist town, Sorrento still manages to preserve the feeling of a civilised coastal retreat. Even the souvenirs are a cut above the norm, with plenty of fine old shops selling ceramics, lacework and marquetry items. It is also the spiritual home of *limoncello*, a delicious lemon liqueur traditionally made from the zest of Femminello St Teresa lemons, also known as Sorrento lemons. Its tart sweetness makes the perfect nightcap, as well as a brilliant flavouring for both sweet and savoury dishes.

🛏 p281

### TOP TIP: PASS TO THE PAST

You can visit all five key sites around Pompeii, including the ruins of Pompeii and Herculaneum as well as the Antiquarium di Boscoreale, Oplontis and Stabiae, with a single pass that costs €20 and is valid for three days. It is available at the ticket offices of all five sites.

# Eating & Sleeping

## Naples 1

**Pizzeria Gino Sorbillo** Pizzeria €

(Via dei Tibunali 32; pizzas from €2.30; lunch & dinner Mon-Sat) The clamouring crowds spilling out into the street say it all: Gino Sorbillo is the official king of the pizza pack. Head in for gigantic, wood-fired perfection.

**Ristorante Radici** Modern Italian €€€

(081 248 11 00; www.ristoranteradici.it, in Italian; Via Riviera di Chiaia 268; meals €50; dinner Mon-Sat) Elegant yet warm, Radici offers respite from the tried-and-tested standards on most local menus. Prime local ingredients are revamped in dishes like melt-in-your-mouth *spigola* (European sea bass) patties. Book ahead.

**Hotel Piazza Bellini** Boutique Hotel €€

(081 45 17 32; www.hotelpiazzabellini.com; Via Costantinopoli 101; d €80-150; ) Naples' newest art hotel inhabits a 16th-century *palazzo*, its cool white spaces spiked with original majolica tiles and the work of emerging artists.

**Hotel San Francescoal Monte** Luxury Hotel €€€

(081 423 91 11; www.sanfrancescoalmonte.it; Corso Vittorio Emanuele I 328; s €160-190, d €170-225; ) The 16th-century monks never had it as good in this monastery as today's pampered guests. The cells have been converted into stylish rooms, the ancient cloisters house an open-air bar, and topping it all off is the 7th-floor swimming pool.

## Herculaneum 

**Vino Lo Re** Modern Italian €€

(081 739 02 07; Corso Resina 261, Ercolano; meals €30; lunch & dinner Tue-Sat, lunch only Sun, closed Aug) In rough-and-tumble Ercolano, the modern town near Herculaneum, Vino Lo Re is a stylish haven, where vintage prints and bookshelves meet a fabulous wine list and revamped regional grub, from ricotta-filled courgette flowers to a heavenly ricotta and chocolate flan.

## Pompeii 8

**Melius** Deli €

(081 850 25 98; Via Lepanto 156-160; 8am-2pm & 4.30-8.30pm Mon-Sat, 8am-2pm Sun) Pack a picnic hamper at this luscious gourmet deli, where local delicacies include fresh *mozzarella di bufala* (buffalo mozzarella), smoked salamis from Cilento, and citrusy Amalfi Coast marmalades.

**President** Traditional Italian €€

(081 850 72 45; Piazza Schettini 12; meals €35; lunch & dinner Mar-Oct, closed Mon & dinner Sun Nov-Feb) With its dripping chandeliers and Bacharach melodies, the President feels like a private dining room in an Audrey Hepburn film. Owner Paolo Gramaglia's passion for local produce is matched only by the menu's creative brilliance.

## Sorrento 10

**Casa Astarita** B&B €

(081 877 49 06; www.casastarita.com; Corso Italia 67; d €80-100) This pocket-sized gem in a 16th-century building in the city centre combines original structural elements with modern comforts. Rooms surround a central parlour where breakfast is served on a large, country-style table.

**Sorrento** *Dine alfresco and savour the zesty limoncello*

# Southern Larder

26

*From the Amalfi Coast to Paestum, this trip packs in both jaw-dropping natural beauty and mouth-watering cuisine built on fresh fish, sun-kissed veggies and the world's finest mozzarella.*

## TRIP HIGHLIGHTS

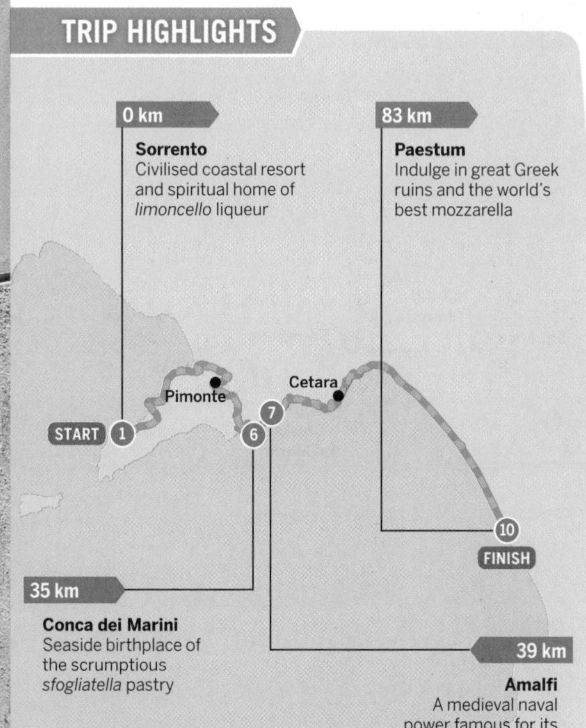


**3–4 DAYS**
**83KM / 52 MILES**

**GREAT FOR...**

**BEST TIME TO GO**

Spring for sunny, clear weather; early autumn for abundant produce.

**ESSENTIAL PHOTO**

Capture the hypnotically terraced cliffs of Agerola at sunset.

**BEST FOR FOODIES**

Going to mozzarella's source in Paestum.

# 26 Southern Larder

Besides the raw natural beauty of the Amalfi Coast and Gulf of Sorrento, this trip is a gourmand's dream. Foodies flock here from the world over for local specialties such as *limoncello* (lemon liqueur), ricotta-stuffed *sfogliatella* pastries, and a wildly creamy concoction made from water-buffalo milk that gives the word 'mozzarella' a whole new meaning. Burn off the extra calories hiking the Amalfi's jaw-dropping coastal trails or clambering over Paestum's majestic Greek ruins.

TRIP HIGHLIGHT

## 1 Sorrento

Most people come to seaside Sorrento as a pleasant stopover between Capri, Naples and the Amalfi Coast. It boasts dramatic views of the Bay of Naples and a festive holiday feel. However, foodies converge here for a very specific treat: *limoncello*, a very simple lemon liqueur made from the zest of lemons (preferably the local Femminello St Teresa lemons), plus

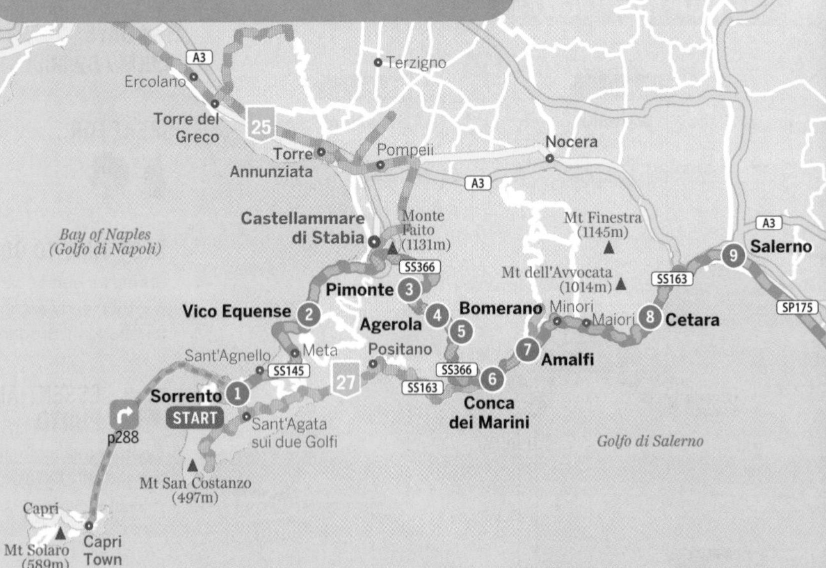

sugar and grain alcohol. It is traditionally served after dinner in chilled ceramic cups, and its combination of sweetness and biting tartness make the perfect end to a meal.

 p289

**The Drive »** Head north on the SS145, including a beautiful stretch along the Bay of Naples, for 12km to Vico Equense.

## ❷ Vico Equense

Known to the Romans as Aequa, Vico Equense is a small cliff-top town east of Sorrento. Largely bypassed by international tourists, it's a laid-back, authentic place worth a quick stopover, if only to experience some of the famous pizza served by the metre at the justly celebrated **Ristorante & Pizzeria da Gigino** (081 879 83 09; Via Nicotera 15; pizza per metre €12-26; noon-1am; ). This is no tourist trap but a beloved local institution due to its fresh ingredients and fluffy dough.

**The Drive »** From Vico Equense to Pimonte is 18km. You'll again hug the beautiful Bay of Naples for a while, reaching the turn-off for the SS366 in Castellammare di Stabia. From here, head inland and uphill as you wind your way to Pimonte.

## ❸ Pimonte

Tucked into the mountains in the easternmost end of the Amalfi peninsula, this small rural town is a far cry from the high-rolling coast, with tractors trundling through the narrow streets. Make a point of stopping at the main piazza for the delicious almond-based speciality *torta palummo* at Caffe Palumma. Expect curious stares; tourists are a rarity here.

**The Drive »** The 8km drive from Pimonte to Agerola takes you along a winding road through forested countryside along the SS366.

## ❹ Agerola

Agerola is located amid a wide green valley approximately 600m above sea level. It is surrounding by natural forests and offers amazing views of the surrounding mountains and Mediterranean Sea. Be sure to make a stop here for the legendary *fior di latte* (cow's-milk mozzarella) and *caciocavallo* (gourd-shaped traditional curd cheese) produced on the fertile slopes around town.

**LINK YOUR TRIP**

**25 Shadow of Vesuvius**

From Sorrento, where this trip begins, head around the Bay of Naples to conquer Naples (Napoli), wander the ruins of Pompeii and Herculaneum, and brave the slopes of Vesuvius (p273).

**27 Amalfi Coast**

Sorrento kicks off this weeklong adventure of hairpin turns and vertical landscapes amid the world's most glamorous stretch of coastline (p291).

**The Drive »** From Agerola to Bomerano, hop back on the SS366 for a quick 3km jaunt to Bomerano, enjoying a forest of beech trees and a backdrop of mountains thickly quilted with pines. You are now in the depths of the verdant Parco Regionale dei Monte Lattari.

## 5 Bomerano

Just a stone's throw from Agerola, you can easily follow your nose to tiny Bomerano for delicious buffalo-milk yogurt, an ultra-rich, mildly tangy and creamy treat. Stop by **Fusco** (Via Principe di Piemonte 3) for a tub of homemade yogurt. While there, you can also feast your eyes on the ornate ceiling frieze in the 16th-century **Chiesa San Matteo Apostolo**.

**The Drive »** From Bomerano to Conca Dei Marini, continue on the same road, SS366, for 9km as it winds dramatically down to the sea, with strategically placed lookouts along the way. From the SS366, you will do more switchbacking down to the town of Conca dei Marini itself.

TRIP HIGHLIGHT

## 6 Conca dei Marini

This charmingly picturesque fishing village has been beloved by everyone from Princess Margaret to Gianni Agnelli, Jacqueline Onassis and Carlo Ponti. Work up an appetite with an excursion to the **Grotta dello Smeraldo** (Green Cavern), a seaside cavern where the waters glow an eerie emerald green. Then head back to the town for a *sfogliatella,* a scrumptious shell-shaped, ricotta-stuffed pastry that was probably invented here in the 18th century in the monastery of Santa Rosa. The local pastry is even honoured with its own holiday: the first Sunday in August.

**The Drive »** Head northeast on the SS163 to the town of Amalfi.

TRIP HIGHLIGHT

## 7 Amalfi

It is hard to believe pretty little Amalfi was once a maritime superpower with a population of more than 70,000. For one thing, it's not a big place – you can easily walk from one end to the other in about 20 minutes. Don't miss the pleasant walk around the headland to neighbouring **Atrani**, a picturesque tangle of whitewashed alleys and arches centred on a lively, lived-in piazza and popular beach. And of course, gourmets shouldn't miss *scialatielli*. Shaped like short, slightly widened strips of tagliatelle, it is a local speciality, most commonly accompanied by zucchini and muscles or clams, or a simple sauce of fresh cherry tomatoes and garlic.

p289

JULIUS.JVLOOTHUIS/GETTY IMAGES ©

**Cetara** Boats clustered in the village harbour

## DETOUR: CAPRI

**Start: 1 Sorrento**

A mass of limestone rock that rises sheer through impossibly blue water, Capri (*ca*-pri) is the perfect microcosm of Mediterranean appeal – a smooth cocktail of chichi piazzas and cool cafes, Roman ruins and rugged seascapes. Need any more reason to go?

OK, here's one more: the *torta capresa*. Back in the 1920s, when an absent-minded baker forgot to add flour to the mix of a cake order, a great dessert was born. Now a traditional Italian chocolate and almond or walnut cake, it is named for the island of Capri from which it originated. The cake has a thin hard shell covering a moist interior. It is usually covered with a light dusting of fine powdered sugar, and sometimes made with a small amount of Strega or other liqueur. It's even gluten-free.

**Gescab-Linee Marittime Partenopee** (☎081 704 19 11; www.consorziolmp.it) runs hydrofoils from Sorrento to Capri from April to November (€15, 20 minutes, 15 daily).

**The Drive »** It's about 15km on the SS163 from Amalfi to Cetara. Silver birches and buildings draped in bougainvillea add to the beauty of the drive.

### 8 Cetara

A picturesque tumble-down fishing village, Cetara is also a gastronomic highlight. Tuna and anchovies are the local specialities, especially the sauce from the latter, appearing in various guises at Al Convento (p289), a sterling seafood restaurant near the small harbour. For your money, you'll probably not eat better anywhere else on the coast; the *puttanesca con alici fresche* (pasta with fresh anchovy sauce, chilli and garlic) sings with flavour.

p289

**The Drive »** Head northeast on SS163 for Salerno. En route, colourful wildflowers spill over white stone walls as you travel the sometimes hair-raising 11km along the coast.

### 9 Salerno

Salerno may seem like a bland big city after the Amalfi Coast's glut of pretty towns, but the place has a charming, if gritty, individuality, especially around its vibrant *centro storico* (historic centre). Don't miss the **cathedral** (Piazza Alfano; ⏰10am-6pm), built in the 11th century and graced by a magnificent main entrance, the 12th-century **Porta dei Leoni**. And for *torta ricotta e pera* (ricotta and pear tart), Sorrento is the *ne plus ultra*. This dessert is an Amalfi speciality, deriving its unique tang from the local sheep's-milk ricotta.

p289

**The Drive »** Head south on the SP175 and hug the coast all the way. Lush palm and lemon trees and the sparkling sea are your escorts for this 38km drive to Paestum.

TRIP HIGHLIGHT

### 10 Paestum

Work up an appetite amid Paestum's fascinating **ancient ruins** (☎0828 81 10 23; admission €4, incl museum €6.50; ⏰8.45am-2hr before sunset), including some of the best-preserved Greek temples in the world. Then head to **Tenuta Vannulo** (☎0828 72 47 65; www.vannulo.it; Via G Galilei Capaccio Scalo; 1hr tour €4, incl lunch €20), a 10-minute drive from Paestum, for a superbly soft and creamy mozzarella made from the organic milk of water buffalo. For a tour and lunch, reservations are essential. You can also stop just to buy the cheese, but be warned: it usually sells out by early afternoon.

p289

# Eating & Sleeping

## Sorrento 1

### Inn Bufalito — Campanian €€

(081 365 69 75; www.innbufalito.it; Vico 1 Fuoro 21; meals €25; Apr-Nov) A mozzarella bar as well as a restaurant, this effortlessly stylish place boasts a menu including delights such as Sorrento-style cheese fondue and buffalo-meat carpaccio. Cheese tastings are a regular event, as are other cultural happenings.

### Aurora Light — Campanian €€

(081 877 26 31; www.auroralight.it; Piazza Tasso 3-4; meals €25) The enthusiastic young owner has created a largely vegetarian menu that taps into traditional dishes while giving them an innovative twist, like fennel salad with beetroot and orange, and aubergine parmigiana with a swordfish sauce.

## Amalfi 7

### Ristorante La Caravella — Campanian €€€

(089 87 10 29; www.ristorantelacaravella.it; Via Matteo Camera 12; meals €60, tasting menu €75; Wed-Mon Jan–mid-Nov) One of the few places in Amalfi where you pay for the food rather than the location, this restaurant has won a Michelin star for regional food that is served either unabashedly simple or with a nouvelle zap. Reservations essential.

### Hotel Lidomare — Hotel €€

(089 87 13 32; www.lidomare.it; Largo Duchi Piccolomini 9; s/d €65/145) This old-fashioned, family-run hotel has real character. The spacious rooms emit an air of gentility, with appealingly haphazard decor.

## Cetara 8

### Al Convento — Seafood €€

(089 26 10 39; Piazza San Francesco 16; meals €25) Enjoy the evocative setting of this restaurant: former church cloisters with faded 17th-century frescoes. You can eat *tagliata di tonna alle erbe* (strips of lightly grilled tuna with herbs) as an antipasto, or anchovies prepared in various ways. Particularly delicious is the spaghetti served with anchovies and wild fennel.

## Salerno 9

### Hotel Plaza — Hotel €

(089 22 44 77; www.plazasalerno.it; Piazza Vittorio Veneto 42; s/d €65/100; ) The Plaza is convenient and comfortable, a stone's throw from the train station. It's a friendly place and the decent-sized rooms, complete with gleaming bathrooms, are pretty good value for money.

## Paestum 10

### Casale Giancesare — B&B €€€

(0828 72 80 61, 333 189 77 37; www.casalegiancesare.it; Via Giancesare 8; d €65-120; P ) This charming stone-clad B&B is run by the delightful Anna, who will happily ply you with her homemade wine and *limoncello*. Located 3km from Paestum and surrounded by vineyards, olive groves and mulberry trees, it has stunning views, particularly from the swimming pool.

***Ravello*** *Jaw-dropping views from Villa Rufolo*

*Classic Trip*

# Amalfi Coast

27

*Not for the fainthearted, this trip along the Amalfi Coast tests your driving skill on a 108km stretch, featuring dizzying hairpin turns and pastel-coloured towns draped over sea-cliff scenery.*

## TRIP HIGHLIGHTS

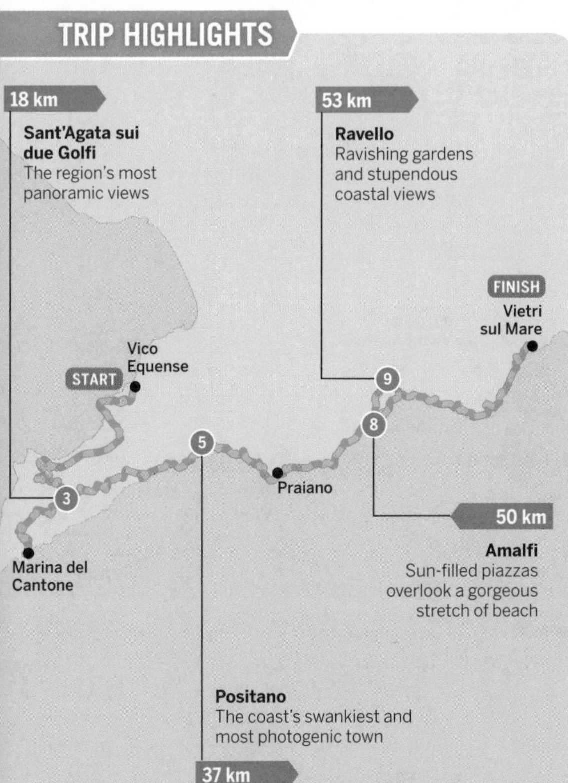


**7 DAYS**
**108KM / 67 MILES**

**GREAT FOR...**

**BEST TIME TO GO**

Summer for best beach weather, but also peak crowds.

**ESSENTIAL PHOTO**

Positano's vertiginous stack of pastel-coloured houses cascading down to the sea.

**BEST FOR OUTDOORS**

Hiking Ravello and its environs.

Classic Trip

# 27 Amalfi Coast

The Amalfi Coast is about drama, and this trip takes you where mountains plunge seaward in a stunning vertical landscape of precipitous crags, forests and resort towns. Positano and Amalfi are fabulously picturesque and colourful, while mountain-top Ravello is a serenely tranquil place with a tangible sense of history. Cars are useful for inland exploration, as are your own two legs. Walking trails provide a wonderful escape from the coastal clamour.

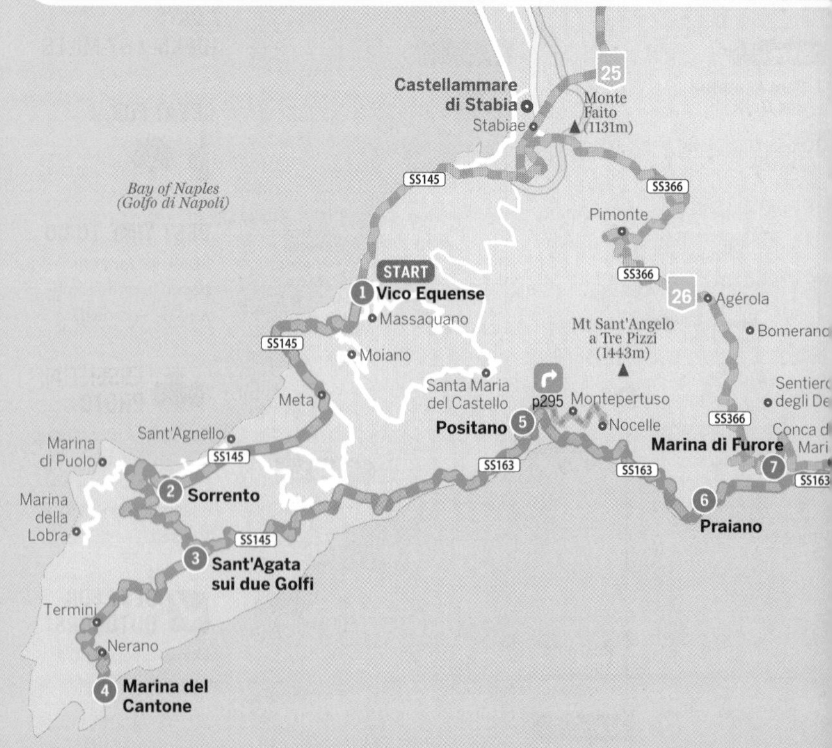

## ❶ Vico Equense

The Bay of Naples is justifiably famous for its pizza, which was invented here as a savoury way to highlight two local specialties: mozzarella and sun-kissed tomatoes. Besides its pretty little *centro storico* (historic centre), this little clifftop town overlooking the Bay of Naples boasts some of the region's best pizza, including a by-the-metre version at **Ristorante & Pizzeria da Gigino** (081 879 83 09; Via Nicotera 15; pizza per metre €12-26; noon-1am; ).

**The Drive »** From Vico Equense to Sorrento, your main route will be the SS145 roadway for 12km. Expect to hug the sparkling coastline after Marina di Equa before venturing inland around Meta.

## ❷ Sorrento

On paper, cliff-straddling Sorrento is a place to avoid – a package-holiday centre with few sights, no beach to speak of and a glut of brassy English-style pubs. In reality, it's strangely appealing, its laid-back southern Italian charm resisting all attempts to swamp it in souvenir tat and graceless development.

According to Greek legend, it was in Sorrento's waters that the mythical sirens once lived. Sailors of antiquity were powerless to resist the beautiful song of these charming maidens-cum-monsters, who would lure them to their doom.

p299

**The Drive »** Take the SS145 (Via Nastro Azzurro) for 11km to Sant'Agata sui due Golfi. Sun-dappled village streets give way to forest as you head further inland.

TRIP HIGHLIGHT

## ❸ Sant'Agata sui due Golfi

Perched high in the hills above Sorrento, sleepy Sant'Agata sui

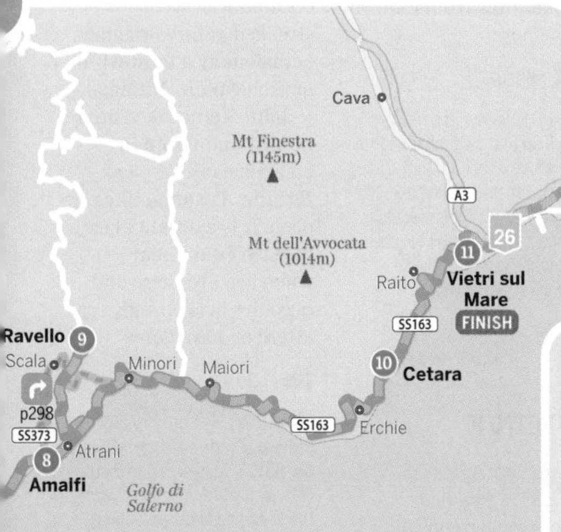


### LINK YOUR TRIP

**25 Shadow of Vesuvius**

Follow the curve of the Bay of Naples, from simmering Vesuvius to roiling Naples (p273).

**26 Southern Larder**

From Sorrento to Paestum, this trip takes you to the heart of mozzarella country (p283).

due Golfi commands spectacular views of the Bay of Naples on one side and the Bay of Salerno on the other (hence its name, Saint Agatha on the two Gulfs). The best viewpoint is the **Deserto** (081 878 01 99; Via Deserto; gardens 7am-7pm, lookout 5-8pm Apr-Sep, 3-4pm Oct-Mar), a Carmelite convent 1.5km uphill from the village centre. The **convent** (s incl meals €45) also offers simple accommodation for those who find the peace and panorama too hard to leave.

**The Drive »** From Sant'Agata sui due Golfi to Marina del Cantone it's a 9km drive, the last part involving some serious hairpin turns. Don't let the gorgeous sea views distract you.

## 4 Marina del Cantone

From Nerano, where you'll park, a beautiful hiking trail leads down to the stunning Bay of Ieranto and one of the coast's top swimming spots, Marina del Cantone. This unassuming village with its small pebble beach is a lovely, tranquil place to stay as well as a popular diving destination. The village also has a reputation as a gastronomic hot spot and VIPs regularly catch a boat over from Capri to dine here.

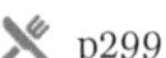
p299

**The Drive »** First, head back up that switchback to Sant'Agata sui due Golfi. Catch the SS145 and then the SS163 as they weave their way along bluffs and cliffsides to Positano. Most of the 24km involve stunning sea views.

TRIP HIGHLIGHT

## 5 Positano

The pearl in the pack, Positano is the coast's most photogenic and expensive town. Its steeply stacked houses are a medley of peaches, pinks and terracottas, and its near-vertical streets (many of which are, in fact, staircases) are lined with voguish shop displays, elegant hotels and smart restaurants. Look closely, though, and you'll find reassuring signs of everyday reality – crumbling stucco, streaked paintwork and occasionally a faint whiff of problematic drainage.

John Steinbeck visited in 1953 and wrote in an article for *Harper's Bazaar*: 'Positano bites deep. It is a dream place that isn't quite real when you are there and becomes beckoningly real after you have gone.'

p299

**The Drive »** From Positano to Praiano it's a quick 8km spin on the SS163, passing Il San Pietro di Positano at the halfway point, then heading southeast along the peninsula's edge.

## 6 Praiano

An ancient fishing village, a low-key summer resort and, increasingly, a popular centre for the arts, Praiano is a delight. With no centre as such,

### THE BLUE RIBBON DRIVE

Stretching from Vietri sul Mare to Sant'Agata sui due Golfi near Sorrento, the SS163 nicknamed the Nastro Azzurro (Blue Ribbon) remains one of Italy's most stunning roadways. Commissioned by Bourbon king Ferdinand II and completed in 1853, it wends its way along the Amalfi Coast's entire length, snaking round impossibly tight curves, over deep ravines and through tunnels gouged out of sheer rock. It's a magnificent feat of civil engineering although, as John Steinbeck pointed out in a 1953 essay, the road is also 'carefully designed to be a little narrower than two cars side by side'.

its whitewashed houses pepper the verdant ridge of Monte Sant'Angelo as it slopes towards Capo Sottile. Formerly an important silk-production centre, it was a favourite of the Amalfi doges (dukes), who made it their summer residence.

For those willing to take the plunge, the **Centro Sub Costiera Amalfitana** (☎089 81 21 48; www.centrosub.it; Via Marina di Praia) runs beginner to expert dives (€80 to €130) exploring the area's coral, marine life and grottoes.

**The Drive »** From Praiano, Marina di Furore is just 3km further on, past beautiful coves that cut into the shoreline.

## 7 Marina di Furore

A few kilometres further on, Marina di Furore sits at the bottom of what's known as the fjord of Furore, a giant cleft that cuts through the Lattari mountains. The main village, however, stands 300m above, in the upper Vallone del Furore. A one-horse place that sees few tourists, it breathes a distinctly rural air despite the presence of colourful murals and unlikely modern sculpture.

**The Drive »** From Marina di Furore to Amalfi, the sparkling Mediterranean Sea will be your escort as you drive westward along the SS163 coastal road for 6km. Look for Vettica Minore and Conca dei Marini along the way, along with fluffy bunches of fragrant cypress trees.

### WALK OF THE GODS

Probably the best-known walk on the Amalfi Coast, the 12km, six-hour **Sentiero degli Dei** (Walk of the Gods) follows the steep paths linking Positano to Praiano. The walk commences at **Via Chiesa Nuova**, just north of the SS163 road, in the northern part of Positano. Not advised for vertigo sufferers, it's a spectacular, meandering trail along the pinnacle of the mountains where caves and terraces plummet dramatically from the cliffs to deep valleys framed by the brilliant blue of the sea. It can sometimes be foggy in the dizzy heights, but that somehow adds to the drama, with the cypresses rising through the mist like dark shimmering sword blades.

TRIP HIGHLIGHT

## 8 Amalfi

It is hard to grasp that pretty little Amalfi, with its sun-filled piazzas and small beach, was once a maritime superpower with a population of more than 70,000. For one thing, it's not a big place – you can easily walk from one end to the other in about 20 minutes. For another, there are very few historical buildings of note. The explanation is chilling – most of the old city, along with its populace, simply slid into the sea during an earthquake in 1343.

One happy exception is the striking **Cattedrale**

### DETOUR: NOCELLE

**Start: 5 Positano**

A tiny, still relatively isolated mountain village above Positano, Nocelle (450m) commands some of the most spectacular views on the entire coast. A world apart from touristy Positano, it's a sleepy, silent place where not much ever happens, nor would its few residents ever want it to. If you want to stay, consider delightful **Villa della Quercia** (☎089 812 34 97; www.villadellaquercia.com; r €70-75; 📶), a former monastery with spectacular views. Nocelle lies eight very windy kilometres northeast of Positano.

Classic Trip

NICHOLA EVANS/GETTY IMAGES ©

PHOTOVOYAGER/ALAMY ©

## WHY THIS IS A CLASSIC TRIP

ROBERT LANDON, AUTHOR

Since the time of the Caesars, the Amalfi Coast has represented the ultimate luxury getaway. It only makes sense, since this coastline – an absurdly beautiful conjunction of craggy cliffs, lush forests, near-vertical townscapes and azure seas – forces you to forget life's daily woes. And when you're ready, you can quickly escape the clamouring coast on some of Italy's most jaw-dropping hikes.

Top: Highway motorcycling on the Amalfi Coast
Left: Cliffside road, Amalfi Coast
Right: Positano

KEVIN VAN DER LEEK/GETTY IMAGES ©

**di Sant'Andrea** (Piazza del Duomo; 9am-6.45pm Apr-Sep, reduced hours off season), parts of which date from the early 10th century. Although the building is a hybrid, the Sicilian Arabic-Norman style predominates, particularly in the two-tone masonry and the 13th-century bell tower.

Be sure to take the short walk around the headland to neighbouring Atrani, a picturesque tangle of whitewashed alleys and arches centred on a lively, lived-in piazza and popular beach.

p299

**The Drive »** Start the 9km trip from Amalfi to Ravello by heading along the coast and then catching the SS373 near Castiglione. Breathtaking views abound on this narrow coastal road, before you head up to hillside Ravello.

TRIP HIGHLIGHT

## 9 Ravello

Sitting high in the hills above Amalfi, refined Ravello is a polished town almost entirely dedicated to tourism. Boasting impeccable bohemian credentials – Richard Wagner, DH Lawrence and Virginia Woolf all lounged here – it's known today for its ravishing gardens and stupendous views, the best in the world according to former resident Gore Vidal.

To enjoy these views, head south of Ravello's cathedral to the 14th-century tower that marks the entrance to **Villa Rufolo** (089 85 76 57; adult/reduced €5/3; 9am-sunset). Created by Scotsman Scott Neville Reid in 1853, these gardens combine celestial panoramic views, exotic colours, artistically crumbling towers and luxurious blooms. Also worth seeking out is the wonderful **Camo** (089 85 74 61; Piazza Duomo 9; 9.30am-noon & 3-5.30pm Mon-Sat). Squeezed between tourist-driven shops, this very special place is, on the face of it, a cameo shop. And exquisite they are too, crafted primarily out of coral and shell. But don't stop here; ask to see the treasure trove of a museum beyond the showroom.

p299

**The Drive »** Head back down to the SS163 for a 19km journey that twists and turns challengingly along the coast to Cetara. Pine trees and a variety of flowering shrubs line the way.

## 10 Cetara

Cetara is a picturesque, tumbledown fishing village with a reputation as a gastronomic delight. Since medieval times it has been an important fishing centre, and today its deep-sea tuna fleet is considered one of the Mediterranean's most important. At night, fishermen set out in small boats armed with powerful lamps to fish for anchovies. No surprise then that tuna and anchovies dominate local menus, especially at Al Convento (p289), a sterling seafood restaurant near the small harbour.

**The Drive »** From Cetara to Vietri sul Mare, head northeast for 6km on the SS163 for more twisting, turning and stupendous views across the Golfo di Salerno.

## 11 Vietri sul Mare

Marking the end of the coastal road, Vietri sul Mare is the ceramics capital of Campania. Although production dates back to Roman times, it didn't take off as an industry until the 16th and 17th centuries. Today, ceramics shopaholics find their paradise at the **Ceramica Artistica Solimene** (089 21 02 43; www.solimene.com; Via Madonna degli Angeli 7), a vast factory outlet. Devotees should also seek out the **Museo della Ceramica** (Museum of Ceramics; 089 21 18 35; Villa Guerriglia; 8am-3pm Tue-Sat, 9am-1pm Sun) in the nearby village of Raito. Housed in a lovely villa surrounded by a park, the museum has a comprehensive collection.

### DETOUR: RAVELLO WALKS

**Start: 9 Ravello**

Ravello is the starting point for numerous walks that follow ancient paths through the surrounding Lattari mountains. If you've got the legs for it, you can walk down to **Minori** via an attractive route of steps, hidden alleys and olive groves, passing the picturesque hamlet of **Torello** en route. Alternatively, you can head the other way, to Amalfi, via the ancient village of **Scala**. Once a flourishing religious centre with more than a hundred churches and the oldest settlement on the Amalfi Coast, Scala is now a pocket-sized sleepy place where the wind whistles through empty streets, and gnarled locals go patiently about their daily chores.

# Eating & Sleeping

## Sorrento 2

**L'Antica Trattoria** Campanian **€€**
(081 807 10 82; Via Padre Reginaldo Giuliani 33; meals from €40) Hailed by locals as the finest restaurant in town; the menu is mainly traditional, with homemade pasta and a daily fresh fish dish, grilled in a crust of salt.

**Hotel Cristina** Hotel **€€**
(081 878 35 62; www.hotelcristinasorrento.it; Via Privata Rubinacci 6, Sant'Agnello; s €90-135, d €90-200; Apr-Oct; ) Perched above Sant'Agnello, Hotel Cristina boasts unrivalled views, best enjoyed from the swimming pool. Elegant rooms fuse inlaid wooden furniture and vintage prints with contemporary touches like Philippe Starck chairs.

## Marina del Cantone 4

**Lo Scoglio** Campanian **€€€**
(081 808 10 26; Marina del Cantone; meals €50) Directly accessible from the sea, Lo Scoglio attracts the likes of Johnny Depp and Stephen Spielberg. The food is top notch (and priced accordingly). But despite the glamorous clientele, this is an unpretentious family-run place, complete with grandma watching the till.

## Positano 5

**Pensione Maria Luisa** Pensione **€**
(089 87 50 23; www.pensionemarialuisa.com; Via Fornillo 42; s €50, d €70-85; @) The best budget choice in town, Maria Luisa's rooms have recently been updated with new blue tiles and fittings. Other perks include a sunny communal area and a jovial, helpful owner. Cash only.

## Amalfi 8

**Marina Grande** Seafood **€€**
(089 87 11 29; www.ristorantemarinagrande.com: Viale Delle Regioni 4; meals €30; Tue-Sun Mar-Oct) Run by the third generation of the same family, patronised primarily by locals and fronting the beach, this restaurant serves fish so fresh it is almost flapping.

**Hotel Luna Convento** Hotel **€€€**
(089 87 10 02; www.lunahotel.it; Via Pantaleone Comite 33; s €220-280, d €240-300; P @) This former convent was founded by St Francis in 1222. Rooms in the original building are in the former nuns' cells, but there's nothing pokey about the bright tiles, balconies and sea views.

## Ravello 9

**Cumpá Cosimo** Trattoria **€€**
(089 85 71 56; Via Roma 44-46; pizzas €6-12, meals €45) Chef Netta Bottone rules the roost at this historic trattoria. Order the *piatto misto* (mixed plate), which may include Ravello's trademark *crespolini* (cheese and prosciutto-stuffed crepes). Evening options include pizza.

**Agriturismo Monte Brusara** Agriturismo **€**
(089 85 74 67; www.montebrusara.com; Via Monte Brusara 32; d €84-90) It's a tough half-hour walk from Ravello's centre, but this authentic mountainside *agriturismo* (farm-stay accommodation) is the real McCoy. It's an ideal spot to escape the crowds and offers three comfortable but basic rooms, fabulous food and big views.

**_Santa Maria di Castellabate_**
_Sun-seekers and statuary adorn this fishing town_

# Cilento Coastal Trail

*Following the wild and rugged coastline of the Cilento peninsula, this trip takes in pristine coastline, fascinating hilltop towns, ancient Greek ruins and atmospheric fishing villages.*

## TRIP HIGHLIGHTS

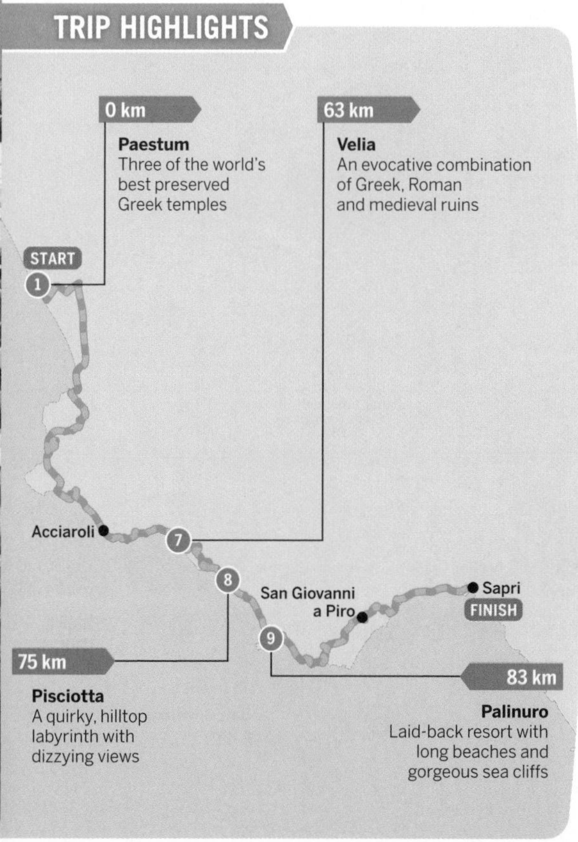

START
1
Acciaroli
7
8
San Giovanni a Piro
9
Sapri
FINISH

**0 km**
**Paestum**
Three of the world's best preserved Greek temples

**63 km**
**Velia**
An evocative combination of Greek, Roman and medieval ruins

**75 km**
**Pisciotta**
A quirky, hilltop labyrinth with dizzying views

**83 km**
**Palinuro**
Laid-back resort with long beaches and gorgeous sea cliffs

**4–5 DAYS**
**148KM / 92 MILES**

### GREAT FOR...

### BEST TIME TO GO

Spring and autumn for hikers; high summer for beach types.

### ESSENTIAL PHOTO

Capture rugged coast and royal blue sea from hilltop Pisciotta.

### BEST FOR OUTDOORS

The Palinura peninsula, where fragrant pines meet sheer cliffs and open sea.

# 28 Cilento Coastal Trail

Barely accessible by road until the 20th century, the jagged cliffs of the Cilento peninsula immerse you in one Italy's least-explored stretches of coastline. After flourishing under the Greeks and Romans, the Cilento was abandoned for centuries to the vagaries of Mediterranean pirates. Today, its fishing villages and pretty hill towns remain largely free of mass development, despite long strands, pristine blue waters and exquisite local seafood.

TRIP HIGHLIGHT

### 1 Paestum

The three stately, honey-coloured temples at Paestum are among the best preserved in Magna Graecia – the Greek colonies that once held sway over much of southern Italy. The Greeks capitulated to the Romans in 273 BC, and Poseidonia, as it was known, remained a thriving trading port until the fall of the Roman Empire.

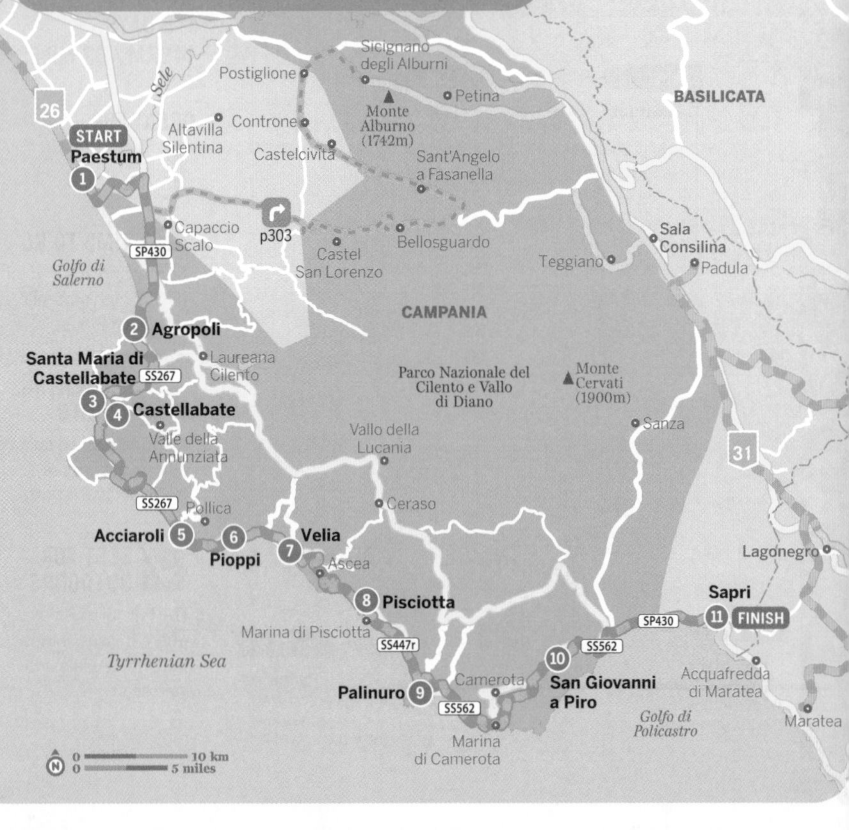

Tickets to the **ruins** (☎0828 81 10 23; admission €4, incl museum €6.50; ⏰8.45am-2hr before sunset) are sold at the main entrance near the tourist office, or, in winter, from the museum, which features frescoes, statuary and lots of historical and archaeological insight.

The first temple you encounter after the main entrance is the 6th-century-BC **Tempio di Cerere** (Temple of Ceres). The smallest of the three temples, it served for a time as a Christian church. The sprawling site also includes remnants of the Roman city, including an amphitheatre, housing complexes and the **foro** (main square and administrative centre). Beyond lies the **Tempio di Nettuno** (Temple of Neptune), the largest and best preserved of the three temples.

Next door, the equally beautiful **basilica** (in reality, a temple to the goddess Hera) is Paestum's oldest surviving monument, dating from the middle of the 6th century BC.

🛏 p307

**The Drive »** Heading 10km south down the SP430 from Paestum, you quickly start winding into the foothills of the Cilento. Agropoli's historic centre will loom up on the right. Follow signs to the 'Centro Storico'.

### DETOUR: PARCO NAZIONALE DEL CILENTO E VALLO DI DIANO

**Start: 1 Paestum**

Italy's second-largest national park, **Parco Nazionale del Cilento e Vallo di Diano** (www.parks.it/parco.nazionale.cilento) occupies the lion's share of the Cilento peninsula. The most interesting and accessible parts of the park lie within an hour's drive northeast of Paestum in the northwest corner of the park. The park's interior offers great opportunities for spelunking, especially the otherworldly caverns at **Grotta di Castelcivita**, near the town of Castelcivita. The town of **Sicignano degli Alburni**, capped by a medieval castle, provides a good base to hike up 1742m-high **Monte Alburno**. Finally, the medieval centre of nearby **Postiglione**, crowned 11th-century Norman castle, makes for a lovely stroll.

### LINK YOUR TRIP

**26 Southern Larder**

Join this culinary adventure through Campania where this trips begins – amid the ancient ruins of Paestum (p283).

**31 Across the Lucanian Appennines**

A short, stunning 20km from Sapri along Basilicata's coastline; Maratea kicks off this journey over the gorgeous Lucanian Appennines to otherworldly Matera (p325).

## 2 Agropoli

Guarding the northern flank of the Cilento peninsula, the ancient town of Agropoli proffers stunning views across the Gulf of Salerno to the Amalfi Coast. The outskirts are made up of a rather faceless grid of shop-lined streets, but the historic kernel, occupying a rocky promontory, is a charming tangle of cobbled streets with ancient churches, the remains of a castle and superlative views up and down the coast.

🍴 p307

**The Drive »** South of Agropoli, the 13km stretch of the SS267 turns inland, giving a taste of Cilento's rugged interior, but you'll quickly head west and to the sea.

## 3 Santa Maria di Castellabate

Because of the danger of sudden pirate attacks, all the coastal towns of Cilento once consisted of a low-lying coastal fishing community and a nearby highly defended hilltop town where peasants and fishermen could find quick refuge.

These days, the fishing district of Castellabate – known as Santa Maria di Castellabate – has outgrown its hilltop protector, thanks to the town's 4km stretch of golden-sand beach. Despite the development, the town's historic centre preserves a palpable southern Italian feel, with dusky-pink and ochre houses blinkered by traditional green shutters. The little harbour is especially charming, with its 19th-century *palazzi* and the remnants of a much older castle. Note that these charms can diminish quickly when summer crowds overwhelm the scant parking.

p307

**The Drive »** Just past the town of Santa Maria di Castellabate along SS267 is the turn-off to Castellabate. The road then winds through orchards and olive groves for 8km.

## 4 Castellabate

With sweeping sea views, medieval Castellabate clings to the top of a steep hill 280m above sea level. One of the most endearing and historic towns on the Cilento coast, its strategic location helped defend residents from pirate incursions throughout the Middle Ages. Its labyrinth of narrow pedestrian streets is punctuated by ancient archways, small piazzas and the occasional *palazzo*.

**The Drive »** Head back down to the SS267 and follow for 21km, which turns inland once again, but you will see the sea soon enough as you twist down to Acciaroli.

## 5 Acciaroli

Despite a growing number of concrete resorts on its outskirts, the tastefully restored historic centre of this fishing village makes it worth a stop, especially for Hemingway lovers. The author spent time here in the 1940s, and some say he based his *The Old Man and the Sea* on a local fisherman.

**The Drive »** After Acciaroli, the coastal highway climbs quickly for 8km to Pioppi, proffering stunning views down the Cilento coast to Capo Palinuro.

## 6 Pioppi

Tiny, seaside Pioppi has the right to feel smug. Based on observations of this town's vigorous older residents in the late 1950s, American medical researcher Dr Ancel Keys launched his famous study concerning the health benefits of the Mediterranean diet. Join a new generation of geezers dozing on the shady benches of lovely Piazza de Millenario. Suitably rested, take a picnic to the pristine, pale pebble beach a few steps away.

**The Drive »** By Cilento standards, it's practically a straight shot for 7km along the coastal highway to the town of Ascea, where coastal mountains make way for the small but rich plains that once fed ancient Velia.

TRIP HIGHLIGHT

## 7 Velia

Founded by the Greeks in the mid-6th century BC, and subsequently a popular resort for wealthy Romans, Velia (formerly Elea) was once home to philosophers Parmenides and Zeno. Today, you can wander around the town's evocative **ruins** (9am-6pm), including intact portions of the original city walls, plus remnants of thermal baths, an Ionic temple, a Roman theatre and even a medieval castle.

**Agropoli** On the Gulf of Salerno

**The Drive »** You are now headed into the most hair-raising stretch of the Cilento's coastal highway, but spectacular views are your reward. Olive trees start multiplying as you near Pisciotta. The total distance is about 24km.

TRIP HIGHLIGHT

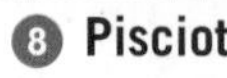

## 8 Pisciotta

The liveliest town in the Cilento and also its most dramatic, hilltop Pisciotta consists of a steeply pitched maze of medieval streets. Life centres on the lively main square where the town's largely elderly residents rule the roost. The hills surrounding the town are terraced into rich olive groves and produce particularly prized oil, while local fishermen specialise in anchovies. When their catch is marinated in the local oil, the result is mouth-wateringly good.

✂ 🛏 p307

**The Drive »** The 15km trip begins with a steep descent from Pisciotta, and a straight road to Palinuro. Before reaching town, you'll see its beautiful, miles-long beach.

TRIP HIGHLIGHT

## 9 Palinuro

The Cilento's main resort, Palinuro remains remarkably low-key (and low rise), with a tangible fishing-village feel, though its beaches become crowded in August. Extending past its postcard-pretty harbour, the remarkable 2km-long promontory known as **Capo Palinuro** proffers wonderful walking trails and views up and down the coast. Better yet, you can visit its sea cliffs and hidden caves, including Palinuro's own version of Capri's famous Grotta Azzurra, with a similarly spectacular display of water, colour and light. To arrange the 90-minute excursion, contact **Da Alessandro** (☎347 654 09 31; www.costieradelcilento.it, in Italian).

✂ p307

**The Drive »** Begin the 27km drive with a beautiful jaunt along the water before heading inland at Marina di Camerota. Get ready for plenty of sharp turns as you wind up stunning SS562.

## 10 San Giovanni a Piro

With its tight-knit historic centre and jaw-dropping views across the Gulf of Policastro to the mountains of La Basilicata and Calabria, this little agricultural town makes a worthy stop as you wind your way around the wild, southern tip of the Cilento peninsula.

**The Drive »** The final 30km of this trip begins with a winding descent from San Giovanni a Piro to the pretty port town of Scario; the road flattens out as you make your way around the picturesque Golfo di Policastro.

## 11 Sapri

Set on an almost perfectly round natural harbour, Sapri is the ideal place to wave goodbye to the Cilento. The peninsula's dramatic interior mountains rear up across the beautiful Golfo di Policastro. Admire the views from the town's seafront promenade or from one of its nearby beaches.

# Eating & Sleeping

## Paestum 1

**Casale Giancesare** B&B €

(☎0828 72 80 61, 333 189 77 37; www.casale-giancesare.it, in Italian; Via Giancesare 8; d €65-120; P ❄ @ ≋) This 19th-century farmhouse-turned-B&B is surrounded by vineyards. The delightful owners produce their own olives, jams, *limoncello* (lemon liqueur) and wine.

## Agropoli 2

**U'Sghiz** Traditional Italian, Pizzeria €

(Piazza Umberto I; pizzas from €3, meals €22; ⊙closed Tue Oct-May) In a 17th-century building on the headland, U'Sghiz specialises in seafood dishes like *spaghetti a vongole* (with mussels) and also has an extensive pizza menu.

## Santa Maria di Castellabate 3

**I Due Fratelli** Seafood €€

(☎0974 968 004; www.ristoranteiduefratelli.net, in Italian; Via San Andrea 13; meals €30-35; ⊙lunch & dinner Thu-Tue, daily Jun-Aug) Housed in an inauspicious concrete building at the side of the highway, this highly respected spot serves up arguably the best seafood in the region.

**Per Bacco** Campanian €€

(☎0974 961 832; Via Andrea Guglielmini 19; meals €35-40; ⊙dinner Wed-Mon, closed Nov) Set on the charming town beach, foodie-favourite Per Bacco proffers a long wine list and creative takes on local specialities, like *tortino di alici* (anchovies with smoked cheese, creamed potatoes and eggplant) and ravioli stuffed with sea urchin.

**Residenza d'Epoca 1861** Guesthouse €

(☎ 0974 961 454; www.residenzadepoca1861.it; Lungomare Perrotti; d €65-90) Occupying an 18th-century mansion on Santa Maria di Castellabate's historic waterfront, this small, impeccably run guesthouse offers sea views from every room, plus whitewashed interiors with discreet splashes of modernist colour. Reserve ahead at weekends and in summer.

## Pisciotta 8

**Osteria del Borgo** Campanian €€

(☎0974 970 113; Via Roma 17; meals €25-35; ⊙lunch & dinner) From your perch on the stone terrace, you'll hear your order loudly repeated to the chef (ie Mamma), followed by the requisite banging of pots and pans. Her perfectly marinated anchovies come sprinkled with lemon and tiny bits of raw garlic, and the seafood risotto is impeccable.

**Mariluvo** Guesthouse €€

(☎0974 973 792; www.marulivohotel.it; Via Castello; r €80-160) Well worth the schlep into the labyrinthine medieval quarters, this tasteful, friendly, immaculately run guesthouse spills down the hill towards the sea. Nearly all the well-appointed rooms have sea views. If not, the panoramic terrace invites beautiful lingering.

## Palinuro 9

**O Guarracino** Seafood €

(☎0974 938 309; www.oguarracino.it; Via Porto; meals €20-25; ⊙lunch & dinner May-Aug, lunch only Mar, Apr, Sep & Oct) This humble beachside eatery is run by a fishing family that still plies the waters in winter. Expect the freshest grilled fish, or try the local speciality *melanzane alla palinurese* (eggplant stuffed with egg and cheese).

**Trani** *Ready your camera for the Cathedral of St Nicholas the Pilgrim*

DAVID MADISON/GETTY IMAGES ©

# Puglia's Pilgrim Trail

29

*From rough-and-ready Bari to the wild Promontorio del Gargano, this trip spotlights Puglia's Norman and German conquerors, whose medieval castles and churches still grace this region.*

## TRIP HIGHLIGHTS

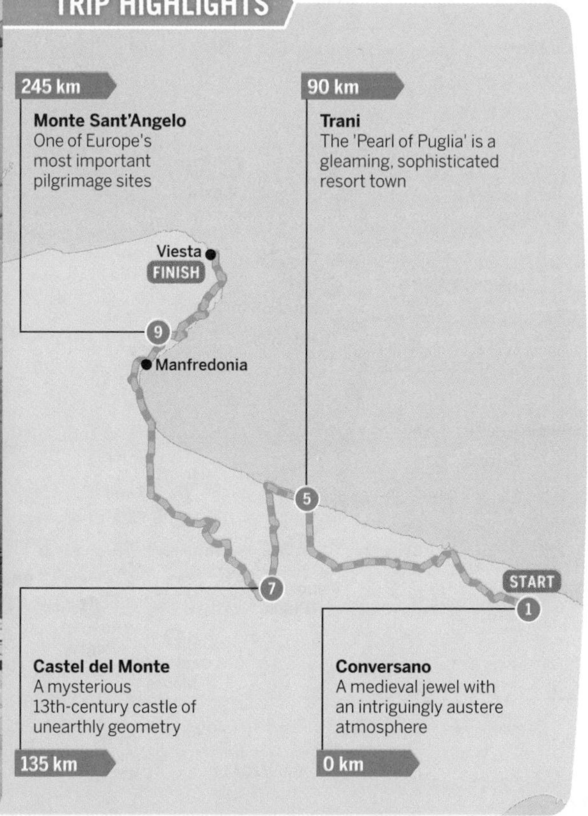

**4 DAYS**
**310KM / 193 MILES**

**GREAT FOR...**

**BEST TIME TO GO**

April to June for hiking amid wildflowers. Fall for mushrooms and mild weather.

**ESSENTIAL PHOTO**

Capture the isolated mountain-top splendour of the Monte Sant'Angelo.

**BEST FOR HISTORY**

Conversano's restrained medieval splendour.

# 29 Puglia's Pilgrim Trail

Both pilgrims and princes have long been partial to this stretch of the Adriatic coast, and you'll know why as you weave your way from sun-kissed seaside to fertile interior plains, which together form the basis for Puglia's extraordinary cuisine. All the way to the dramatic Promontorio del Gargano, you'll see splendid evidence of Puglia's medieval prosperity, when Norman and Swabian overlords built both bristling castles and the region's distinctive Romanesque churches.

TRIP HIGHLIGHT

## 1 Conversano

Conversano's historic centre is a medieval jewel that generates its own austerely intriguing atmosphere. The main attraction is the medieval **Castello di Conversano**, which commands views over the coastal plains all the way to Bari. And don't miss the beautiful Romanesque **cathedral** (Largo Cattedrale). Built between the 9th and the 14th centuries, it has a typical graven portal,

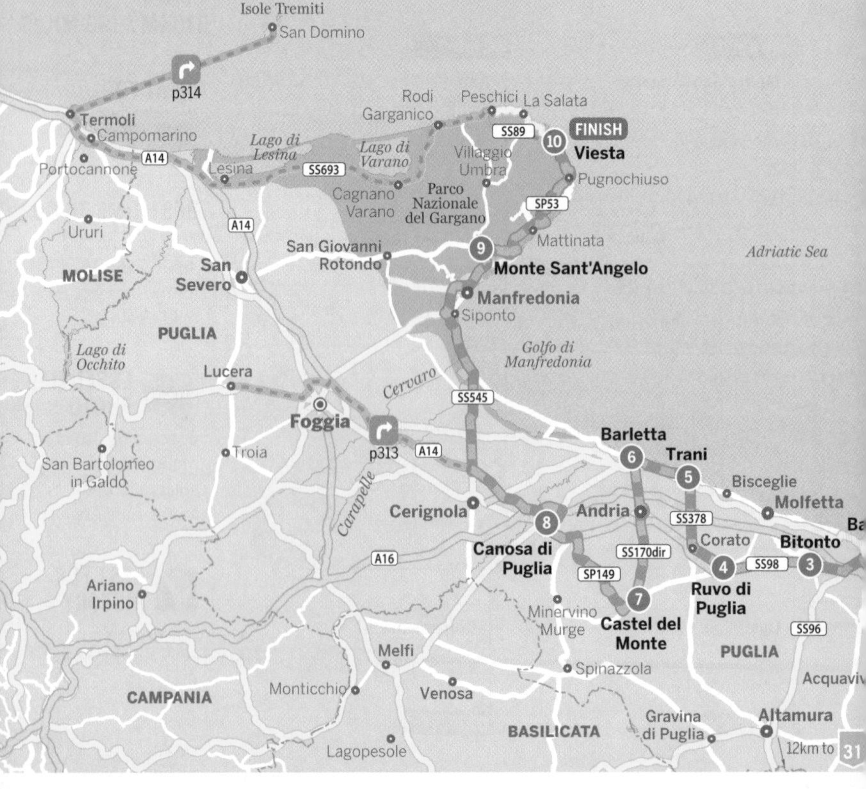

large rose window and pointy gabled roof.

**The Drive »** Head northwest through Puglia's rich agricultural flatlands along the SS634 to Bari for 29km.

## 2 Bari

Once regarded as the Bronx of southern Italy, Puglia's capital – one of the south's most prosperous cities – deserves more than a cursory glance. Spruced up and rejuvenated, Bari Vecchia, the historic old town, is an atmospheric warren of tight alleyways and graceful piazzas that also manages to cram in 40 churches. In the evenings, piazzas buzz with trendy restaurants and bars, though parts of the old town carry a gritty undertone and require some caution. Bari's **Basilica di San Nicola** (Piazza San Nicola; ⌚7am-1pm & 4-7pm Mon-Sat, 7am-1pm & 4-9pm Sun), one of the south's first Norman churches, is a splendid example of Puglian-Romanesque style.

p315

**The Drive »** A not-very-interesting 19km drive heads into Bari's flat, industrial suburbs along the SS96 until the town of Modugno, where you will catch the SS98 to Bitonto.

## 3 Bitonto

Surrounded as it is by olive groves, it's no surprise Bitonto produces a celebrated extra-virgin oil. However, it is the town's medieval core that makes it worth seeking out. Its magnificent 12th-century **cathedral** (Piazza Cattedrale) is romantically dedicated to St Valentine. There is also an impressive Norman castle and smaller medieval churches to refresh the spirit.

**The Drive »** Heading west along the SS98, the flat Puglia landscape will turn more rural, until you reach the outskirts of Ruvo di Puglia, 19km to the west.

## 4 Ruvo di Puglia

Situated on the eastern slopes of the Murgia plateau and surrounded by olive and almond orchards, Ruvo is one of the most attractive country towns in Puglia. The old town is dominated by a famous 13th-century **cathedral**, a gorgeous example of Puglia's distinctive version of Romanesque architecture. The town also is home to the

### LINK YOUR TRIP

**30 Salento Surprises**

From Bari, head 150km along coastal highways SS16, SS379 and SS613 until you reach jewel-like Lecce, then along the fascinating, beach-lined high heel of the Italian boot (p317).

**31 Across the Lucanian Appennines**

About 67km south of Bari via the SS96 and SS99 lies Matera, the culmination of this trip over the gorgeous and little-explored Lucanian Appenines (p325).

**Museo Nazionale Jatta** (www.palazzojatta.org; Piazza Bovio 35), with its remarkable collection of ancient Greek ceramics. And don't leave without trying the exquisite cakes and pastries made from Ruvo's prized local almonds.

**The Drive »** Head through fields and olive orchards along the SP2 for 8km to Corato, where you'll catch the SS378 – a straight shot north for 14km through dozens of olive groves to seaside Trani.

TRIP HIGHLIGHT

## 5 Trani

Known as the 'Pearl of Puglia', Trani is sophisticated, particularly in summer when well-heeled visitors pack the bars on the marina. The marina is the place to promenade and watch the boats, while the historic centre, with its medieval churches, glossy limestone streets and faded yet charming *palazzi,* is enchanting. The most arresting sight is the austere, 12th-century **Cathedral of St Nicholas the Pilgrim** (Piazza del Duomo; ⌚9am-12.30pm & 3-6.30pm), white against the deep-blue sea.

✕ 🛏 p315

**The Drive »** Following the coastline, SS16bis heads quickly again into agricultural land until you reach Barletta's suburbs after 12km.

## DETOUR: VALLE D'ITRIA

**Start: 1 Conversano**

Just south of Conversano rises the great limestone plateau of the Murgia (473m), a strange landscape riddled with holes and ravines through which small streams and rivers gurgle. At the heart of the Murgia lies the idyllic Valle d'Itria, famous for its *trulli.* Unique to Puglia, these Unesco-protected circular stone houses boast curious conical roofs.

The Murgia is also famous for its *masserie*. Modelled on the classical Roman villa, these fortified farmhouses – equipped with oil mills, storehouses, chapels and accommodation for workers and livestock – functioned as self-sufficient communities. These days, many have become country inns, including lovely **Biomasseria Lama di Luna** (☎0883 56 95 05; www.lamadiluna.com; Montegrosso; s/d €100/130; P❄), a working farm redesigned according to principles of green architecture.

## 6 Barletta

Barletta's crusading history is a lot more exotic than the modern-day town, although the historic centre is pretty enough with its cathedral and fine castle. However, the history of the town is closely linked with the nearby archaeological site of **Canne della Battaglia** (☎0883 51 09 93; adult/reduced €2/1; ⌚8.30am-7.30pm), where Carthaginian Hannibal whipped the Romans. Barletta also boasts some of the nicest beaches along this stretch of coast.

Isole Tremiti Take a detour to this rugged archipelago

**The Drive »** From Barletta it's a straight drive south for 14km along Via Andria to Andria, where you'll get the SS170dir. For the remaining 16km, the land begins to rise as you near Castel del Monte, which is visible for miles.

TRIP HIGHLIGHT

## 7 Castel del Monte

With its unearthly geometry and hilltop location, this 13th-century, Unesco-protected **castle** (☎0883 569 997; http://casteldelmonte.beniculturali.it; Piazza Federico II di Svevia; admission €5; ⏰9am-6.30pm) is visible for miles. No one knows why Frederick II built this mysterious structure. There's no nearby town or strategic crossroads, and it lacks typical defensive features like a moat or arrow slits. Some theories claim that, in accordance with mid-13th-century beliefs, the octagon represented

## DETOUR: LUCERA

**Start: 8 Canosa di Puglia**

About 85km north of Canosa di Puglia, Lucera has one of Puglia's most impressive castles and a handsome old town centre of mellow sand-coloured brick and stone, with chic shops lining wide, shiny stone streets. Frederick II's enormous **castle** (admission free; ⏰9am-2pm year-round, plus 3-7pm Apr-Sep), built in 1233, lies 14km northwest of the town on a rocky hillock surrounded by a perfect 1km pentagonal wall, guarded by 24 towers.

the union of the circle (representing the sky and the infinite) and square (the Earth and the temporal).

**The Drive »** From Castel del Monte this leg is 31km, heading south again along the SP170dir, then catching the SP149, which winds through a hilly and rather barren stretch until you reach the SS98 and the flatter lands around Canosa di Puglia.

## 8 Canosa di Puglia

Predating the arrival of the Romans by many centuries, this rather drab provincial town was once rich and powerful Canusium, Roman capital of the region. Today you can see remnants of this prosperity in the massive **Arco Traiano**, the **Roman Bridge**, and **Basilica di San Leucio**. Once a Roman temple (the biggest in southern Italy), it was converted into a massive Christian basilica in the 4th and 5th centuries; today only tantalising fragments remain.

**The Drive »** This 84km trip starts on the A14 toll road. At the Cerignola exit, take SS545 through fields and olive groves to the main coastal highway. Passing Manfredonia, you will reach the Promontorio del Gargano. Watch out for the SP55, which takes you up to hilltop Monte Sant'Angelo.

TRIP HIGHLIGHT

## 9 Monte Sant'Angelo

One of Europe's most important pilgrimage sites; it was here in AD 490 that St Michael the Archangel is said to have appeared in a grotto. During the Middle Ages, the **Santuario di San Michele** (Via Reale Basilica; 7.30am-7.30pm Jul-Sep, 7.30am-12.30pm & 2.30-7pm Apr-Jun & Oct, to 5pm Nov-Mar) marked the end of the Route of the Angel, which began in Mont St-Michel (Normandy) and passed through Roma (Rome). Today the sanctuary is a remarkable conglomeration of Romanesque, Gothic and baroque elements. Etched bronze and silver doors, cast in Constantinople in 1076, open into the grotto itself. Inside, a 16th-century statue of the archangel covers a sacred spot: the site of St Michael's footprint.

**The Drive »** From Monte Sant'Angelo, you head back towards the sea, eventually reaching SS89 and then the fiercely winding SP53 as you head to the tip of the peninsula. This 60km drive is the most scenic of the trip.

## 10 Viesta

Jutting off the Gargano's easternmost promontory into the Adriatic, Vieste is an attractive whitewashed town that sits above the area's most spectacular beach – a gleaming wide strip backed by sheer white cliffs and overshadowed by the towering rock monolith, Scoglio di Pizzomunno. It's packed in summer and ghostly quiet in winter.

### DETOUR: ISOLE TREMITI

**Start: 10 Viesta**

This three-island archipelago is a picturesque vision of rugged cliffs, medieval structures, lonesome caves, sandy coves and thick pine woods – all surrounded by a glittering, dark-blue sea. It's packed to the gills in July and August, but makes a wonderful off-season getaway. Ferries depart in summer from Vieste, and year-round from Termoli, about a two-hour drive up the Adriatic coast.

# Eating & Sleeping

## Bari 2

**La Locanda di Federico** Trattoria €€
(☎080 522 77 05; www.lalocandadifederico.com; Piazza Mercantile 63-64; meals €30; ⏱lunch & dinner) This restaurant oozes medieval atmosphere. The menu is typical Pugliese, offering delicious food at reasonable prices. *Orecchiette con le cime di rape* ('little ears' pasta with turnip greens) is highly recommended.

**Caffé Borghese** Cafe €
(☎080 524 21 56; Corso Vittorio Emanuele II 22; dishes €6-10; ⏱8am-2am Tue-Sun) You'll experience genuine hospitality and friendly service in this small cafe. Its understated charm and simple dishes will have you returning for breakfast, lunch and *aperitivi*.

**B&B Casa Pimpolini** B&B €
(☎080 521 99 38; www.casapimpolini.com; Via Calefati 249; s/d €60/80; ❄@) This lovely B&B in the new town is within easy walking distance of shops, restaurants and Bari Vecchia. Rooms are warm and welcoming, and the breakfast is homemade.

## Trani 5

**U'Vrascir** Trattoria €
(☎0883 49 18 40; www.uvrascir.it; Piazza Cesare Battisti 9; meals €25; ⏱Wed-Mon) With a cosy atmosphere, friendly service and a menu written in dialect, this inviting trattoria and pizzeria is sure to satisfy.

**Albergo Lucy** Hotel €
(☎0883 48 10 22; www.albergolucy.com; Piazza Plebiscito 11; d/tr/q €65/85/105; wifi) In a restored 17th-century *palazzo* overlooking a leafy square and close to the shimmering port, this family-run place offers both charm and value.

## Monte Sant'Angelo 9

**La Jalantuu'mene** Trattoria €€
(☎0884 56 54 84; Piazza de Galganis 5; meals €35-40; ⏱lunch & dinner daily summer, lunch only Wed-Mon winter) This renowned restaurant, starring eccentric chef Gegè Mangano, serves excellent regional fare. It's intimate, there's a select wine list and, in summer, tables spill into the piazza.

## Viesta 10

**Taverna Al Cantinone** Traditional Italian €€
(☎0884 70 77 53; Via Mafrolla 26; meals €25-30; ⏱lunch & dinner Wed-Mon) Run by a charming Italian-Spanish couple, this place serves exceptional food that is also exquisitely presented. The menu changes with the seasons.

**B&B Rocca sul Mare** B&B €
(☎0884 70 27 19; www.roccasulmare.it; Via Mafrolla 32; per person €25-70; wifi) In a former convent in the old quarter, this charming place offers large, comfortable high-ceilinged rooms. There's a vast rooftop terrace with panoramic views and a suite with a steam bath. Meals and bike hire available.

**Hotel Seggio** Hotel €€
(☎0884 70 81 23; www.hotelseggio.it; Via Veste 7; d €80-150; ⏱Apr-Oct; P❄@ wifi pool) In a butter-coloured *palazzo*, this hotel in the town's historic centre has steps that spiral down to a pool, and a sunbathing terrace with the sea as its backdrop. The rooms are modern and plain, but the entire effect of the family-run place is welcoming.

***Santa Cesarea Terme*** *Take time out in this lovely spa town*

# Salento Surprises

30

*This journey into Italy's heel takes you to a land of crickets and cacti. You'll find Greek, Roman and much older relics, but also gorgeous beaches lined by a new generation of sun worshippers.*

## TRIP HIGHLIGHTS

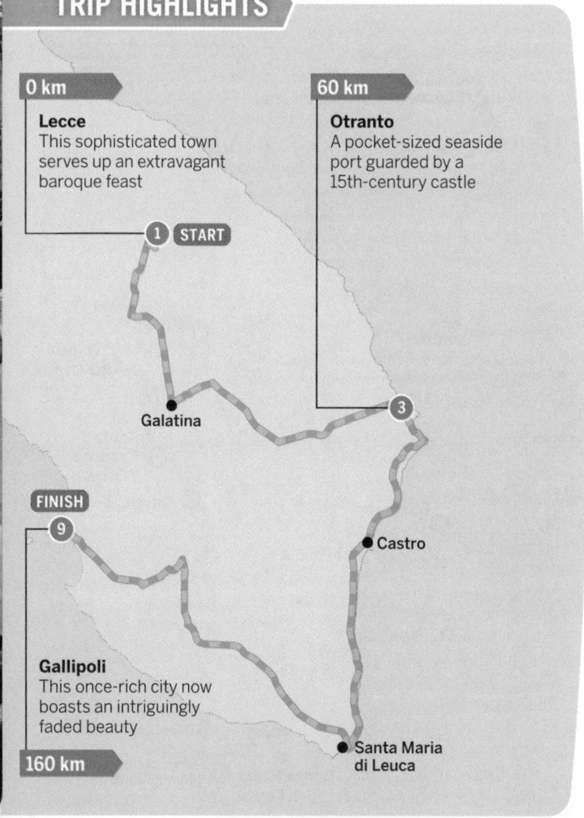

0 km
**Lecce**
This sophisticated town serves up an extravagant baroque feast

1 START

60 km
**Otranto**
A pocket-sized seaside port guarded by a 15th-century castle

3

Galatina

Castro

FINISH
9

**Gallipoli**
This once-rich city now boasts an intriguingly faded beauty

160 km

Santa Maria di Leuca

**5–7 DAYS**
**160KM / 99 MILES**

**GREAT FOR...**

**BEST TIME TO GO**

Summers are scorching and crowded, but good for beach lovers.

**ESSENTIAL PHOTO**

Capture Lecce's Basilica di Santa Croce illuminated at night.

**BEST FOR HISTORY**

Gape at Lecce's hypnotic baroque treasures.

# 30 Salento Surprises

Until quite recently the Salento was a poor, isolated region littered with the broken relics of a better past, from crumbling Greek ports to Bronze Age dolmens. But with flashy new neighbours in town, such as Lord MacAlpine and Helen Mirren, it's enjoying a cultural renaissance, and this trip will justify all the buzz, taking you from Lecce's baroque splendours to some of the Mediterranean's finest beaches.

TRIP HIGHLIGHT

### 1 Lecce

As you stare open-mouthed at Lecce's madcap baroque architecture, it's almost hard not to laugh. It's so joyously extravagant that it can be considered either grotesquely ugly or splendidly beautiful. The 18th-century traveller Thomas Ashe called it the most beautiful city in Italy, while the Marchese Grimaldi called the facade of Santa Croce the nightmare of a lunatic.

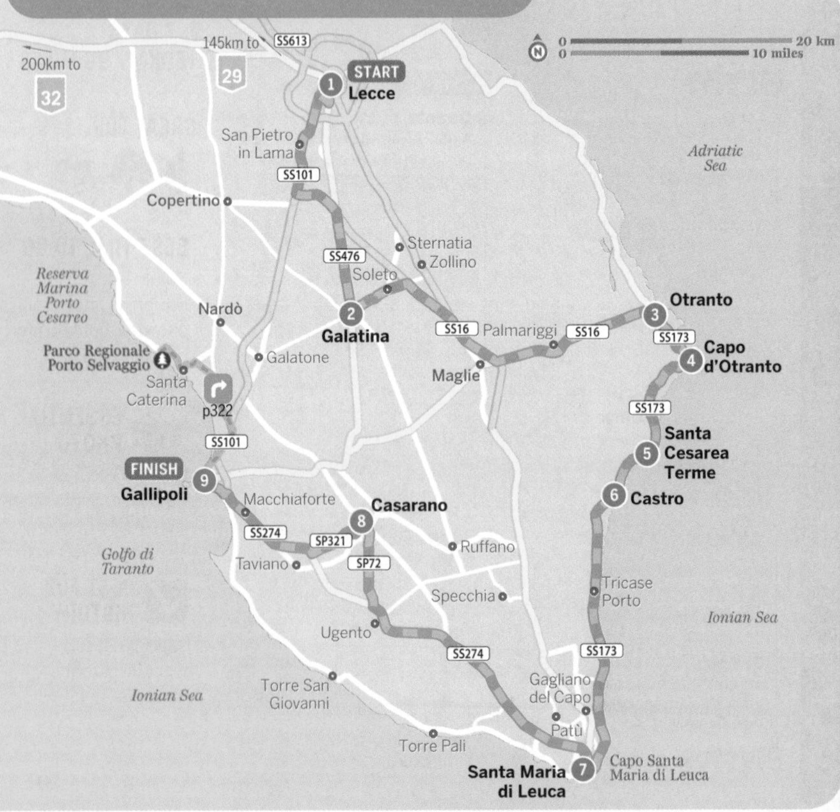

What is certain is that, with more than 40 churches and at least as many *palazzi* (mansions) from the 17th and 18th centuries, the city has an extraordinary cohesion.

A baroque feast, Piazza del Duomo is the city's focal point and a sudden open space amid the surrounding enclosed lanes. However, the most hallucinatory facade has to be **Basilica di Santa Croce** (www.basilicasantacroce.eu; Via Umberto I; ⏲9am-noon & 5-8pm), a swirling allegorical feast of sheep, dodos, cherubs and unidentified

## LOCAL KNOWLEDGE: PUGLIA ON YOUR PLATE

Puglia's bold, brawny cuisine adheres very closely to its roots in *cucina povera* – literally, 'cooking of the poor'. Yet that cuisine is built on an incredibly rich set of raw ingredients: seafood from the long coastline; durum wheat, olives and extraordinary produce from its rich plains; abundant grapes that are being turned into rapidly improving wines; and some of the world's best almonds. For pasta, Puglians tend to favour broccoli or *ragù* (meat sauce) topped with the pungent local *ricotta forte*. Like their Greek forbears, they're also partial to lamb and kid. And raw fish (such as anchovies or baby squid) are marinated to perfection in olive oil and lemon juice.

beasties. And the **Museo Provinciale** (☎0832 68 35 03; Via Gallipoli 28; admission free; ⏲8.30am-7.30pm Mon-Sat, to 1.30pm Sun) stylishly displays 10,000 years of history, from Palaeolithic bits and bobs to Greek and Roman art and ceramics.

✕ 🛏 p323

**The Drive »** Head south for 26km, first on the SS101, then catch SS664 and SS476 through fertile plains to Galatina.

### ❷ Galatina

With a charming historic centre, Galatina is the capital of the Salento's Greek-inflected culture. It is almost the only place where the ritual of tarantism – a folk cure for the bite of a tarantula – is still remembered. The *taranta* folk dance evolved from it, and each year on the feast day of Sts Peter and Paul the ritual is performed. However, most people come to Galatina to see the incredible 14th-century **Basilica di Santa Caterina d'Alessandria** (⏲8am-12.30pm & 4.30-6.45pm Apr-Sep, 8am-12.30pm & 3.45-5.45pm Oct-Mar), its interior a kaleidoscope of Gothic frescoes set off by the serenity of a pure-white altarpiece

🛏 p323

**The Drive »** Head back to the SS16 and head east for a total of 34km, mostly through flat agricultural fields and olive orchards.

TRIP HIGHLIGHT

### ❸ Otranto

Overlooking a pretty harbour on the blue Adriatic, whitewashed Otranto is today a pocket-sized resort town, but for 1000 years it was

## LINK YOUR TRIP

### 29 Puglia's Pilgrim Trail

From Lecce, head about 120km north along SS613, SS379 and SS16 to Conversano, which kicks off this journey through northern Puglia's sun-kissed sea resorts (p309).

### 32 The Calabrian Wilderness

From the wild snow-capped peaks of the Pollino to Tropea's violet-coloured seas, get lost in Italy's least-explored region – about a four-hour drive from Lecce along E90 and SP263. (p333).

Italy's main port to the East. The small historic centre is watched over by a beautiful 15th-century castle. Long a target of jealous neighbours, Otranto was besieged by Turks, in league with Venezia (Venice), in 1480. They brutally murdered 800 of Otranto's faithful who refused to convert to Islam. Their bones are preserved in a chapel of the 11th-century **Norman cathedral** (☎0836 80 27 20; Piazza Basilica; ⌚8am-noon & 3-6pm). The cathedral also features a vast 12th-century mosaic of a stupendous tree of life balanced on the back of two elephants. The town itself has a pretty beach, though there are much longer strands just outside of town.

 p323

**The Drive »** It is a fairly straight shot for 7km through the farmland south of Otranto to Capo d'Otranto. As you get close, you'll see the white lighthouse against the blue Adriatic.

## 4 Capo d'Otranto

As you head down Salento's dreamy coast, take a pit stop on this small peninsula, which serves as the official division between the Ionian and Adriatic Seas. Its recently restored 19th-century lighthouse sits picturesquely at its tip. On clear days you can see the mountains of Albania across a sparkling blue Adriatic Sea.

**The Drive »** Heading south for 13km, the coastal highway SS173 (Via Roma) suddenly starts twisting and turning as the coastline turns more rugged, with broad rocky flatlands.

## 5 Santa Cesarea Terme

Santa Cesarea Terme boasts a number of Liberty-style (art nouveau) villas, reminiscent of the days when spa-going was all the rage. There are still hotels that cater to the summer crowds of Italians who come to bathe in the thermal spas. But don't have visions of stylish hammams and soothing massages; here spa-going is a serious medical business, and the **Terme di Santa Cesarea** (☎0836 944314; Via Roma 40; www.termesantacesarea.it; ⌚Apr-Dec) feels a like a fusty old hospital with a lingering smell of sulphur about it. Still, this makes a great stop to ease the aches and pains of life on the road.

**The Drive »** From Santa Cesarea Terme to Castro, it is a quick 7km drive along the coastal highway.

## 6 Castro

Almost midway between Santa Maria and Otranto lies the town of Castro, which is dominated by

Gallipoli

an austere, Romanesque cathedral and forbidding castle. Just downhill, its marina serves as a popular boating and diving hub for the rocky coastline, which is riddled with fascinating sea caves. Most famous is the **Grotta Zinzulusa**, which is filled with stalactites that hang like sharp daggers from the ceiling. It can only be visited on a guided tour. Note that in summer it gets maniacally busy.

**The Drive »** Keep hugging the coastline south along SS173 for 31km as you pass pine and eucalyptus groves, farmland and a series of small resort towns until you reach the very southern tip of the peninsula.

## 7 Santa Maria di Leuca

At the very tip of Italy's high heel, the resort town of Santa Maria di Leuca occupies what Romans called *finibus terrae,* the end of the earth. The spot is marked by the **Chiesa di Santa Maria di Leuca**, an important place of pilgrimage built over an older Roman temple dedicated to Minerva. These days, with its Gothic- and Liberty-style villas, this is a holiday resort, pure and simple. Many people come here to take one of the boat trips to visit the sea grottoes like the **Grotta del Diavolo**, the **Grotta della Stalla** and the **Grotta Grande di Ciolo**. Trips depart from the little *porto* between June and September.

**The Drive »** Head inland along SS274 25km through seemingly endless olive groves and sunburnt farms to around Ugento, then 12km along SP72 to Casarano.

## 8 Casarano

Sitting amid the Salento's rich olive groves, laid-back Casarano is home of **Chiesa di Santa Maria della Croce**. One of the oldest sites in Christendom, it holds mosaics that date to the 5th century as well as frescoes from the Byzantine period.

**The Drive »** From Casarano to Gallipoli, head west on the SP321 and SS274 roadways. You'll drive 20km through olive trees and ochre-coloured fields, passing Taviano and Macchiaforte en route.

TRIP HIGHLIGHT

## 9 Gallipoli

Kallipolis, the 'beautiful city' of the Greeks, may be a faded beauty now, but it still retains its island charm. The Salentines see it as a kind of southern Portofino, and its weathered white *borgo* (historic centre) has a certain grungy chic: part fishing village, part fashion model.

In the 16th and 17th centuries, Gallipoli was one of the richest towns in the Salento, exporting its famous olive oil to Napoli (Naples), Paris and London to illuminate their street lamps. That explains the rather elegant air of the old town, which is divided into two distinct halves: the patrician quarter, which housed the wealthy merchant class, to the north of Via Antonietta de Pace; and the popular quarter, with its rabbit-warren of streets to the south.

p323

### DETOUR: PARCO REGIONALE PORTO SELVAGGIO

**Start: 9 Gallipoli**

The Ionian coast can be holiday hell, but head about 25km north from Gallipoli and you'll soon see the real belle of region, the **Parco Regionale Porto Selvaggio** (www.portoselvaggio.net, in Italian), a protected area of rocky coastline covered with umbrella pines, eucalyptus trees and olives. Right in the middle of the park is the elegant **Santa Caterina**, a quiet seaside centre.

# Eating & Sleeping

## Lecce ①

### Cucina Casareccia — Apulian €

(☎0832 24 51 78; Viale Colonnello Archimede Costadura 19; meals €20; ⊙lunch Tue-Sun) Chef Carmela Perrone will gladly whisk you through a dazzling array of Salentine dishes from the true *cucina povera* (literally 'cooking of the poor'). Reservations recommended.

### Pasticceria Natale — Gelateria €

(Via Trinchese 7a) Lecce's best ice-cream parlour also has an array of fabulous baked goods and chocolates. Try the *mustazzolo* gelato, based on the local cookie of the same name, featuring wine must, toasted local almonds and spices.

### Risorgimento Resort — Hotel €€

(☎0832 24 63 11; www.risorgimentoresort.it; Via Imperatore Augusto 19; d from €145; P ❄ @ ☜) Expect a warm welcome at this stylish, five-star, centrally located hotel. Rooms are spacious and refined, with high ceilings and contemporary details reflecting the colours of the Salento.

### Suite 68 — Boutique Hotel €

(☎0832 30 35 06; www.kalekora.it; Via Prato; d €80-120; ❄) Strong colours, abstract canvases and vividly patterned rugs in the large, bright rooms define this simple but stylish spot.

## Galatina ②

### Samadhi — Agriturismo €

(☎0836 60 02 84; www.agricolasamadhi.com; Via Stazione 116, Zollino; per person from €40; ❄ ☜ ≈) Soothe the soul on this 10-hectare organic farm 7km east of Galatina in tiny Zollino. As well as ayurvedic treatments and yoga courses, there's a vegan and organic restaurant.

## Otranto ③

### La Bella Idrusa — Pizzeria €

(☎0836 80 14 75; Via Lungomare degli Eroi; pizza €5; ⊙dinner Thu-Tue) You can't miss this pizzeria right by the huge Porta Terra in the historic centre. Outdoor seating is great for people-watching, while indoors is atmospheric and romantic.

### Palazzo Papaleo — Hotel €€

(☎0836 80 21 08; www.hotelpalazzopapaleo.com; Via Rondachi 1; r €119-490; P ❄ @ ☜) Located next to the cathedral, this sumptuous hotel has magnificent rooms with original frescoes, exquisitely carved antique furniture and panoramic views from the rooftop Jacuzzi.

## Gallipoli ⑨

### La Puritate — Trattoria €€

(☎0833 26 42 05; Via S Elia 18; meals €40-45; ⊙Thu-Tue) This place in the old town is great for fish and also proffers sea views. Follow the excellent antipasti with delicious *primi* (first courses) such as seafood spaghetti. And consider the daily catch – swordfish is usually a good bet.

### La Casa del Mare — B&B €

(☎333 474 57 54; www.lacasadelmare.com; Piazza de Amicis 14; d €60-110; ❄ @ ☜) In a butter-coloured 16th-century building, this B&B in the town centre is a great choice. Helpful and friendly Federico has also restored a beautiful 18th-century *palazzo* nearby, **Palazzo Flora** (www.palazzoflora.com; Via d'Ospina 19; d €65-120, house €150-300), which sleeps four to six and has fantastic views.

***Viggiano*** *Enjoy enchanting views from this hilltop town*

# Across the Lucanian Appennines

*From seaside Maratea to otherworldly Matera, this trip crosses the hinterlands of Basilicata, a gorgeous region of hilltop towns, purple peaks, fertile valleys and possibly the world's best cheese.*

## TRIP HIGHLIGHTS

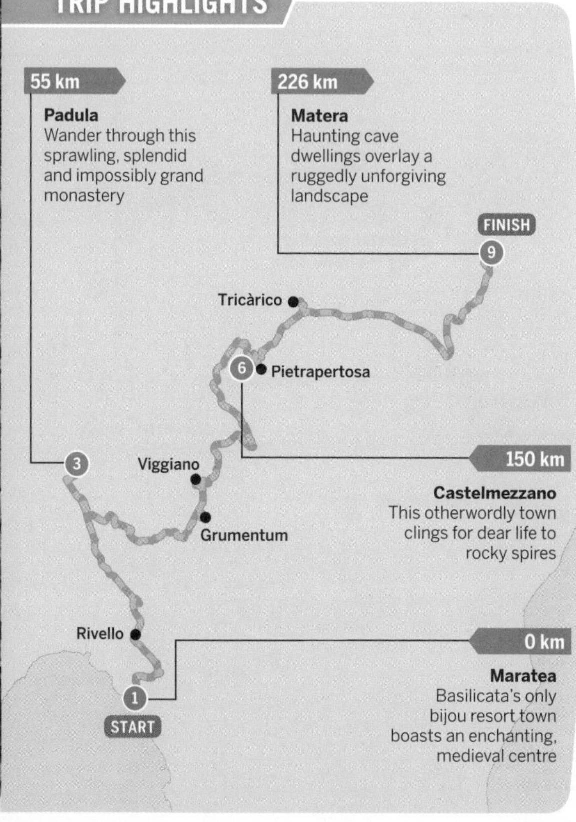

**55 km**
**Padula**
Wander through this sprawling, splendid and impossibly grand monastery

**226 km**
**Matera**
Haunting cave dwellings overlay a ruggedly unforgiving landscape

**150 km**
**Castelmezzano**
This otherwordly town clings for dear life to rocky spires

**0 km**
**Maratea**
Basilicata's only bijou resort town boasts an enchanting, medieval centre

FINISH 9 · Tricàrico · 6 Pietrapertosa · 3 · Viggiano · Grumentum · Rivello · 1 START

**5–7 DAYS**
**226KM / 140 MILES**

**GREAT FOR...**

**BEST TIME TO GO**

Spring and autumn for sunny weather without summer heat and crowds.

**ESSENTIAL PHOTO**

Capture Matera's ancient cave dwellings at sunset.

**BEST FOR FOODIES**

Try the heavenly local cheeses in Castelmezzano's Al Becco della Civetta.

# Across the Lucanian Appennines

This trip begins on Basilicata's Tyrrhenian coast, which may be diminutive but rivals Amalfi for sheer drama. The trip ends in a completely different world – the chalky, sunburnt landscape around Matera, a strange and remarkable city with timeless troglodyte dwellings that are Unesco-protected. In between, you'll cross the dramatic peaks of the Lucanian Apennines, a gorgeous land of alpine forests, green valleys and bristling hilltop downs.

TRIP HIGHLIGHT

### 1 Maratea

Sitting in stately fashion above the cliffs and pocket-sized beaches of Golfo di Policastro, Maratea is Basilicata's only bijou resort town. Uphill, the enchanting medieval centre, which dates to the 13th century, boasts elegant hotels, pint-sized piazzas, wriggling alleys and startling coastal views. Down at sea level, **Porto di Maratea**, the town's harbour, shelters sleek

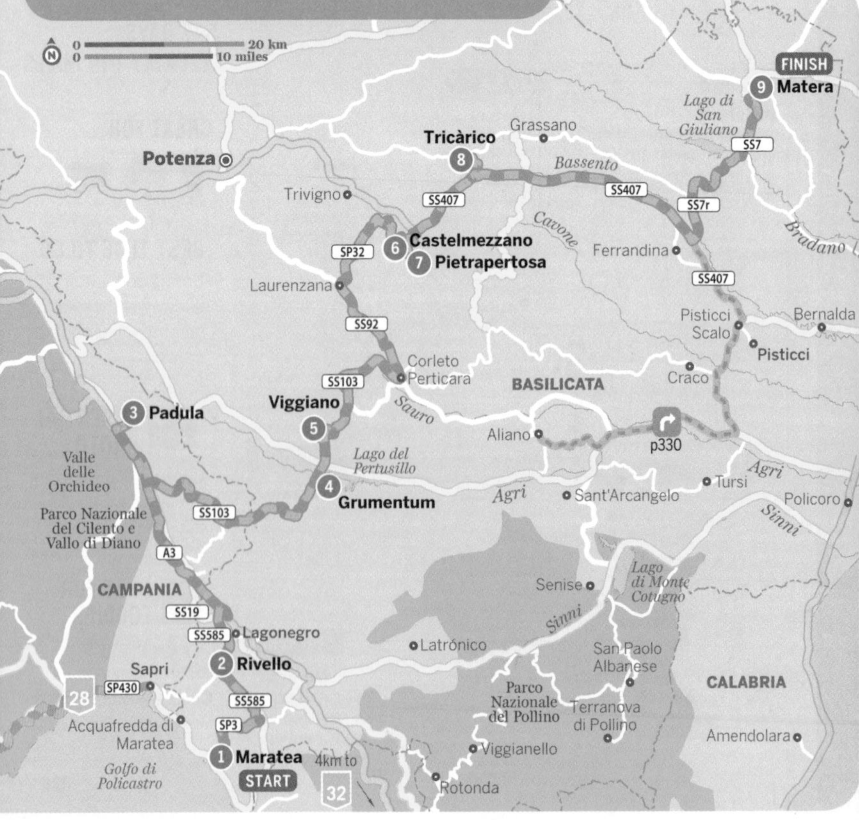

yachts and bright-blue fishing boats. The deep green hillsides that encircle this tumbling conurbation offer excellent walking trails, while the surrounding coastline hides dozens of tiny beaches.

p331

**The Drive »** The 23km to Rivello takes you into the heights of the coastal range. From Maratea, follow signs north to Trecchina. Expect great sea views along the way. At Trecchina, head down to a short but blessedly straight stretch of highway SS585. Rivello will appear quickly at your left. The total distance is 23km.

## 2 Rivello

Perched on a high ridge and framed by the southern Apennines, Rivello is not just another picture-pretty medieval village. Due to its strategic position, it was contested for centuries by both Lombards and Byzantines. Eventually, they reached an unlikely compromise – the Lombards settled in the lower part of town, the Byzantines in the upper. This resulted in two separate centres with two diverse cultures developing in a single town. Today, Rivello's charm lies in its narrow alleys, where homes both grand and humble are graced with wrought-iron balconies.

**The Drive »** For the 40km to Padula, return to the SS585 and head to the A3 autostrada. Rugged mountains will suddenly open out into the wide, fertile Valle del Diano. Take the Padula exit and follow signs to the abbey.

TRIP HIGHLIGHT

## 3 Padula

In the plains just below hilltop Padula lies one of southern Italy's most extraordinary sites. The **Certosa di San Lorenzo** (☎0975 77 45; Padula; adult/child €4/2; ⏰9am-7.30pm) is among the largest monasteries in southern Europe, with 320 rooms and halls, 13 courtyards, 100 fireplaces, 52 stairways, 41 fountains and the world's largest cloisters. Founded in 1306, its buildings represent more than four centuries of construction, though primarily it is a 17th- and 18th-century baroque creation.

**The Drive »** From Padula, head back along Via Nazionale (SS19). Just past Montesano Scalo, follow signs to Sarconi along the SS103. Here begins a beautiful, winding ascent into the Lucanian Appennines, then back down toward the verdant Val d'Agri.

## 4 Grumentum

Set amid the fertile Val d'Agri valley, Grumentum was once an important enough Roman city that the invading Hannibal made it his headquarters. Eventually it was abandoned for hilltop Grumento Nova in the 9th century. Today, the **ruins** (adult/child €4/2; ⏰9am-7.30pm) sit humbly amid agricultural fields and leave much to the imagination. Still, they make for a fascinating and atmospheric ramble, especially the miniature version of the Colosseum.

**The Drive »** Head back to the SS103 for a 15km drive along the pastoral valley floor following signs to Viggiano. The last few kilometres are pure switchback.

## 5 Viggiano

Hilltop Viggiano stands guard above the beautiful Val d'Agri. Aside from its fine views, Viggiano has an illustrious music history for a town of a few thousand souls. Since the 18th century, it has been celebrated for

### LINK YOUR TRIP

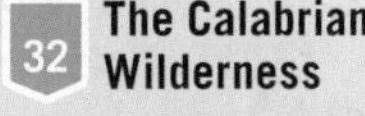

**28 Cilento Coastal Trail**

From Maratea, take the coastal SS18 north to Sapri to explore this wild coastline (p301).

**32 The Calabrian Wilderness**

From Rivello take the A3 south to Mormanno to get lost in Italy's least-explored region (p333).

harp makers and players, and the town has a long tradition of producing lively street musicians. For centuries, the town has also been a centre of local pilgrimage, thanks to its ancient statue of a Black Madonna.

p331

**The Drive »** The 63km ride to Castelmezzano is breathtaking. Head back down the switchback and look for the SS103 and signs to the town Corleto Perticara. At Corleto Perticara, pick up the SS92 and wind past Laurenzana with its beautiful Romanesque church and castle. Then catch the SP32 and head north. After passing a pretty reservoir and just before reaching SS407, signs will lead to Castelmezzano.

TRIP HIGHLIGHT

## 6 Castelmezzano

Clinging to a series of impossibly narrow ledges, the houses of tiny Castelmezzano look like something out of a fairytale, bounded on one side by rocky spires and on the other by the vertigo-inducing gorges of the Caperrino river. When the mist swirls in (as it often does) the effect is otherworldly.

For an adrenaline rush, fly across the gorge to neighbouring Pietrapertosa at 120km/h attached to a steel cable via **Il Volo dell'Angelo** (www.volodellangelo.com; €40; 9.30am-6.30pm Sun May & Jun, daily Jul & Aug).

This region is also know for its incomparable goat's milk and sheep's milk, the best of which are on the menu at Al Becco della Civetta.

p331

**The Drive »** Though you could practically throw a stone across the gorge separating Castelmezzano from Pietrapertosa, the 10km drive requires dozens of hairpin turns and a strong stomach. But views of the gorges are gorgeous indeed. The way is well marked.

## 7 Pietrapertosa

As the highest town in Basilicata, Pietrapertosa is possibly even more dramatically situated than neighbouring Castelmezzano. Pietrapertosa literally translates as 'perforated stone' and, indeed, the village sits in the midst of bizarrely shaped rocky towers. Literally carved into the mountainside, its 10th-century **Saracen fortress** is difficult to spot, but once you've located it you won't regret the long climb up. The views are breathtaking.

**The Drive »** After the winding descent from Pietrapertosa, take SS407 to the Tricàrio exit, 29km from Pietrapertosa. You'll notice the peaks of the Dolomiti Lucani disappear in favour of the chalky plains and gorges that define the landscape around Matera.

ANGELA SORRENTINO/GETTY IMAGES ©

Castelmezzano

## DETOUR: CARLO LEVI COUNTRY

**Start: 9 Matera**

Aliano, a tiny and remote village about 80km south of Matera, would still languish unknown had not writer, painter and political activist Carlo Levi been exiled here in the 1930s during Mussolini's regime. In his extraordinary book *Christ Stopped at Eboli*, Levi graphically describes the aching hardship of peasant life in 'Gagliano' (in reality, Aliano) where 'there is no definite boundary between the world of human beings and that of animals and even monsters'.

Today, Aliano is a sleepy town that only seems to come alive late in the afternoon when old men congregate on the park benches in the pleasant tree-lined Via Roma, and black-shrouded women exchange news and gossip on the streets.



### 8 Tricàrico

Perched on a ridge above the Bassento river valley, Tricàrio may not be as dazzlingly odd as Castelmezzano and Pietrapertosa, but it does have one of the best-preserved medieval cores in Basilicata, with Gothic and Romanesque religious buildings capped by a picturesque Norman **tower**. Its ramparts also proffer lovely views over the surrounding countryside.

**The Drive »** Head back to the SS407 highway and east along the snaking Bassento river valley, until you see the castle of Migliònico. Shortly after lies the exit to Matera. Signs will lead you along the SS7 to Matera.

TRIP HIGHLIGHT

### 9 Matera

Haunting and beautiful, Matera's **sassi** (stone houses carved out of the caves and cliffs) sprawl below the rim of a yawning ravine like a giant nativity scene. Although many buildings are crumbling and abandoned, more and more are being restored and transformed into cosy abodes, restaurants and swish cave-hotels.

On the plains just above the cliff, the new town is a lively place, with its elegant **baroque churches**, exquisite **Romanesque cathedral**, and elegant **palazzi** (mansions). Yet, thanks to the deep gorge on which it sits, you can escape with just a few steps into a wild and beautiful countryside.

Matera is said to be one of the world's oldest towns, inhabited since the Palaeolithic Age. The simple natural grottoes that dotted the gorge were adapted to become homes, and an ingenious system of canals regulated the flow of water and sewage. The town was an important regional centre for centuries, but began its long decline when power moved to Potenza in 1806. In his great book, *Christ Stopped at Eboli*, Carlo Levi describes how in the 1930s children would beg passers-by for quinine to stave off the deadly malaria. Ironically, the town's history of misery has transformed it into Basilicata's leading tourist attraction.

p331

# Eating & Sleeping

## Maratea 1

**Da Cesare** Seafood **€€**

(0973 871 840; Coastal Hwy 18, Cersuta; meals around €35; lunch & dinner) On the main coastal highway in the village of Cersuta about 4km north of Maratea, Da Cesare is worth seeking out for its simple, delicate and masterful handling of local seafood.

**B&B Nefer** B&B **€**

(0973 871 828; www.bbnefer.it; Via Cersuta; s/d €60/90; P) Set just off the coastal highway in a small seaside community 5km northwest of Maratea, this family-run affair has four pretty, immaculate rooms, all with views down an olive orchard to the sea. There's a lovely garden and outdoor kitchen for guest use.

**Locanda delle Donne Monache** Hotel **€€€**

(0973 876 139; www.locandamonache.com; Via Carlo Mazzei 4; r €130-310; P) This 18th-century convent-turned-exclusive-hotel is a charming hotchpotch of vaulted corridors, terraces and gardens fringed with bougainvillea and lemon trees.

## Viggiano 5

**Hotel dell'Arpa** Hotel **€**

(0975 311 303; www.hoteldellarpa.it; Corso Giorgio Marconi 34; s/d €62/77; P) Sitting conveniently at the foot of historic Viggiano, this modern hotel is more comfortable than charming, but most rooms have fantastic views across the Val d'Agri.

## Castelmezzano 6

**Al Becco della Civetta** Traditional **€€**

(0971 986 249; www.beccodellacivetta.it; Vico I Maglietta 7; meals around €40; lunch & dinner Wed-Mon Nov-Mar, daily Apr-Oct) This place offers outstanding cuisine built on local ingredients, from superlative local cheeses to wild chicory and asparagus culled from the surrounding hillsides. Reservations recommended at weekends. Just upstairs, the same owners offer simple whitewashed rooms (double from €80) with traditional furnishings.

## Matera 9

**Le Botteghe** Traditional **€€**

(0835 344 072; Piazza San Pietro Barisano 22; meals €30-40; lunch & dinner, closed two weeks Jan or Feb) A cluster of cosy, rustic rooms are ranged around the restaurant's key feature – a wood-burning grill on which cooks prepare local lamb, beef and goat to perfection. Adhering strictly to local traditions, this place also offers fine wine and cheese options.

**Ostello & Hotel Le Monacelle** Inn **€**

(0835 334 097; www.lemonacelle.it; Via Riscatto 9; d from €86; ) This former monastery has been transformed into a sprawling, beautifully whitewashed inn. One half is a hostel with cavernous dorms (€18 per person), while the other half offers simple, well-kept private rooms, most with canyon views.

**Sassi Hotel** Hotel **€**

(0835 331 009; www.hotelsassi.it; Via San Giovanni Vecchio 89; d from €90; ) With a cluster of cave-like rooms and fantastic views over the *sassi*, this extraordinary hotel is considered one of the city's best.

**Calabria** *Off-the-beaten-track adventures await*

# The Calabrian Wilderness

32

*From the peaks of the Pollino to the crystalline waters of the Tropea peninsula, this trip immerses you in the natural beauty of Calabria, one of Italy's wildest and least explored regions.*

## TRIP HIGHLIGHTS

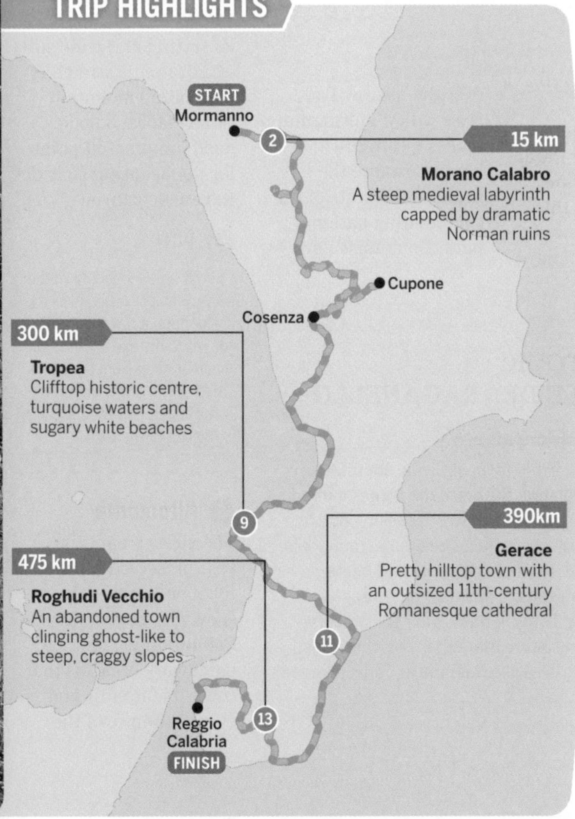

START
Mormanno

15 km
**Morano Calabro**
A steep medieval labyrinth capped by dramatic Norman ruins

Cupone

Cosenza

300 km
**Tropea**
Clifftop historic centre, turquoise waters and sugary white beaches

390km
**Gerace**
Pretty hilltop town with an outsized 11th-century Romanesque cathedral

475 km
**Roghudi Vecchio**
An abandoned town clinging ghost-like to steep, craggy slopes

Reggio Calabria
FINISH

**8–10 DAYS**
**627KM / 390 MILES**

### GREAT FOR...

### BEST TIME TO GO

Spring and autumn for sunny weather without summer heat and crowds.

### ESSENTIAL PHOTO

Capture sweeping views of mountains and sea from Capo Vaticano.

### BEST FOR OUTDOORS

From Cupone, strike out into the wilds of Calabria's Sila mountain range.

# 32 The Calabrian Wilderness

From the alpine Pollino to the thickly forested slopes of the Aspromonte, Calabria possesses some of Italy's wildest landscapes. Avoid the overbuilt coast and you'll often feel you have the place to yourself. Plagued by earthquakes, poverty and organised crime, its artistic heritage is limited, yet its rough beauties are gripping. Besides three sprawling national parks, ancient towns seem to grow out of craggy hilltops, while amethyst waters wash Tropea's beaches.

## 1 Mormanno

In the heart of the **Parco Nazionale del Pollino** (www.parcopollino.it), this bristling hilltop town of 3000 souls stands guard over the narrow Lao river valley. Mormanno makes a convenient base to explore the peaks and forests of the surrounding national park. Don't miss its prized local lentils, best served in a deliciously simple soup loaded with oregano.

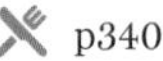

p340

**The Drive »** Instead of the A3 autostrada, take the pleasant SS19, which winds its way for 21km through forested hills and green valleys as you sneak up on the back side of Morano Calabro.

### DETOUR: GOLE DEL RAGANELLO

**Start: 2 Morano Calabro**

Located just outside the town of Civitá, about 20km east of Morano Calabro, the dramatic gorges carved by the Raganello river are well worth seeking out. In addition to the majesty of their sheer limestone walls, the gorges are also home to rich flora and fauna, from foxes and martens to soaring golden eagles. Note also that the towns in this region still preserve traces of Albanian culture more than five centuries after their ancestors fled to Calabria as Turks invaded Albania.

TRIP HIGHLIGHT

## 2 Morano Calabro

One of the most dramatic hill towns in southern Italy, Morano Calabro is a dense, steeply rising medieval labyrinth capped by the dramatic ruins of a **Norman castle**. Just as extraordinary is its setting at the foothills of a dramatic stretch of the Pollino mountain range. Morano makes a good jumping-off point for the beautiful Gole del Raganello canyon.

p340

**The Drive »** Head down the A3, dramatically framed by the Pollino mountain range, until you reach the exit for Altomonte, which is 30km from Morano Calabro. The town itself sits at the end of a series of well-marked country roads.

## 3 Altomonte

The views from this well-preserved hilltop town encompass the snowy heights of the Pollino range, the rich patchwork of farms that cover its foothills and even a glimpse of the blue Mediterranean off to the east. Don't miss the 14th-century **Chiesa di Santa Maria della Consolazione**, one of the finest examples of Gothic architecture in Calabria.

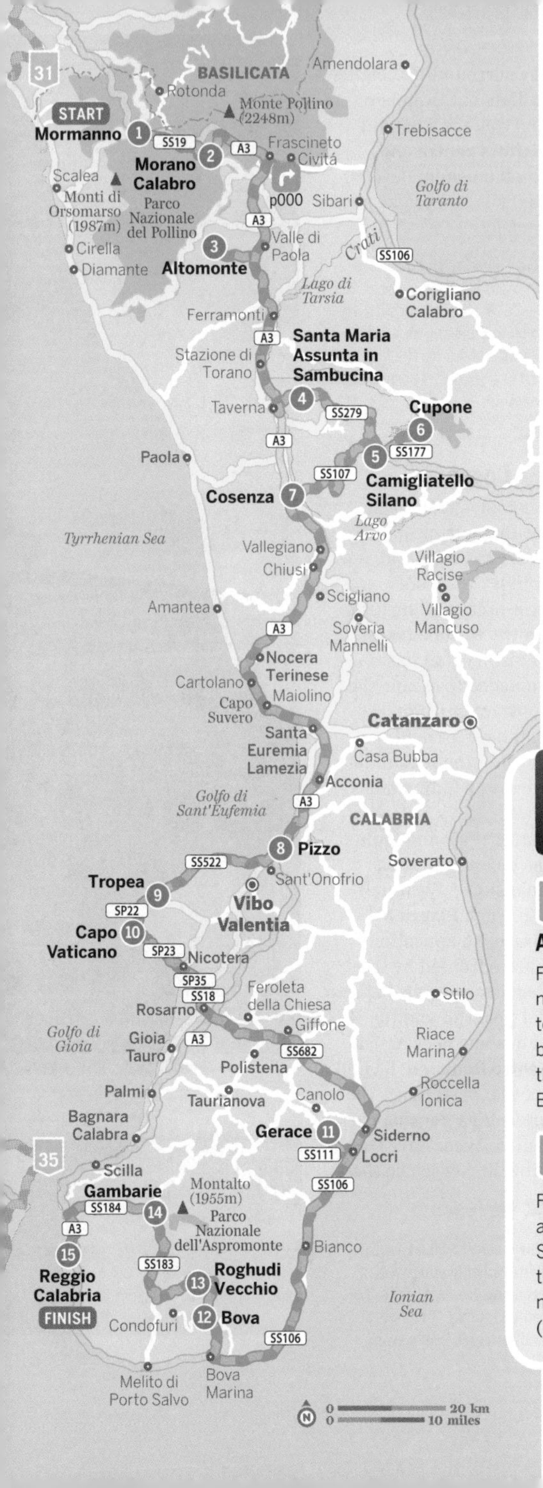

**The Drive »** For this 51km leg, head back to the A3, then south to the Montalto exit, where you'll then twist and turn along SS559 as you head into the foothills of the Sila.

## 4 Santa Maria Assunta in Sambucina

Tucked in the foothills of the Sila mountains, this once-vast **abbey** has, over the centuries, been reduced to just a few atmospheric remnants, thanks to a

### LINK YOUR TRIP

#### 31 Across the Lucanian Appennines

From Mormanno, head north 66km (41 miles) to seaside Maratea to begin your adventure into the beautiful interior of Basilicata (p325).

#### 35 Sicilian Island Hop

From Reggio Calabria, it's a half-hour ferry ride to Sicily, where you can join this trip to the beautiful and mysterious Aeolian Islands (p365).

devastating combination of earthquakes and landslides. Today, all that is left is a transept of the original church, which mixes elements of both Romanesque and Gothic.

**The Drive »** Back on the SS559, you will soon wind your way up to the SS279, then along a high plain, where pastureland alternates with pine and oak forests offering a distinct alpine flavour. Signs lead you the 38km to Camigliatello Silano

## 5 Camigliatello Silano

A popular ski-resort town with 6km of trails, Camigliatello Silano looks much better under snow – think Swiss chalets in poured concrete. However, even in the summer it makes a comfortable base to explore the Sila mountains, with their upland meadows, pine and oak forests and well-marked hiking trails.

p340

**The Drive »** As you gently wind you way along the 6km jaunt on SS177 to Cupone, you will soon see the blue waters of Lago Cecita appear through the trees.

## 6 Cupone

Home to the headquarters of **Parco Nazionale della Sila** (www.parcosila.it), Cupone sits on the edge of pretty, meandering Lago Cecita. Well-marked hikes into the surrounding heights radiate out from here, and there is a helpful **visitors centre** and small **museum** devoted to the local ecology and geology.

**The Drive »** Head back to Camigliatello Silano, then catch the SS107, which winds its way down to Cosenza, for a total distance of 43km. The last part of the drive is particularly beautiful.

## 7 Cosenza

Though surrounded by uninspiring sprawl, Cosenza's medieval core is Calabria's best-preserved historic centre, the one piece of history that has managed to escape the constant earthquakes that have levelled so much in the region. Its narrow, winding lanes have a gritty feel, with dark streets and fading, once-elegant *palazzi* (mansions). Eventually, you reach **Piazza XV Marzo**, an appealing square fronted by the Renaissance-style **Palazzo del Governo** and the handsome neoclassical **Teatro Rendano**. Behind the piazza stretches the lovely **Villa Vecchia** park, with lofty mature trees providing welcome shade.

p340

**The Drive »** Head south on the A3 until you reach sweeping views of the Gulf of Santa Eufemia. Pizzo sits at its southern end, 90km away.

Tropea

## 8 Pizzo

Stacked high on a sea cliff with sweeping views down to the Tropean peninsula, Pizzo has a distinct ramshackle charm. On its main square, cafes compete to offer the town's best *tartufo,* a death-by-chocolate ice-cream ball. A kilometre north of town, the **Chiesa di Piedigrotta** (www.chiesettadipiedigrotta.it; admission €2.50; ⌚9am-1pm & 3-7.30pm) was first carved into the tufa rock by Neapolitan shipwreck survivors in the 17th century and has since been filled with tufa saints as well as less godly figures like Fidel Castro and JFK.

 p340

**The Drive »** Head 30km south along coastal route SS522, which winds its way through uninspired beach resorts that alternate with farmland prized for its sweet red onions.

TRIP HIGHLIGHT

## 9 Tropea

Much of the Calabrian coast has been decimated by poorly planned mass development. Tropea is a jewel-like exception. Set on a rocky promontory, the town's small but well-preserved historic centre sits above a sugary, white-sand beach. At sunset, the clear turquoise waters are known to turn garish shades of purple. And don't miss the sweet fire of the region's prized red onions, which come from the surrounding peninsula.

Note that the town's attractions are compromised in high summer by teeming crowds, when parking can become a blood sport.

p341

**The Drive** It is a lovely drive to Capo Vaticano for 13km along SP22, mostly following the coastline. When you reach the little town of San Nicolò, follow signs to Faro Capo Vaticano.

## 10 Capo Vaticano

Even if you don't have time to explore its beaches, ravines and limestone sea cliffs, stop at the southwestern corner of Tropean peninsula for its jaw-dropping views. On a clear day, you can see past the Aeolian Islands all the way to Sicily.

**The Drive »** For this 83km drive, wind your way along the coastal bluffs of SP23, skirting Rosarno until you reach SS682, which whisks across the pretty northern reaches of the Aspromonte. At the Ionian coast, head south to Locri. From Locri's Via Garibaldi, follow signs inland along the torturously winding SS111 to hilltop Gerace.

TRIP HIGHLIGHT

## 11 Gerace

Hilltop Gerace is worth a detour for the views alone. On one side lies the Ionian Sea, and on the other the dark, dramatic heights of the Aspromonte mountains. The hilltop town also boasts Calabria's largest Romanesque **cathedral** (Piazza Tribuna; ⌚10am-noon & 3-5pm Tue-Sun), a majestically simple structure that dates to 1045 and incorporates

### DREADED 'NDRANGHETA

While Sicily's Mafia gets more press, Calabria's 'Ndrangheta is one of the most fearsome organised crime networks in the world. EURISPES, an independent Italian think tank, estimates the 'Ndrangheta's annual income reached more than €40 billion in 2007. The *Guardian* has reported that the loosely organised group is cemented by family bonds, with at least 6000 members overall. And according to Wikileaks, a leaked US embassy cable declared that, if Calabria were independent, it would be a failed state. The Aspromonte mountains have long served as the group's refuge and traditional headquarters.

columns pilfered from nearby Roman ruins.

p341

The Drive » After heading back down SS111, turn south on SS106 along the blue waters of the Ionic coast. At the town of Bova Marina, follow signs inland along the sharply twisting road to hilltop Bova. The total distance is 77km.

## 12 Bova

This mountain eyrie possesses a photogenic ruined **castle**, plus stupendous surf-and-turf views that rival Gerace's. Don't miss the bilingual signage – the townspeople are among the few surviving speakers of Griko, a Greek dialect that dates at least to the Byzantine period and possibly to the times when ancient Greeks ruled here.

The Drive » The 19km road from Bova to Roghudi Vecchio boasts the most stunning stretch of driving on this trip, though it's also the most serious twisting and turning – plus some pretty rough patches. Note that it's important to ask about road conditions before heading from Bova to Roghudi as roads can be washed out. It may be advisable to skip Roghudi and head straight to Gambarie via SS183.

TRIP HIGHLIGHT

## 13 Roghudi Vecchio

The wild, winding ride to Roghudi Vecchio takes you through a stunning stretch of the Aspromonte mountains. This ghostly town clings limpet-like to a steep, craggy slope above an eerily white bed of the Amendolea river, which is formed by limestone washed down from the surrounding peaks. The river is barely a trickle most of the year, but two terrible floods in the 1970s caused the town itself to be abandoned. Note that the town is still uninhabited and unpoliced, so wandering off the main road is not recommended.

The Drive » On the 59km drive to Gambarie, it's more dramatic switchbacks down to the Amendolea river and back up, past the very poor town of Roccaforte del Greco and eventually back to SS183, which climbs quickly from the olive trees and cactus of the lower altitudes to pines, oaks and chestnut trees along the flat peaks of the Aspromonte.

## 14 Gambarie

Headquarters of the **Parco Nazionale dell'Aspromonte** (www.parcoaspromonte.it) and the region's largest town, faux-Swiss Gambarie is more convenient than charming. It does make a great base to explore the pine-covered heights that surround it. This is wonderful walking country, and the park has several colour-coded trails. There is also skiing in winter, with a lift right from the town centre.

p341

The Drive » It's now time to return to sea level. This 32km leg begins on the SS184 as it winds its way down through the towns of San Stefano and Sant'Alessio in Aspromonte, all the way to the A3. On the way down, gape at the views across the Straits of Messina to Sicily, weather permitting.

## 15 Reggio Calabria

Reggio is the main launching point for ferries to Sicily, which sparkles temptingly across the Strait of Messina. Though the city's grid of dusty streets have the slightly dissolute feel shared by most port cities, Reggio's wide, seafront promenade, lined with art deco palaces, is delightful.

The city is also home to the spectacular **Bronzi di Riace**, two full-sized Greek bronze nudes. At the time of research, the **Museo Nazionale della Magna Grecia** (☎0965 81 22 55; www.museonazionalerc.it; Piazza de Nava 26; adult/child €7/3; ⌚9am-7.30pm Tue-Sun), where they usually reside, was closed, but the statues themselves were still on view.

p341

# Eating & Sleeping

## Mormanno 1

**Osteria del Vicolo** Calabrese €

(☎0881 804 75; www.osteriadelvicolo.it; Vico Primo San Francesco 5; meals €15-25; lunch & dinner Thu-Tue) Follow signs from Mormanno's church to this humble but much-lauded eatery. The menu stars the region's highly prized lentils, which accompany local grilled meats, form the base for pasta sauce, or come infused with oregano in a divinely simple soup. The family also runs a B&B nearby.

## Morano Calabro 2

**Albergo Villa San Domenico** Inn €€

(☎0981 399 991; www.albergovillasandomenico.it; Via Sotto gli Olmi; r €110-160; P ❄ @ 📶) This hotel occupies an 18th-century palace that sits picturesquely next to Santa Magdalena church at the foot of the old town. Digs are furnishing in traditional style, but also fitted out with all the modern comforts.

## Camigliatello Silano 5

**La Tavernetta** Calabrese $$

(☎0984 579 026; www.latavernetta.info; Campo San Lorenzo 14; meals €40-50; lunch & dinner Mon-Sat) Among Calabria's best eats, La Tavernetta marries rough country charm with citified elegance in warmly colourful dining rooms. The food is first-rate and based on the best local ingredients, from wild anise seed and essence of bergamot to mountain-raised lamb and kid. Reserve ahead on Sundays and holidays.

**Albergo San Lorenzo** Inn €

(☎0984 570 809; www.sanlorenzosialberga.it; Campo San Lorenzo 14; s/d €80/110; P ❄ @ 📶) Above their famous restaurant, the owners of La Tavernetta have opened the area's most stylish sleep, with large, well-equipped rooms done up in colourful, modernist style.

## Cosenza 7

**La Graticola** Calabrese €

(☎0984 790 318; Via Capoderose 13; meals €20-25; lunch & dinner Mon-Sat) This unpretentious trattoria just off the city's pedestrian district offers excellent takes on Calabrese classics, like *lagana e ceci* (hearty pasta with chick peas), *paccheri alla Norma* (pasta with eggplant, tomatoes and smoked ricotta) and a remarkable *semifreddo di amaretto* (almond-flavoured ice).

**Royal Hotel** Hotel $

(☎0984 412 165; www.hotelroyalsas.it; Via Molinella 24e; s/d €50/75; P ❄ @) Near the city's lively pedestrian district and a short walk to the historic quarters, this 1980s-style modern hotel offers convenience, value and comfort, if not great charm.

## Pizzo 8

**Bar Gelateria Ercole** Gelato €

(☎0963 531 149; www.barercole.com; Piazza della Repubblica) On Pizzo's main square, Ercole is by many accounts the winner of Pizzo's gelato wars, for which the town is famous. The most admired flavours include *tartuffo* (chocolate and hazelnut) and *cassate* (egg cream with candied fruit).

**Piccolo Grand Hotel** Boutique Hotel $$

(☎0963 533 293; www.piccolograndhotel.com; Via Leoluca Chiaravalloti 32; s €95-110, d €138-158; ❄ @ 📶) This shining new boutique hotel is hidden on an unlikely and rather dingy side street of Pizzo. But its exuberant blue-and-white design, upscale comforts and panoramic rooftop breakfasts have quickly made it among the city's top sleeps.

## Tropea 9

**Pimm's** Seafood €€

(0963 666 105; Largo Migliarese; meals €35-45; lunch & dinner) Set on the lip of Tropea's stunning cliffs, Pimm's serves up simple but excellent local seafood, plus wonderful salads starring Tropea's prized red onions. This place earns its nautical-themed decor.

**Residenza Il Barone** Inn €€

(0963 607 181; www.residenzailbarone.it; Largo Barone; d from €100; P) With rooms in a 19th-century mansion as well as in newer outbuildings, this well-run inn sits just a block outside Tropea's historic centre. Expect discounts in winter and a surcharge in July and August.

**Residenza Il Duomo** B&B €€

(0963 666 006; www.residenzailduomo.it; Via Boiano 3; d from €86; ) On the top floor of an old baronial home in Tropea's historic centre, this comfortable and well-run B&B offers bright, prettily decorated rooms and a rooftop breakfast with stunning views.

## Gerace 11

**La Casa di Gianna** Calabrese €€

(0964 355 024; www.lacasadigianna.it; Via Paola Frascà 4; meals €30-40; lunch & dinner) Halfway between mountains and sea in the heart of Gerace, this foodie favourite tackles both meat and seafood with aplomb.

**I Giardino di Gerace** B&B €

(0964 356 732; www.ilgiardinodigerace.com; Via Fanfani 8; d €80; ) Set amid hillside gardens, this place is well worth the winding walk along pedestrian-only alleys from the central square. Rooms are small but cosy. Breakfast is served in the gardens, weather permitting. Other meals are available upon request.

## Gambarie 14

**Hotel Miramonti** B&B €

(0965 743 190; www.hotelmiramontigambarie.it; Via degli Sci 10; r €40-80; ) A few hundred metres uphill from the main square, this inn provides all the necessary comforts, steps from the ski lifts. The restaurant serves hearty mountain fare, including soups and stews, mountain-grown meats, and first-rate local cheeses.

## Reggio Calabria 15

**Le Nasse U Bais** Seafood €€

(0965 897 266; www.ubais.it; Via Lemos 6; meals €30-45; lunch & dinner Tue-Sun) Offering a long wine list and fresh local seafood, this restaurant looks like a very sophisticated version of a fisherman's whitewashed shack. The food follows the same theme – simple, fresh ingredients, but served up with care and intelligence.

**Cèsare** Gelateria €

(Piazza Indipendenza; 6am-1am) The most popular gelateria in town serves classic flavours as well as a few local twists like bergamot. Look for the green kiosk at the end of the *lungomare* (seafront).

**Casa Blanca** B&B €

(347 945 92 10, 342 066 89 22; www.bbcasablanca.it; Via Arcovito 24; d €65-90; ) A little gem in Reggio's heart, this 19th-century *palazzo* has spacious rooms gracefully furnished with romantic white-on-white decor. There's a self-serve breakfast nook, a small breakfast table in each room and two apartments available. Great choice.

**Segesta** *Explore temple ruins set on the edge of a canyon*

Classic Trip

# Wonders of Ancient Sicily

*More than a trip around la bella Sicilia, this is also a journey through time, from spare Greek temples to Norman churches decked out with Arab and Byzantine finery.*

## TRIP HIGHLIGHTS

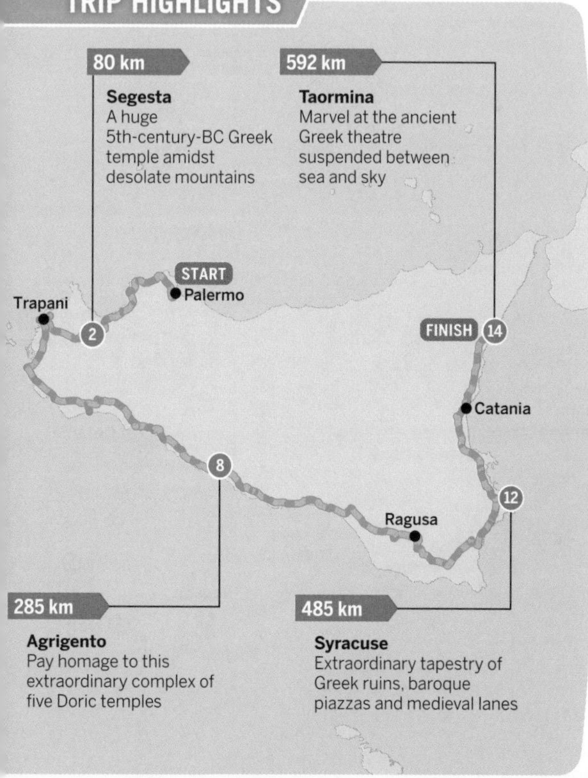

80 km
**Segesta**
A huge 5th-century-BC Greek temple amidst desolate mountains

592 km
**Taormina**
Marvel at the ancient Greek theatre suspended between sea and sky

START Palermo

Trapani

2

FINISH 14

Catania

8

12

Ragusa

285 km
**Agrigento**
Pay homage to this extraordinary complex of five Doric temples

485 km
**Syracuse**
Extraordinary tapestry of Greek ruins, baroque piazzas and medieval lanes

**12–14 DAYS**
**592KM / 368 MILES**

**GREAT FOR...**

**BEST TIME TO GO**

Spring and autumn are best. Avoid the heat and crowds of high summer.

**ESSENTIAL PHOTO**

Capture Mt Etna from Taormina's Greek theatre.

**BEST FOR HISTORY**

Explore layer upon layer of Sicily's past in glorious Syracuse.

Classic Trip

# 33 Wonders of Ancient Sicily

A Mediterranean crossroads for 25 centuries, Sicily is heir to an unparalleled cultural legacy, from the temples of Magna Graecia to Norman churches made kaleidoscopic by Byzantine and Arab craftsmen. This trip takes you from exotic, palm-fanned Palermo to the baroque splendours of Syracuse and Catania. On the way, you'll also experience Sicily's startlingly diverse landscape, including bucolic farmland, smouldering volcanoes and long stretches of aquamarine coastline.

## ❶ Palermo

These days Palermo is a fascinating conglomeration of splendour and decay. Unlike Florence or Rome, many of the city's treasures are hidden rather than scrubbed up for endless streams of tourists. The evocative history of the city infuses its daily life, and the dusty backstreets of the old quarter have a distinct Middle Eastern feel. Palermo is also home to Sicily's **Regional Archaeological Museum** (☎091 611 68 05; Piazza Olivella 24), one of the most important museums of its kind in Europe. At research time, it was closed for renovations.

A trading port since Phoenician times, Palermo first came to prominence as the capital of Arab Sicily in the 9th century AD. When the Normans rode into town in the 11th century, they used Arab know-how to turn Palermo into Christendom's richest and most sophisticated city. The incredible **Cappella Palatina** (Palatine Chapel; ☎091 626 28 33; www.federicosecondo.org; Piazza Indipendenza 1; adult/reduced €7/5; ⏲8.15am-5pm Mon-Sat, to 12.15pm Sun) is the perfect expression of the marriage, with its gold-inflected Byzantine mosaics crowned by a honeycomb *muqarnas* ceiling – a masterpiece of Arab craftsmanship. See more of Palermo's historic architecture on our walking tour (p354).

✕ 🛏 p352

**The Drive »** From Palermo the 82km trip to Segesta starts along the fast-moving A29 as it skirts the mountains west of Palermo, then runs along agricultural plains until you reach the hills of Segesta. The Greek ruins lie just off the A29dir.

### LINK YOUR TRIP

**32 The Calabrian Wilderness**

To experience the wild snow-capped peaks of the Pollino pick up this trip across the Strait of Messina from Taormina in Reggio Calabria (p333).

**35 Sicilian Island Hop**

In Taormina, you can join this trip, which begins on the high slopes of Etna and ends in the beautiful and mysterious Aeolian Islands off Sicily's northeast shores (p365).

TRIP HIGHLIGHT

## ❷ Segesta

Set on the edge of a deep canyon in the midst of desolate mountains, Segesta's huge **Greek temple** (☎0924 95 23 56; adult/reduced €6/3; ⏲9am-1hr before sunset) is a magical site. On windy days its 36 giant columns are said to act like an organ, producing mysterious notes. The city, founded by the ancient Elymians, was in constant conflict with Selinunte, whose destruction it sought with dogged determination and singular success. Time, however, has done to Segesta what violence inflicted on Selinunte; little remains now, save the **theatre** and the never-completed temple, the latter dates from around 430 BC and is remarkably well preserved.

**The Drive »** Keep heading along A29dir through a patchwork of green and ochre fields and follow signs for the 40km to Trapani. As you reach its outskirts, you'll head up the very windy SP3 to Erice, with great views of countryside and sea.

## ❸ Erice

A spectacular hilltown, Erice combines medieval charm with astounding 360-degree views from the legendary **Mt Eryx** (750m). On a clear day, you can see Cape Bon in Tunisia. Wander the medieval streets interspersed with churches, forts and tiny cobbled piazzas. Little remains from its ancient past, though as a centre for the cult of Venus, it has a seductive history.

The best views can be had from **Giardino del Balio**, which overlooks the rugged turrets and wooded hillsides down to the saltpans of Trapani and the sea. Adjacent to the gardens is the Norman **Castello di Venere** (Via Castello di Venere), built in the 12th and 13th centuries over the ancient Temple of Venus.

p352

**The Drive »** For the 12km from Erice to Trapani, it's back down the switchbacks of SP3.

### 4 Trapani

Once a key link in a powerful trading network that stretched from Carthage to Venice, Trapani occupies a sickle-shaped spit of land that hugs its ancient harbour. Although Trapani's industrial outskirts are rather bleak, its historic centre is filled with atmospheric pedestrian streets and some lovely churches and baroque buildings. The narrow network of streets remains a Moorish labyrinth, although it takes much of its character from the fabulous 18th-century baroque of the Spanish period.

p352

**The Drive »** For the 33km trip from Trapani to Marsala, head south on the SS115 as small towns alternate with farmland until you reach Marsala at the westernmost reaches of Sicily.

### 5 Marsala

Best known for its eponymous sweet dessert wines, Marsala is an elegant town of stately baroque buildings within a perfect square of city walls. Founded by Phoenicians escaping Roman attacks, the city still has remnants of the Phoenicians' 7m-thick ramparts, ensuring that it was the last Punic settlement to fall to the Romans. Marsala's finest treasure is the partially reconstructed remains of a Carthaginian *liburna* (warship) – the only remaining physical evidence of the Phoenicians' seafaring superiority in the 3rd century BC. You can visit it at the **Museo Archeologico Baglio Anselmi** (0923 95 25 35; Lungomare Boeo; admission €4; 9am-7pm Tue-Sun, to 1.30pm Mon).

p352

**The Drive »** For this 52km leg, once again head down the SS115, passing through farmland and scattered towns until you reach the A29. Then it's more rural country to Campobello di Mazara, where the SP81 heads south through orchards and fields to seaside Selinunte.

### 6 Selinunte

Built on a promontory overlooking the sea, the Greek **ruins of Selinunte** (0924 465 40; adult/reduced €6/3; 9am-1hr before sunset) are among the most impressive in Sicily, dating to around the 7th century BC. The city's history has been largely lost; though its sheer size indicates wealth and importance, even the names of the various temples have been forgotten and are now identified only by letters. The most impressive, **Temple E**, has been partially rebuilt, its columns pieced together from their fragments with part of its tympanum. Many of the carvings, the quality of which is on par with the Parthenon marbles, particularly from **Temple C**, are now in Palermo's archaeological museum (p345).

**The Drive »** Head back up to the SS115 and past a series of hills and plains for the trip to Sciacca.

### 7 Sciacca

Founded in the 5th century BC as a thermal resort for nearby Selinunte, seaside Sciacca still attracts visitors, who come to take the waters at **Nuovo Stabilimento**

**Termale** (☎0925 080 462; www.grandhoteldelleterme.com, in Italian; Viale Nuove Terme 1), a thermal-baths complex next door to the Grand Hotel delle Terme. Sciacca also boasts an attractive medieval core and some excellent seafood restaurants.

**The Drive »** Back on the SS115 you'll hug the shore briefly around Porto Empedocle, then head uphill and inland on the SS189 to Agrigento.

## DETOUR: VILLA ROMANA DEL CASALE

**Start: 8 Agrigento**

Near the town of Piazza Armerina in central Sicily, the stunning 3rd-century Roman **Villa Romana del Casale** (☎0935 68 00 36; www.villaromanadelcasale.org; adult/reduced €10/5; ⏲9am-6pm) was once a sumptuous hunting lodge, possibly belonging to Diocletian's co-emperor Marcus Aurelius Maximianus. Buried under mud in a 12th-century flood, it remained hidden for 700 years before its magnificent floor mosaics – considered unique for their narrative style – were discovered in the 1950s. Visit from November to March or early in the day to avoid the hordes of motor-coach tourists.

TRIP HIGHLIGHT

## 8 Agrigento

Seen from a distance, the modern city's rows of unsightly apartment blocks loom incongruously on the hillside. Never fear: once you get among the **ruins** (☎0922 49 72 26; adult/reduced/child €8/4/free, incl archaeological museum €10/5/free; ⏲9am-11.30pm Jul & Aug, to 7pm Tue-Sat & to 1pm Sun & Mon Sep-Jun) of ancient Akagras, you will understand how this remarkable complex of temples became Sicily's pre-eminent travel destination, thanks to the five Doric temples that once stood on a ridge, designed as a beacon to homecoming sailors.

The ruins are divided into two main sections, known as the eastern and western zones. In the eastern zone, the magnificent **Tempio della Concordia** (Temple of Concord) is the only temple to survive relatively intact. Built around 440 BC, it was transformed into a Christian church in the 6th century. Agrigento's medieval district also has its charms, with its 14th-century **cathedral** and a number of medieval and baroque structures.

✕ 🛏 p352

**The Drive »** For this 133km run head back to the SS115, which veers from inland farmland to brief encounters with the sea. Past the town of Gela, you will head into more hilly country, including a steep climb past Comiso, followed by a straight shot along the SP52 to Ragusa.

## 9 Ragusa

Set amid the rocky peaks northwest of Modica, Ragusa has two faces. Atop the hill sits **Ragusa Superiore**, a busy town with all the trappings of a modern provincial capital, while etched into the hillside is **Ragusa Ibla**. This sloping area of tangled alleyways, grey stone houses and baroque *palazzi* (mansions) is Ragusa's magnificent historic centre.

Like other towns in the region, Ragusa Ibla collapsed after the 1693 earthquake. But the aristocracy, ever impractical, rebuilt their homes on exactly the same spot. Grand baroque churches and *palazzi* line the twisting, narrow lanes, which then open suddenly onto sun-drenched piazzas. Palm-planted Piazza del Duomo, the centre of town, is dominated by the 18th-century baroque **Cattedrale di San Giorgio** (⏲10am-12.30pm & 4-6.30pm), with its magnificent neoclassical dome and stained-glass windows.

PETER ADAMS/GETTY IMAGES ©

MARK BASSETT/ALAMY ©

**EDWARD BOTTONE**
PROFESSOR OF GASTRONOMY, DREXEL UNIVERSITY

Sicilians are known for their prodigious memories. Like all of Sicilian culture, its cuisine is a palimpsest of everything that has come before. Each occupying force is remembered at the table, including ancient Greeks and Romans (wine, olive oil, artichokes), Byzantines (honey, sesame seeds), Arabs (almonds, pistachios, saffron, cumin, sumac), Normans (salt cod) and Spanish (cocoa, peppers, potatoes, finesse).

Top: Sciacca's harbour
Left: Ruins at Agrigento
Right: The road to Ragusa

SABINE LUBENOW/GETTY IMAGES ©

**The Drive »** It's a short, winding, up-and-down drive for 15km through rock-littered hilltops along the SS194 to Modica.

## ⑩ Modica

Modica is a wonderfully atmospheric town with ancient medieval buildings climbing steeply up either side of a deep gorge. But unlike some of the other Unesco-listed cities in the area, it doesn't package its treasures into a single easy-to-see street or central piazza: rather, they are spread around the town and take some discovering. The highlight has to be the baroque **Chiesa di San Giorgio** (Corso San Giorgio; ⏲9am-noon & 4-7pm), which stands in isolated splendour atop a majestic 250-step staircase.

**Corso Umberto I** is the place to lap up the lively local atmosphere. A wide avenue flanked by graceful palaces, churches, restaurants, bars and boutiques, it is where the locals come to parade during the evening *passeggiata* (stroll). Originally a raging river ran through town, but after major flood damage in 1902 it was dammed and Corso Umberto was built over it.

🛏 p353

The Drive » Head back onto SS115, which will turn quite twisty as you close in on Noto, 40km away.

## 11 Noto

Flattened in 1693 by an earthquake, Noto was rebuilt quickly and grandly, and its golden-hued sandstone buildings make it the finest baroque town in Sicily, especially impressive at night when illuminations accentuate its intricately carved facades. The *pièce de résistance* is **Corso Vittorio Emanuele**, an elegantly manicured walkway flanked by thrilling baroque *palazzi* and churches.

The only one of Noto's *palazzi* that is open to the public, **Palazzo Villadorata** (Palazzo Nicolaci; ☎320 5568038; www.palazzonicolaci.it; Via Nicolaci; adult/reduced €4/2; ⏲10am-1pm & 3-7.30pm), reveals the luxury to which the local nobility were accustomed. The decor is as opulent as the facade, with heavy glass chandeliers, frescoed ceilings and crafty wall paintings designed to look like brocaded wallpaper.

✕ p353

The Drive The 39km drive to Syracuse from Noto takes you down SP59 and then northeast on the A18, past the majestic Riserva Naturale Cava Grande del Cassibile as you parallel Sicily's eastern coast.

TRIP HIGHLIGHT

## 12 Syracuse

Encapsulating Sicily's timeless beauty, Syracuse is a dense tapestry of overlapping cultures and civilisations. Ancient Greek ruins rise out of lush citrus orchards, cafe tables spill out onto baroque piazzas, and medieval lanes meander to the sea. Your visit, like the city itself, can be split into two easy parts: one dedicated to the archaeological site, the other to the island of Ortygia, which is just offshore.

It's difficult to imagine now but in its heyday Syracuse was the largest city in the ancient world, bigger even than Athens and Corinth. The **Parco Archeologico della Neapolis** (☎0931 6 50 68; Viale Paradis; adult/reduced €9/4.50; ⏲9am-1hr before sunset) is home to a staggering number of well-preserved Greek (and Roman) remains, with the huge 5th-century-BC Greek theatre as the main attraction. In the grounds of Villa Landolina, about 500m east of the archaeological park, is the **Museo Archeologico Paolo Orsi** (☎0931 46 40 22; Viale Teocrito; adult/reduced €8/4; ⏲9am-6pm Tue-Sat, to 1pm Sun).

Despite the labyrinthine streets, it is hard to get lost on the island of **Ortygia**, since it measures less than 1 sq km. And yet it also manages to encompass 25 centuries of history. Architectural styles vary widely, including ancient ruins and medieval Norman buildings as well as **Piazza del Duomo** – a masterpiece in baroque

### THE 1693 EARTHQUAKE

On 11 January 1693, a devastating, 7.4-magnitude earthquake hit southeastern Sicily, destroying buildings from Catania to Ragusa. The destruction was terrible, but it also created a blank palette for architects to rebuild the region's cities and towns out of whole cloth, in the latest style and according to rational urban planning – a phenomenon practically unheard of since ancient times. In fact, the earthquake ushered in an entirely new architectural style known as Sicilian baroque, defined by its seductive curves and elaborate detail, which you can see on display in Ragusa, Modica, Catania and many other cities in the region.

town planning. Look down the outer flank of the **Duomo** (Cathedral; 8am-7pm) for thick Doric columns incorporated into the cathedral's structure – all that survive from the mighty Greek temple that once stood here.

 p353

**The Drive ››** From Syracuse to Catania, it is a 66km drive north along the A18. This is orange-growing country and you will see many orchards, which can be gorgeously fragrant when in bloom.

**Porto Empedocle** On the way to Agrigento

## 13 Catania

Catania is a true city of the volcano, much of it constructed from the lava that poured down on it during a 1669 eruption. The baroque centre is lava-black in colour, as if a fine dusting of soot permanently covers its elegant buildings, most of which are the work of Giovanni Vaccarini. The 18th-century architect almost single-handedly rebuilt the civic centre into an elegant, modern city of spacious boulevards and set-piece piazzas.

Long buried under the lava, the **Graeco-Roman Theatre & Odeon** (Via Vittorio Emanuele II 262; adult/reduced €4/2; 9am-1pm & 2.30pm-1hr before sunset Tue-Sun) remind you that the city's history goes back much further. Picturesquely sited in the thick of a crumbling residential area, the ruins are bedecked with laundry flapping on the rooftops of neighbouring buildings that seem to have sprouted organically from the stage.

p353

**The Drive ››** The 53km drive to Taormina along the A18 is a coast-hugging northern run, taking in more orange groves as well as glimpses of the sparkling Ionian Sea.

TRIP HIGHLIGHT

## 14 Taormina

Over the centuries, Taormina has seduced an exhaustive line of writers and artists, from Goethe to DH Lawrence. The main reason for their swooning? The perfect horseshoe-shaped **Greek theatre** (0942 2 32 20; Via Teatro Greco; adult/reduced €8/4; 9am-1hr before sunset), suspended between sea and sky, with glorious views to brooding Mt Etna through the broken columns. Built in the 3rd century BC, the theatre is the most dramatically situated Greek theatre in the world and the second largest in Sicily (after Syracuse). The 9th-century capital of Byzantine Sicily, Taormina also boasts a very well-preserved, if touristy, medieval town – and gorgeous views up and down the Strait of Messina.

p353

# Eating & Sleeping



## Palermo 1

**Trattoria Ai Cascinari** Sicilian €

(☎091 651 98 04; Via d'Ossuna 43/45; meals €20-25; ⊙lunch Tue-Sun, dinner Wed-Sat) Friendly service, simple straw chairs and blue-and-white-checked tablecloths set the relaxed tone at this Slow Food–recommended neighbourhood trattoria, 1km north of the Cappella Palatina.

**Butera 28** Apartment €€

(☎333 316 54 32; www.butera28.it; Via Butera 28; 2-/4-/8-person apt per day from €50/100/150; ❄ 📶) Delightful bilingual owner Nicoletta offers 11 well-equipped and comfortable apartments of varying sizes in her elegant *palazzo* near Piazza della Kalsa. Nicoletta also offers cooking classes in her gorgeous blue-and-white-tiled kitchen.

## Erice 3

**Hotel Elimo** Hotel €€

(☎0923 86 93 77; www.hotelelimo.it; Via Vittorio Emanuele 23; d €90-130; P @ 📶) Communal spaces at this historic house are filled with tiled beams, marble fireplaces, intriguing art, knick-knacks and antiques. The bedrooms are more mainstream, but many have breathtaking views.

## Trapani 4

**Osteria La Bettolaccia** Sicilian €€

(☎0923 2 16 95; Via Generale Enrico Fardella 25; meals €30-40; ⊙lunch & dinner Mon-Fri, dinner Sat) An unwaveringly authentic, Slow Food–recommended restaurant, this is the perfect place to try *couscous con zuppa di mare* (couscous with mixed seafood in a spicy fish sauce, with tomatoes, garlic and parsley).

## Marsala 5

**Il Gallo e l'Innamorata** Modern Sicilian €

(☎0923 195 44 46; Via Bilardello 18; meals €25; ⊙lunch & dinner) Warm orange walls and arched stone doorways lend an artsy, convivial atmosphere to this Slow Food–acclaimed eatery with its superb fixed-price menu (€25 including appetisers, pasta, main course, fruit, dessert, water and wine).

**Hotel Carmine** Hotel €€

(☎0923 71 19 07; www.hotelcarmine.it; Piazza Carmine 16; s €70-90, d €100-125; P ❄ @ 📶) This lovely hotel in a 16th-century monastery has elegant rooms (especially numbers 7 and 30), with original blue-and-gold majolica tiles, stone walls, antique furniture and lofty beamed ceilings.

## Agrigento 8

**Kokalos** Pizzeria €

(☎0922 60 64 27; Via Magazzeni 3; pizzas €5-11, meals €17-30; ⊙lunch & dinner) This eatery, resembling a Wild West ranch, is the perfect place to enjoy wood-fired pizza on the summer terrace while gazing out over the temples. You'll find it up a dusty track a couple of kilometres southeast of town.

**Villa Athena** Luxury Hotel €€€

(☎0922 59 62 88; www.hotelvillaathena.it; Via Passeggiata Archeologica 33; d €190-350; P ❄ @ 📶 🏊) With the Tempio della Concordia lit up in the near distance and palm trees lending an exotic Arabian-nights feel, the views from this historic five-star, housed in an aristocratic 18th-century villa, are magnificent.

## Modica ⑩

**Villa Quartarella** Agriturismo €

(☎360 654 829; www.quartarella.com; Contrada Quartarella; s €40, d €70-80) Rooms are spacious at this countryside villa south of Modica, and owners Francesco and Francesca are generous in sharing their love and encyclopaedic knowledge of local history, flora and fauna.

## Noto ⑪

**Ristorante Il Cantuccio** Modern Sicilian €€

(☎0931 83 74 64; Via Cavour 12; meals €30-35; ⏲dinner Tue-Sun, lunch Sun) Chef Valentina presents a seasonally changing menu that combines familiar Sicilian ingredients in exciting new ways. Try her exquisite gnocchi with basil, parsley, mint, capers, almonds and cherry tomatoes, and then move on to memorable main courses such as lemon-stuffed bass with orange-fennel salad.

## Syracuse ⑫

**Red Moon** Seafood €

(☎0931 6 03 56; Riva Porto Lachio 36; meals €25; ⏲lunch & dinner Thu-Tue) Serving some of the best seafood in Syracuse under its tented octagonal roof, this reasonably priced family-run place on the mainland makes a pleasant refuge from Ortygia's well-worn tourist track.

**Villa dei Papiri** Agriturismo €€

(☎0931 72 13 21; www.villadeipapiri.it; Contrada Cozzo Pantano, Fonte Ciane; d €70-132, 2-person ste €105-154, 4-person ste €140-208; P ❄ @ ≈) Immersed in orange groves and papyrus reeds 8km outside Syracuse, this lovely *agriturismo*, next to Ovid's Fonte Ciana spring, offers suites in a beautifully converted 19th-century farmhouse as well as double rooms dotted around the lush grounds.

## Catania ⑬

**Trattoria di De Fiore** Trattoria €

(☎095 31 62 83; Via Coppola 24/26; meals €15-25; ⏲Tue-Sun) This neighbourhood trattoria is presided over by septuagenarian chef Mamma Rosanna, who uses organic flour and fresh, local ingredients to recreate her great-grandmother's recipes. Service is slow, but worth the wait.

**5 Balconi B&B** B&B €

(☎095 723 45 34; www.5balconi.it; Via Plebiscito 133; s €30-35, d €50-65, tr €70-75; ❄ ≈) You won't find a nicer low-end option than this lovingly remodelled antique *palazzo* in a workaday neighbourhood. The friendly owners offer three high-ceilinged rooms with a pair of shared bathrooms down the hall, plus a breakfast featuring local organic bread and fresh fruit.

## Taormina ⑭

**Licchio's** Seafood €€

(☎0942 62 53 27; Via Patricio 10; meals €30-40; ⏲lunch & dinner, closed Thu Nov-Mar) The seafood antipasti at this classy little eatery are delicious and varied enough to constitute a meal in themselves, but the menu's full of other enticements: tempura-fried zucchini flowers, fabulously fresh spinach-ricotta gnocchi and divine desserts.

**Villa Belvedere** Hotel €€

(☎0942 2 37 91; www.villabelvedere.it; Via Bagnoli Croce 79; d with inland view €124-184, with sea view €144-236; ⏲Mar-Nov; P ❄ @ ≈ ≋) Built in 1902, the exquisite Villa Belvedere offers both class and a family atmosphere. Rooms are simple but refined with cream linens and terracotta floors, and the luxurious garden commands majestic sea views.

# STRETCH YOUR LEGS PALERMO

**Start/Finish:** Palazzo dei Normanni

**Distance:** 2.8km

**Duration:** Three hours

Take in the complex warp and weave of Sicily's capital, from baroque fountains and dazzling Arab-Norman mosaics to the vivid sights and sounds of its sprawling outdoor markets – all in just a few hours.

Take this walk on Trip

## Palazzo dei Normanni

This austere palace, once the seat of a magnificent court, today houses Sicily's parliament. In addition to political haggling, the palace holds Palermo's greatest treasure, the **Cappella Palatina** (Palatine Chapel; ☎091 626 28 33; www.federicosecondo.org; Piazza Indipendenza 1; adult/reduced €7/5; ⏲8.15am-5pm Mon-Sat, 8.15-9.45am & 11.15am-12.15pm Sun). Begun by Norman King Roger II in the 1130s, this mosaic-clad chapel swarms with figures in glittering gold.

**The Walk »** The short walk to the cathedral takes you along Corso Vittorio Emanuele, the city's main east–west thoroughfare, and through the baroque Porta Nuova, once the city's main gate.

## Cattedrale

A feast of geometric patterns, ziggurat crenulations and majolica cupolas, Palermo's **cathedral** (www.cattedrale.palermo.it; Corso Vittorio Emanuele; ⏲8am-5.30pm Mon-Sat, 7am-1pm & 4-7pm Sun) is an extraordinary example of the Arab-Norman style. The interior was stripped and modernised in the 18th century, though its atmospheric **crypt** (adult/reduced €3/1.50; ⏲9.30am-5.30pm Mon-Sat), the final resting place of Sicily's Norman royals, remains fascinating.

**The Walk »** Head straight down Corso Vittorio Emanuele and admire the decaying splendour of its elaborate baroque facades.

## Quattro Canti

The intersection of Corso Vittorio Emanuele and Via Maqueda forms the civic heart of Palermo. Built in the early 17th century, the crossroads is adorned with four elaborate facades. The intersection represents one of Europe's first coordinated efforts at urban planning since ancient times.

**The Walk »** Continuing along Corso Vittorio Emanuele, you'll soon see Casa Merlo.

## Casa Merlo

Inside a beautifully preserved art-nouveau pharmacy, Casa Merlo is

more than a shop, it's a little museum of Sicilian ceramics. With a range of styles and materials, it sells both large, elaborate pieces and smaller keepsakes.

The Walk » Heading back along Corso Vittorio Emanuele, you'll see stairs on the left just before Quattro Canti. They'll take you to Piazza Pretoria.

## Fontana Pretoria

This huge and ornate fountain originally graced a garden in Florence, but was bought by Palermo in 1573. Its naked nymphs proved too much for Sicilian tastes, and it was prudishly dubbed the Fountain of Shame, but the city has since come around.

The Walk » Exiting the piazza onto Via Maqueda, you will find the next two churches just a few steps to the south.

## Chiesa Capitolare di San Cataldo & La Martorana

With its cubic simplicity, Arabic dome and delicate tracery, the 12th-century **Chiesa Capitolare di San Cataldo** (Piazza Bellini 3; admission €2; ⏲9.30am-1.30pm & 3.30-5.30pm Mon-Sat, 9.30am-1.30pm Sun) is one of Palermo's most striking buildings. Disappointingly, it's almost bare inside. That's not the case for the adjacent **La Martorana** (Piazza Bellini 3; ⏲8.30am-1pm & 3.30-5.30pm Mon-Sat, 8.30am-1pm Sun), a 12th-century church whose interior is a profusion of colour. At writing, the interiors of both churches were closed for restorations.

The Walk » On the right just a few steps down Via Maqueda, look for Via del Ponticello, which leads directly into the Mercato di Ballarò.

## Mercato di Ballarò

Snaking for several city blocks east of Palazzo dei Normanni is Palermo's busiest street market, which throbs with activity well into the early evening. It's a fascinating mix of noises, smells and street life, and the cheapest place for everything from Chinese padded bras to fresh produce, fish and cheese.

The Walk » Head along Via Porta di Castro. Eventually the walls of the Palazzo dei Normanni will loom up on your right.

***Polizzi Generosa*** *Stunning landscapes make for a hiker's paradise*

# Into the Madonie Mountains

*The perfect escape from the bustle of the island's coast, this trip whisks you into the craggy peaks of the Madonie mountains – a hiker's dream, rising majestically from Sicily's northern coast.*

## TRIP HIGHLIGHTS

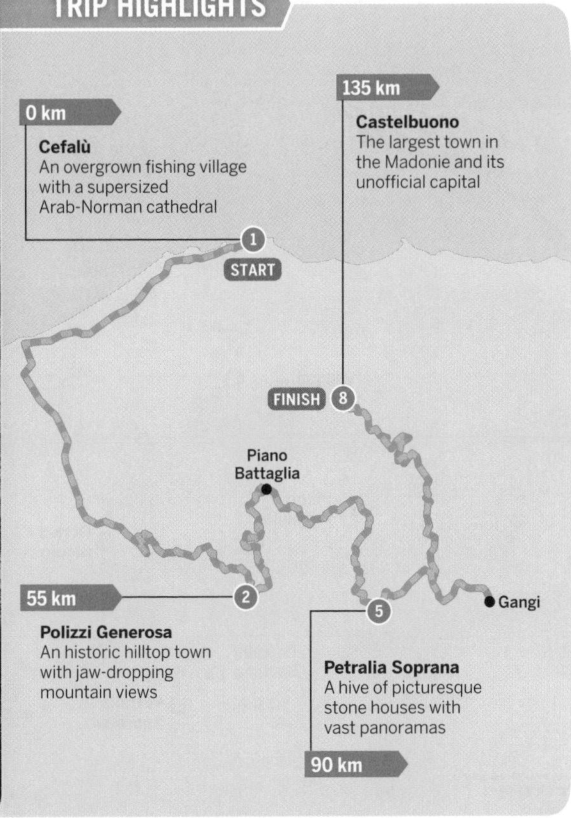

**0 km**

**Cefalù**
An overgrown fishing village with a supersized Arab-Norman cathedral

1 START

**135 km**

**Castelbuono**
The largest town in the Madonie and its unofficial capital

FINISH 8

Piano Battaglia

Gangi

**55 km** 2

**Polizzi Generosa**
An historic hilltop town with jaw-dropping mountain views

5

**Petralia Soprana**
A hive of picturesque stone houses with vast panoramas

**90 km**

**3–5 DAYS**
**135KM / 84 MILES**

**GREAT FOR…**

**BEST TIME TO GO**

Late spring for wildflowers and winter for skiing.

**ESSENTIAL PHOTO**

Capture patchwork farms and dramatic peaks from Petralia Soprana.

**BEST HIKING**

The most exciting trails start around Piano Battaglia.

# 34 Into the Madonie Mountains

Most travellers only catch a glimpse of the Madonie mountains from Sicily's Tyrrhenian coast. This trip immerses you in their craggy peaks, where the wooded slopes shelter wolves, wildcats, eagles and the near-extinct ancient Nebrodi fir trees. Besides stunning vistas down to the Mediterranean, ramblers (and in winter, skiers) can replenish their energy with rustic mountain fare, from outstanding local pecorino to pastas made fragrant with mountain-gathered herbs and mushrooms.

TRIP HIGHLIGHT

## 1 Cefalù

Giuseppe Tornatore filmed scenes from his *Cinema Paradiso* in this lovely, overgrown fishing village. Of course, his nostalgic camera carefully avoids both summer hordes and the cement hotels that accommodate them. Still, the old town is enchanting for its honey-hued stone buildings and supersized **cathedral** (☎0921 92 20 21; Piazza del Duomo; admission free;

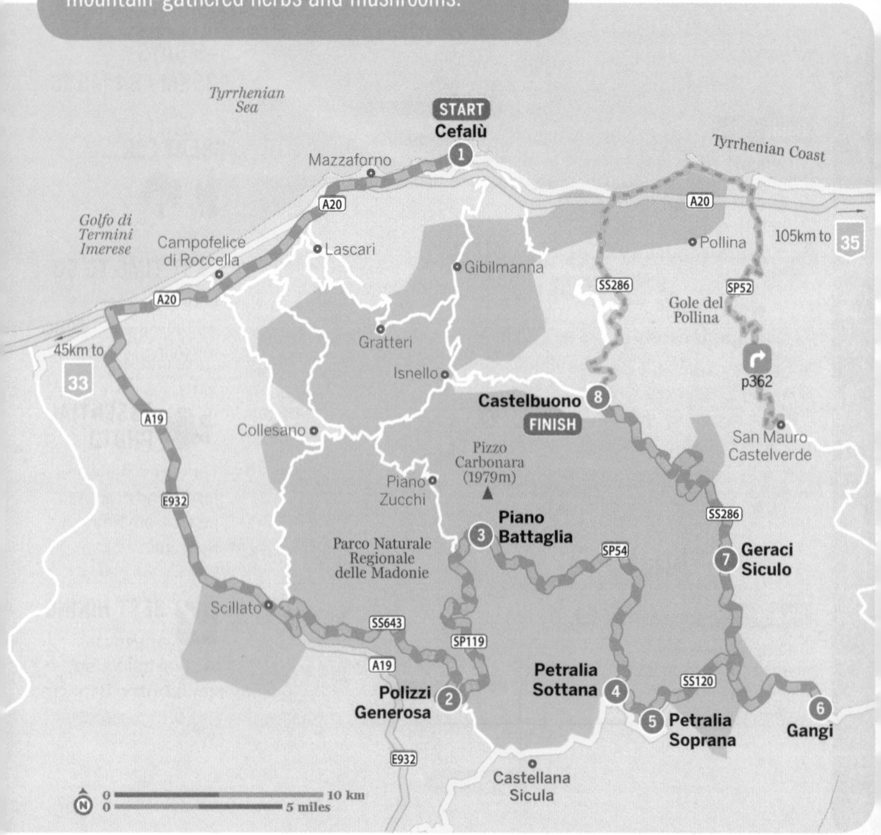

8am-7pm Apr-Sep, to 5pm Oct-Mar). A jewel in Sicily's Arab-Norman crown with its elaborate mosaics, the cathedral is equalled in magnificence only by the Cattedrale di Monreale and Palermo's Cappella Palatina. Its 16 interior columns were likely pilfered from a Roman temple atop the adjacent **La Rocca** (admission free; 9am-7pm May-Sep, to 5pm Oct-Apr). This rock outcrop looms 278m above the town, providing outstanding views up and down Sicily's northern coast.

Note that parking in Cefalù is notoriously bad in summer, and not particularly good in winter, either.

p363

LINK YOUR TRIP

**Wonders of Ancient Sicily**

From Cefalù, catch the A20 west to Palermo, which kicks off this tour of Sicily's coastline and its key monuments, both ancient and modern (p343).

**Sicilian Island Hop**

From Cefalù, head east along the A20 to Milazzo, the best place to catch a ferry to the Aeolian islands (p365).

**The Drive »** This 56km leg should be pretty quick, as you head west along the coast via superhighway A20, then south along its twin, A19. The Madonie will start rearing up quickly on your left. A long, wending, but also stunning ride from along highway SS643 leads to lonely, hilltop Polizzi Generosa.

TRIP HIGHLIGHT

## 2 Polizzi Generosa

With a well-preserved historic centre and jaw-dropping views of the dramatic western flanks of the Madonie, Polizzi Generosa is arguably the region's mostly beautiful town. With its strategic views up and down the Imera river valley, you can understand why the Normans made it a stronghold against Arab incursions. Foodies come for the celebrated *fagiolo badda nera* – a rich, multicoloured local bean. The town is especially magical on crisp mornings when fog turns the hilltop town into an island floating amid the clouds.

p363

**The Drive »** Possibly the most stunning leg of this trip winds 18km, first along the SP119 along the western flanks of the Madonie and then along the SP54 up into the middle of its highest peaks.

## 3 Piano Battaglia

Skiing in the middle of the Mediterranean? In Piano Battaglia, it's possible. More Swiss than Sicilian, this town, nestled in a bowl-like valley amid the Madonie's highest peak, comes alive only in the winter when the surrounding slopes are blanketed in snow. However, in the warmer months the area attracts lots of hikers, since some of the best (and most challenging) trails of the **Parco Regionale delle Madonie** (www.parks.it/parco.madonie) radiate out from here.

**The Drive »** The curves of SP54 on the 14km road to Petralia Sottana are less radical than other parts of the Madonie, though the views are no less impressive.

## 4 Petralia Sottana

Perched at the edge of a cliff with fine views over the surrounding peaks, the town makes a convenient base for exploring the surrounding countryside, especially since it is home to a helpful information office of the **Ente Parco delle Madonie** (www.parks.it/parco.madonie; Corso Paolo Agliata 16; 9am-3.30pm Sun & Mon, 3.30-7.30pm Tue-Sat). You can get good, free hiking maps, themed walks and more. In addition, Petralia Sottana itself is home to a surprisingly rich architectural legacy, paid for by the particular fecundity of the surrounding fields.

The 17th-century **Chiesa Madre**, with a *campanile* (bell tower) that doubles as a beautiful Gothic passageway, is the town's principal landmark.

🛏 p363

**The Drive »** The short but steep 7km climb to Petralia Soprana, Petralia Sottana's sister city, combines hairpin turns and more gorgeous views.

TRIP HIGHLIGHT

## 5 Petralia Soprana

Occupying a strategic ridge at the southern end of the Madonie, proud little Petralia Soprana is the highest town of the Madonie at 1145m, and also one of the best preserved. The historic centre is a hive of picturesque stone houses decked out with wrought-iron balconies. Despite their sombre outward bearing, the town's churches hide surprisingly elegant interiors – restrained baroque confections in white and gold. The **Chiesa Madre** – with its medieval base and elegant Renaissance porch – sits on a handsome stone square. Above it, the elliptical Chiesa Santissimo Salvatore is believed to have been built on the ruins of a mosque – hence its unusual shape.

The town's most dramatic feature is its **belvedere**, the cliffside terrace that sits just off the town's main square. It offers splendid views across a great expanse of fertile wheat fields and steep, green pastures to the stony peaks of the Madonie.

🍴 🛏 p363

**The Drive »** Wind along the SS120 through a patchwork of wheat fields and pastureland as the landscape changes quickly from alpine heights to the rolling hills and plains of Sicily's interior. The total distance is 15km.

## 6 Gangi

From afar, the hilltown of Gangi looks more like a sculptural experiment than a human habitat. Its oddly elliptical shape completely covers the hillside it occupies, while Mt Etna looms dreamily in the background, far across Sicily's interior plains. Beware that Gangi's absurdly steep streets will test your thighs. Hint: drive to the very top of town, where most of the sites are clustered. Don't miss the 13th-century Gothic **Torre Ventimiglia**, a military watchtower that has been turned into the *campanile* of the town's main church.

**The Drive »** Head back about 7km along the SS120 to the SS286, which winds its way along the Madonie's precipitous eastern flanks for 6km. Soon, the ruins of Geraci Siculo's castle will rear up and, beyond it, a sliver of the Tyrrhenian Sea.

SABINE LUBENOW/GETTY IMAGES ©

**Madonie mountains** A shepherd tends his flock

## DETOUR: GOLE DEL POLLINA & SAN MAURO CASTELVERDE

**Start: 8 Castelbuono**

In the valley that separates the Madonie from the neighbouring Nebrodi, the Pollina river has carved the deep and picturesque Gole del Pollina, also known as the Gole di Tiberio. The canyon is worth seeking out, but check ahead at one of the park's **information offices** (www.parcodellemadonie.it) to ensure waters are low enough to allow exploration by foot.

If you continue past the canyon along the twisting SP52, you'll eventually reach **San Mauro Castelverde** – but only after dozens of hairpin (and rather hair-raising) turns. While the town itself is quite humble, the views are extraordinary, encompassing green valleys, craggy peaks, the blue of the Mediterranean and, when the air is crisp, the distant Aeolian islands. The best time to come is in the morning, when the sun lights up the eastern flanks of the Madonie.

## 7 Geraci Siculo

This slip of a town enjoys some of the most dramatic panoramas in the Madonie, though in fact mostly what you are seeing are the Monti Nebrodi, the neighbouring mountains just to the east across the Pollina valley. The tangle of Geraci Siculo's streets culminates with the forlorn but atmospheric ruins of a once-formidable Norman **castle** that occupies the highest point of the rocky promontory. The rest of the town doesn't have much in the way of sites, but makes for atmospheric strolling.

**The Drive »** A long and very twisty 24km descent along SS286 takes you through a gorgeous sea of Holm oaks. Off to the right across the Pollina valley, look for the precariously perched San Mauro Castelverde.

TRIP HIGHLIGHT

## 8 Castelbuono

Set amid ancient manna ash and chestnut forests in the eastern foothills of the Madonie, Castelbuono is both the largest town in the Madonie and its unofficial capital. It owes its name to the 14th-century **castello** (☎0921 67 12 11; Piazza Castello; admission €4; ⏰9.30am-1pm & 4-8pm Tue-Sun) of the powerful Ventimiglia family. At the heart of the fortress is the **Cappella Palatina** (Palace Chapel), which dates from 1683 and is decorated with marvellous stuccowork. The castle is rare in that it stands largely intact, retaining the same rectilinear bearing for over 700 years.

Town life centres on Piazza Margherita, where a series of men's social clubs compete to see who can attract the largest crowd of loitering seniors. Also on the square is the odd and intriguing **Chiesa Madre**, with its strange extra nave and ancient crypt awash in 15th-century frescoes of Christ's Passion.

p363

# Eating & Sleeping

## Cefalù ❶

**La Tavernetta** Seafood **€€**

(☎0921 422 510; www.la-tavernetta.com; Corso da Presidiana; pizza €6-10, meals around €30; ⏲lunch & dinner Tue-Sun, daily Jun-Aug, closed Jan) Tucked away in the marina (called Porto Turistico) east of the historic centre, this first-rate seafood place is a favourite among locals. The pasta with swordfish, eggplant, tomatoes and mint is magnificent.

**B&B Dolce Vita** B&B **€**

(☎0921 923 151; www.dolcevitabb.it; Via Carlo Ortolani di Bordonaro 8; d €45-110; ❄@) Cefalù's most popular B&B is close to the *duomo* and overlooks the sea – a winning combination. Rooms feature bright paint schemes, terracotta tiles and simple furnishings. A panoramic roof terrace is the crowning touch.

## Polizzi Generosa ❷

**Ristorante Itria** Trattoria **€€**

(☎0921 688 790; Via Beato Guglielmo Gnoffi 8; meals €25-35; ⏲lunch & dinner Thu-Tue) This foodie favourite specialises in asparagus and mushrooms gathered from surrounding hillsides. Don't expect a menu, just expertly prepared dishes crafted from local ingredients.

## Petralia Sottana ❹

**Hotel Pomiere** Inn **€**

(☎0921 649 998; www.hotelpomieri.it; Strada Provinciale 54; d €60-70; P❄) This Swiss-style chalet is worth the stunning 11km drive from Petralia Sottana. Rooms are adequate rather than luxurious, but almost all have winning views. The extraordinary restaurant (meals around €30) offers a menu based on ingredients gathered from the surrounding mountainsides, including wild mushrooms, fennel and asparagus. Pastas and sausage are homemade – and exquisite.

## Petralia Soprana ❺

**Da Salvatore** Trattoria **€**

(☎0921 680 169; Piazza San Michele 3; meals €20-25; ⏲lunch & dinner Wed-Mon) Much of your meal is prepared in a wood-burning oven at this beloved trattoria. You won't regret the generous antipasti tray of local cheeses and cured meats. Pastas and grilled meats are rustically simple but first-rate.

**Hotel Residenza Petra** Inn **€**

(☎0921 681 321; www.residenzapetra.it, in Italian; Via Errante 9; s/d €65/85) This new inn occupies a series of typical stone houses clustered around an atmospheric courtyard. Rooms are well appointed, with comfy beds and handsome wood furnishings.

## Castelbuono ❽

**A Rua Fera** Trattoria **€**

(☎0921 676 723; Via Roma 71; pizza €6-10; ⏲lunch & dinner Wed-Mon, closed Oct) This place packs in the crowds with dependably great pizza served in stone-vaulted dining rooms or, weather permitting, on the large terrace.

**Relais Santa Anastasia** Luxury Hotel **€€€**

(☎0921 672 233; www.santa-anastasia-relais.it; Località Santa Anastasia; r from €210; P❄@≋ᯤ) A rare bit of luxury in these parts, this 12th-century abbey boasts beautifully appointed rooms, a great pool and fine gardens.

***Lipari*** *Island-hop around the captivating Aeolians*

# Sicilian Island Hop

*Starting on Mt Etna and ending in the mysterious Aeolian Islands, this journey takes you from windswept mountains to cobalt seas, from Greek ruins to tiny villages lost in time.*

## TRIP HIGHLIGHTS

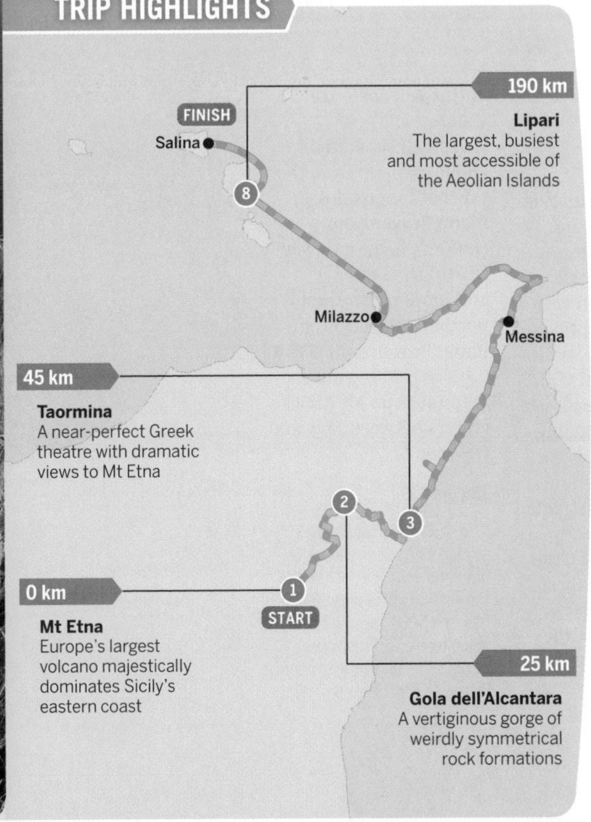

FINISH
Salina
Milazzo
Messina
START

**190 km**
**Lipari**
The largest, busiest and most accessible of the Aeolian Islands

**45 km**
**Taormina**
A near-perfect Greek theatre with dramatic views to Mt Etna

**0 km**
**Mt Etna**
Europe's largest volcano majestically dominates Sicily's eastern coast

**25 km**
**Gola dell'Alcantara**
A vertiginous gorge of weirdly symmetrical rock formations

**7 DAYS**
**255KM / 158 MILES**

**GREAT FOR...**

**BEST TIME TO GO**

Avoid August, when high crowds test patience. Spring and autumn are best for hiking Etna.

**ESSENTIAL PHOTO**

Capture all the Aeolian Islands from a Salina cliff top.

**BEST FOR OUTDOORS**

Frollick in the cool canyon waters of Gola dell'Alcantara.

# 35 Sicilian Island Hop

From the slopes of Mt Etna, you can view all the splendour that awaits you on this trip, from bijou resort town Taormina to the Aeolian Islands shimmering at Sicily's northeast tip. Along the way, you'll visit timeless towns like Savoca, where Coppola filmed scenes for *The Godfather*. At Milazzo, you'll catch a ferry to the Aeolian Islands, with their cobalt seas, splendid beaches and awe-inspiring volcanic landscape.

TRIP HIGHLIGHT

## 1 Mt Etna

Majestically dominating Sicily's eastern coast, **Mt Etna** (www.parcoetna.it) is Europe's largest volcano – and still very much active. Eruptions occur frequently, and its slopes are littered with fissures and craters. Locals understandably keep a close eye on the smouldering peak – at least when not distracted by beautiful views. Sicily's hinterlands, the mountains of Calabria across the Strait of Messina, and even the Aeolians – ultimate goal of this journey – are visible.

A small ski station about 16km up from the town of Linguaglossa, **Piano Provenzano** (1800m), is the gateway to Mt Etna's quieter and more picturesque northern slopes. From Piano Provenzano, **STAR** (☎347 495 70 91) runs Jeep tours up Mt Etna's craters between May and October.

🛏 p371

**The Drive »** This 32km stretch starts with a series of dramatic switchbacks down to the outskirts of Linguaglossa, then the SP64, eventually reaching the SP71, which crosses the Alcantara River on its way to Francavilla di Sicilia.

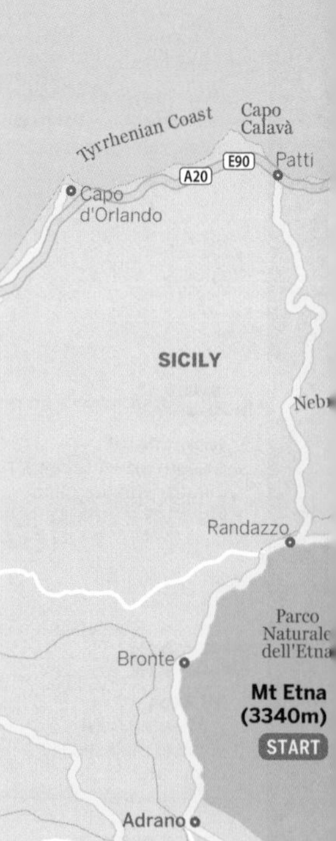

TRIP HIGHLIGHT

## 2 Gola dell'Alcantara

The beautiful **Gola dell'Alcantara** (www.terralcantara.it) is a vertiginous, 25m-high natural gorge bisected by the freezing waters of the Alcantara River. Characterised by its weirdly symmetrical rock formations, it's a spectacular sight. Off-limits from November to March (due to flash flooding), it is open for the rest of the year for hiking, climbing and wading. For more info, check out the park's website. Note that near the car park in the town

### 32 The Calabrian Wilderness

Just a ferry trip across the Strait of Messina, this journey immerses you in Italy's least-explored region, from the snow-capped peaks of the Pollino to Tropea's violet-coloured seas (p333).

### Wonders of Ancient Sicily

From Taormina you can join Sicily's coastline and its remarkable monuments, both ancient and modern (p343).

of Francavilla di Sicilia, there is a visitor centre, where you can hire waders – recommended since waters are ice-cold even in high summer. More extensive trips by canoe should be booked in advance.

**The Drive »** From Francavilla di Sicilia to Taormina is a 26km drive that sends you southeast toward the sea on the SS185. At Giardini-Naxos, turn north onto the SS114, following signs for Taormina. Sandwiched between the Peloritani mountains and the sea, the SS114 hugs the coast. It's a slow drive, past never-ending towns that merge one into another, but the sparkling blue sea makes delightful company.



TRIP HIGHLIGHT

## 3 Taormina

With its pristinely preserved medieval town and stunning views up and down the Strait of Messina, Taormina has seduced an exhaustive line of writers and artists, aristocrats and royalty, and nowadays it's host to a summer arts festival that packs the town with international visitors. However, it's the **Teatro Greco** (Greek Theatre; ☎0942 2 32 20; Via Teatro Greco 40; adult/reduced €6/3, audio guide €5; ⏰9am-7pm) that is the crowning touch. One of Sicily's great sights, it is a near-perfect ancient amphitheatre with dramatic views over snow-capped Etna.

p371

**The Drive »** From Taormina to Savoca is another gorgeous 22km coastal drive. You'll spin past the sea on the SS114. Head inland on SP19, which then makes the steep climb to hilltop Savoca.

## 4 Savoca

Savoca's claim to fame is its association with *The Godfather,* parts of which were filmed here – including Michael Corleone's marriage to Apollonia. Still a tiny, trapped-in-time village, it seems unchanged since medieval times, with its gated walls, stone cottages and haunting churches. It even has its own **catacombs** (admission by donation; ⏰9am-noon & 3-7pm Tue-Sat, 3-7pm Sun) beneath a Capuchin monastery, where the macabre bodies of a few mummified bigwigs stand in wall niches.

**The Drive »** From Savoca, head back to the sea and then back up the SS114, eventually catching the much faster A18 for another glorious ride along the cobalt blue seas. You'll pass Sant'Alessio Saculo, Roccalumera and Scaletta Zanclea during the 42km drive.

## 5 Messina

For centuries an important transport hub, Messina sits on the northernmost point of Sicily's Ionian coast. It is busy and congested, but does possess an

PHILIP & KAREN SMITH/GETTY IMAGES ©

impressive historic centre with elegant 19th-century buildings, and its **cathedral** (Piazza del Duomo; ⏰7am-7pm Mon-Sat, 7.20am-1pm & 4-7.30pm Sun) is one of Sicily's finest.

**The Drive »** From Messina to Ganzirri, it's a quick 10km hop on the SP43 (Via Consolare Pompea), heading north along the coast. The gorgeous mountains of southern Calabria are clearly visible across the Strait of Messina.

## 6 Ganzirri

The coast curves around to Sicily's most northeasterly point, Capo Peloro, just 3km

Savoca

across the water from the Italian mainland. South of the cape is the lakeside town of Ganzirri, a popular summer hang-out famous for its seafood. Succulent mussels are the local speciality, cultivated in the salty lake waters.

**The Drive »** The 50km trip sees you heading around Sicily's northeast tip via SS113dir, and if the weather is clear you will see the Aeolians (your eventual destination) offshore to the north. To the west you will also see the spit of land that protects Milazzo's harbour, your next destination. To speed things along, get on the A20 and exit at Milazzo.

## 7 Milazzo

The main reason for the traveller to visit this industrial port town is to catch a ferry to the Aeolian Islands. That said, it does have a pretty *borgo antico* (old town), including a 13th-century castle built by Frederick II. And the isthmus that juts out to the north is an area of great natural beauty dotted with rocky coves and wonderful views of Sicily's rugged northern coastline.

**The Drive »** Actually, it's a sail. You'll board the ferry at Via Nino Bixio in Milazzo for the hour's crossing of the Tyrrhenian Sea to Lipari. Note that between July and September, you can only take a car if you have booked accommodation in the Aeolians for at least seven days.

TRIP HIGHLIGHT

## 8 Lipari

Lipari is the largest, busiest and most accessible of the Aeolian Islands. The island's rugged shoreline offers excellent opportunities for hiking, boating and swimming, with some of the best beaches in the archipelago. The main focus is Lipari Town, the archipelago's

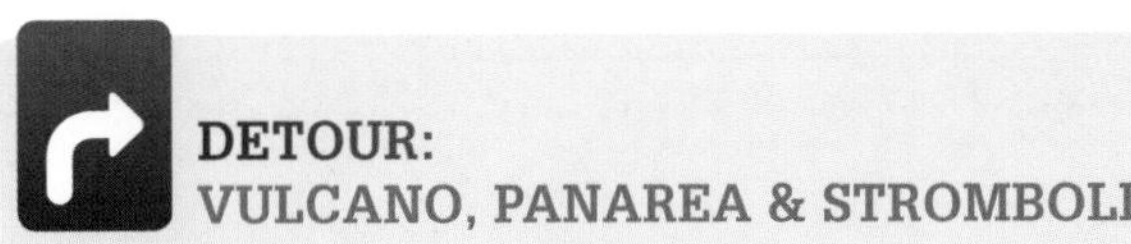

## DETOUR: VULCANO, PANAREA & STROMBOLI

**Start: 8 Lipari**

It is an easy day hop to the other Aeolian islands, each of which has its own unique character. You will find the most regular connections from Lipari, the Aeolians' travel hub.

**Vulcano** White smoke trails rise from the island's ominous peaks, a ghostly image quickly overwhelmed by the smell of sulphur. Celebrated for its therapeutic mud baths and hot springs, the island's main attraction remains the *Gran Cratere* (Large Crater), the steaming volcano that towers over the island's northeast shores.

**Panarea** Exclusive and expensive, Panarea is the smallest and most fashionable of the Aeolians, attracting the international set and Milanese fashionistas with yacht-friendly harbours, designer restaurants and discreet pebble beaches.

**Stromboli** The island of Stromboli is the tip of a vast underwater volcano. The most isolated and captivating of the Aeolian Islands, it's a hugely popular day-trip destination and the site of Roberto Rossellini's 1949 classic *Stromboli*, starring Ingrid Bergman.

principal transport hub and the nearest thing that islanders have to a capital city. Atop a volcanic crag sits the town's charming citadel, which is guarded by 16th-century walls. A busy little port with a pretty, pastel-coloured seafront and plenty of accommodation, it makes the best base for island hopping.

A boat tour around Lipari is a good way of seeing the island, and the only way of getting to some of the more inaccessible swimming points (unless you rent your own boat). Away from the more obvious coastal pleasures, there's some lovely hiking on Lipari. Most walks involve fairly steep slopes, although the summer heat is as likely to wear you down as the terrain.

p371

**The Drive »** Catch the ferry at the Via Tenente M Amendola for the 45-minute ride to Salina. Once there, it's about 7km to the town of Salina on the SP182.

### 9 Salina

In stark contrast to the exposed volcanic terrain of the other Aeolian Islands, Salina boasts a lush, verdant landscape, supporting the Aeolians' famous Malvasia wine as well as the fat, juicy capers that flavour many local dishes. Salina's main port, **Santa Marina Salina** is a typical island settlement with a lively main drag and steeply stacked houses rising up the hillside.

For jaw-dropping views, climb to Salina's (and indeed the Aeolians') highest point, **Monte Fossa delle Felci** (962m). And seek out the gorgeous beach at Pollara, featured in the 1994 film *Il Postino*.

p371

# Eating & Sleeping

## Mt Etna 1

### Agriturismo San Marco — Agriturismo €

(☎389 423 7294; www.agriturismosanmarco.com; Rovittello, Castiglione di Sicilia; per person B&B/half-board/full board €35/53/68) This delightful *agriturismo* on Mt Etna's north slope requires a drive and a good map, but the bucolic setting, rustic rooms and superb country cooking more than compensate. Call ahead for directions.

## Taormina 3

### Al Duomo — Sicilian €€

(☎094 262 56 56; Vico Ebrei 11; meals €35-40, tasting menu €60; ⏲lunch & dinner, closed Mon Nov-Mar) Right in the heart of the action, this highly acclaimed restaurant specialises in traditional, even historic, regional cuisine – among its specialities are *fava a maccu* (fava-bean puree), stewed lamb, and fresh fish with olives and capers.

### Licchio's — Seafood €€

(☎0942 62 53 27; Via Patricio 10; meals €30-40; ⏲lunch & dinner, closed Thu Nov-Mar) The seafood antipasti at this classy little eatery are delicious and varied enough to constitute a meal in themselves, but the menu is full of other enticements: tempura-fried zucchini flowers, fabulously fresh spinach-ricotta gnocchi, and divine desserts.

### Isoco Guest House — B&B €

(☎0942 2 36 79; www.isoco.it; Via Salita Branco 2; s €65-120, d €85-120; ⏲Mar-Nov; P ❄ @) Every room in this exceptionally welcoming, gay-friendly B&B is dedicated to an artist – from the angels of Botticelli to the sculpted buttocks of the Herb Ritts room. The excellent breakfast, sun decks and outdoor Jacuzzi are great as well.

## Lipari 8

### E Pulera — Sicilian €€

(☎090 981 11 58; www.pulera.it; Via Isabella Vainicher Conti; meals €35-45; ⏲dinner Apr-Sep) This especially romantic restaurant features specialities like *pecorino* cheese with balsamic vinegar and fresh mint, and swordfish caked in ground almonds. Service and wine list are also excellent. Reservations are required.

### Casajanca — Guesthouse €€

(☎090 988 02 22; ww.casajanca.it; Marina Garibladi 115, Località Canneto; d €60-200; ⏲May-Oct) Just off the beach at Canneto, this charming little hotel's 10 rooms are impeccably decorated with polished antiques. The dappled courtyard is perfect for breakfast, and boasts a natural thermal water pool that's perfect for winter stays.

## Salina 9

### Da Alfredo — Sandwich Shop €

(Piazza Marina Garibaldi, Lingua; granite €2.50, sandwiches €7-10) This place is renowned all over Sicily for its *granite:* ices made with coffee, fresh fruit or locally grown pistachios and almonds. It's also worth a visit for its *pane cunzato* – open-faced sandwiches piled high with tuna, ricotta, eggplant, tomatoes, capers and olives.

### Hotel Signum — Hotel €€€

(☎090 984 42 22; www.hotelsignum.it; Via Scalo 15; d €130-280) Salina's best hotel boasts antique-clad rooms, a terrace restaurant, a fabulous wellness centre complete with natural spa baths, and a superb infinity pool looking straight out to smoking Stromboli.

**Noto** *Baroque beauties await in this grand town*

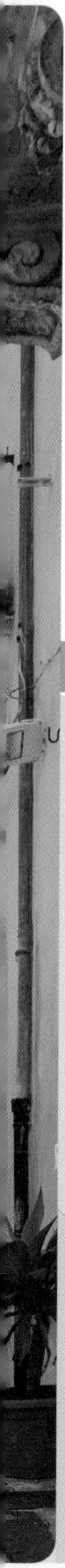

# Sicilian Baroque

*From the sparkling blue waters of the Ionic Sea to the hills and gorges of the interior, this trip stars a series of Unesco-listed towns that showcase Sicily's version of baroque grandeur.*

## TRIP HIGHLIGHTS

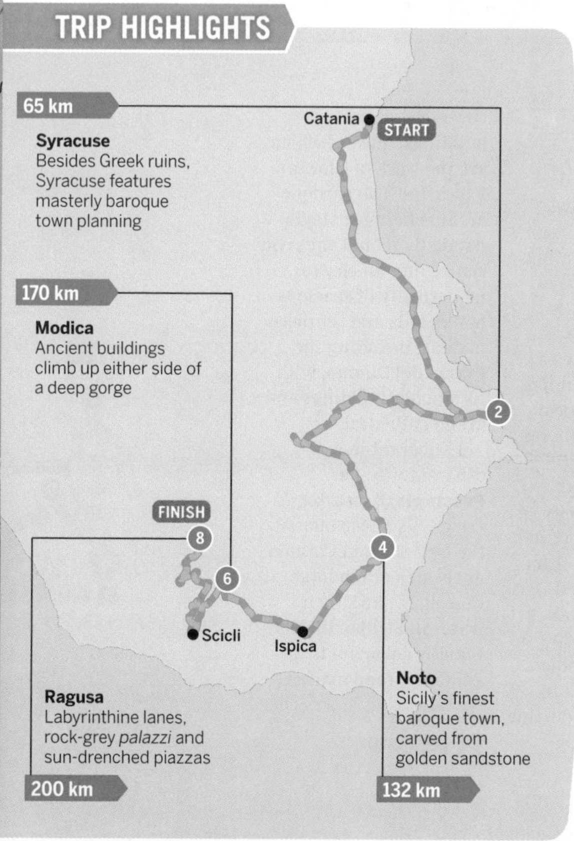

65 km
**Syracuse**
Besides Greek ruins, Syracuse features masterly baroque town planning

170 km
**Modica**
Ancient buildings climb up either side of a deep gorge

Catania START

2

FINISH 8

6

4

Scicli

Ispica

**Ragusa**
Labyrinthine lanes, rock-grey *palazzi* and sun-drenched piazzas
200 km

**Noto**
Sicily's finest baroque town, carved from golden sandstone
132 km

**5 DAYS**
**200KM / 124 MILES**

**GREAT FOR...**

**BEST TIME TO GO**

Spring and autumn bring fewer crowds and better weather for hiking in the hillsides of the Monti Iblei.

A night-time shot of Noto's Corso Vittorio Emanuele.

Wander the labyrinthine lanes of Ragusa Ibla.

# 36 Sicilian Baroque

Dominated by the Monti Iblei hills, this journey through Sicily's southeast takes you to some of the island's most beautiful towns. Shattered by a devastating earthquake in 1693, they were rebuilt in Sicily's own brand of baroque, lending the region a rare, honey-coloured cohesion and collective beauty. The towns sit delightfully amid a region of rich citrus and olive groves, and checkerboard fields shot through with limestone cliffs and rocky gorges.

## 1 Catania

Though surrounded by ugly urban sprawl, Catania's baroque heart is lively and captivating exactly because this is a working city rather than a boutique resort. A thriving centre with a large university, it has a tough, resilient local population that adheres to the motto of *carpe diem* (seize the day).

It is also a true city of the volcano, much of it being constructed from the lava that poured down from Mt Etna's slopes during a 1669 eruption. The baroque centre is lava-black in colour, as if a fine dusting of soot permanently covers its elegant buildings, most of which are the work of Giovanni Vaccarini. The baroque architect almost single-handedly rebuilt the civic centre into an elegant, modern city of spacious boulevards and set-piece piazzas, including the **Piazza del Duomo**, with its sinuous buildings and grand cathedral.

Exuberant in a different way, **La Pescheria** (Fish Market; Via Pardo; ⌚7am-2pm) offers the best show in Catania as theatrical vendors raucously hawk their wares in Sicilian dialect. Equally colourful is the adjoining **food market** (Via Naumachia; ⌚7am-3pm).

p379

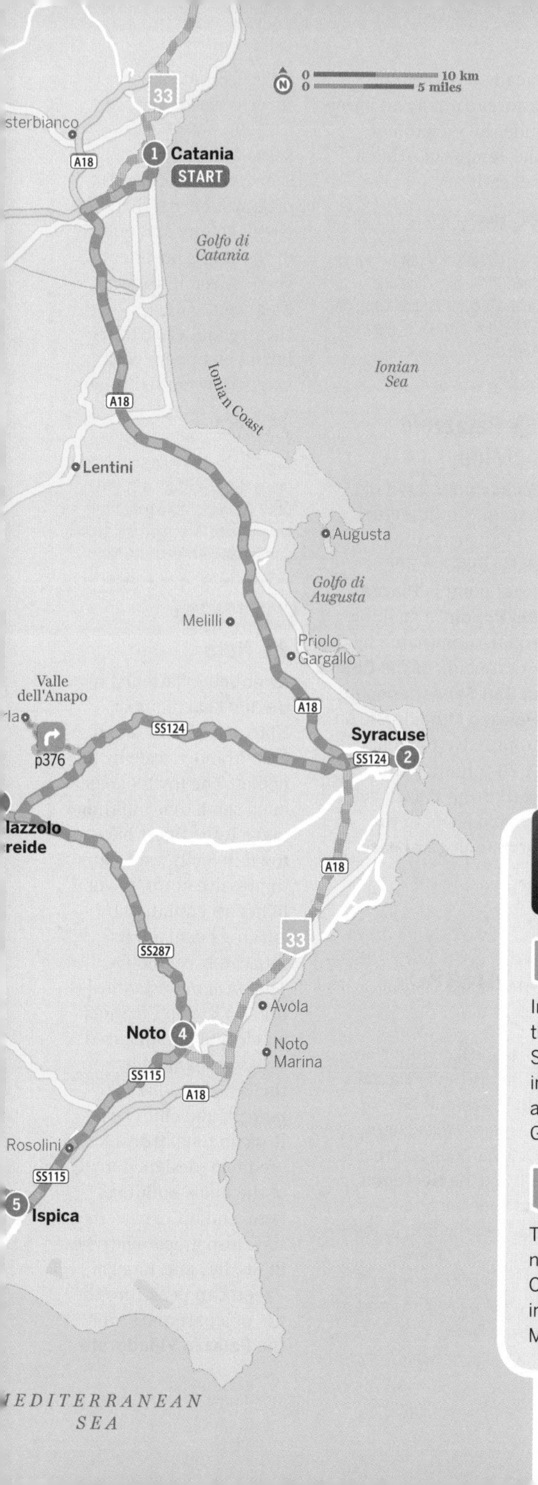

0 10 km
0 5 miles

sterbianco
A18
1 Catania
START
33
Golfo di Catania
Ionian Coast
Ionian Sea
A18
Lentini
Augusta
Golfo di Augusta
Melilli
Priolo Gargallo
Valle dell'Anapo
p376
SS124
A18
Syracuse
SS124 2
lazzolo
reide
A18
33
SS287
Avola
Noto 4
Noto Marina
SS115
A18
Rosolini
SS115
5 Ispica
MEDITERRANEAN SEA

**The Drive ›› From Catania to Syracuse, it is a 72km drive along the A18. This is orange-growing country and you'll see many orchards, which are gorgeously fragrant when in bloom. Exit onto SS124 for the short 4km jaunt into central Syracuse.**

TRIP HIGHLIGHT

## 2 Syracuse

Settled by colonists from Corinth in 734 BC, Syracuse was considered the most beautiful city of the ancient world, rivalling Athens in power and prestige. You can still encounter the city's ancient heart at the extraordinary **Parco Archeologico della Neapolis** (☎0931 6 50 68; Viale Paradis; adult/reduced €9/4.50; ⏰9am-1hr before sunset, to 4.30pm during theatre festival), the

## LINK YOUR TRIP

### 33 Wonders of Ancient Sicily

In Catania, you can join the grand tour of Ancient Sicily, which begins in Arab-inflected Palermo and ends at Taormina's spectacular Greek theatre (p343).

### 34 Into the Madonie Mountains

Take the A19 then A20 north from Catania to Cefalù to pick up this trip into the craggy peaks of the Madonie Mountains (p357).

star attraction of which is the huge 5th-century-BC Greek theatre. In the wake of the 1693 earthquake, Syracuse, like the rest of the cities in the region, got a baroque facelift. You can see a number of baroque masterpieces at the **Museo Regionale d'Arte Medioevale e Moderna** (☎0931 6 95 11; www.regione.sicilia.it/beniculturali/palazzobellomo; Via Capodieci 16; adult/reduced €8/4; ⏰9am-7pm Tue-Sat, to 1pm Sun), which is housed in a 13th-century *palazzo* (mansion). However, the real masterpiece is the **Piazza del Duomo**, considered a marvel of baroque town planning. But despite its baroque veneer, the Greek essence of Syracuse is everywhere in evidence, including the baroque **duomo** (Piazza del Duomo; ⏰8am-7pm). Even the sumptuous facade designed by Andrea Palma can barely hide the skeleton of the Temple of Athena beneath.

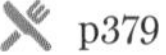 p379

**The Drive »** From Syracuse, head through rolling and unspoilt countryside along the SS124 for 42km to Palazzolo Acreide.

## ❸ Palazzolo Acreide

A charming town of baroque architecture and ancient ruins, Palazzolo Acreide's focal point is **Piazza del Popolo**, a striking square dominated by the ornate bulk of the **Chiesa di San Sebastiano** and **Palazzo Municipale**, an impressive town hall. A 20-minute uphill walk from Piazza del Popolo leads to the **archaeological park** (☎0931 88 14 99; Colle dell'Acromonte; admission €4; ⏰9am-7pm Mon-Sat & 9am-5pm Sun Apr-Oct, 9am-4pm Mon-Sat Nov-Mar) of Akrai, once a thriving Greek colony and one of the area's best-kept secrets. You'll discover an ancient Greek theatre and Christian burial chambers with exquisitely carved reliefs.

✕ p379

**The Drive »** Head southeast along the SS287 for a 30km drive through more beautiful countryside. The road will grow curvier as you head into Noto.

TRIP HIGHLIGHT

## ❹ Noto

After being flattened by the 1693 earthquake, Noto was rebuilt on an even grander scale by its nobles. The town's golden-hued sandstone buildings make it the finest baroque town in Sicily, especially impressive at night when lights accentuate the curving beauty of its intricately carved facades. The *pièce de résistance* is Corso Vittorio Emanuele, an elegantly manicured walkway flanked by thrilling baroque *palazzi* and churches. Rosario Gagliardi, a local architect, designed many of the finest buildings here, and his extroverted style also graces churches in Modica and Ragusa.

You can peak into the life of a baroque baron at the **Palazzo Villadorata**

### DETOUR: VALLE DELL'ANAPO

**Start: ❷ Syracuse**

For some beautifully wild and unspoilt countryside, turn off the SS124 between Syracuse and Palazzolo Acreide and head down into the beautiful Valle dell'Anapo – a deep limestone gorge. Follow signs to **Ferla**, with its small but lovely baroque centre. Another 11km past Ferla, you'll find the **Necropoli di Pantalica** (admission free), an important Iron and Bronze Age necropolis. Dating from the 13th to the 8th century BC, it is an extensive area of limestone rocks honeycombed by more than 5000 tombs. There's no ticket office – just a car park at the end of the long, winding road down from Ferla.

SALVATOR BARKI/GETTY IMAGES ©

**Ragusa** Views over the historic city

(☎320 55 68 038; www.palazzonicolaci.it, in Italian; Via Nicolaci; adult/reduced €4/2; ⏲10am-1pm & 3-7.30pm), once a private palace. The decor is as opulent as the facade, with heavy glass chandeliers, frescoed ceilings, and wall paintings designed to look like brocaded wallpaper.

✕ p379

**The Drive »** Head southwest 22km along SS115 through more fields and orchards, passing through the town of Rosolini. Hilltop Ispica will rise up in front of you. Catch the sharply winding SP47 to the town centre.

## 5 Ispica

On the way from Noto to Modica, this hilltop town boasts a number of fine baroque buildings. However, the real reason to stop is to peer into the **Cava d'Ispica**. Stretching for some 13km between Modica and Ispica, this verdant gorge is studded with thousands of natural caves and grottoes. Over the millennia, the caves have served as Neolithic tombs, early Christian catacombs and medieval dwellings.

**The Drive »** Start this 19km leg on the SS115 through relatively flat agricultural land. As you reach the suburbs of Noto, follow signs to Via Nazionale and then to Corso Umberto I, the town's main drag.

TRIP HIGHLIGHT

## 6 Modica

Modica is a wonderfully atmospheric town with ancient medieval buildings climbing steeply up either side of a deep gorge. But unlike some of the other Unesco-listed cities in the area, it doesn't package its treasures into a single easy-to-see street or central piazza.

## LOCAL KNOWLEDGE: HITTING THE HIGH NOTE

Catania's most famous native son, Vincenzo Bellini (1801–1835), is the quintessential composer of bel canto opera. With his inimitable ability to combine sensuality with melodic clarity, he still woos audiences today. **Museo Belliniano** (☎095 715 05 35; Piazza San Francesco 3; ⏰9am-1pm Mon-Sat), in the composer's former Catania home, has an interesting collection of his memorabilia. Catania's lavish, 19th-century **Teatro Massimo Bellini** (☎095 730 61 11; www.teatromassimobellini.it; Via Perrotta 12) is the place to hear *I Puritani*, *Norma* and his other masterworks. At the time of writing, the theatre was closed for renovation.

The highlight is the baroque **Chiesa di San Giorgio** (Corso San Giorgio; ⏰9am-noon & 4-7pm), which stands in isolated splendour atop a majestic 250-step staircase.

**Corso Umberto I** is the place to lap up the lively local atmosphere. A wide avenue flanked by graceful palaces, churches, restaurants, bars and boutiques, it is here that locals come to parade during the evening *passeggiata*. Originally a raging river ran through town, but after major flood damage in 1902 it was dammed and Corso Umberto I was built over it.

🛏 p379

**The Drive »** From Modica to Scicli, wind your way southwest along the SP54 for 12km through rugged country.

### 7 Scicli

This pleasant country town boasts a small but charming baroque centre, including the pretty, palm-fringed **Piazza Italia**. Overlooking everything is a rocky peak topped by an abandoned church, the **Chiesa di San Matteo**. The 10-minute walk up rewards you with fine views over the town.

**The Drive »** The first half of this 26km stretch winds north on SP94, passing along the rim of a pretty canyon typical of the region. Then catch the winding SS115 as it heads up to Ragusa. Across a small canyon, you will see the old, hillside historic centre of Ragusa rising grandly.

TRIP HIGHLIGHT

### 8 Ragusa

Set amid rocky peaks, Ragusa Ibla – Ragusa's historic centre – is a joy to wander, with its labyrinthine lanes weaving through rock-grey *palazzi*, then opening suddenly onto beautiful, sun-drenched piazzas. After the 1693 earthquake, the aristocracy, ever optimistic, rebuilt Ragusa on exactly the same spot. It's easy to get lost but you can never go too far wrong, and sooner or later you'll end up at **Piazza Duomo**, Ragusa's sublime central square. At the top end of the sloping square is the town's pride and joy, the 1744 **Cattedrale di San Giorgio** (⏰10am-12.30pm & 4-6.30pm), set high on a grand staircase. It's one of Rosario Gagliardi's finest accomplishments; the extravagant convex facade rises like a three-tiered wedding cake supported by gradually narrowing Corinthian columns.

Atop the hill sits Ragusa Superiore, a busy town with all the trappings of a modern provincial capital.

p379

# Eating & Sleeping

## Catania 1

**Trattoria di De Fiore** Trattoria €

(☎095 31 62 83; Via Coppola 24/26; meals €15-25; closed Mon) This neighbourhood trattoria is presided over by septuagenarian chef Mamma Rosanna, who uses organic flour and fresh local ingredients to recreate her great-grandmother's recipes. Service is slow, but worth the wait.

**5 Balconi B&B** B&B €

(☎095 723 45 34; www.5balconi.it; Via Plebiscito 133; s €30-35, d €50-65, tr €70-75; ) This great low-end option is in lovingly remodelled antique *palazzo* in a workaday neighbourhood. The gracious owners offer high-ceilinged rooms with shared bathrooms, plus a breakfast featuring local organic bread and fresh fruit.

## Syracuse 2

**Red Moon** Seafood €

(☎0931 603 56; Riva Porto Lachio 36; meals €25; lunch & dinner Thu-Tue) Serving some of the best seafood in Syracuse, this reasonably priced family-run place on the mainland makes a pleasant refuge from the well-worn tourist track.

**Villa dei Papiri** Agriturismo €€

(☎0931 72 13 21; www.villadeipapiri.it; Contrada Cozzo Pantano, Fonte Ciane; d €70-132, 2-person ste €105-154, 4-person ste €140-208; P@) Immersed in orange groves and papyrus reeds 8km outside Syracuse, this lovely *agriturismo* offers suites in a beautifully converted 19th-century farmhouse, plus double rooms set around the lush grounds.

**B&B dei Viaggiatori, Viandanti e Sognatori** B&B €

(☎0931 247 81; www.bedandbreakfastsicily.it; Via Roma 156; s €35-50, d €55-70; ) An old *palazzo* at the end of Via Roma cradles this lovely B&B. Rooms are colourfully and stylishly decorated, with super-comfy beds – there's also a terrace with sweeping sea views.

## Palazzolo Acreide 3

**Il Portico** Sicilian €

(☎0931 88 15 32; Via Orologio 6; pizza from €4, meals €25; closed Tue) This formally decorated restaurant focuses on local Iblean mountain dishes, so expect plenty of grilled meats, mushrooms and cheeses.

## Noto 4

**Ristorante Il Cantuccio** Modern Sicilian €€

(☎0931 83 74 64; Via Cavour 12; meals €30-35; dinner Tue-Sun, lunch Sun) Chef Valentina presents a seasonally changing menu that combines familiar Sicilian ingredients in exciting new ways.

## Modica 6

**Villa Quartarella** Agriturismo €

(☎360 654829; www.quartarella.com; Contrada Quartarella; s €40, d €70-80) Rooms are spacious at this countryside villa south of Modica, and owners Francesco and Francesca are generous in sharing their encyclopaedic knowledge of local history, flora and fauna.

## Ragusa 8

**Ristorante Duomo** Gastronomic €€€

(☎0932 65 12 65; Via Capitano Bocchieri 31; meals €90-100, tasting menus €135-140) Hailed by some as Sicily's best restaurant, Duomo serves nouvelle Sicilian cuisine in a quintet of small rooms outfitted like private parlours, ensuring a suitably romantic atmosphere.

**Capo Testa** *Don't forget your swimsuit in this stunning coastal playground*

WALTER ZERLA/GETTY IMAGES ©

# Emerald Coast

37

*This journey takes you around Sardinia's extraordinary northern coast, a land of wind-carved rocks, pearly white beaches and emerald-green seas that entertain divers and dolphins alike.*

## TRIP HIGHLIGHTS

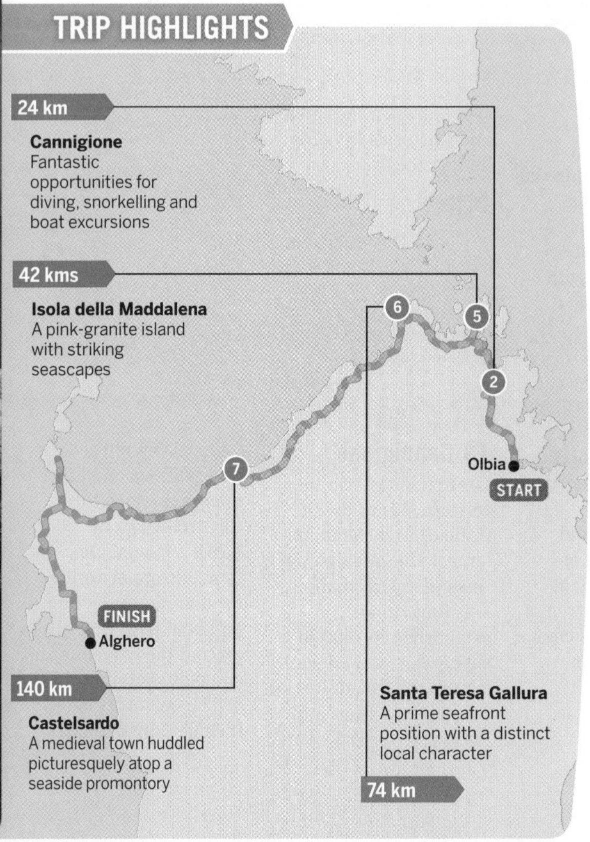

24 km
**Cannigione**
Fantastic opportunities for diving, snorkelling and boat excursions

42 kms
**Isola della Maddalena**
A pink-granite island with striking seascapes

140 km
**Castelsardo**
A medieval town huddled picturesquely atop a seaside promontory

**Santa Teresa Gallura**
A prime seafront position with a distinct local character
74 km

Olbia START
Alghero FINISH

**5–7 DAYS**
**273KM / 170 MILES**

**GREAT FOR...**

**BEST TIME TO GO**

May, June, September and October, for beach weather without huge crowds.

**ESSENTIAL PHOTO**

The bizarre shapes of Capo Testa's natural sculpture garden.

**BEST FOR OUTDOORS**

Dive into the crystalline waters of the Maddalena Archipelago.

# 37 Emerald Coast

From unassuming Olbia, this trip rockets you into the dazzling coastline that the Aga Khan has turned into a playground for oligarchs and their bikini-clad admirers. Head further north, however, and the coast grows wilder, with rocky coves washed by the startlingly blue waters of La Maddalena marine reserve. Rounding Sardinia's northwest corner, popular resorts alternate with timelessly silent stretches of coast, until finally you arrive at lovely, Spanish-inflected Alghero.

## 1 Olbia

Scratch Olbia's industrial outskirts and find a fetching city with a *centro storico* (historic centre) crammed with boutiques, wine bars and cafe-rimmed piazzas. Olbia is also a refreshingly authentic and affordable alternative to the purpose-built resorts stretching to the north and south.

To get a feel of old Olbia, head south of Corso Umberto to the tightly packed warren of streets that represents the original fishing village. You'll find it has a special charm, particularly in the evening when the cafes and trattorias fill with hungry locals.

p387

**The Drive »** Heading north on the SS125 and then the SP13 for this 29km leg, you'll pass through a rocky, sun-bleached landscape that alternates with patchwork farmland.

TRIP HIGHLIGHT

## 2 Cannigione

Cannigione sits on the western side of the Golfo di Arzachena, the largest *ria* (inlet) along this coast. Originally a fishing village established in 1800 to supply the Maddalena islands with food, it is now a prosperous, and reasonably priced, tourist town. Down at the port, various operators offer excursions to the Arcipelago di La Maddalena, plus fantastic opportunities for diving, snorkelling and boat trips that nose around the gorgeous and complex shoreline.

The operators here include **Consorzio del**

**Golfo** (☎0789 8 84 18; www.consorziodelgolfo.it) and **Anthias** (☎0789 8 63 11; www.anthiasdiving.com; Tanca Manna).

**The Drive »** Hugging the coast as you head north along the SP13, this beautiful 8km drive is defined by the famously beautiful blue-green waters of Costa Smerelda. Near the town of Le Saline, you'll see the inlet on which the Capo d'Orso sits.

## LINK YOUR TRIP

### Shadow of Vesuvius

Regular ferries connect Sardinia's Cagliari port with Naples for this journey around the Bay of Naples (p273).

### Historic Sardinia

This trip into the Sardinian heartland starts in Oristano, 105km south of Alghero on the SS292 (p389).

### 3 Capo d'Orso

Watching over the strait that separates Sardinia from Isola della Maddalena, Capo d'Orso (Cape Bear) owes its name to a granite outcropping that, over the millennia, has been modelled by wind and rain to resemble a rather ferocious-looking bear. The ursine enjoys a particularly dramatic view that, in a single sweep of the eye, takes in Sardinia's rugged northern coast, the Arcipelago di La Maddalena and, to the north, the mountains of Corsica.

**The Drive »** From Capo d'Orso, head northwest along the SP121 to Palau, just 5km away.

### 4 Palau

Palau is a lively summer resort and also the main gateway to the granite islands and jewel-coloured waters of the Arcipelago di La Maddalena. Three kilometres west of town, you can tour the **Fortezza di Monte Altura**, a 19th-century sentinel standing guard over the rocky crag. **Petag Boat Tours** (☎0789 70 86 81; www.petag.it; Piazza del Molo 4) offers boat excursions around the Maddalena islands. Trips cost around €35 per person and include lunch and time to swim on famous beaches. Fancy a dive? Check out the **Nautilus Dive Centre** (☎0789 709 058; www.divesardegna.com; Piazza G Fresi 8; ). There's excellent diving in the marine park.

p387

**The Drive »** Actually, it's a sail. From Palau, there are at least hourly passenger and car ferry services to Isola della Maddalena. The journey takes 15 minutes.

TRIP HIGHLIGHT

### 5 Isola della Maddalena

Just over the water from Palau, the pink-granite island of Maddalena lies at the heart of the La Maddalena islands. From the moment you dock at **Cala Gavetta** (La Maddalena's main port), you'll be in the thrall of its cobbled piazzas and infectious holiday atmosphere.

Beyond the harbour, the island offers startlingly lovely seascapes. Divers sing the praises of the sapphire waters here, which are among the cleanest in the Mediterranean and teem with marine life. A 20km panoramic road circles the island, allowing easy access to several attractive bays.

Worth a stop is **La Maddalena Hotel & Yacht Club** (☎0789 794 273; www.lamaddalenahyc.com; Piazza Faravelli, Località Moneta; d €200-500, ste €450-1100; ). After the US Navy withdrew from here in 2008, derelict garrisons were turned into a strikingly contemporary luxury getaway of vast, light-filled spaces and minimalist chic. If your budget doesn't stretch

## DETOUR: ISOLA CAPRERA

**Start: 5 Isola della Maddalena**

Just over a causeway from Isola Maddalena, Isola Caprera was once Giuseppe Garibaldi's 'Eden' – a wild, wonderfully serene island, covered in green pines which look stunning against the ever-present seascape and ragged granite cliffs. The green, shady Caprera is ideal for walking, and there are plenty of trails weaving through the pines. The island's rugged coast is indented with several tempting coves. You can also visit **Compendio Garibaldino** (☎0789 72 71 62; adult/reduced €5/2.50; 9am-7.15pm Tue-Sun), the serene compound the Italian revolutionary built for himself here.

GERMANO ZUCCA/GETTY IMAGES ©

Isola Caprera

to the five-star price tag, you can book a spa treatment or just have a drink at the bar.

The ravishing **Parco Nazionale dell'Arcipelago di La Maddalena** (www.lamaddalenapark.it) consists of seven main islands, including Maddalena, and 40 granite islets, plus several small islands to the south. They form the high points of an underwater valley that once joined Sardinia and Corsica. Over the centuries, the *maestrale* (northwesterly wind) has moulded the granite into bizarre natural sculptures. But the great delight lies in its crystalline waters, which are rich in marine life and also assume priceless shades of emerald, aquamarine and sapphire.

p387

**The Drive »** Hop the ferry back to Palau, then head northeast on the SS133, which will veer off as the SS133bis. Along the 24km, mostly inland, journey you'll pass Mediterranean scrub and granite boulders, with a brief seaside encounter at Porto Pozzo.

TRIP HIGHLIGHT

## 6 Santa Teresa di Gallura

Bright, breezy and relaxed, Santa Teresa di Gallura bags a prime seafront position on Gallura's north coast. The resort gets extremely busy in high season, yet somehow retains a distinct local character. When not on the beach, most people hang out at cafe-lined Piazza Vittorio Emanuele. Otherwise, you can wander up to the 16th-century **Torre di Longonsardo**, a defensive tower near the entrance to **Spiaggia Rena Bianca**, the town's idyllic (but crowded) beach.

Well worth the 4km hike west of Santa Teresa, the small peninsula known as **Capo Testa** resembles a bizarre sculpture garden. Giant boulders lay strewn about the grassy slopes, their weird and wonderful forms the result of centuries of wind erosion. The walk itself is also stunning, passing through boulder-strewn scrub and affording magnificent views of rocky coves and the cobalt Mediterranean. Stop en route for a swim and to admire the views of not-so-distant Corsica.

p387

**The Drive »** It's rugged, hilly terrain on this 70km southwestern route along the SP90, with a brief stint along the winding SS134 to Castelsardo and the sea.

## LOCAL KNOWLEDGE: MUST-TRY SARDINIAN DISHES

» **Zuppa gallurese** Layers of bread and cheese drenched in broth and baked to a crispy crust.

» **Ortidas** Fried sea anemones.

» **Capretto al mirto** Roast kid infused with myrtle.

» **Fregola con cozze e vongole** Sardinian granular pasta with mussels and clams.

» **Mazzafrissa** Creamy fried semolina.

TRIP HIGHLIGHT

### 7 Castelsardo

Medieval Castelsardo huddles atop a high, cone-shaped promontory that juts picturesquely into the Mediterranean. Originally designed as a defensive fort by a 12th-century Genoese family, the dramatic, hilltop *centro storico* is an ensemble of dark alleyways and medieval buildings seemingly melded into the rocky grey peak.

**The Drive »** Hug Sardinia's rugged northern coastline as you head west to Porto Torres along the SS200 and SP81. Head inland and into desolately beautiful country after Porto Torres, heading to Stintino, 63km from Castelsardo, on the SP34.

### 8 Stintino

With its saltpans and hardscrabble landscape, the northwest corner of Sardinia has a particularly desolate feel, especially when the *maestrale* blows in, whipping the *macchia* (Mediterranean scrub) and bleak rocks. But it also shelters the welcoming and laid-back resort town of Stintino and the fabulous **Spiaggia della Pelosa**, one of Sardinia's most celebrated beaches.

**The Drive »** For this 54km drive, head back down south along the SP34 to coastal route SP57, followed by SP69. Soon you will reach the flat agricultural plain just north of Alghero. Then it's a straight shot on SS291 into Alghero itself.

### 9 Alghero

For many people a trip to Sardinia means a trip to Alghero, the main resort in the northwest and an easy flight from many European cities. Although largely given over to tourism, the town has managed to avoid many of its worst excesses, and it retains a proud and independent spirit.

The main focus is the picturesque *centro storico*, one of the best preserved in Sardinia. Enclosed by robust, honey-coloured seawalls, this is a tightly knit enclave of shady cobbled lanes, Spanish Gothic *palazzi* (mansions) and cafe-lined squares. Below, yachts crowd the marina and long, sandy beaches curve away to the north. Hanging over everything is a palpable Spanish atmosphere, a hangover of the city's past as a Catalan colony. Even today, more than three centuries after the Iberians left, the Catalan tongue is still spoken and street signs and menus are often in both languages. Alghero also boasts a long, sandy, family-friendly beach.

p387

# Eating & Sleeping

## Olbia 1

**Ristorante Gallura** Sardinian €€€

(0789 2 46 48; Corso Umberto 145; meals €40-60; Tue-Sun) Rita runs a tight ship at the homely Gallura, one of northern Sardinia's best restaurants. Fresh seasonal ingredients go into specialities like sea anemones fried in yogurt, and suckling pig perfumed with myrtle.

**Hotel Panorama** Hotel €€

(0789 266 56; www.hotelpanoramaolbia.it; Via Mazzini 7; s €65-119, d €79-159; P) The rooftop terrace of this friendly, central hotel has unbeatable views of city, sea and Monte Limbara. Rooms are spacious and contemporary, with gleaming wood floors and marble bathrooms.

## Palau 4

**San Giorgio** Pizzeria, Seafood €€

(0789 70 80 07; Via La Maddalena 4; pizza €6-9, meals €30; Wed-Mon) The open-plan kitchen tells you all you need to know about this pizzeria-cum-restaurant. Grilled fish and spaghetti *allo scoglio* (with mixed seafood) are excellent bets.

**L'Orso e Il Mare** B&B €

(331 222 20 00; www.orsoeilmare.com; Vicolo Diaz 1; d €60-100, tr €70-120; ) Pietro gives a genuinely warm welcome at this B&B, just steps from Piazza Fresi. The spacious rooms sport breezy blue-and-white colour schemes. Breakfast is a fine spread.

## Isola della Maddalena 5

**B&B Petite Maison** B&B €

(0789 73 84 32; www.lapetitmaison.net; Via Livenza 7, La Maddalena; d €70-110) Liberally sprinkled with paintings and art-deco furnishings, this B&B is a five-minute amble from the main square and offers excellent breakfasts in a bougainvillea-draped garden. Credit cards (and kids) are not accepted.

## Santa Teresa di Gallura 6

**Il Chiostro** Seafood €€

(0789 74 10 56; Porto Turistico; meals €25-45) Overlooking the marina, this inviting restaurant prides itself on the freshness of its fish. Try to snag a table on the terrace.

**B&B Domus de Janas** B&B €€

(338 499 02 21; www.bbdomusdejanas.it; Via Carlo Felice 20a; d €60-120, tr €80-140; ) Daria and Simon are your affable hosts at this sweet B&B in the centre of town. Rooms are cheery, and the terrace boasts cracking sea views.

## Alghero 9

**La Botteghina** Sardinian €€

(079 97 38 375; www.labotteghina.biz; Via Principe Umberto 63; meals €25-30) A crisp new place in the *centro storico*, La Botteghina only deals in food from small, local producers. Try the *fregola* (small pasta made similar to couscous) with seafood.

**Angedras Hotel** Hotel €€

(079 973 50 34; www.angedras.it; Via Frank 2; s €60-140, d €75-150; @) A model of whitewashed Mediterranean style, the Angedras has bright rooms with big French doors opening onto sunny patios. It's a good 15-minute walk south from the *centro storico*.

***Oristano*** *Come for Carnevale, or to wander the historic centre*

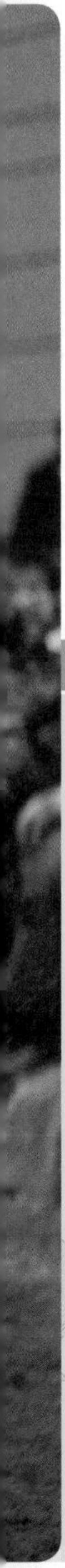

# Historic Sardinia

*Head straight into the wild heart of Sardinia, a strange landscape littered with citadels of the Bronze Age Nuragic people and isolated mountain towns legendary for feuding and banditry.*

## TRIP HIGHLIGHTS

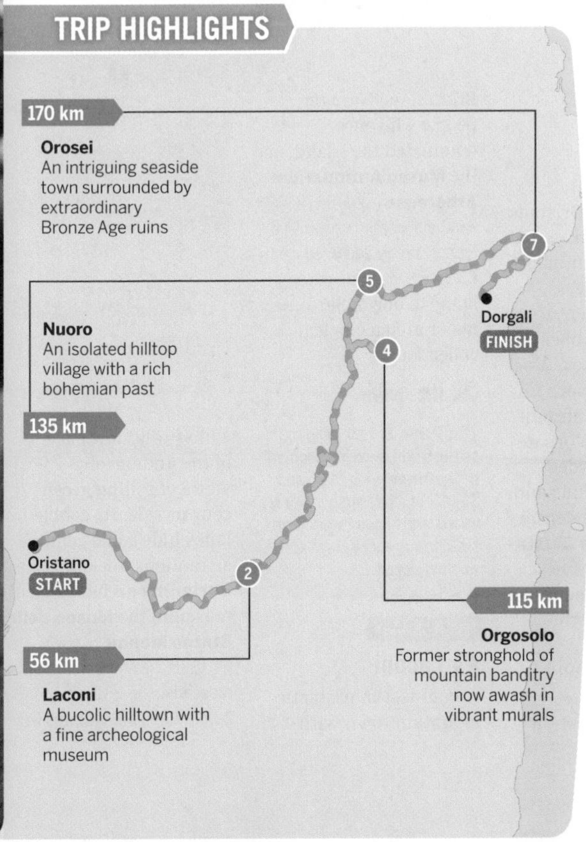

170 km

**Orosei**
An intriguing seaside town surrounded by extraordinary Bronze Age ruins

**Nuoro**
An isolated hilltop village with a rich bohemian past

135 km

Dorgali
FINISH

Oristano
START

115 km

**Orgosolo**
Former stronghold of mountain banditry now awash in vibrant murals

56 km

**Laconi**
A bucolic hilltown with a fine archeological museum

**7 DAYS**
**234KM / 145 MILES**

**GREAT FOR...**

**BEST TIME TO GO**

March to May for wildflowers and green hillsides.

**ESSENTIAL PHOTO**

Capture the granite peak of Monte Ortobene, Nuoro's spectacular backdrop.

**BEST FOR OUTDOORS**

Great hikes abound around Dorgali.

# 38 Historic Sardinia

This trip immerses you in Sardinia's strange and captivating hinterlands. You will discover remnants of the prehistoric *nuraghi* (Bronze Age fortified settlements) and the lonesome villages of the Barbagia, which are still steeped in bandit legend. You'll end up in the wilds of the eastern coast, where limestone mountains and deep canyons roll down to the aquamarine waves of the Golfo di Orosei.

## 1 Oristano

Sardinia's most important city in medieval times, Oristano has a historic centre that still preserves reminders of former greatness, including 12th-century towers and a number of Gothic churches. It's also a pleasant place to wander, with its elegant shopping streets, ornate piazzas and crowded cafes. Located 3km south of town, the 12th-century **Basilica di Santa Giusta** – one of Sardinia's finest Tuscan-style Romanesque churches – is worth seeking out.

The region around Oristano was an important centre of the Bronze Age Nuragic people who once dominated the island, and the **Museo Antiquarium Arborense** (☎0783 79 12 62; www.antiquariumarborense.it; Piazza Corrias; adult/reduced €3/1; ⊙9am-2pm & 3-8pm) is home to one of Sardinia's major archaeological collections.

p395

**The Drive »** Your main routes on the 58km drive to Laconi will be the meandering SP35 and SS442. You'll traverse a widely varied land of patchwork farms, small towns, rocky crags and wooded slopes.

TRIP HIGHLIGHT

## 2 Laconi

Laconi is a charismatic mountain town with a blissfully slow pace of life and bucolic views of rolling green countryside. Its cobbled lanes hide some genuine attractions, including an intriguing archaeological museum, the **Museo delle Statue Menhir** (☎0782 69 32 38; Via Amsicora; adult/reduced €5/3; ⊙10am-1pm & 3-6pm Tue-Sun). Occupying

an elegant 19th-century *palazzo* (mansion), this museum beautifully exhibits a collection of 40 menhirs – starkly anthropomorphic slabs probably connected with prehistoric funerary rites.

Just outside town, **Parco Laconi** (⏲8am-7pm summer, to 4pm winter) is

## LINK YOUR TRIP

### 25 Shadow of Vesuvius

Regular ferries connect Sardinia's port of Cagliari with Naples to pick up this trip from the ruins of Pompeii to the slopes of Vesuvius (p273).

### 37 Emerald Coast

Starting 83km up the coast from Orosei, this trip reveals Sardinia's wind-carved northern coast (p381).

a gorgeous 22-hectare park with exotic trees, lakes, grottoes, great views and the remains of 11th-century **Castello Aymerich**.

p395

The Drive » For this 27km leg, you'll head northeast along the SS128 and then the SS295 as you enter a wilder, more barren landscape, eventually reaching the pine-covered slopes around Aritzo.



## 3 Aritzo

With its cool climate and Alpine character, this vivacious mountain resort (elevation 796m) has been attracting visitors since the 19th century, when it caught the imagination of boar-hunting Piedmontese nobility. But long before tourism took off, the village flourished thanks to its lucrative trade in snow gathering. For five centuries, Aritzo supplied the whole of Sardinia with ice, and snow farmers, known as *niargios*, collected the white stuff from the slopes of **Punta di Funtana Cungiada** (1458m) and stored it in straw-lined wooden chests before sending it off to the high tables of Cagliari.

The Drive » Heading northeast along the Via Marginigola, turn onto the sharply curving SP7 for the 60km to Orgosolo through the deserted mountains and valleys of central Sardinia. At the town of Mamoiada, the SP22 will wind sharply up to Orgosolo.

TRIP HIGHLIGHT

## 4 Orgosolo

High in the brooding mountains, Orgosolo is Sardinia's most notorious town, its name long a byword for the banditry and bloody feuds that once blighted this region. Between 1901 and 1950, the village was averaging a murder every two months as rival families feuded over a disputed inheritance. In the 1950s and '60s, feuding gave way to more lucrative kidnapping, led by the village's most infamous son, Graziano Mesina, a self-styled Robin Hood.

The problem of violence now largely resolved, Orgosolo is drawing visitors with the vibrant graffiti-style **murals** that adorn its town centre. Like satirical caricatures, they depict all the big political events of the 20th century and are often very moving. But in the evening, the villagers reclaim their streets – the old boys staring at anyone they don't recognise and the lads with crew cuts racing up and down in their mud-splattered cars.

p395

The Drive » For the 26km to Nuoro, head back down the SP22 to Mamoiada, and take the SS389 northeast through a particularly sun-bleached landscape of cacti and maquis.

TRIP HIGHLIGHT

## 5 Nuoro

Once an isolated hilltop village synonymous with banditry, Nuoro had its cultural renaissance in the 19th and early 20th centuries, attracting a hotbed of artistic talent, from author Grazia Deledda to sculptor Francesco Ciusa. This legacy is reflected in the fine **Museo d'Arte**

Dorgali

(☎0784 25 21 10; www.museoman.it; Via Satta 15; adult/reduced €3/2; ⏰10am-1pm & 4.30-8.30pm Tue-Sun). The only serious contemporary art gallery in Sardinia, it displays more than 400 works by the island's top 20th-century painters. Nuoro is also home to the **Museo della Vita e delle Tradizioni Sarde** (☎0784 25 70 35; Via Antonio Mereu 56; adult/reduced €3/1; ⏰9am-8pm daily summer, 9am-1pm & 3-6pm Tue-Sun winter), a peerless collection of Sardinian arts and crafts, from filigree jewellery and rich embroidery to weapons and masks.

The city's spectacular backdrop is the granite peak of **Monte Ortobene** (955m). Capped by a 7m-high bronze statue of the Redentore (Christ the Redeemer), it makes for good hiking.

p395

**The Drive »** Head 33km east along SS129 as mountains give way to a green and ochre checkerboard of farmland.

## 6 Galtelli

Crouched at the foot of **Monte Tuttavista** and hemmed in by olive groves, vineyards and sheep-nibbled pastures, Galtelli is quite the village idyll. Its tiny medieval centre is a joy to wander, with narrow lanes twisting to old stone houses and sun-dappled piazzas. If you fancy tiptoeing off the map for a while, this is the place.

**The Drive »** It's a quick and relatively straight 9km jaunt along SS129 to Orosei, as rugged limestone peaks rear up again on your right.

TRIP HIGHLIGHT

## 7 Orosei

Scenically positioned at the gulf's northernmost point and surrounded

## DETOUR: GOLA SU GORROPU & TISCALI

**Start: 8 Dorgali**

Dubbed the 'Grand Canyon of Europe', the **Gola Su Gorropu** (☎328 897 65 63; www.gorropu.info; adult/reduced €5/3; ⏰tours 10.30am-3.30pm) is a spectacular gorge flanked by vertical 400m rock walls that, at their narrowest point, stand just 4m apart. The day-long return hike down to and through the canyon floor takes you into a strangely silent world of gnarled holm oaks, sheer limestone slopes and pockmarked cliffs. There are two main approach routes. The more dramatic begins from the car park opposite Hotel Silana at the **Genna 'e Silana** pass on the SS125 at kilometre 183. The second and slightly easier route is via the **Sa Barva bridge** over the Rio Flumineddu, about 15km from Dorgali.

Also at the Sa Barva bridge is the trailhead for the walk to one of Sardinia's archaeological highlights. Hidden in a mountaintop cave deep in the Valle Lanaittu is the Nuragic village of **Tiscali** (adult/reduced €5/2; ⏰9am-7pm summer, to 5pm winter). The hike up to the village is part of the pleasure, as you strike into the heart of the limestone Supramonte highlands. You'll need sturdy footwear for some easy rock hopping, but most of the path – marked with red arrows – is easygoing, and canopies of juniper and cork oaks afford shady respite. Allow five hours for the return hike, including breaks and visiting Tiscali.

by marble quarries and fruit orchards, Orosei is an unsung treasure. Over the centuries the silting of the Cedrino river, plus malaria, pirate raids and Spanish neglect, took their toll on the town, once an important Pisan port. However, its demise left behind an atmospheric historic centre laced with cobbled lanes, pretty stone-built houses, medieval churches and leafy piazzas.

Just south of town lies one of Sardinia's most extraordinary *nuraghe*. Follow signs along the Cala Gonone–Dorgali road to **Nuraghe Mannu** (adult/reduced €3/2; ⏰9am-noon & 3-6pm winter, to 7pm summer). First inhabited around 1600 BC, the ruins are modest but set picturesquely above a lush gorge. The ruins captured ancient Roman imaginations too, and you can see the rectilinear remnants for their constructions alongside the elliptical shapes of their predecessors.

p395

**The Drive »** From the plains around Orosei, head southwest on the SS125 for 21km. Expect glimpses of both mountains and sea as you wind your way to Dorgali.

### 8 Dorgali

Nestled at the foot of **Monte Bardia** and framed by vineyards and olive groves, Dorgali is a down-to-earth town with a grandiose backdrop. Its pastel-coloured houses and steep, narrow streets are charming, and the town is also famous for its leatherwork. However, the best thing about Dorgali is its spectacular natural environs, above all the nearby Gola Su Gorropu, about 15km south of town.

p395

# Eating & Sleeping

## Oristano 1

**Trattoria Gino** Trattoria €€

(☎0783 714 28; Via Tirso 13; meals €25-30; ⊙Mon-Sat) This wonderful and simple trattoria set in one neat room has offered excellent local cuisine since the 1930s, from sage-and-ricotta ravioli to char-grilled cuttlefish studded with fresh cherry tomatoes.

**Eleonora B&B** B&B €

(☎0783 704 35; www.eleonora-bed-and-breakfast.com; Piazza Eleonora d'Arborea 12; s €35-50, d €60-70, apt €80; ❄) This particularly charming B&B is housed in a medieval *palazzo* on Oristano's central piazza. The rooms are tastefully decorated with antique furniture, with floors covered in gorgeous old tiles.

## Laconi 2

**Albergo Ristorante Sardegna** Sardinian €€

(☎0782 86 90 33; www.albergosardegna.it; meals €25-30) By the northern entrance to the village, this family-run restaurant serves good old-fashioned Sardinian cooking such as *culurgiones* (ravioli) and pasta with *cinghiale* (wild boar) *ragù*.

## Orgosolo 4

**Portico** Pizzeria €

(☎0784 40 29 29; Via Giovanni XXIII; pizza €3.50-6, meals €15-20) This excellent pizzeria-cum-restaurant serves fulsome, woody pizzas and superb local vegetables and meats. The airy dining room and friendly service add to the pleasure.

## Nuoro 5

**La Locanda** Sardinian €

(☎0784 3 10 32; Via Brofferio 31; meals €15-20; ⊙Mon-Sat) It's all about the food at this friendly, down-to-earth trattoria. The set lunch at €10 is a bargain to write home about.

**Silvia e Paolo** B&B €

(☎0784 312 80; www.silviaepaolo.it, Corso Garibaldi 58; s €30-35, d €50-60, tr €70; ❄@) Silvia and Paolo run this sweet B&B. Family treasures from dolls to old leather trunks make you feel right at home in the bright, spacious rooms. There's also a roof terrace for observing the action on Corso Garibaldi.

## Orosei 7

**La Taverna** Sardinian €€

(☎0784 99 83 30; Piazza G Marconi 6; meals €25-30; ⊙May-Oct) Tuck into fresh gulf fish and earthy meat dishes such as wild boar at this authentic taverna. It spills out onto a tree-shaded square just off Piazza Sas Animas.

## Dorgali 8

**Ristorante Colibrí** Sardinian €€

(☎0784 9 60 54; Via Gramsci 14; meals €30; ⊙Mon-Sat) Tucked away in an incongruous residential area (follow the signs), this is the bee's knees for meat eaters, with dishes like wild boar with rosemary and *porceddu* (traditional suckling pig).

**Sa Corte Antica** B&B €

(☎0784 9 43 17; www.sacorteantica.it; Via Mannu 17; d €50-60, tr €65-75; ❄) Gathered around an old stone courtyard, this B&B radiates old-world charm, with traditional reed ceilings, wrought-iron bedsteads and homemade bread at breakfast.

# ROAD TRIP ESSENTIALS

# Italy Driving Guide

*Italy's stunning natural scenery, comprehensive road network and passion for cars makes it a wonderful road-trip destination.*

### Driving Fast Facts

- **Right or left?** Drive on the right
- **Manual or automatic?** Mostly manual
- **Legal driving age** 18
- **Top speed limit** 130km/h to 150km/h (on autostradas)
- **Signature car** Flaming red Ferrari or Fiat 500

## DRIVING LICENCE & DOCUMENTS

When driving in Italy you are required to carry with you:

- The vehicle registration document
- Your driving licence
- Proof of third-party liability insurance

### Driving Licence

- All EU member states' driving licences are fully recognised throughout Europe.
- Travellers from other countries should obtain an International Driving Permit (IDP) through their national automobile association. This should be carried with your licence; it is not a substitute for it.
- No licence is needed to ride a scooter under 50cc. To ride a motorcycle or scooter up to 125cc, you'll need a licence (a car licence will do). For motorcycles over 125cc you need a motorcycle licence.

## INSURANCE

- Third-party liability insurance is mandatory for all vehicles in Italy, including cars brought in from abroad.
- If driving an EU-registered vehicle, your home country insurance is sufficient. Ask your insurer for a European Accident Statement (EAS) form, which can simplify matters in the event of an accident.
- Hire agencies provide the minimum legal insurance, but you can supplement it if you choose.

## HIRING A CAR

Car-hire agencies are widespread in Italy but pre-booking on the internet is often cheaper. Considerations before renting:

- Bear in mind that a car is generally more hassle than it's worth in cities, so only hire one for the time you'll be on the open road.
- Consider vehicle size carefully. High fuel prices, extremely narrow streets and tight parking conditions mean that smaller is often better.
- Road signs can be iffy in remote areas, so consider booking and paying for satnav.

Standard regulations:

- Many agencies have a minimum rental age of 25 and a maximum of 79. You can sometimes hire if you're over 21 but supplements will apply.

### Local Expert: Driving Tips

A representative of the Automobile Club d'Italia (ACI) offers these pearls to ease your way on Italian roads:

➡ Pay particular attention to the weather. In summer when it gets very hot, always carry a bottle of water with you and have some fresh fruit to eat. Italy is a sunny country but, in winter, watch out for ice, snow and fog.

➡ On the extra-urban roads and autostradas, cars have to have their headlights on even during the day.

➡ Watch out for signs at the autostrada toll booths – the lanes marked 'Telepass' are for cars that pay through an automatic electronic system without stopping.

➡ Watch out in the cities – big and small – for the Limited Traffic Zones (ZTL) and pay parking. There is no universal system for indicating these or their hours.

➡ To rent you'll need a credit card, valid driver's licence (with IDP if necessary) and passport or photo ID. Note that some companies require that you've had your licence for at least a year.

➡ Hire cars come with the minimum legal insurance, which you can supplement by purchasing additional coverage.

➡ Check with your credit-card company to see if it offers a Collision Damage Waiver, which covers you for additional damage if you use that card to pay for the car.

The following are among the most competitive multinational and Italian car-hire agencies.

**Avis** (☎199 100133; www.avis.com)

**Budget** (☎800 4723325; www.budget.com)

**Europcar** (☎199 307030; www.europcar.com)

**Hertz** (☎199 112211; www.hertz.com)

**Italy by Car** (☎091 6393120; www.italyby car.it) Partners with Thrifty.

**Maggiore** (☎199 151120; www.maggiore.it) Partners with Alamo and National.

### Motorcycles

Agencies throughout Italy rent motorbikes, ranging from small Vespas to larger touring bikes. Prices start at around €80/400 per day/week for a 650cc motorcycle.

## BRINGING YOUR OWN VEHICLE

There are no major obstacles to driving your own vehicle into Italy. But you will have to adjust your car's headlights if it's a left-hand-drive UK model. You'll need to carry the following in the car:

➡ A warning triangle

➡ A fluorescent reflective vest to wear if you have to stop on a major road

➡ Snow chains if travelling in mountainous areas between 15 October and 15 April

## MAPS

We recommend you purchase a good road map for your trip. The best driving maps are produced by the **Touring Club Italiano** (www.touringclub.com), Italy's largest map publisher. They are available at bookstores across Italy or online at the following:

**Stanfords** (www.stanfords.co.uk)

**Omni Resources** (www.omnimap.com)

## ROADS & CONDITIONS

Italy's extensive road network covers the entire peninsula and with enough patience you'll be able to get just about anywhere. Road quality varies – the autostradas are generally excellent but smaller roads, particularly in rural areas, are not always great. Heavy rain can cause axle-busting potholes to form and road surfaces to crumble.

## Coins

Always try to keep some coins to hand. They come in very useful for parking meters.

Traffic in and around the main cities is bad during morning and evening rush hours. Coastal roads get very busy on summer weekends. As a rule, traffic is quietest between 2pm and 4pm.

### Road Categories

**Autostradas** Italy boasts an extensive network of autostradas, represented on road signs by a white 'A' followed by a number on a green background. The main north–south link is the Autostrada del Sole (the 'Motorway of the Sun'), which runs from Milan (Milano) to Reggio di Calabria. It's called the A1 from Milan to Rome (Roma), the A2 from Rome to Naples (Napoli), and the A3 from Naples to Reggio di Calabria. There are tolls on most motorways, payable by cash or credit card as you exit. To calculate the toll price for any given journey, use the route planner on www.autostrade.it.

**Strade statali** State highways; represented on maps by 'S' or 'SS'. Vary from four-lane highways to two-lane main roads. The latter can be extremely slow, especially in mountainous regions.

**Strade regionali** Regional highways connecting small villages. Coded 'SR' or 'R'.

**Strade provinciali** Provincial highways; coded 'SP' or 'P'.

**Strade locali** Often not even paved or mapped.

Along with their A or SS number, some Italian roads are labelled with an E number – for example, the A4 autostrada is also shown as the E64 on maps and signs. This E number refers to the road's designation on the Europe-wide E-road network. E routes, which often cross national boundaries, are generally made up of major national roads strung together. The E70, for example, traverses 10 countries and includes the Italian A4, A21 and A32 autostradas, as it runs from northern Spain to Georgia.

### Limited Traffic Zones

Many town and city centres are off-limits to unauthorised traffic at certain times. If you drive past a sign with the wording *Zona a Traffico Limitato* you are entering a Limited Traffic Zone (ZTL) and risk being caught on camera and fined. Being in a hire car will not exempt you from this rule.

If you think your hotel might be in a ZTL, contact them beforehand to ask about access arrangements.

## ROAD RULES

- Drive on the right side of the road and overtake on the left. Unless otherwise indicated, give way to cars entering an intersection from a road on your right.
- Seatbelt use (front and rear) is required by law; violators are subject to an on-the-spot fine.
- In the event of a breakdown, a warning triangle is compulsory, as is use of an approved yellow or orange safety vest if you leave your vehicle. Recommended accessories include a first-aid kit, spare-bulb kit and fire extinguisher.
- Italy's blood-alcohol limit is 0.05%, and random breath tests take place. If you're involved in an accident while under the influence, the penalties can be severe.

## Road-Trip Websites

AUTOMOBILE ASSOCIATIONS

**Automobile Club d'Italia** (www.aci.it) Has a comprehensive online guide to motoring in Italy. Provides 24-hour roadside assistance.

CONDITIONS & TRAFFIC

**Autostrade** (www.autostrade.it) Route planner, weather forecasts and the traffic situation in real time. Also lists service stations, petrol prices and toll costs.

MAPS

**Michelin** (www.viamichelin.it) Online road-trip planner.

**Tutto Città** (www.tuttocitta.it) Good for detailed town and city maps.

## Driving Problem-Buster

**I can't speak Italian, will that be a problem?** When at a petrol station you might have to ask the attendant for your fill-up. The thing to do here is ask for the amount you want, so *venti euro* for €20 or *pieno* for full. And always specify *benzina senza piombo* for unleaded petrol and *gasolio* for diesel. At autostrada toll booths, the amount you owe appears on a read-out by the booth.

**What should I do if my car breaks down?** Call the service number of your car-hire company. The Automobile Club d'Italia (ACI) provides a 24-hour roadside emergency service – call ☎803 116 from a landline or mobile with an Italian provider or ☎800 116800 from a foreign mobile phone. Foreigners do not have to join but instead pay a per-incident fee. Note that in the event of a breakdown, a warning triangle is compulsory, as is use of an approved yellow or orange safety vest if you leave your vehicle.

**What if I have an accident?** For minor accidents there's no need to call the police. Fill in an accident report – Constatazione Amichevole di Incidente (CAI; Agreed Motor Accident Statement) – through your car-hire firm or insurance company.

**What should I do if I get stopped by the police?** The police will want to see your passport (or photo ID), licence, car registration papers and proof of insurance.

**What if I can't find anywhere to stay?** Always book ahead in summer and popular holiday periods. Italy doesn't have chains of roadside motels so if it's getting late head to the nearest town and look for signs for an *albergo* (hotel).

**Will I be able to find ATMs?** Some autostrada service stations have ATMs (known as *bancomat* in Italian). Otherwise, they are widely available in towns and cities.

**Will I need to pay tolls in advance?** No. When you join an autostrada you have to pick up a ticket at the barrier. When you exit you pay based on the distance you've covered. Pay by cash or credit card. Avoid Telepass lanes at toll stations.

**Are the road signs easy to read?** Most signs are fairly obvious but it helps to know that town/city centres are indicated by the word *centro* and a kind of black-and-white bullseye sign; *divieto fermata* means 'no stopping'; and *tutte le direzione* means 'all directions'.

➡ Headlights are compulsory day and night for all vehicles on autostradas and main roads.

➡ Helmets are required on all two-wheeled transport.

➡ Motorbikes can enter most restricted traffic areas in Italian cities.

➡ Speeding fines follow EU standards and are proportionate with the number of kilometres that you are caught driving over the speed limit, reaching up to €2000 with possible suspension of your driving licence. Speed limits are as follows:

**Autostradas** 130km/h to 150km/h
**Other main highways** 110km/h
**Minor, non-urban roads** 90km/h
**Built-up areas** 50km/h

### Road Etiquette

➡ Italian drivers are fast, aggressive and skilful. Lane hopping and late braking are the norm and it's not uncommon to see cars tailgating at 130km/h. Don't expect cars to slow down for you or let you out. As soon as you see a gap, go for it. Italians expect the unexpected and react swiftly, but they're not used to ditherers, so be decisive.

➡ Flashing is common on the roads and has several meanings. If a car behind you flashes it means: 'Get out of the way' or 'Don't pull out, I'm not stopping'. But if an approaching car flashes you, it's warning you that there's a police check ahead.

➡ Use of the car horn is widespread. It might be a warning but it might equally be an expression of frustration at slow-moving traffic or celebration that the traffic light's turning green.

## PARKING

➡ Parking is a major headache. Space is at a premium in towns and cities and Italy's traffic wardens are annoyingly efficient.

➡ Parking spaces outlined in blue are designated for paid parking – get a ticket from the nearest meter (coins only) or *tabaccaio* (tobacconist) and display it on your dashboard. Note, however, that charges often don't apply overnight, typically between 8pm and 8am.

➡ White or yellow lines almost always indicate that residential permits are needed.

➡ Traffic police generally turn a blind eye to motorcycles or scooters parked on footpaths.

## FUEL

➡ You'll find filling stations all over, but smaller ones tend to close between about 1pm and 3.30pm and on Sunday afternoons.

➡ Many have *fai da te* (self-service) pumps that you can use any time. Simply insert a bank note into the payment machine and press the number of the pump you want.

➡ Italy's petrol prices are among the highest in Europe and vary from one service station *(benzinaio, stazione di servizio)* to another. When this book was researched, lead-free petrol *(benzina senza piombo)* averaged €1.93 per litre, with diesel *(gasolio)* averaging €1.81 per litre.

## SAFETY

The main safety threat to motorists is theft. Hire cars and foreign vehicles are

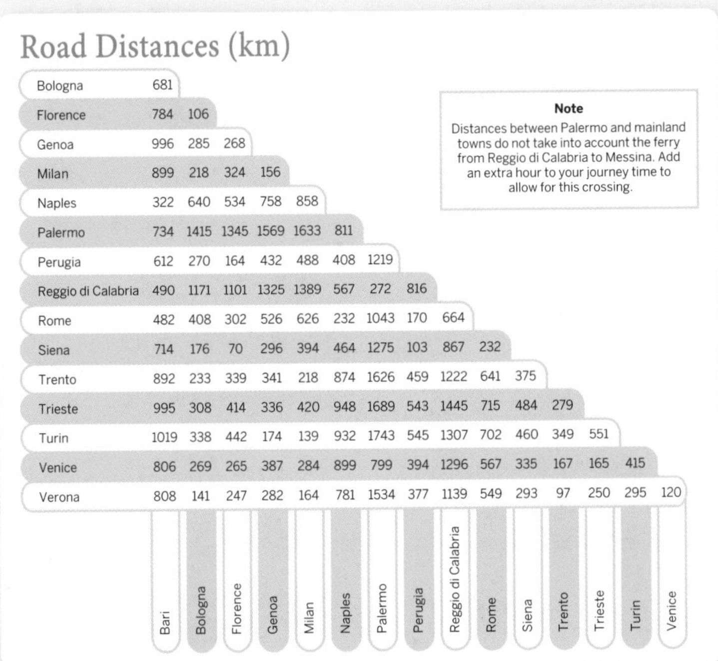

### Road Distances (km)

| | Bari | Bologna | Florence | Genoa | Milan | Naples | Palermo | Perugia | Reggio di Calabria | Rome | Siena | Trento | Trieste | Turin | Venice |
|---|---|---|---|---|---|---|---|---|---|---|---|---|---|---|---|
| Bologna | 681 | | | | | | | | | | | | | | |
| Florence | 784 | 106 | | | | | | | | | | | | | |
| Genoa | 996 | 285 | 268 | | | | | | | | | | | | |
| Milan | 899 | 218 | 324 | 156 | | | | | | | | | | | |
| Naples | 322 | 640 | 534 | 758 | 858 | | | | | | | | | | |
| Palermo | 734 | 1415 | 1345 | 1569 | 1633 | 811 | | | | | | | | | |
| Perugia | 612 | 270 | 164 | 432 | 488 | 408 | 1219 | | | | | | | | |
| Reggio di Calabria | 490 | 1171 | 1101 | 1325 | 1389 | 567 | 272 | 816 | | | | | | | |
| Rome | 482 | 408 | 302 | 526 | 626 | 232 | 1043 | 170 | 664 | | | | | | |
| Siena | 714 | 176 | 70 | 296 | 394 | 464 | 1275 | 103 | 867 | 232 | | | | | |
| Trento | 892 | 233 | 339 | 341 | 218 | 874 | 1626 | 459 | 1222 | 641 | 375 | | | | |
| Trieste | 995 | 308 | 414 | 336 | 420 | 948 | 1689 | 543 | 1445 | 715 | 484 | 279 | | | |
| Turin | 1019 | 338 | 442 | 174 | 139 | 932 | 1743 | 545 | 1307 | 702 | 460 | 349 | 551 | | |
| Venice | 806 | 269 | 265 | 387 | 284 | 899 | 799 | 394 | 1296 | 567 | 335 | 167 | 165 | 415 | |
| Verona | 808 | 141 | 247 | 282 | 164 | 781 | 1534 | 377 | 1139 | 549 | 293 | 97 | 250 | 295 | 120 |

**Note**

Distances between Palermo and mainland towns do not take into account the ferry from Reggio di Calabria to Messina. Add an extra hour to your journey time to allow for this crossing.

### Italy Playlist

**Nessun Dorma** Puccini

**O sole mio** Traditional

**Tu vuoi fare l'americano** Renato Carsone

**Vieni via con me** Paolo Conte

**That's Amore** Dean Martin

**Four Seasons** Vivaldi

a target for robbers and although you're unlikely to have a problem, thefts do occur. As a general rule, always lock your car and never leave anything showing, particularly valuables, and certainly not overnight. If at all possible, avoid leaving luggage in an unattended car. It's a good idea to pay extra to leave your car in supervised car parks.

## RADIO

RAI, Italy's state broadcaster, operates three national radio stations – Radio 1, 2 and 3 – offering news, current affairs, classical and commercial music, and endless phone-ins. Isoradio, another RAI station, provides regular news and traffic bulletins. There are also thousands of commercial radio stations, many broadcasting locally. Major ones include Radio Capital, good for modern hits; Radio Deejay, aimed at a younger audience; and Radio 24, which airs news and talk shows.

# Italy Travel Guide

## GETTING THERE & AWAY

### AIR

Italy's main international airports:

**Rome Leonardo da Vinci** (Fiumicino; www.adr.it) Italy's principal airport.

**Rome Ciampino** (www.adr.it) Hub for Ryanair flights to Rome (Roma).

**Milan Malpensa** (www.milanomalpensa1.eu, www.milanomalpensa2.eu) Main airport of Milan (Milano).

**Milan Linate** (www.milanolinate.eu) Milan's second airport.

**Bergamo Orio al Serio** (www.sacbo.it)

**Turin** (www.turin-airport.com)

**Bologna Guglielmo Marconi** (www.bologna-airport.it)

**Pisa Galileo Galilei** (www.pisa-airport.com) Main international airport for Tuscany.

**Venice Marco Polo** (www.veniceairport.it)

**Naples Capodichino** (www.gesac.it)

**Bari Palese** (www.aeroportidipuglia.it)

**Catania Fontanarossa** (www.aeroporto.catania.it) Sicily's busiest airport.

**Palermo Falcone-Borsellino** (www.gesap.it)

**Cagliari Elmas** (www.sogaer.it) Main gateway for Sardinia.

Car hire is available at all of these airports.

### CAR & MOTORCYCLE

Driving into Italy is fairly straightforward – thanks to the Schengen Agreement, there are no customs checks when driving in from neighbours France, Switzerland, Austria and Slovenia.

Aside from the coast roads linking Italy with France and Slovenia, border crossings into Italy mostly involve tunnels through the Alps (open year-round) or mountain passes (seasonally closed or requiring snow chains). The list below outlines the major points of entry.

**Austria** From Innsbruck to Bolzano via A22/E45 (Brenner Pass); Villach to Tarvisio via A23/E55.

**France** From Nice to Ventimiglia via A10/E80; Modane to Turin (Torino) via A32/E70 (Fréjus Tunnel); Chamonix to Courmayeur via A5/E25 (Mont Blanc Tunnel).

**Slovenia** From Sežana to Trieste via SS58/E70.

**Switzerland** From Martigny to Aosta via SS27/E27 (Grand St Bernard Tunnel); Lugano to Como via A9/E35.

### SEA

International car ferries sail to Italy from Albania, Croatia, Greece, Malta, Montenegro, Morocco, Slovenia, Spain and Tunisia. Some routes only operate in summer, when ticket prices rise. Prices for vehicles vary according to their size. Car hire is not always available at ports, so check beforehand on the nearest agency.

The website www.traghettionline.com (in Italian) details all of the ferry companies in the Mediterranean. The principal operators serving Italy:

**Agoudimos Lines** (www.agoudimos.it) Greece to Bari (11 to 16 hours) and Brindisi (seven to 14 hours).

**Endeavor Lines** (www.endeavor-lines.com) Greece to Brindisi (seven to 14 hours).

**Grandi Navi Veloci** (www.gnv.it) Barcelona to Genoa (18 hours).

### Practicalities

- **Smoking** Banned in all closed public spaces.
- **Time** Italy uses the 24-hour clock and is on Central European Time, one hour ahead of GMT/UTC.
- **TV & DVD** The main TV channels: state-run RAI-1, RAI-2 and RAI-3; Canale 5, Italia 1 and Rete 4; and La 7. Italian DVDs are regionally coded 2.
- **Weights & Measures** Italy uses the metric system, so kilometres not miles, litres not gallons.

**Jadrolinija** (www.jadrolinija.hr) Croatia to Ancona (from nine hours) and Bari (10 hours).

**Minoan Lines** (www.minoan.gr) Greece to Venice (22 to 30 hours) and Ancona (16 to 22 hours).

**Montenegro Lines** (www.montenegrolines.net) Bar to Bari (nine hours).

**Superfast** (www.superfast.com) Greece to Bari (11 to 16 hours) and Ancona (16 to 22 hours).

**Ventouris** (www.ventouris.gr) Albania to Bari (eight hours).

## TRAIN

Regular trains on two western lines connect Italy with France (one along the coast and the other from Turin into the French Alps). Trains from Milan head north into Switzerland and on towards the Benelux countries. Further east, two lines connect with Central and Eastern Europe.

**Trenitalia** (www.trenitalia.com) offers various train and car-hire packages that allow you to save on hire charges when you book a train ticket – see the website for details.

# DIRECTORY A–Z

## ACCOMMODATION

From dreamy villas to chic boutique hotels, historic hideaways and ravishing farmstays, Italy offers accommodation to suit every taste and budget.

### Seasons & Rates

- Hotel rates fluctuate enormously from high to low season, and even from day to day depending on demand, season and booking method (online, through an agency etc).
- As a rule, peak rates apply at Easter, in summer and over the Christmas/New Year period. But there are exceptions – in the mountains, high season means the ski season (December to late March). Also, August is high season on the coast but low season in many cities where hotels offer discounts.
- Southern Italy is generally cheaper than the north.

### Reservations

- Always book ahead in peak season, even if it's only for the first night or two.
- In the off-season, it always pays to call ahead to check that your hotel is open. Many coastal hotels close for winter, typically opening from late March to late October.
- Hotels usually require that reservations be confirmed with a credit-card number. No-shows will be docked a night's accommodation.

### B&Bs

B&Bs can be found throughout the country in both urban and rural settings. Options include restored farmhouses, city *palazzi* (mansions), seaside bungalows and rooms in family houses. Prices vary but as a rule B&Bs are often better value than hotels in the same category. Note that breakfast in an Italian B&B will often be a continental combination of bread rolls, croissants, ham and cheese. For more information, contact **Bed & Breakfast Italia** (www.bbitalia.it).

### Hotels & Pensioni

A *pensione* is a small, family-run hotel or guesthouse. Hotels are bigger and more expensive than *pensioni*, although at the

### Sleeping Price Ranges

The price ranges listed in this book refer to a double room with bathroom.

**€** less than €100

**€€** €100–€200

**€€€** more than €200

cheaper end of the market, there's often little difference between the two. All hotels are rated from one to five stars, although this rating relates to facilities only and gives no indication of value, comfort, atmosphere or friendliness.

Breakfast in cheaper hotels is rarely worth setting the alarm for. If you have the option, save your money and pop into a bar for a coffee and *cornetto* (croissant).

- One-star hotels and *pensioni* tend to be basic and often do not offer private bathrooms.
- Two-star places are similar but rooms will generally have a private bathroom.
- Three-star hotel rooms will come with a hairdryer, minibar (or fridge), safe and air-con. Many will also have satellite TV and wi-fi.
- Four- and five-star hotels offer facilities such as room service, laundry and dry-cleaning.

### Agriturismi

From rustic country houses to luxurious estates and fully functioning farms, Italian farmstays, known as *agriturismi* (singular – *agriturismo*) are hugely popular. Comfort levels, facilities and prices vary accordingly but the best will offer swimming pools and top-class accommodation. Many also operate restaurants specialising in traditional local cuisine.

*Agriturismi* have long thrived in Tuscany and Umbria, but you'll now find them across the country. For listings and further details, check out the following sites:

**Agritour** (www.agritour.net)

**Agriturismo.com** (www.agriturismo.com)

**Agriturismo.it** (www.agriturismo.it)

**Agriturismo-Italia.net** (www.agriturismo-italia.net)

**Agriturismo.net** (www.agriturismo.net)

**Agriturismo Vero** (www.agriturismovero.com)

**Agriturist** (www.agriturist.com)

### Other Options

**Camping** A popular summer option. Most campsites are big, summer-only complexes with swimming pools, restaurants and supermarkets. Many have space for RVs and offer bungalows or simple, self-contained flats. Minimum stays sometimes apply in high season. Check out www.campeggi.com and www.camping.it.

**Hostels** Hostels around the country offer dorm beds and private rooms. Breakfast is usually included in rates and dinner is sometimes available for about €10. For listings and further details, see www.aighostels.com or www.hostelworld.com.

**Convents & Monasteries** Some convents and monasteries provide basic accommodation. Expect curfews, few frills and value for money. Useful resources include www.monasterystays.com, www.initaly.com/agri/convents.htm and www.santasusanna.org/comingToRome/convents.html.

**Refuges** Mountain huts kitted out with bunk rooms sleeping anything from two to a dozen or more people. Many offer half-board (bed, breakfast and dinner) and most are open from mid-June to mid-September.

**Villas** Villas and *fattorie* (farmhouses) can be rented in their entirety or sometimes by the room. Many have swimming pools.

### Book Your Stay Online

For more accommodation reviews by Lonely Planet authors, check out http://hotels.lonelyplanet.com/italy. You'll find independent reviews, as well as recommendations on the best places to stay. Best of all, you can book online.

## ELECTRICITY

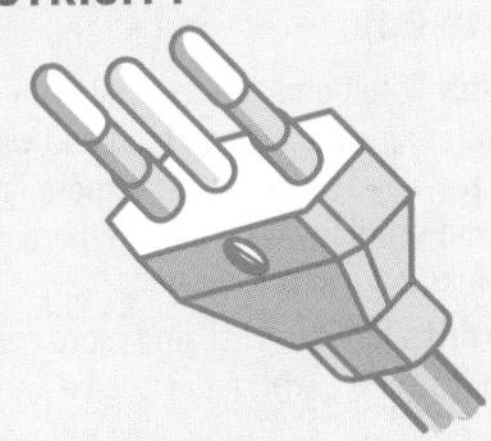

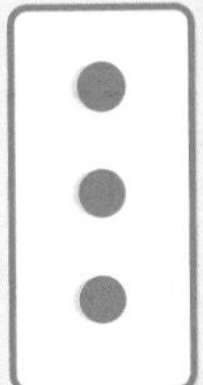

120V/60Hz

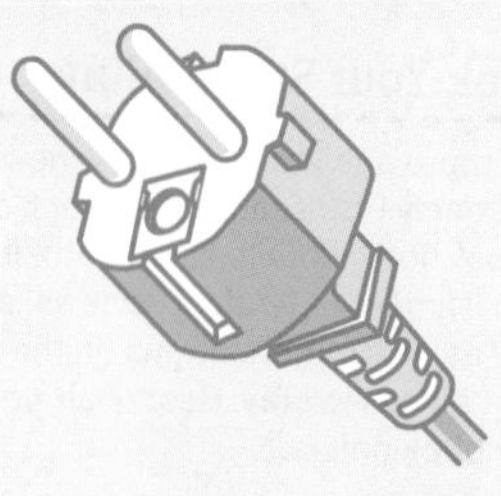

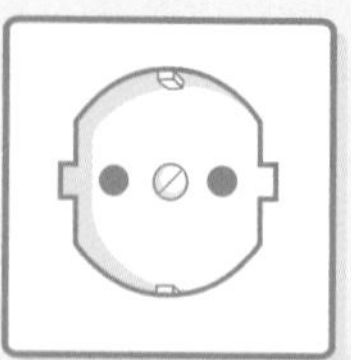

120V/60Hz

## FOOD

A full Italian meal consists of an antipasto (appetiser), *primo* (first course, usually a pasta, risotto or polenta), *secondo* (second course, meat or fish) with *contorno* (vegetable side dish) or *insalata* (salad), and *dolce* (dessert) and/or fruit. When eating out it's perfectly OK to mix and match and order, say, a *primo* followed by an *insalata* or *contorno*.

### Where to Eat

**Trattorias** Traditional, often family-run eateries offering simple, local food and wine. Some newer-wave trattorias offer more creative fare and scholarly wine lists. Generally cheap to midrange in price.

**Restaurants** More formal, and more expensive, than trattorias, with more choice and smarter service. Reservations are generally required for popular and top-end places.

**Pizzerias** Alongside pizza, many pizzerias also offer antipasti, pastas, meat and vegetable dishes. They're often only open in the evening. The best have a wood-oven *(forno a legna)*.

**Bars & Cafes** Italians often breakfast on *cornetti* and coffee at a bar or cafe. Many bars and cafes sell *panini* (bread rolls with simple fillings) at lunchtime and serve a hot and cold buffet during the early evening *aperitivo* (aperitif) hour.

**Wine Bars** At an *enoteca* (plural – *enoteche*) you can drink wine by the glass and eat snacks such as cheeses, cold meats, bruschette and *crostini* (little toasts). Some also serve hot dishes.

**Markets** Most towns and cities have morning produce markets where you can stock up on picnic provisions. Villages might have a weekly market.

### Eating Price Ranges

The following price ranges refer to a meal consisting of a *primo* (first course), *secondo* (second course), *dolce* (dessert) and a glass of house wine for one:

**€** less than €25

**€€** €25–€45

**€€€** more than €45

## GAY & LESBIAN TRAVELLERS

➡ Homosexuality is legal in Italy and well tolerated in the major cities. However, overt displays of affection by homosexual couples could attract a negative response, particularly in the more conservative south and in smaller towns.

➡ There are gay clubs in Rome, Milan and Bologna, and a handful in places such as Florence (Firenze). Some coastal towns and resorts (such as Viareggio in Tuscany and Taormina in Sicily) see much more action in summer.

Useful resources:

**Arcigay & Arcilesbica** (www.arcigay.it) Bologna-based national organisation for gays and lesbians.

**GayFriendlyItaly.com** (www.gayfriendlyitaly.com) English-language site produced by Gay.it, with information on everything from hotels to homophobia issues and the law.

**Gay.it** (www.gay.it) Website listing gay bars and hotels across the country.

**Pride** (www.prideonline.it) National monthly magazine of art, music, politics and gay culture.

## HEALTH

➡ Italy has a public health system that is legally bound to provide emergency care to everyone.

➡ EU nationals are entitled to reduced-cost, sometimes free, medical care with a European Health Insurance Card (EHIC), available from your home health authority.

➡ Non-EU citizens should take out medical insurance.

➡ For emergency treatment, you can go to the *pronto soccorso* (casualty) section of an *ospedale* (public hospital), though be prepared for a long wait.

➡ Pharmacists can give advice and sell over-the-counter medication for minor illnesses. Pharmacies generally keep the same hours as other shops, closing at night and on Sundays. A handful remain open on a rotation basis *(farmacie di turno)* for emergency purposes. These are usually listed in newspapers. Closed pharmacies display a list of the nearest ones open.

➡ In major cities you are likely to find English-speaking doctors or a translator service available.

➡ Italian tap water is fine to drink.

➡ No vaccinations are required for travel to Italy.

### Italian Wine Classifications

Italian wines are classified according to strict quality-control standards and carry one of four denominations:

**DOCG** (Denominazione di Origine Controllata e Garantita) Italy's best wines; made in specific areas according to stringent production rules.

**DOC** (Denominazione di Origine Controllata) Quality wines produced in defined regional areas.

**IGT** (Indicazione di Geografica Tipica) Wines typical of a certain region.

**VdT** (Vino da Tavola) Wines for everyday drinking; often served as house wine in trattorias.

## INTERNET ACCESS

➡ An increasing number of hotels, B&Bs, hostels and even *agriturismi* offer free wi-fi. You'll also find it in many bars and cafes.

➡ The [wi-fi] icon used throughout this book indicates wi-fi is available.

➡ Rome and Bologna are among the cities that provide free wi-fi, although you'll have to register for the service at www.romawireless.com (Rome) and www.comune.bologna.it/wireless (Bologna) and have an Italian mobile phone number.

➡ Venice (Venezia) offers pay-for wi-fi packages online at www.veniceconnected.com.

➡ Internet access is not as widespread in rural and southern Italy as in urban and northern areas.

➡ Internet cafes are thin on the ground. Typical charges range from €2 to €6 per hour. They might require formal photo ID.

➡ Many top-end hotels charge upwards of €10 per day for access.

## MONEY

Italy uses the euro. Euro notes come in denominations of €500, €200, €100, €50, €20, €10 and €5; coins come in denominations of €2 and €1, and 50, 20, 10, five, two and one cents.

For the latest exchange rates, check out www.xe.com.

### Admission Prices

➡ There are no hard and fast rules, but many state museums and galleries offer discounted admission to EU seniors and students.

➡ Typically, EU citizens under 18 and over 65 enter free and those aged between 18 and 24 pay a reduced rate.

➡ EU teachers might also qualify for concessions. In all cases you'll need photo ID to claim reduced entry.

### ATMs

ATMs (known as *bancomat*) are widely available throughout Italy and are the best way to obtain local currency.

### Credit Cards

➡ International credit and debit cards can be used in any ATM displaying the appropriate sign. Visa and MasterCard are among the most

## Tipping Guide

| | |
|---|---|
| **Taxis** | Round the fare up to the nearest euro. |
| **Restaurants** | Many locals don't tip waiters, but most visitors leave 10% if there's no service charge. |
| **Cafes** | Leave a coin (as little as €0.10 is acceptable) if you drank your coffee at the counter, or 10% if you sat at a table. |
| **Hotels** | Bellhops usually expect €1 to €2 per bag; it's not necessary to tip the concierge, cleaners or front-desk staff. |

widely recognised, but others such as Cirrus and Maestro are also well covered.

➡ Only some banks give cash advances over the counter, so you're better off using ATMs.

➡ Cards are good for paying in most hotels, restaurants, shops, supermarkets and toll booths. Some cheaper *pensioni*, trattorias and pizzerias only accept cash. Don't rely on credit cards at museums or galleries.

➡ Check any charges with your bank. Most banks now build a fee of around 2.75% into every foreign transaction. Also, ATM withdrawals can attract a further fee, usually around 1.5%.

➡ In an emergency, call to have your card blocked:

**Amex** (☎06 7290 0347 or your national call number)

**Diners Club** (☎800 393939)

**MasterCard** (☎800 870866)

**Visa** (☎800 819014)

### Moneychangers

You can change money in banks, at post offices or at a *cambio* (exchange office). Post offices and banks tend to offer the best rates; exchange offices keep longer hours, but watch for high commissions and inferior rates.

## OPENING HOURS

Opening times are only spelled out in this guide when they deviate from the standard hours outlined here:

**Banks** 8.30am to 1.30pm and 2.45pm to 4.30pm Monday to Friday.

**Bars & Cafes** 7.30am to 8pm, sometimes until 1am or 2am.

**Clubs** 10pm to 4am.

**Post Offices** Main offices 8am to 7pm Monday to Friday, 8.30am to noon Saturday; branches 8am to 2pm weekdays, 8.30am to noon Saturday.

**Restaurants** Noon to 3pm and 7.30pm to 11pm; sometimes later in summer and in the south. Kitchens often shut an hour earlier than final closing time; most places close at least one day a week.

**Shops** 9am to 1pm and 3.30pm to 7.30pm (or 4pm to 8pm) weekdays. In larger cities, department stores and supermarkets typically open 9am to 7.30pm or 10am to 8pm Monday to Saturday, some also on Sunday.

## PUBLIC HOLIDAYS

Individual towns have public holidays to celebrate the feasts of their patron saints. National public holidays:

**Capodanno** (New Year's Day) 1 January

**Epifania** (Epiphany) 6 January

**Pasquetta** (Easter Monday) March/April

**Giorno della Liberazione** (Liberation Day) 25 April

**Festa del Lavoro** (Labour Day) 1 May

**Festa della Repubblica** (Republic Day) 2 June

**Festa dei Santi Pietro e Paolo** (Feast of St Peter & St Paul) 29 June

**Ferragosto** (Feast of the Assumption) 15 August

**Festa di Ognisanti** (All Saints' Day) 1 November

**Festa dell'Immacolata Concezione** (Feast of the Immaculate Conception) 8 December

**Natale** (Christmas Day) 25 December

**Festa di Santo Stefano** (Boxing Day) 26 December

## SAFE TRAVEL

Italy is a safe country but petty theft can be a problem. There's no need for paranoia but be aware that thieves and pickpockets operate in touristy areas, so watch out when exploring the sights in Rome, Florence, Venice, Naples (Napoli) etc.

Cars, particularly those with foreign number plates or rental-company stickers, provide rich pickings for thieves – see p401.

In case of theft or loss, report the incident to the police within 24 hours and ask for a statement. Some tips:

- Keep essentials in a money belt but carry your day's spending money in a separate wallet.
- Wear your bag/camera strap across your body and away from the road – thieves on mopeds can swipe a bag and be gone in seconds.
- Never drape your bag over an empty chair at a street-side cafe or put it where you can't see it.
- Always check your change to see you haven't been short changed.

## TELEPHONE

### Domestic Calls

- Italian telephone area codes all begin with 0 and consist of up to four digits. Area codes are an integral part of all Italian phone numbers and must be dialled even when calling locally.
- Mobile-phone numbers are nine or 10 digits and have a three-digit prefix starting with a 3.
- Toll-free (free-phone) numbers are known as *numeri verdi* and usually start with 800.
- Non-geographical numbers start with 840, 841, 848, 892, 899, 163, 166 or 199. Some six-digit national rate numbers are also in use (such as those for Alitalia, rail and postal information).

### International Calls

- To call Italy from abroad, call the international access number (☎011 in the USA, ☎00 from most other countries), Italy's country code (☎39) and then the area code of the location you want, including the leading 0.
- The cheapest options for calling internationally are free or low-cost computer programs such as Skype, cut-rate call centres and international calling cards.
- Cut-price call centres can be found in all of the main cities, and rates can be considerably lower than from Telecom payphones.
- Another alternative is to use a direct-dialling service such as AT&T's USA Direct (access number ☎800 172444) or Telstra's Australia Direct (access number ☎800 172610), which allows you to make a reverse-charge (collect) call at home-country rates.
- To make a reverse-charge international call from a public telephone, dial ☎170.

### Mobile Phones (Cell Phones)

- Italy uses GSM 900/1800, which is compatible with the rest of Europe and Australia but not with North American GSM 1900 or the totally different Japanese system.
- Most modern smart phones are multiband, meaning that they are compatible with a variety of international networks. Check with your service provider to make sure it is compatible and beware of calls being routed internationally (very expensive for a 'local' call). In many cases you're better off buying an Italian phone or unlocking your phone for use with an Italian SIM card.
- If you have a GSM multiband phone that you can unlock, it can cost as little as €10 to activate a prepaid SIM card in Italy. **TIM** (Telecom Italia Mobile; www.tim.it), **Wind** (www.wind.it) and **Vodafone** (www.vodafone.it) offer SIM cards and have retail outlets across Italy. You'll usually need your passport to open an account.
- Once you're set up with a SIM card, you can easily purchase recharge cards (allowing you to top up your account with extra minutes) at

### Important Numbers

**Italy country code** (☎39)

**International access code** (☎00)

**Police** (☎113)

**Carabinieri** (military police; ☎112)

**Ambulance** (☎118)

**Fire** (☎115)

**Roadside assistance** (☎803 116 from a landline or mobile with an Italian provider; ☎800 116800 from a foreign mobile phone)

tobacconists and news stands, as well as some bars, supermarkets and banks.

➡ You can buy or lease an inexpensive Italian phone for the duration of your trip.

### Payphones & Phonecards

➡ You'll find payphones on the streets, in train stations and in Telecom offices. Most accept only *carte/schede telefoniche* (phonecards), although some accept credit cards.

➡ Telecom offers a range of prepaid cards; for a full list, see www.telecomitalia.it/telefono/carte-telefoniche.

➡ You can buy phonecards at post offices, tobacconists and news stands.

## TOILETS

➡ Public toilets are thin on the ground in Italy. You'll find them in autostrada service stations (generally free) and in main train stations (usually with a small fee of between €0.50 and €1).

➡ Often, the best thing is to nip into a cafe or bar, although you'll probably have to order a quick drink first.

➡ Keep some tissues to hand as loo paper is rare.

## TOURIST INFORMATION

Practically every village, town and city in Italy has a tourist office of sorts. These operate under a variety of names: Azienda di Promozione Turistica (APT), Azienda Autonoma di Soggiorno e Turismo (AAST), Informazione e Assistenza ai Turisti (IAT) and Pro Loco. All deal directly with the public and most will respond to written and telephone requests for information.

Tourist offices can usually provide a city map, lists of hotels and information on the major sights. In larger towns and major tourist areas, English is usually spoken.

Main offices are generally open Monday to Friday; some also open on weekends, especially in urban areas and in peak summer season. Info booths (at train stations, for example) may keep slightly different hours.

### Tourist Authorities

The **Italian National Tourist Office** (ENIT; www.enit.it) maintains international offices. See the website for contact details.

Regional tourist authorities are more concerned with planning, marketing and promotion than with offering a public information service. However, they offer useful websites:

**Abruzzo** (www.abruzzoturismo.it)

**Basilicata** (www.aptbasilicata.it)

**Calabria** (www.turiscalabria.it)

**Campania** (www.in-campania.com)

**Emilia-Romagna** (www.emiliaromagnaturismo.it)

**Friuli Venezia Giulia** (www.turismo.fvg.it)

**Lazio** (www.ilmiolazio.it)

**Le Marche** (www.le-marche.com)

**Liguria** (www.turismoinliguria.it)

**Lombardy** (www.turismo.regione.lombardia.it)

**Molise** (www.regione.molise.it/turismo)

**Piedmont** (www.piemonteitalia.eu)

**Puglia** (www.viaggiareinpuglia.it)

**Sardinia** (www.sardegnaturismo.it)

**Sicily** (www.regione.sicilia.it/turismo)

**Trentino-Alto Adige** (www.visittrentino.it, www.suedtirol.info)

**Tuscany** (www.turismo.intoscana.it)

**Umbria** (www.regioneumbria.eu)

**Valle d'Aosta** (www.regione.vda.it/turismo)

**Veneto** (www.veneto.to)

Other useful websites include www.italia.it and www.easy-italia.com.

## TRAVELLERS WITH DISABILITIES

Italy is not an easy country for travellers with disabilities. Cobbled streets, blocked pavements and tiny lifts cause problems for wheelchair users. Not an awful lot has been done to make life easier for the deaf or blind, either.

A handful of cities publish general guides on accessibility, among them Bologna, Milan, Padua (Padova), Reggio Emilia, Turin, Venice and Verona. Contact the relevant tourist authorities for further information. Other helpful resources:

**Handy Turismo** (www.handyturismo.it) Information on Rome.

**Milano per Tutti** (www.milanopertutti.it) Covers Milan.

Useful organisations:

**Accessible Italy** (www.accessibleitaly.com) Specialises in holiday services for travellers with disabilities. This is the best first port of call.

**Consorzio Cooperative Integrate** (www.coinsociale.it) This Rome-based organisation provides information on the capital (including transport and access) and is happy to share its contacts throughout Italy. Its **Presidio del Lazio** (www.presidiodellazio.it) program seeks to improve access for tourists with disabilities.

**Tourism for All** (www.tourismforall.org.uk) This UK-based group has information on hotels with access for guests with disabilities, where to hire equipment and tour operators dealing with travellers with disabilities.

## VISAS

➡ EU citizens do not need a visa for Italy.

➡ Residents of 28 non-EU countries, including Australia, Brazil, Canada, Israel, Japan, New Zealand and the USA, do not require visas for tourist visits of up to 90 days.

➡ Italy is one of the 15 signatories of the Schengen Convention. The standard tourist visa for a Schengen country is valid for 90 days. You must apply for it in your country of residence and you cannot apply for more than two in any 12-month period. They are not renewable within Italy.

➡ For full details of Italy's visa requirements check www.esteri.it/visti/home_eng.asp.

# Language

Italian sounds can all be found in English. If you read our coloured pronunciation guides as if they were English, you'll be understood. Note that ai is pronounced as in 'aisle', ay as in 'say', ow as in 'how', dz as the 'ds' in 'lids', and that r is strong and rolled. If the consonant is written as a double letter, it's pronounced a little stronger, eg *sonno* son·no (sleep) versus *sono* so·no (I am). The stressed syllables are indicated with italics.

## BASICS

| | | |
|---|---|---|
| **Hello.** | *Buongiorno.* | bwon·*jor*·no |
| **Goodbye.** | *Arrivederci.* | a·ree·ve·*der*·chee |
| **Yes./No.** | *Sì./No.* | see/no |
| **Excuse me.** | *Mi scusi.* | mee *skoo*·zee |
| **Sorry.** | *Mi dispiace.* | mee dees·*pya*·che |
| **Please.** | *Per favore.* | per fa·*vo*·re |
| **Thank you.** | *Grazie.* | *gra*·tsye |

**You're welcome.**
*Prego.* — *pre*·go

**Do you speak English?**
*Parli inglese?* — *par*·lee een·*gle*·ze

**I don't understand.**
*Non capisco.* — non ka·*pee*·sko

**How much is this?**
*Quanto costa questo?* — *kwan*·to *kos*·ta *kwe*·sto

## ACCOMMODATION

**Do you have a room?**
*Avete una camera?* — a·*ve*·te *oo*·na *ka*·me·ra

**How much is it per night/person?**
*Quanto costa per una notte/persona?* — *kwan*·to *kos*·ta per *oo*·na *no*·te/per·*so*·na

## DIRECTIONS

**Where's ...?**
*Dov'è ...?* — do·*ve* ...

**Can you show me (on the map)?**
*Può mostrarmi (sulla pianta)?* — pwo mos·*trar*·mee (*soo*·la *pyan*·ta)

## EATING & DRINKING

**What would you recommend?**
*Cosa mi consiglia?* — *ko*·za mee kon·*see*·lya

**I'd like ..., please.**
*Vorrei ..., per favore.* — vo·*ray* ... per fa·*vo*·re

**I don't eat (meat).**
*Non mangio (carne).* — non *man*·jo (*kar*·ne)

**Please bring the bill.**
*Mi porta il conto, per favore?* — mee *por*·ta eel *kon*·to per fa·*vo*·re

## EMERGENCIES

**Help!**
*Aiuto!* — a·*yoo*·to

**I'm lost.**
*Mi sono perso/a.* (m/f) — mee *so*·no *per*·so/a

**I'm ill.**
*Mi sento male.* — mee *sen*·to *ma*·le

**Call the police!**
*Chiami la polizia!* — *kya*·mee la po·lee·*tsee*·a

**Call a doctor!**
*Chiami un medico!* — *kya*·mee oon *me*·dee·ko

### Want More?

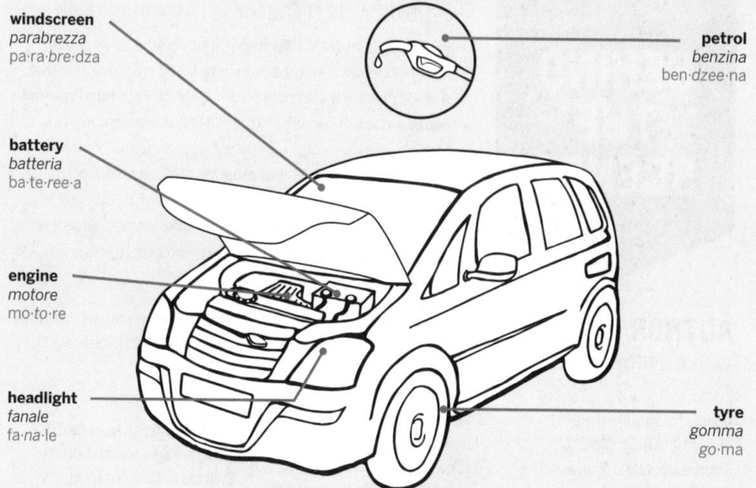


## Signs

| | |
|---|---|
| **Alt** | Stop |
| **Dare la Precedenza** | Give Way |
| **Deviazione** | Detour |
| **Divieto di Accesso** | No Entry |
| **Entrata** | Entrance |
| **Pedaggio** | Toll |
| **Senso Unico** | One Way |
| **Uscita** | Exit |

## ON THE ROAD

| | | |
|---|---|---|
| **I'd like to hire a/an ...** | *Vorrei noleggiare ...* | vo·*ray* no·le·*ja*·re ... |
| **4WD** | *un fuoristrada* | oon fwo·ree·*stra*·da |
| **automatic/ manual** | *una macchina automatica/ manuale* | *oo*·na *ma*·kee·na ow·to·*ma*·tee·ka/ ma·noo·a·le |
| **motorbike** | *una moto* | *oo*·na *mo*·to |

| | | |
|---|---|---|
| **How much is it ...?** | *Quanto costa ...?* | *kwan*·to *kos*·ta ... |
| **daily** | *al giorno* | al *jor*·no |
| **weekly** | *alla settimana* | a·la se·tee·*ma*·na |

**Does that include insurance?**
*E' compresa l'assicurazione?* — e kom·*pre*·sa la·see·koo·ra·*tsyo*·ne

**Does that include mileage?**
*E' compreso il chilometraggio?* — e kom·*pre*·so eel kee·lo·me·*tra*·jo

**What's the city/country speed limit?**
*Qual'è il limite di velocità in città/campagna?* — kwa·le eel *lee*·mee·te dee ve·lo·chee·*ta* een chee·*ta*/kam·*pa*·nya

**Is this the road to (Venice)?**
*Questa strada porta a (Venezia)?* — *kwe*·sta *stra*·da *por*·ta a (ve·*ne*·tsya)

**(How long) Can I park here?**
*(Per quanto tempo) Posso parcheggiare qui?* — (per *kwan*·to *tem*·po) *po*·so par·ke·*ja*·re kwee

**Where's a service station?**
*Dov'è una stazione di servizio?* — do·*ve oo*·na sta·*tsyo*·ne dee ser·*vee*·tsyo

**Please fill it up.**
*Il pieno, per favore.* — eel *pye*·no per fa·*vo*·re

**I'd like (30) litres.**
*Vorrei (trenta) litri.* — vo·*ray* (*tren*·ta) *lee*·tree

**Please check the oil/water.**
*Può controllare l'olio/ l'acqua, per favore?* — pwo kon·tro·*la*·re *lo*·lyo/ *la*·kwa per fa·*vo*·re

**I need a mechanic.**
*Ho bisogno di un meccanico.* — o bee·*zo*·nyo dee oon me·*ka*·nee·ko

**The car/motorbike has broken down.**
*La macchina/moto si è guastata.* — la *ma*·kee·na/*mo*·to see e gwas·*ta*·ta

**I had an accident.**
*Ho avuto un incidente.* — o a·*voo*·to oon een·chee·*den*·te

# BEHIND THE SCENES

## SEND US YOUR FEEDBACK

We love to hear from travellers – your comments help make our books better. We read every word, and we guarantee that your feedback goes straight to the authors. Visit **lonelyplanet.com/contact** to submit your updates and suggestions.

Note: We may edit, reproduce and incorporate your comments in Lonely Planet products such as guidebooks, websites and digital products, so let us know if you don't want your comments reproduced or your name acknowledged. For a copy of our privacy policy visit lonelyplanet.com/privacy.


## AUTHOR THANKS

### PAULA HARDY

I'd like to thank the following people for sharing the best of northern Italy: Claudio Buonasera, Mario Pietraccetta, Francesca at Villa Rosmarino, Alessandro Manzana, Contessa Caroline di Levetzow Lantieri Piccolomini, Lorenzo Bagnara and the staff at Rosa Alpina. Also thanks to co-authors Duncan and Robert, and Joe Bindloss for his steady guidance.

### DUNCAN GARWOOD

Thanks to Joe Bindloss for the commission and to fellow author Paula Hardy for her advice. I also owe thanks to Caterina Bencistà Falorni in Greve in Chianti and Paolo Borgognone at ACI in Rome. And, as always, *grazie mille* to Lidia, Ben and Nick.

### ROBERT LANDON

Thanks to Joe Bindloss and Paula Hardy for their expertise, Bo Fowlkes for the rupesters and sass, Nicoletta Lampedusa for surprising insights and uncommon hospitality, Thiago Fico for his patience on the home front, and especially Caterina Enni, who saw me off and welcomed me back with her usual élan.

## PUBLISHER THANKS

Climate map data adapted from Peel MC, Finlayson BL & McMahon TA (2007) 'Updated World Map of the Köppen-Geiger Climate Classification', *Hydrology and Earth System Sciences*, 11, 163344.

Cover photographs

Front (clockwise from top): Val d'Orcia, Fabio Muzzi/Corbis; Staircase, Vatican Museums, Stefano Amantini/Corbis; Vintage Italian race car, Guido Cozzi/Corbis

Back: Field of poppies and cypress trees, near Montalcino, David Tomlinson/Getty Images

## THIS BOOK

This 1st edition of Lonely Planet's *Italy's Best Trips* guidebook was researched and written by Paula Hardy, Duncan Garwood and Robert Landon. This guidebook was commissioned in Lonely Planet's London office, and produced by the following:
**Commissioning Editor** Joe Bindloss **Coordinating Editors** Carolyn Boicos, Monique Perrin **Coordinating Cartographer** Brendan Streager **Coordinating Layout Designer** Joseph Spanti **Managing Editor** Bruce Evans **Senior Editors** Andi Jones, Catherine Naghten **Managing Cartographers** Mark Griffiths, Alison Lyall **Managing Layout Designer** Chris Girdler **Assisting Editors** Kate James, Helen Koehne **Assisting Cartographers** Valeska Cañas, Karusha Ganga, Cameron Romeril **Cover Research** Timothy O'Hanlon **Internal Image Research** Kylie McLaughlin **Language Content** Branislava Vladisavljevic

**Thanks to** Jennifer Bilos, Laura Crawford, Janine Eberle, Ryan Evans, Jennye Garibaldi, Joshua Geoghegan, Liz Heynes, Laura Jane, Jennifer Johnston, David Kemp, Gabriel Lindquist, Wayne Murphy, Trent Paton, Jessica Rose, Mik Ruff, Julie Sheridan, Laura Stansfeld, Matt Swaine, John Taufa, Gerard Walker, Juan Winata

# INDEX

## E



## F



## G



## H



## I



## J



## L

## S



## T

## U



## V



## W



## Z

**Robert Landon** Ten minutes into his maiden voyage to Italy, Robert was pickpocketed in a Florence church, yet he has been returning obsessively ever since, including stints living in Rome and Florence. He has authored Lonely Planet guides to *Florence*, *Venice* and *Brazil*, and has also written about travel, art and architecture for the *Los Angeles Times*, *Dwell*, *Metropolis* and many other publications.

**My Favourite Trip** 31 **Across the Lucanian Appennines** is a gorgeous and surprising journey the whole way, but especially memorable for a particular goat's-milk cheese plate in otherworldly Castelmezzano.

Read more about Robert at: lonelyplanet.com/members/robertlandon

# OUR WRITERS

## OUR STORY

A beat-up old car, a few dollars in the pocket and a sense of adventure. In 1972 that's all Tony and Maureen Wheeler needed for the trip of a lifetime – across Europe and Asia overland to Australia. It took several months, and at the end – broke but inspired – they sat at their kitchen table writing and stapling together their first travel guide, *Across Asia on the Cheap*. Within a week they'd sold 1500 copies. Lonely Planet was born.

Today, Lonely Planet has offices in Melbourne, London and Oakland, with more than 600 staff and writers. We share Tony's belief that 'a great guidebook should do three things: inform, educate and amuse'.

**Paula Hardy** Paula's first experience of northern Italy was Furniture Fair madness in Milan, braving frigid lake waters out of season and a suitcase full of impractical shoes. Now with over a decade of experience in contributing to Lonely Planet's Italy books, including five editions of *Italy*, *Pocket Milan*, *Puglia & Basilicata*, *Sicily* and *Sardinia*, she knows better and now shops in sensible shoes to work off the worst excesses of the Italian table. You can find her tweeting from the lakes and mountains @paula6hardy.

**My Favourite Trip** 12 **Grande Strada delle Dolomiti** because, secretly, I'd like to be Heidi living amid the pink rock walls and oceans of wildflowers.

**Duncan Garwood** Ever since moving to Italy in 1997, Duncan has spent much of his time driving the country on assignment for Lonely Planet. He's clocked up tens of thousands of kilometres and contributed to a whole host of Lonely Planet guidebooks, including *Italy*, *Rome*, *Sicily*, *Sardinia* and *Naples*, as well as the *Food Lover's Guide to the World*. He currently lives in the Castelli Romani hills just outside of Rome.

**My Favourite Trip** 18 **Abruzzo's Wild Landscapes** for the magnificent, unspoiled mountain scenery in this often-overlooked part of Italy.

Read more about Duncan at: lonelyplanet.com/members/duncangarwood

MORE WRITERS

**Published by Lonely Planet Publications Pty Ltd**
ABN 36 005 607 983
1st edition – Mar 2013
ISBN 978 1 74220 987 6

10 9 8 7 6 5 4 3 2 1
Printed in China